Journal of Pentecostal Theology
Supplement Series
11

D1342331

Editors
John Christopher Thomas
Rickie D. Moore
Steven J. Land

Sheffield Academic Press
Sheffield

Pentecostalism

in Context

Essays in Honor of

William W. Menzies

edited by
Wonsuk Ma & Robert P. Menzies

Sheffield Academic Press

Published by Sheffield Academic Press Ltd
Mansion House
19 Kingfield Road
Sheffield S11 9AS
England

Printed on acid-free paper in Great Britain
by Cromwell Press
Melksham, Wiltshire

British Library Cataloguing in Publication Data

A catalogue record for this book is available
from the British Library

ISBN 1-85075-803-4

CONTENTS

Part III
THE MISSIOLOGICAL CONTEXT

PREFACE

We joyfully offer this Festschrift to William W. Menzies on the occasion of his sixty-fifth birthday. We believe that *Pentecostalism in Context* is a fitting tribute to his ministry, which has touched the lives of so many colleagues, students and friends. The book contains essays which examine Pentecostalism in three specific contexts: biblical, theological and missiological. This is appropriate in that William Menzies, during the course of his ministry, has been involved in a significant way in each one of these areas. The contributors to this book—all friends, colleagues or students—also approach their subjects from within their unique contexts: North America, Europe and Asia. In view of the numerous years William Menzies has served the cause of Christ in the Asia-Pacific region, we are especially delighted to include a number of articles from this dynamic context.

From the outset, we had little difficulty finding willing contributors. The eager responses reflected the respect and affection William Menzies has earned throughout his life and ministry. When we turned our sight to Asia, we were especially pleased to see many, relatively young, Asian Pentecostal thinkers. However, it was not easy for them to find the time and resources needed to produce an article. All of them were very active and filling more than one role, often teaching, pastoring and traveling. Some initially accepted the challenge, but later gave up due to the pressures of time or lack of resources. Others simply felt overwhelmed to have their works printed with those of well-known theologians from the West. However, their courage, coupled with a bit of editorial encouragement, enabled them to complete the fine work contained in this volume. Asian women contributors were difficult to find, so we feel doubly fortunate to have Julie Ma's fine article grace the pages of this book. We do feel this volume is especially significant in that it introduces a number of new and emerging Asian Pentecostal writers to a wide range of readers. The Western contributors, by standing together with their Asian counterparts, have encouraged them in this enterprise and for this we are most thankful. We hope this volume will stimulate more cooperative and intercultural efforts of this kind. There is a great need today for Asian Pentecostals to engage in theological reflection. Their voices need to be heard in their respective settings and in the larger Pentecostal world. William Menzies and his wife, Doris, have invested many years in Asia with the hope that this dream might be realized. This book, then, is indeed a fitting tribute to their labors.

We had hoped that this volume might include theological as well as geographical diversity. This would appropriately reflect William Menzies' wide influence among diverse evangelical, charismatic and pentecostal groups, in addition to his profound contribution to the Assemblies of God. In achieving this aim, we were only modestly successful, although the contributions by Peter Hocken and Cecil M. Robeck, with their respective charismatic and ecumenical emphases, stand out in this regard.

We would like to express our deep appreciation to those who made this publication possible. First of all, our contributors deserve a word of appreciation. In the face of busy schedules and deadlines, they produced fine articles. Their enthusiasm has been a source of great encouragement to the editors. We also owe a great debt to John Christopher Thomas, the editor of the *Journal of Pentecostal Theology* Supplement Series. From the beginning, he encouraged the inclusion of contributors from diverse backgrounds and regions. He also spent considerable time reading the contributions and offered many valuable suggestions. His willingness to include this volume in the *JPT* Supplement Series is greatly appreciated. Glen Menzies kindly labored to compile a bibliography of the honoree's published works. It was not an easy job since William Menzies produced, in addition to his academic writings, many popular works printed in various periodicals. Sung-Kyu Hong of Korea has elevated the visual appeal of the book with his graceful Oriental drawing. Several individuals and churches in Korea, particularly Sung-Kyu Choi of Full Gospel Inchon Church, kindly offered financial assistance and thus helped to make this publication possible.

This volume involved several years of planning and preparation. It was therefore inevitable that some works might appear elsewhere. This is indicated in the footnotes.

There are two articles (Li Yue Hong and Cornelis van der Laan) where Chinese names appear frequently. The Chinese names are written according to the Chinese convention: the surname preceding the given name.

Along with the many colleagues, students and friends of William Menzies, the editors of this Festschrift would like to extend our heartfelt appreciation to the honoree himself for his many contributions to the Pentecostal movement, his gentle spirit and his devotion to God—all of which have impacted us deeply. Above all, we praise God for his precious gifts to his church. We consider the life and ministry of William Menzies to be a manifestation of God's grace, a precious gift to the pentecostal church today.

Wonsuk Ma and Robert P. Menzies
Christmas Day, 1995

ABBREVIATIONS

AB	Anchor Bible
BARev	*Biblical Archaeology Review*
BDB	F. Brown, S.R. Driver and C.A. Briggs, *A Hebrew and English Lexicon of the Old Testament*
BZAW	Beihefte zur Zeitschrift für die alttestamentliche Wissenschaft
HeyJ	*Heythrop Journal*
HSM	Harvard Semitic Monographs
ICC	International Critical Commentary
Int	*Interpretation*
JBL	*Journal of Biblical Literature*
JETS	*Journal of Evangelical Theological Society*
JPTSup	*Journal of Pentecostal Theology*, Supplement Series
JSNTSup	*Journal for the Study of the New Testament*, Supplement Series
JSOTSup	*Journal for the Study of the Old Testament*, Supplement Series
NASB	*New American Standard Bible*
NCB	New Century Bible
NICNT	New International Commentary on the New Testament
NIV	New International Version
NTS	*New Testament Studies*
OTL	Old Testament Library
RSV	Revised Standard Version
SJT	*Scottish Journal of Theology*
SNTU	Studien zum Neuen Testament und seiner Umwelt
TNTC	Tyndale New Testament Commentary
TS	*Theological Studies*
VT	*Vetus Testamentum*
WBC	Word Biblical Commentary
ZAW	*Zeitschrift für die alttestamentliche Wissenschaft*

LIST OF CONTRIBUTORS

Simon Chan, Lecturer in Systematic Theology, Trinity Theological College, Singapore

Gordon D. Fee, Professor of New Testament, Regent College, Vancouver, British Columbia, Canada

Peter D. Hocken, Executive Secretary of the Society for Pentecostal Studies, and Chaplain, Mother of God Community, Gaithersburg, Maryland, USA

Stanley M. Horton, Professor of Bible and Theology Emeritus, Assemblies of God Theological Seminary, Springfield, Missouri, USA

Walter C. Kaiser, Jr, Colman M. Mockler Distinguished Professor of Old Testament, Gordon–Conwell Theological Seminary, South Hamilton, Massachusetts, USA

Li Yue Hong, Lecturer, Chinese Literature Department, Minority Nationalities University, Kunming, Yunnan Province, People's Republic of China

Julie Ma, Lecturer of Intercultural Studies, Asia Pacific Theological Seminary, Baguio City, Philippines

Wonsuk Ma, Academic Dean and Lecturer in Old Testament Studies, Asia Pacific Theological Seminary, Baguio City, Philippines

Gary B. McGee, Professor of Church History, Assemblies of God Theological Seminary, Springfield, Missouri, USA

Glen Menzies, Associate Professor, Pastoral Ministries Department, North Central Bible College, Minneapolis, Minnesota, USA

Robert P. Menzies, Director of the China Studies Program and Lecturer in New Testament Studies, Asia Pacific Theological Seminary, Baguio City, Philippines

Cecil M. Robeck, Jr, Associate Professor of Church History and Ecumenics, Fuller Theological Seminary, Pasadena, California, USA

Russell P. Spittler, Provost/Vice President for Academic Affairs, and Professor of New Testament, Fuller Theological Seminary, Pasadena, California, USA

Roger Stronstad, Dean of Education, Western Pentecostal Bible College, Clayburn, British Columbia, Canada

Benjamin Sun, Bible School Coordinator, Asia Pacific Education Office, Laguna Hills, California, USA.

Del Tarr, President and Professor of Cross-Cultural Communication, Assemblies of God Theological Seminary, Springfield, Missouri, USA

Cornelis van der Laan, President, Centrale Pinkster Bijbelschool, Lunteren, Netherlands

Miroslav Volf, Associate Professor of Systematic Theology, Fuller Theological Seminary, Pasadena, California, USA

Xu Qin Sun, Instructor, Foreign Languages Department, Yunnan University, Kunming, Yunnan Province, People's Republic of China

RETROSPECTIVE BIBLIOGRAPHY OF WILLIAM W. MENZIES

Glen Menzies

1993   Review of G. Fee, *Gospel and Spirit: Issues in New Testament Hermeneutics*, *Paraclete* 27.1 (Winter): 29-32.

1992   'Prized Blanket', *Pentecostal Evangel* 4093 (18 Oct.): 12.
Understanding Bible Doctrine (All Church Training Series; 2 vols.; Springfield, MO: Gospel Publishing House, 1992).

1990   'The Movers and Shakers (Biographies)', in H.B. Smith (ed.), *Pentecostals from the Inside Out* (The Christianity Today Series; Wheaton: Victor Books): 29-41.
'Toward a Theology of Suffering: A Pentecostal Perspective', in *Pan Asia Pacific Conference, Presented Papers* (Kuala Lumpur, Malaysia: Asia Pacific Theological Seminary Press): 85-95.

1989   'Confessions of a Preacher', *Advance* 25.3 (March): 8.
Review of P. Elbert (ed.), *Faces of Renewal: Studies in Honor of Stanley M. Horton*, *Paraclete* 23.2 (Spring): 27-29.
Review of D.R. McConnell, *A Different Gospel*, *Cultic Studies Journal* 6.1: 105-107.
Review of D.R. McConnell, *A Different Gospel*, *Paraclete* 23.2 (Spring): 31-32.
'Will Charismatics Go Cultic?', Review of D.R. McConnell, *A Different Gospel*, *Christianity Today* 33.4 (3 March): 59-60.

1988   Review of S.M. Burgess, *The Spirit and the Church: Antiquity*, and Ronald A. Kydd, *Charismatic Gifts in the Early Church*, *Paraclete* 22.1 (Winter): 30-31.
Review of D.W. Dayton, *Theological Roots of Pentecostalism*, *Paraclete* 22.3 (Summer): 27-29.
Review of G. Fee, *The First Epistle to the Corinthians*, *Paraclete* 22.3 (Summer): 29-31.
Review of R.W. Graves, *Praying in the Spirit*, *Paraclete* 22.4 (Fall): 29-30.

1987   Review of H.D. Hunter, *Spirit Baptism: A Pentecostal Alternative*, *Paraclete* 21.2 (Spring): 31-32.

1986   Review of F.L. Arrington, *Maintaining the Foundations: A Study of 1 Timothy*, *Paraclete* 20.3 (Summer): 31-32.

1985   'The Methodology of Pentecostal Theology: An Essay on Hermeneutics', in P. Elbert (ed.), *Essays on Apostolic Themes: Studies in Honor of Howard M. Ervin* (Peabody, MA: Hendrickson): 1-14.

Review of M. Harper, *The Love Affair*, *Paraclete* 19.1 (Winter): 31-32.

Review of M. Harper, *Walking in the Spirit*, *Paraclete* 19.2 (Spring 1985): 31-32.

1984   Review of T.A. Smail, *The Forgotten Father*, *Paraclete* 18.1 (Winter): 31-32.

1983   'Biblical Hermeneutics', in G. Jones (ed.), *Conference on the Holy Spirit Digest* (2 vols.; Springfield, MO: Gospel Publishing House): 62-69.

'The Lord Will Intervene!', *Pentecostal Evangel* 3592 (13 March): 20-22.

Review of W.A. Grudem, *The Gift of Prophecy in 1 Corinthians*, *Paraclete* 17.4 (Fall): 29-30.

Review of C.E. Hummel, *Fire in the Fireplace*, *Paraclete* 17.1 (Winter): 31-32.

'Roy Wead: Interviewed by William Menzies' (VHS video cassette; Springfield, MO: Assemblies of God Graduate School).

1982   'Biblical Hermeneutics' (audio cassette; Conference on the Holy Spirit; Springfield, MO: Assemblies of God Audiovisual Services).

Review of F.L. Arrington, *Divine Order in the Church: A Study of First Corinthians*, *Paraclete* 16.3 (Summer): 32.

Review of S.M. Horton, *The Book of Acts*, *Paraclete* 16.1 (Winter): 31-32.

Review of J. Rodman Williams, *The Gift of the Holy Spirit Today*, *Paraclete* 16.2 (Spring): 31-32.

1981   'Divorce and Remarriage: A Biblical Theology' (audio cassette; San Jose, CA: Bethel Church).

Philippians: The Joyful Life (Springfield, MO: Gospel Publishing House; trans. into Spanish as *Filipenses: La epistola del gozo* [Miami: Editorial Vida]).

Review of V. De Leon, *The Silent Pentecostals*, *Paraclete* 15.2 (Spring): 32.

Review of M. Harper, *Live by the Spirit*, *Paraclete* 15.3 (Summer): 30.

Review of C.F.D. Moule, *The Holy Spirit*, *Paraclete* 15.3 (Summer 1981): 30-31.

Review of L.W. Wood, *Pentecostal Grace*, *Paraclete* 15.3 (Summer): 31-32.

1980   'The Contribution of the Reformation to Pentecostalism' (audio cassette; Symposium on the Legacy of the Reformation; Springfield, MO: Assemblies of God Graduate School).

1979   '[Inaugural] Editorial', *Pneuma* 1.1 (Spring): 3-5.

'The Holy Spirit in Christian Theology', in K.S. Kantzer (ed.), *Perspectives on Evangelical Theology: Papers from the Thirteenth Annual Meeting of the Evangelical Theological Society* (Grand Rapids: Baker): 67-69.

1978   Review of D. Gee, *The Fruit of the Spirit*, *Paraclete* 12.3 (Summer): 32.

Review of D. Gee, *A Word to the Wise*, *Paraclete* 12.1 (Winter 1978): 31-32.

'A Taxonomy of Charismatic Theologies, *Pneuma* 1978' (audio cassette; Springfield, MO: Assemblies of God Audiovisiual Services).

1977   'Grace Recovered: Luther's Gift to us', *Advance* 13.10 (Oct.): 4-5.

Review of S.M. Horton, *What the Bible Says about the Holy Spirit, Paraclete* 11.3 (Summer): 31-32.

1976   *Apologetics* (ICI College Division Degree Program Study Guide; Brussels: International Correspondence Institute).

1975   'The Non-Wesleyan Origins of the Pentecostal Movement', in V. Synan (ed.), *Aspects of Pentecostal-Charismatic Origins* (Plainfield, NJ: Logos International): 81-98.

Review of D.W. Faupel, *The American Pentecostal Movement: A Bibliographical Essay, JETS* 18.1 (Winter): 56-57.

1974   'Giving Thanks for our Heritage', *Pentecostal Evangel* 3159 (24 Nov.): 4-6.

Review of C.W. Carter, *The Person and Ministry of the Holy Spirit: A Wesleyan Perspective, Paraclete* 14.2 (Spring 1980): 30-32.

'Revival—A Work of God the Holy Spirit', *Pentecostal Evangel* 3116 (27 Jan.): 8-9.

1972   'Lessons from Great Revivals' (Audio cassette; Council on Spiritual Life, 1972; Springfield, MO: Assemblies of God Audiovisual Services).

Review of V. Synan, *The Holiness-Pentecostal Movement, JETS* 15.4 (Fall): 240-41.

'The Theistic View of Man', *Advance* 8.10 (Oct.): 4-5, 35.

1971   *Anointed to Serve: The Story of the Assemblies of God* (Springfield, MO: Gospel Publishing House).

'Anointed to Serve', *Advance* 7.9 (Sept.): 4-5.

'The Resurrection: Voice of Verification', *Advance* 7.4 (April): 4-5.

'The Scriptures Inspired', *Sunday School Counselor* 31.1 (Jan.): 7-8.

Understanding our Doctrine (Fundamentals for Sunday School Workers, 3; Springfield, MO: Gospel Publishing House; subsequently rev. and expanded by S.M. Horton as *Bible Doctrines: A Pentecostal Perspective* [Springfield, MO: Logion Press, 1993]).

1969   *Understanding the Times of Christ* (Workers' Training Textbook; Springfield, MO: Gospel Publishing House).

Review of F.B. Craddock, *The Pre-Existence of Christ in the New Testament, JETS* 12.4 (Fall): 241-42.

1968   'The Assemblies of God, 1941–1947: The Consolidation of a Revival Movement' (PhD diss., University of Iowa; Ann Arbor: University Microfilms).

Review of H.B. Swete, *The Holy Spirit in the New Testament, Paraclete* 2.2 (Spring): 31-32.

1967   'Where Does the Pulpit Belong?', *Advance* 3.5 (May): 13-14

1965   'The Bible College–Classroom in Commitment', *Pentecostal Evangel* 2680 (Sept. 19): 16-18.

'The Incarnation—Battleground of Faith', *Advance* 1.3 (Dec.): 21-22.

1961   'College—The Mission Field Next Door', *Pentecostal Evangel* 2448 (April 9): 12-13.

'South of the Border in '62', *Pentecostal Evangel* 2469 (3 Sept.): 23.

1960   'Be Biblical', *C.A. Herald* (Feb.): 11-12.
              'Keeping Collegians Christian', *Pentecostal Evangel* 2419 (18 Sept.):
              28-29.
1957   'An Examination of Christian Perfection in the New Testament' (MA
              Thesis, Wheaton College, IL).
1954   'Good and Bad', *C.A. Herald* (July): 19.
1953   'Declare your Independence', *C.A. Herald* (Sept.): 9-10.
              'Why Should I Be Pentecostal?', *C.A. Herald* (Aug.): 19-21.
              'The True Story of Harry Hodge', *C.A. Herald* (July): 8-10.

Collaborative Efforts

1992   Menzies, R.P. (ed.), 'The Essence of Pentecostalism' (a forum on
              theology, hermeneutics, and evangelicalism with David Bundrick, Ian
              Henderson, Robert Menzies, William Menzies Dave Oleson, Jack
              Rozell, and Robert Soderberg participating), *Paraclete* 26.3 (Summer):
              1-9.
1981   *et al.*, *Divorce and Remarriage in the Church: A Practical Guide for
              Church Leaders* (Symposium on Divorce and Remarriage, 1981; San
              Jose, CA, Bethel Church).

REFLECTIONS ON THE LIFE AND MINISTRY
OF WILLIAM W. MENZIES

Stanley M. Horton

William Watson Menzies was born July 1, 1931 to William E. and Sophie
B. Menzies in New Kensington, Pennsylvania. His parents were powerful Pentecostal pioneers who gave him a rich spiritual heritage. Bill has
served God in an outstanding way as a pastor, teacher, missionary, college and seminary administrator, and scholar.

He earned a BA in Bible from Central Bible College and a second BA
from Wheaton College, then an MA in Theology from Wheaton College
Graduate School. He met his wife, formerly Doris Dresselhaus, while
studying at Wheaton College. They were married in 1955. He holds the
PhD degree in Religion from the University of Iowa, where he majored
in American Church History.

I remember him first as a young freshman student at Central Bible
College, full of zeal, ready to turn the world upside down for Jesus. He
sensed the urgency of the times and was ready to quit school and go out
into the harvest field. But he responded to a little counseling that
reminded him that Jesus trained his disciples for three and a half years.
He recognized that the Lord had brought him to school and he needed
to be found faithful where he was. He has continued to be faithful in the
various fields where the Lord has led him. His kind and compassionate
spirit have made him well-loved by his students and fellow workers
everywhere.

He was ordained in 1956 while pastoring in Michigan. In 1958 he
became my colleague on the faculty of Central Bible College. Then from
1970 to 1980 he taught at Evangel College, giving scholarly substance
to their Bible and Philosophy Department. From 1980 to 1984 he
taught and chaired the Biblical Studies Department at the Assemblies of
God Theological Seminary. It was a pleasure for me to work under him
during that time. He was so gracious and encouraging.

He had a missionary's heart and took many opportunities to teach and preach in Europe, South America, Asia and the islands of the Pacific. He provided valuable help in the formation and development of the curriculum of the Far East Advanced School of Theology in Manila, the Philippines, and served as its president in 1984–85. From 1985 to 1987 he served as Vice-President for Academic Affairs at the California Theological Seminary in Fresno, still keeping in touch with the Far East where his heart was. In 1988 he returned to the Philippines as President of the Asia Pacific Theological Seminary in Baguio where he has developed an outstanding program for the training of ministers and missionaries. It was my privilege to be with him in Baguio in 1994. There I observed the great work he was doing and the way he was building up the seminary to meet the needs of the people of the Pacific Rim. The gracious hospitality and encouragement shown me by Bill and his wife Doris will never be forgotten. In March, 1996, he resigned from the President's office and became Chancellor.

During his career he has served his denomination, the Assemblies of God, in many additional ways. He was editor of the *Campus Ambassador* (the Assemblies of God college youth magazine). He served on many committees and provided wise counsel in many theological discussions.

His concern for Pentecostal theology led him to join with Vinson Synan and Horace Ward to found the Society for Pentecostal Studies in 1970. He became its first President. Then from 1979–83 he served as editor of its journal, *Pneuma*. In 1984 he participated as an outstanding Pentecostal theologian in the Lausanne Consultation and after that on its committees. Then in 1986 he was selected to be a consulting editor for *Christianity Today*.

His book, *Anointed to Serve*,[1] was an adaptation of his doctoral dissertation and remains as the most outstanding history of the first half-century plus of the Assemblies of God. Other books include *Understanding our Doctrine*,[2] *Understanding the Times of Christ*,[3] and *Philippians: The Joyful Life*.[4] He graciously gave me permission to revise and enlarge

---

1. W.W. Menzies, *Anointed to Serve: The Story of the Assemblies of God* (Springfield, MO: Gospel Publishing House, 1971).

2. W.W. Menzies, *Understanding our Doctrine* (Fundamentals for Sunday School Workers, 3; Springfield, MO: Gospel Publishing House, 1971).

3. W.W. Menzies, *Understanding the Times of Christ* (Worker's Training Textbook: Springfield, MO: Gospel Publishing House, 1969).

4. W.W. Menzies, *Phillipians: The Joyful Life* (Springfield, MO: Gospel Publishing House, 1981).

Understanding our Doctrine which was renamed *Bible Doctrines: A Pentecostal Perspective.*[5] It contains a chapter on each of the 16 points of the 'Statement of Fundamental Truths', as held by the Assemblies of God.

Like many of the pioneers he described in *Anointed to Serve*, Bill will be remembered as a godly example and a pillar in the Church of our Lord Jesus Christ. Those of us who know him share warm feelings of appreciation and thanksgiving for his faithful ministry.

5. W.W. Menzies, *Bible Doctrines: A Pentecostal Perspective* (rev. and ex-panded, S.M. Horton; Springfield, MO: Logion Press, 1993).

Part I

THE BIBLICAL CONTEXT

TOWARD A PAULINE THEOLOGY OF GLOSSOLALIA[1]

Gordon D. Fee

There can be little question that the experience and theological articulation of speaking in tongues is one of the primary 'contexts' of Pentecostalism. Because of the Pentecostals' understanding of the baptism in the Spirit as subsequent to conversion and evidenced by glossolalia, much of their theological energy on the matter of 'tongues' has understandably been devoted to the Book of Acts. This does not mean that Paul's discussion of the phenomenon has been irrelevant to Pentecostals; on the contrary, it has held high court among them, but has usually been understood as the 'same in kind but different in purpose' from the experience of tongues which serves as evidence of 'the baptism' according to the traditional interpretation of Acts.[2]

This reading of Acts and Paul resulted in a twofold understanding of glossolalia among historic Pentecostals: tongues as 'sign', as the 'initial physical evidence' for the baptism in the Spirit; and tongues as 'spiritual gift', expressed privately as 'prayer language' and publicly when accompanied by interpretation as 'a message in tongues'. The latter is thus understood to function in the same role as, and in my own experience in the church, far more often than, prophetic utterances.[3]

1. An earlier version appeared in *Crux* 31 (March, 1995), pp. 22-23, 26-31.
2. See, for example, the extensive citation from W.T. Gaston in G.B. McGee (ed.), *Initial Evidence* (Peabody, MA: Hendrickson, 1991), pp. 127-29; cf. more recently, D. Lim, *Spiritual Gifts; A Fresh Look* (Springfield, MO: Gospel Publishing House, 1991), pp. 85-86.
3. For the high value placed on this phenomenon *in the assembly* see, for example, the considerable defense of this practice found in R.M. Riggs, *The Spirit Himself* (Springfield, MO: Gospel Publishing House, 1949), pp. 162-66. Thus, in my own experience in Pentecostalism I have often heard both clergy and laity bemoan the absence of such 'messages' in the assembly but never the absence of prophecy as an evidence of a lack of spiritual vigor in the church. And this despite the clear focus of the Pauline injunctions in 1 Corinthians 14. One wonders whether

The net result is that glossolalia has played a much higher role in the public gatherings of Pentecostalism than Paul himself would probably have been comfortable with, especially in light of his reordering of Corinthian priorities in 1 Corinthians 12–14. To be sure, most Pentecostals do not think of glossolalia as either the most important or least important aspect of their life in Christ. Traditionally, they have put their overall theological emphasis precisely where other evangelicals do on the person and work of Christ. Nonetheless, the public expression of tongues, which has so often characterized Pentecostal worship, has also served as much as anything else to distinguish Pentecostals, and very often therefore to separate them, from their other brothers and sisters in Christ. Unfortunately, because glossolalia is seen as the point of demarcation, tongues has sometimes come to be viewed—by both Pentecostals and others—in a much more triumphalistic way than either historic Pentecostalism intended or Scripture warrants.

The thesis of this paper is that Paul's understanding of glossolalia is to be found in the paradox of 2 Cor. 12.9, that '[God's] power finds perfection in [human] weakness', and that speaking in tongues therefore reflects a position of weakness, not of strength. Thus I propose: 1) briefly to overview the theme of power and weakness in Paul; 2) to examine the Pauline data regarding glossolalia from 1 Corinthians; 3) to suggest that these data correspond to Paul's cryptic reference to praying in the Spirit in Rom. 8.26-27; and 4) to conclude by showing how these data regarding 'prayer in the Spirit' fit into the theme of strength in weakness.[4]

this unbiblical emphasis is an unconscious transfer of tongues as 'initial evidence' of the individual believer's baptism in the Spirit to tongues as evidence of genuine spirituality in the church.

4.   I offer these musings on this aspect of Pauline theology and spirituality out of deep respect and appreciation for the honoree of this Festschrift, whose life and work among us have been exemplary of the servant ministry commanded by our Lord and modeled by Paul. I am also well aware that this is not the first attempt at a 'theology of glossolalia'. See, for example, J. Massingberd Ford, 'Toward a Theology of "Speaking in Tongues"', *TS* 32 (1971), pp. 3-29 (whose journey through Jewish literature led her to an understanding of tongues as God's way of re-creating the organ necessary for praise); cf. F.D. Macchia, 'Sighs Too Deep for Words: Toward a Theology of Glossolalia', *Journal of Pentecostal Theology* 1 (1992), pp. 47-73, who offers four theological reasons for the gift. Almost all of the older Pentecostal literature had sections that wrestled with 'why tongues', or 'the value of tongues', which very often took the form of theological reflection; cf. more recently,

1. *The Context*

One understands Paul and his gospel poorly who does not recognize the crucial role the Spirit plays in his entire theological enterprise;[5] and crucial to the Spirit's central role is the thoroughly eschatological framework within which Paul both experienced and understood the Spirit. The gift of the out-poured Spirit, who had played a fundamental role in his and others' eschatological expectations, came to serve for Paul, along with the resurrection of Christ, as the primary cause of his radically altered eschatological perspective. On the one hand, the coming of the Spirit fulfilled the Old Testament eschatological promises, the sure *evidence* that the future had *already* been set in motion; on the other hand, since the final expression of the Eschaton had *not yet* taken place, the Spirit also served as the sure *guarantee* of the final glory. It is quite impossible to understand Paul's emphasis on the experienced life of the Spirit apart from this thoroughgoing eschatological perspective that dominated his thinking.

It is within this context that one is to understand the inherent ambivalence one finds in Paul's letters between the themes of 'power' and 'weakness'. Indeed, 'power' is something of an elusive term in Paul's writings. It often refers to clearly visible manifestations that evidence the Spirit's presence (e.g., 1 Cor. 2.4-5; Gal. 3.5; Rom. 15.19). The evidence from 1 Thess. 5.19-22; 1 Corinthians 12–14; Rom. 12.6; and especially Gal. 3.2-5 with its matter-of-fact appeal to the continuing presence of miracles in the churches, makes it certain that the Pauline churches were 'charismatic' in the sense that a dynamic presence of the Spirit was manifested in their gatherings.[6] And even where 'power' means that believers apprehend and live out the love of Christ in a greater way (Eph. 3.16-20), Paul recognizes here a miraculous work of the Spirit that will be *evidenced* by the way renewed people behave toward one another. Whatever else, the Spirit was *experienced* in the Pauline churches; he was not simply a matter of creedal assent.

On the other hand, Paul also assumes the closest correlation between

---

R.W. Graves, *Praying in the Spirit* (Old Tappen, NJ: Chosen, 1987), pp. 38-43.

5.   On this matter see G.D. Fee, *God's Empowering Presence: The Holy Spirit in the Letters of Paul* (Peabody, MA: Hendrickson, 1994).

6.   On this matter see J.D.G. Dunn, *Jesus and the Spirit* (Philadelphia: Westminster Press, 1975), pp. 260-65; cf. Fee, *Presence*, pp. 894-95.

the Spirit's power and present weaknesses. Such passages as Rom. 8.17-27; 2 Cor. 12.9; and Col. 1.9-11[7] indicate that the Spirit is seen as the source of empowering in the midst of affliction or weakness. In Paul's view, 'knowing Christ' means to know '*both* the power of his resurrection *and* the fellowship of his sufferings' in which life in the 'already' means to be 'conformed to his death' as we press toward the 'not yet' final prize (Phil. 3.9-13).[8] Suffering means to be as one's Lord, following his example and thus 'filling up what was lacking in his sufferings' (Col. 1.24).

Even so, Paul also expects God's more visible demonstrations of power through the Spirit to be manifested in the midst of weakness, as God's 'proof' that his power resides in the message of a crucified Messiah. In 1 Cor. 2.3-5, therefore, Paul can appeal simultaneously to the reality of his own weaknesses and the Spirit's manifest power in his preaching and the Corinthians' conversion; and in 1 Thess. 1.5-6 he reminds these new believers that they became so by the power of the Spirit, but in the midst of suffering that was also accompanied by the joy of the Holy Spirit.

All of this reflects Paul's basic eschatological understanding of Christian existence as 'already/not yet', a tension that Paul was able to keep together in ways that many later Christians have not. For him it was not simply a tension in which the present was all weakness and the (near) future all glory. The future had truly broken into the present, evidenced by the gift of the Spirit; and since the Spirit meant the presence of God's power, that dimension of the future was also already present in some measure. Thus present suffering is a mark of discipleship, whose paradigm is our crucified Lord. But the same power that raised the crucified one from the dead is also already at work in our present mortal bodies.

It is precisely this paradox in Paul's own understanding that creates so

7. For the exegesis of the passages see Fee, *Presence*, *ad loc*. In the latter passage Paul prays for the Colossians to be filled with all the Spirit's wisdom and insight so as to walk worthy of Christ, one dimension of which includes 'being *empowered* for endurance and patience *with all power* in keeping with God's *might*'.

8. This is almost certainly how one is to understand the καὶς that follow τοῦ γνῶναι αὐτόν (to know him). There are not three things that Paul longs to know; rather it is one thing: to know Christ. But in context that means to know him simultaneously in two ways, both the power of his resurrection and the fellowship of his sufferings. Cf. the discussion in G.D. Fee, *Philippians* (Grand Rapids: Eerdmans, 1995), pp. 327-35.

many difficulties for moderns. Indeed, as much as anything else, it is the church's subsequent failure to embrace both power and weakness, simultaneously and vigorously, that has led to so much of the ebb and flow of Spirit life in the church over the centuries. Paul and the rest of the New Testament writers held these expressions of Spirit and power in happy tension.[9] Thus Paul in particular steered a path through the 'radical middle' that is often missed by both evangelicals and Pentecostals, who traditionally tend to place their emphasis on one side or the other.[10]

I propose in this paper that Paul's stance in the eschatological 'radical middle' is the key to his understanding of glossolalia, not simply because he himself stands so squarely over against the Corinthians, whose enchantment with tongues and triumphalism apparently went hand in glove, but also because what Paul says positively about tongues leads in this same direction. Thus we turn to a (very) brief examination of the Pauline data.

2. *The Pauline Data*

It is well known that Paul specifically mentions the phenomenon of glossolalia ('speaking in tongues') only in 1 Corinthians 12–14. It is also generally agreed, although not always in the same way, that Paul's discussion of the phenomenon was primarily for the purpose of *correcting a Corinthian abuse*, not of instructing them theologically in an area where they needed further teaching. For this reason a certain tenuousness exists for us in the task of theologizing. What we get from Paul are his emphases in correcting the Corinthians rather than full-orbed instruction or reflection.

Nonetheless, several significant conclusions can be drawn from a careful analysis of this section of 1 Corinthians. I simply list them here; they will be elaborated in the next section:

1.   Whatever else, glossolalia is Spirit-inspired utterance, as 1 Cor. 12.7-11 and 14.2 make plain.

9.   After all, for Paul the preaching of the crucified One is precisely where God's power is at work in the world (1 Cor. 1.18-25), and his own preaching in a context of weakness and fear and trembling certified that the power that brought about the Corinthians' conversion lay in the work of the Spirit, not in the wisdom or eloquence of the preacher.

10.   For a further discussion of these two tendencies in the church see Fee, *Presence*, pp. 822-26.

2.   Whether Paul also understood it to be an actual earthly language is a moot point, but the overall evidence suggests not.

3.   It is speech essentially unintelligible both to the speaker (14.14) and to other hearers (14.16), which is why it must be interpreted in the assembly.

4.   The regulations for its community use in 14.27-28, plus the declaration in 14.32 that the 'Spirit of the prophets is subject to the prophets', make it clear that the speaker is not in 'ecstasy' or 'out of control'.

5.   It is speech directed basically toward God (14.2, 5, 28), whose content takes the form of prayer, song, blessing (praise) and thanksgiving.

6.   Although he does not forbid its use in the assembly, Paul clearly does not encourage it; rather he insists that they 'seek earnestly' to speak what is intelligible to the others, thus to prophesy (14.1, 3-5, 6, 9, 12, 16, 19, 24-25, 28).

7.   As a gift for private prayer, Paul held it in the highest regard (14.2, 4a, 15, 17-18). Even though unintelligible to the speaker, such prayer 'in the Spirit' edifies the one thus speaking (14.4).

My immediate concern is to point out the significant correspondences between these conclusions (esp. 1, 3, 4, 5 and 7) and what Paul says about 'praying in the Spirit' in Rom. 8.26-27. In my recent study on the Spirit in Paul, I have argued at length that one can make the best exegetical and phenomenological sense of the Romans passage if we understand the Spirit's making appeal for us 'with inarticulate groanings' as referring primarily to glossolalia.[11]

What convinced me to change my mind on this matter[12] was a combination of three realities: 1) The essential matters as to what Paul says about the Spirit's praying through us in Rom. 8.26-27 correspond precisely with his description of praying in tongues in 1 Cor. 14.14-19, namely, (a) the Spirit is understood to be praying in/through the believer (cf. items 1, 4 and 5 above), and (b) the one so praying does not understand with his or her mind what the Spirit is saying (cf. items 2, 3 and 7). 2) The experience which Paul describes in Rom. 8.26-27 as 'the Spirit's interceding with ἀλαλήτος groanings' is expressed in such a way that

---

11. See Fee, *Presence*, pp. 575-86.

12. Cf. my article on the 'Pauline Literature' in S.M. Burgess, G.B. McGee and P.H. Alexander, *Dictionary of Pentecostal and Charismatic Movements* (Grand Rapids: Regency Reference Library, 1988), pp. 665-83 (esp. p. 680).

he is obviously appealing to something that is commonplace among early believers (after all, in this case he is writing to a church that knows him only by reputation not in person). But in fact there is no other evidence of any kind in the New Testament or beyond for such a phenomenon. Glossolalia, on the other hand, has all the earmarks of being commonplace.[13] (3) In that case Paul's use of the phrase στεναγμὸς ἀλαλήτος (probably = 'inarticulate groanings') rather than 'glossolalia' (if that is the phenomenon being described in this way) is purely contextual, having been dictated by what he has previously said in vv. 22-23 about the present 'groaning' of creation as it awaits the 'not yet' of final redemption and of believers' 'joining with creation' in that 'groaning'. Thus, despite his use of ἀλαλήτος,[14] Paul almost certainly does not intend to describe silent praying, but praying that is 'too deep for words' in the sense of 'the ordinary words of the speaker's native language'. It is therefore 'inarticulate' not in the sense that one does not 'mouth words',[15] but in the sense that what is said is not understood by the mind of the speaker.

In any case, what Paul describes in Rom. 8.26-27 is clearly a form of 'praying in the Spirit', the language he also uses for 'speaking in tongues' in 1 Cor. 14.15-16.[16] Thus, in light of these correspondences,

13. To those who point to its mention only in 1 Corinthians as evidence that it was more or less a strictly Corinthian phenomenon, I point out (a) that only in 1 Corinthians, where he is also correcting an abuse, does Paul mention the Lord's Table(!), and (b) that the nature of Paul's argument in 1 Cor. 12–14, just as in 11.17-34, assumes a widely-known and practiced phenomenon, which was out of control in Corinth. After all, although obviously tailored to their situation, 1 Cor. 14.26 gives expression to Christian worship that has all the hallmarks of being broadly, not locally, conceived. Here, I might add, is the significance of the spurious ending of Mark (16.9-20), an ending which reflects very early tradition, but has no evident association with Corinth. In a quite matter-of-fact way this early tradition says, among other things, that 'they will speak in new tongues'.

14. By derivation this word literally means 'unspoken'; it is quite unlikely that it also means 'inexpressible [= too deep for words]', since there is a perfectly good Greek word for that idea (ἀνεκλάλητος; cf. 1 Pet. 1.8; *Phil.* 1.3). In the context of Romans the word can hardly mean 'silent'; therefore, 'inarticulate', meaning 'without *known* words', seems to be the best option in this passage.

15. All the more so when one realizes that both praying and reading in antiquity were articulated in the sense of 'mouthing the words'; hence they both prayed and read 'aloud', as it were.

16. Cf. A.J.M. Wedderburn, 'Romans 8.26—Towards a Theology of Glossolalia?' *SJT* 28 (1975), pp. 369-77, who rejects this interpretation of Rom. 8.26 (at

my attempt at theologizing this phenomenon will embrace the data from both passages and should therefore be understood as 'toward a theology of praying in the Spirit' which for Paul would most often have been 'in tongues'. After all, he can say without proof, but also without fear of contradiction, that 'I speak [pray] in tongues more than all of you' to a congregation that has (apparently) taken special pride in the public expression of this phenomenon (1 Cor. 14.18).

3. *A Theological Proposal*

Although Paul does not himself offer theological reflection on the phenomenon of speaking in tongues, what he does say and to a degree what he does not say allows us to make several significant affirmations as to his understanding of it. Picking up on the conclusions noted above, I offer the following reflections:

1.   That Paul understood glossolalia as Spirit-inspired utterance is clearly expressed in the combination of statements in 1 Cor. 12.7-8, 10-11. In 12.7 he begins by saying that 'to each is given the manifestation of the Spirit for the common good', which is followed in vv. 8-10 by a listing of nine such 'manifestations', the first four of which are explicitly attributed to the Spirit in such a way ('to one...through the Spirit', 'to another...by the same Spirit') so as to imply that the final five are to be understood in the same way. This is made certain by the wrap-up sentence in v. 11: '*All these things* the one and the same Spirit works [among you], distributing to each one just as he wills'.

This is also explicitly stated in 1 Cor. 14.2, where Paul affirms that 'the one who speaks in tongues...speaks mysteries [to God] by the Spirit',[17] which is then picked up in v. 15 as 'I will pray/sing with my S/spirit'.[18] Such praying 'by the Spirit' which is unintelligible to the speaker but effective with God is also explicitly stated in Rom. 8.26-27.

This theological reality in itself should cause some to speak more cautiously when trying to 'put tongues in their place' (usually meaning

least in the form it is presented by E. Käsemann), but allows that it still might function as a basis for a Pauline theology of glossolalia.

17. In one of their less insightful moments, the NIV translators, against the clear usage in context and Pauline usage in general, translated this occurrence of πνεύματι as 'with his spirit'. For Pauline usage in this regard, see ch. 2 in Fee, *Presence*, pp. 15-26.

18. For this translation and understanding of this passage, see Fee, *Presence*, pp. 228-33.

'to eliminate them altogether') in the contemporary church. Paul does not damn tongues with faint praise, as some have argued, nor does he stand in awe of the phenomenon, as apparently the Corinthians had done and some later Pentecostals and charismatics as well. As with all Spirit-empowered activity, Paul held it in high regard *in its proper place*.

2.   About the actual phenomenon itself, two things need to be noted. First, the regulations for its community use in 1 Cor. 14.27-28 make it clear that the speaker is not in 'ecstasy' or 'out of control'. Quite the opposite; the speakers are instructed to speak in turn, one at a time, and they must remain silent if there is no one to interpret. Such instruction makes little or no sense if the speaker is in a kind of 'ecstasy' whereby one is understood to be under the 'power of the Spirit' and thus out of personal control. What Paul says of prophecy in v. 32, therefore, applies equally to those who would speak in tongues in the assembly: 'The S/spirits of the prophets are subject to the prophets.' This also means that the outsiders who would view the believers as 'mad' if all speak in tongues (simultaneously, seems to be implied) in their gatherings, do not see the 'madness' in the *nature* of the activity itself (= 'mania') but in its lack of intelligibility and lack of order. Likewise, although Paul does not speak to this issue as such in Rom. 8.26-27, there is nothing in that description that implies that the speaker is 'out of control'.

Secondly, that Paul did not think of glossolalia as an actual earthly language is indicated by several pieces of converging evidence. He certainly does not envisage the likelihood of someone's being present who might understand without interpretation; and the analogy of earthly language in 14.10-12 implies that it is not an earthly language (a thing is not usually *identical* with that to which it is merely *analogous*). Our most likely entrée into Paul's understanding is to be found in his description of the phenomenon in 1 Cor. 13.1 as 'the tongues of angels'. The context itself demands that this phrase refers to glossolalia. The more difficult matter is its close conjunction with 'the tongues of people'. Most likely this refers to two kinds of glossolalia: human speech, inspired of the Spirit, but unknown to the speaker or hearers; and angelic speech, inspired of the Spirit to speak in the heavenly dialect. The historical context in general suggests that the latter is what the Corinthians themselves understood glossolalia to be, and therefore considered it one of the evidences of their having already achieved something of their future heavenly status.[19]

19. The question as to whether the 'speaking in tongues' in contemporary

3. According to all the available evidence, Paul understood glossolalia as speech directed toward God, not toward other believers. This comes out in a variety of ways. First, this is expressly said in every case where Paul explicitly refers to the direction of the speaking, and in one case this is said in specific contrast to prophecy, which is directed toward other people. Thus in 1 Cor. 14.2 Paul says that the one who speaks in a tongue does *not* speak to people, but to God. Likewise in 14.28, if no one is present to interpret the tongue, the speaker is to keep silent *in the church* and to 'speak by him or herself and to God'. The same is implied in vv. 14-16, where the one speaking in tongues is said variously to be 'praying' (vv. 14-15), 'blessing God' (v. 16), and 'giving thanks' (to God, is implied, v. 17). So also, finally, in Rom. 8.26-27 the Spirit is presented as praying to God through the believer on the believer's behalf.

Two important considerations arise out of this reality. First, there seems to be little Pauline evidence for the traditional Pentecostal phrase, 'a message in tongues', to describe the phenomenon of tongues and interpretation as it has been practiced historically in Pentecostal churches. This language apparently was based on 1 Cor. 14.5,[20] where Paul gives equal value to prophecy and an interpreted tongue for edifying the believing community. But it seems to have been reading into the text what is not there to suggest that prophecy and interpreted tongues thereby become *equatable phenomena*, since vv. 2 and 28 make it clear that they are not. This is especially so in v. 28 where Paul argues that there must be no glossolalia without interpretation in *the church*; rather the speaker is told to speak *'by himself and to God'*. The clear implication is that what is interpreted in every case is the speech that in v. 2 is called 'speaking mysteries to God'. To be sure, one cannot thereby

---

pentecostal and charismatic communities is the *same* in kind as that in the Pauline churches is moot—and probably somewhat irrelevant. There is simply no way to know. As an *experienced* phenomenon, it is at the very least *analogous* to theirs, meaning that it is understood to be a supernatural activity of the Spirit which functions in many of the same ways, and for many of its practitioners has value similar to that described by Paul.

20. See, for example, Riggs, *The Spirit Himself*, p. 87: 'tongues and interpretation are the equivalent of prophecy'. He then goes on to offer a considerable apologetic, in light of this assertion, as to why there should be both prophecy and interpreted tongues in the assembly. This is a less common view among more recent Pentecostals; see, for example, S.M. Horton, *What the Bible Says about the Holy Spirit* (Springfield, MO: Gospel Publishing House, 1976).

demonstrate that public speaking in tongues is never directed toward the community; what one can say is that Paul never says or implies that it is.

Secondly, all of the available data, therefore, also indicate that while Paul will not forbid interpreted glossolalia in the assembly, neither is he enthusiastic about it. This is made evident by his explicit preference for prophecy in the church, as well as by the clear implication in 1 Cor. 14.18-19 ('I speak in tongues more than all of you, but *in church* five intelligible words is preferable to thousands that are unintelligible') and v. 28 (to the one speaking in tongues, 'if there is no one to interpret remain silent *in church* and speak to God by yourself').

4.   That leads me to note further and to isolate specifically for the sake of the theological reflections that follow that the reason for 'silence' in church with regard to uninterpreted glossolalia vis-à-vis prophecy is that in both cases Paul's concern is with edification. What happens in the gathered community must be intelligible, precisely so that it can edify the rest of the community. Thus, in the case of uninterpreted glossolalia, the one speaking in tongues 'thanks God' to be sure, but the rest of the community cannot be edified and thus say the 'Amen' (1 Cor 14.16-17), because they are unable to understand what is being said to God.

But the opposite prevails for the individual believer who prays in tongues in the private place. Such a person 'speaks mysteries to God', and even though the mind is at rest and thus unfruitful, it is not detached or out of control. On the contrary, such prayer is a means of edification for the one so praying (1 Cor. 14.4) despite the 'unfruitfulness' regarding one's own understanding of what is being said.

While such an understanding runs counter to the heavily enlightenment-influenced self-understanding of Western Christendom, Rom. 8.27 offers the theological key to such edification. It is a matter of trusting God that the one to whom we thus pray by the Spirit 'knows the *mind of the Spirit*, that the Spirit is praying *on behalf of the saints* what is *according to God* [in keeping with his purposes]'. Paul is obviously at rest much more than later Christendom with the Spirit's edifying one's spirit, without such edification needing to be processed in the cortex of the brain. And it is at this point where my final, more theological, reflection emerges, as an attempt to tie parts 1 and 3 of this paper together.

5.   The Pauline context for 'praying in the Spirit', and thus for glossolalia, is his thoroughgoing eschatological framework, in which he understands the Spirit as the certain evidence that the future has already

made its appearance in the present[21] and the sure guarantee of its final consummation.[22] Within this framework glossolalia for Paul serves the believer *not* as evidence that the future is already present (vis-à-vis Corinth), but that the future is 'not yet' consummated.[23] It is because of our 'between the times' existence that we desperately need the Spirit's help in our present frailty. This is quite the point of Rom. 8.26-27. The Spirit comes alongside, prays through us with 'inarticulate groanings', as our help in this present time of weakness. At the same time glossolalia serves as a constant reminder that we, along with the whole of creation, continue to anticipate our final redemption.

This is why tongues, as well as prophecy and all other Spirit charismata, are for the present time only (1 Cor. 13.8-13). Tongues and prophecy and knowledge belong to this time of present weakness, when we 'know in part' and need the Spirit's help. The believers' praying in tongues echoes the 'groaning' of the whole creation, while together we await the final consummation of the future that God has already ushered in by the Resurrection and the gift of the Spirit.

The theological implications of such an understanding are large. In contrast to what is often implied in Pentecostal and charismatic circles, for Paul one does not 'pray in tongues' from a position of 'strength', as though being filled with the Spirit puts one in a position of power before God. Rather, one prays in tongues from a position of weakness, because we 'do not know how to pray as we ought'. At such times we desperately need the Spirit to help us, for the Spirit to pray through us what is

---

21. On this matter see esp. Fee, *Presence*, pp. 803-13. The Spirit is both the 'down payment' and the 'firstfruits' of the future that has already dawned with the prior coming of Christ and his resurrection and subsequent gift of the eschatological Spirit.

22. See esp. Eph. 4.30; cf. G.D. Fee, 'Some Exegetical and Theological Reflections on Ephesians 4.30 and Pauline Pneumatology', in M.W. Wilson (ed.), *Spirit and Renewal: Essays in Honor of J. Rodman Williams* (JPTSup, 5; Sheffield: Sheffield Academic Press, 1994), pp. 129-44.

23. Whether or not the Corinthians understood tongues as 'showy' is debatable; only the second application of the body analogy in 1 Cor. 12.22-24 would seem to suggest as much. That they considered tongues as evidence that they had already achieved something of their heavenly status seems much more in keeping with the Pauline argument. But in either case, their view of glossolalia and its purposes was utterly wrong from Paul's point of view. Praying in tongues belongs primarily in the privacy of one's own life of prayer; and such 'inarticulate groanings' reflect God's power at work even in our present weakness.

in keeping with God's purposes. And we need especially to learn the kind of trust that such praying inherently demands, namely that God does indeed know the mind of the Spirit, that his intercession for us is right on in terms of God's own purposes in our lives and in the world.

Such an understanding of glossolalia implies weakness in yet another way. Although the one speaking in tongues is not 'out of control' in the ecstatic sense of such phenomena, one is not 'in control' in the more biblical sense. One gives up control of one's life and agendas, so as to put one's whole self—especially those most unruly parts of oneself, the mind and the tongue—at God's disposal,[24] believing that his love for us is absolutely pure, totally 'without dissimulation' (to use an old King James phrase), and that he purposes only good for 'the saints'. This is why Paul insists that he will do both: that he will pray and sing with his mind (for the sake of others), and that he will pray and sing in the Spirit (for his own sake).

At the same time, by urging that we pray out of a stance of weakness, Paul also affirms our utter dependence upon God for all things; and here is where the 'power in weakness' comes in. By praying through us in tongues, the Spirit is the way whereby God's strength is made perfect in the midst of our weakness, which is where the ultimate strength lies for the believer. Thus our praying in tongues, while evidence for us that we have entered the new, eschatological age ushered in by the Spirit, serves especially as evidence that we are still 'not yet' regarding the consummation of that age. Because we have not yet arrived, and await with the whole of creation our final redemption, we thus pray in the Spirit out of weakness, implicitly trusting the Spirit to pray in keeping with God's purposes. Such praying is thus freedom and power, God's power being perfected in the midst of our weakness.

I note finally that if the view presented here is in fact faithful to Paul, one can also understand why, on the one hand, he speaks so little of it, but speaks so positively of it, on the other; and why also he himself was

24. I admit to wondering at times whether present resistance to glossolalia on the part of so many is not a combination of both a misunderstanding of Paul's own perspective on this matter and of a need to be 'in control'. Maybe the bottom line of such resistance is our lip-service to putting ourselves at God's disposal in our weakness, yet insisting that all praying should be from a stance of strength—the form of strength found in praying only with one's mind and seldom in the Spirit. This is another place where cessationism fails in all its forms. Not only is it exegetically and hermeneutically unsupportable, but it ends up being a form of 'living from a position of strength', in this case in the strength of a rationalistic mindset.

given to it in his private praying far more than any of the Corinthians who appeared to prize it so highly. Paul's entire understanding of present existence in Christ by the Spirit is one in which God's power and wisdom are best exhibited through human weakness and frailty. This is why he refused to know anything among the Corinthians except 'Christ and him crucified'; this is why he argues with them as he does in 2 Corinthians 11–12; and this is why he can speak so confidently of the Spirit's empowering even while he himself knows weakness, suffering, imprisonment, scoffing.

In sum, understood from Paul's perspective, speaking in tongues fits the whole of his theological outlook. Here is our opportunity to express our deepest selves to God in praise, thanksgiving, prayer and intercession. And this is so especially when we do not ourselves know what to pray in the midst of present weakness; but what we do know, Paul goes on, is that by thus praying in our behalf in our present weakness, 'the Spirit works all things together for good, for us who love God and are called in keeping with God's purposes' (Rom. 8.28).[25]

25. For this understanding of this familiar passage, see Fee, *Presence*, pp. 587-90.

THE HOLY SPIRIT IN THE OLD TESTAMENT

Walter C. Kaiser, Jr

One of the most important, but yet the most notoriously difficult, aspects of salvation in the Old Testament is to describe the precise work of the Holy Spirit in the individual's experience of regeneration and sanctification in that testament.

1. *Jesus and Nicodemus*

There can be no question but that the Spirit had to be part of every new birth during that era before the cross of Christ for several reasons. Most significantly, this was the view that Jesus held. Did he not remind Nicodemus that a person could not enter the kingdom of God without being 'born again' and being born 'of the Spirit' (Jn 3.3, 5, 8)?

Apparently this was a totally new concept for Nicodemus—which deficiency in Nicodemus's education, in turn, amazed Jesus. How could this man be a teacher of the Jews and not know either about being born again or being born of the Spirit? Where must this man have gone to Yeshiva or seminary? Had he never read Ezek. 36.25-32 with its teaching about the 'new heart' and the 'new Spirit'?

The point must be faced: Jesus expected Nicodemus (and all subsequent interpreters) to understand that no one (in any period of time) is ever converted into the kingdom of God without experiencing the new birth and the regenerating work of the Holy Spirit. If the God of the New Testament is the God of the Old Testament, then the Holy Spirit of the New Testament is the Holy Spirit of the Old Testament—he is one, not several divided deities.

My argument here is not to use the New Testament to settle doctrine for the Old Testament, but only to show that Jesus thought it was altogether reasonable for a person to experience both being born again and the work of regeneration by the Holy Spirit in the process of experiencing the new birth as judged by the writings of the Old Testament—especially since the New Testament had not yet been written and Christ had not yet gone to the cross and been raised from the dead.

2. *Paul and 'The Same Spirit'*

But the argument for the presence and work of the Holy Spirit in the Old Testament involves much more than this confrontation between Nicodemus and Jesus. If the reference to 'the same spirit of faith' is a reference to the Holy Spirit in 2 Cor. 4.13, then the apostle Paul adds another definitive touch to this argument, that is, that the act of believing during the days of the Old Testament was no less a result of the Holy Spirit's ministry in each new birth than is New Testament faith in this Christian era a product of the same Holy Spirit's work. This point seems to be substantiated by the citation by Paul from Ps. 116.10 in 2 Cor. 4.13. The very same Holy Spirit, Paul's argument seems to say, who was at work in the psalmist who said, 'I believe; therefore I spoke', is the Holy Spirit that is now present in Christian believers. He is also the same Holy Spirit of faith during both the old and the new eras.

This is the argument that Geoffrey W. Grogan set forth in his pioneering article on the work of the Holy Spirit entitled, 'The Experience of Salvation in the Old and New Testaments'. There Grogan suggested, 'It may be that "the same spirit of faith" in 2 Cor. 4.13 is a reference to the divine Spirit, in which case Paul is saying that our faith is the product of the same Spirit who was at work in the author of Psalm cxvi. 10'.[1] Even though many deny the reference is to the Holy Spirit in 2 Cor. 4.13, the fact that it is a quotation from Ps. 116.10 which, similar to Paul, also focuses on belief is crucial to the case: 'I believe; therefore [or: "even when"] I said'. Accordingly, Paul argued: 'It is written: "I believed; therefore I have spoken"'.[2]

---

1.   G.W. Grogan, 'The Experience of Salvation in the Old and New Testaments', *Vox Evangelica* 5 (1967), p. 13.

2.   While most commentators agree that the Hebrew construction of the clause in Ps. 116.10 is extremely difficult, they almost all join in declaring that the Greek Septuagint rendering that Paul follows is 'certainly wrong'. The LXX rendered it: Ἐπίστευσα διὸ ἐλάλησα, 'I believed, therefore I have spoken'. Some think that the LXX διό, 'therefore' was corrupted from διότι, 'because'. But in the Greek Psalter διότι is never found and διό only here (according to L.C. Allen, *Psalms 101–150*; WBC; Waco, TX: Word Books, 1983, p. 113). To complicate matters further, the LXX, Syriac, Arabic and Ethiopic agree on cutting Ps. 116 into two, making

3. *Psalm 51.11*

Certainly, the *crux interpretum* in this discussion of the Holy Spirit's work and presence in the Old Testament is Ps. 51.11: 'Do not cast me from your presence or take your Holy Spirit from me. Restore to me the joy of your salvation.' It is doubtful if this plea by David could simply refer, as many interpreters prefer to explain it, to a request that he not loose the gift of government, which came upon him at his anointing from the Holy Spirit and that he not be removed from his office (1 Sam. 16.13-14). The context in Ps. 51.10 would be decidedly against such a limitation of his plea to apply merely to this desire to be able to continue to govern, for David had just prayed, 'Create in me a pure heart, O God, and renew a right Spirit within me'. It is little wonder, then, that a few, such as A.B. Simpson believed that David's mention of the Spirit referred to the one who 'will come into the heart that has been made right, and dwell within us in His power and holiness'.[3]

Most discussions of the work of the Holy Spirit in the Old Testament limit his ministry to equipping people for particular acts or spheres of service, giving them wisdom and the gifts of craftsmanship, using them as channels of his power, being the Spirit of prophetic inspiration, and working in the creation of the world. But the Holy Spirit also was at work in regenerating every believer that ever experienced the new birth in those days before Calvary, just as he was present after Pentecost. If

---

Ps. 116.10 the beginning of Ps. 116 and uniting the first nine verses of Ps. 116 to the end of Ps. 115. The Hebrew text reads: האמנתי כי אדבר. Usually, when כי follows a hiphil, it means 'that'; however in all other instances the subject of the verb in the subordinate clause is different from that in the principal clause, for example, Exod. 4.5, 'that they may believe *that* Yahweh has appeared'. But could not Ps. 116.10 be rendered as 'I believe that I should speak'? M. Dahood, *Psalms III: 101–150* (AB, 17A; Garden City, NY: Doubleday, 1970), p. 148, rendered the verb 'to believe' as 'I have remained faithful', and then argued that כי should be understood as an adversative 'though' in accordance with instances cited in BDB, 474b ('I remained faithful though I was pursued'—thereby repointing the word for 'spoke' to mean 'pursue'!). The mystery seems almost insoluble. To add just one more piece in favor of Paul's rendering, the Syriac in the Hexapla reads, 'I have believed; therefore have I spoken'. (But in the margin it reads: 'I have believed that I should speak').

3.   A.B. Simpson, *The Holy Spirit* (2 vols.; Harrisburg: Christian Publications, n.d.), I, p. 137.

men and women were justified by faith through grace from Adam's day until the time of Jesus, and if faith is and was the gift of God, and not of works, lest anyone should boast (Eph. 2.5b, 9), then it is a given that this faith came as a result of the inner working of the Holy Spirit, and that they, like us, were also regenerated by the Holy Spirit.

4. *The New Testament Promise of the Holy Spirit*

But what shall we do with the passages in the New Testament that seem to claim that the Holy Spirit had not yet been given until he came at Pentecost? There are a large number of passages that are usually raised at this point to counter the certainty of any permanent activity of the Spirit in the life of the believer before Pentecost (Mt. 3.11 [and its parallels]; Jn 1.33; 7.37-39; 14.16-19, 26; 15.26; 16.7-15; Acts 1.4-8; 11.15-17; 15.8).

If these passages were intended to indicate that the Holy Spirit had never ministered prior to the days of Jesus and the apostles, what would we ever do with passages such as Ps. 51.11 and Ezekiel 36? John 3.5-8 certainly indicates that Jesus held Nicodemus and all teachers of the Jews responsible for knowing and teaching that the Holy Spirit was involved in the work of each person's new birth prior to the cross. There were also the additional evidences, such as Jesus' encouragement when he sent out the twelve prior to his crucifixion in Mt. 10.20, that it would not be the twelve themselves who would be doing the speaking, 'but the Spirit of your Father speaking through you'. Another argument favoring that same thesis could be raised from Lk. 11.13. While Jesus was teaching on prayer, he urged, 'If you then, though you are evil, know how to give good gifts to your children, how much more will your Father in heaven give the Holy Spirit to those who ask him!'—this while the age of the older covenant was in force. That also is why believers who were jailed on false charges were not to worry what they would say in their defense as believers, 'for the Holy Spirit will teach you at that time what you should say' (Lk. 12.12). All of these examples were before Pentecost, even though some of these promises anticipated Pentecost as well.

There are two groups of passages mentioned above that should be set off to one side, since they have no effect on this issue of the presence and work of the Holy Spirit in the Old Testament. The first group deals exclusively, not with the individual believer, but with the promise that the Holy Spirit would assist those who would write the New Testament canon, by reminding them of everything that happened while Jesus was with them (Jn 14.26), testifying about Jesus' works to those who had been with him since the beginning of his ministry (Jn 15.26-27), and by taking the doctrine that was the Father's teaching and making it known to these writers of the New Testament (Jn 16.12-15). These texts should not be confused with the concern about the experience of regeneration by the Holy Spirit in the Old Testament.

Likewise, there is a second group of texts about the coming baptism of the Holy Spirit and fire (Mt. 3.11 [and its synoptic parallels]; Jn 1.33; Acts 1.4-8; 11.15-17; 15.8), which pointed to a new, but distinct, work of the Holy Spirit. Here was another dissimilarity with the revelation that had preceded the New Testament. In this unique baptism of the Holy Spirit, new believers were incorporated into the universal body of believers, Christ's Church. The gospels and the book of Acts saw this work as a future work, whereas 1 Cor. 12.13 viewed it as a completed action: 'For we were all baptized by one Spirit into one body.' Therefore, that new work of the Holy Spirit came somewhere between these two terminal points of the Gospels and Paul's word to the Corinthians. The natural suggestion, since the promised new event was 'not many days' off, when it was mentioned in the beginning of Acts (1.5), was that this baptism of the Holy Spirit referred to the Jewish (Acts 2), Samaritan (Acts 8) and Gentile (Acts 10) Pentecosts, and to all who subsequently confessed Christ as their Lord and Savior, by which all so endowed with the Holy Spirit were in turn incorporated into the universal body of Christ, his Church.

But for the question of the role of the Holy Spirit in the Old Testament, Jn 14.16-17 is extremely important and textually difficult. In that Upper Room discourse, just prior to his death, Jesus declared,

> And I will ask the Father, and he will give you another Counselor to be with you forever—the Spirit of Truth. The world cannot accept him, because it neither sees him or knows him. But you know him, for he lives with you and will be [or 'is'] in you.

The resolution to the problem of the Holy Spirit's presence in the Old Testament stands or falls, for those who receive the witness only of the New Testament as definitive for Church doctrine (a practice in itself very dubious), on the correct reading of the verb 'to be' in v. 17. Is it a future verb (ἔσται) or the present tense (ἔστι)?[4]

---

4.   B.F. Westcott, *The Gospel of St John* (The Speaker's Commentary; Cam-

If one is to choose the more difficult reading (*lectio deficilior*), a principle that is usually recommended in cases such as this one (since copyists tended to level out their readings), favor must be given to the present tense form of the verb: the Holy Spirit 'is' with you. Moreover, the use of the preposition παρά, 'with', pointed not to a fluctuating relationship, but to one of the same permanence as that of the Father with the Son. Thus they made their home 'with' that person (Jn 14.23). If the present tense is the correct reading here, as I believe it is, then the Holy Spirit was already 'Liv[ing] with' believers prior to Pentecost.

The more difficult text, from the standpoint of the position that I have taken here, is Jn 7.38-39.

> Whoever believes in me, as the Scripture has said, streams of living water will flow from within him. By this [Jesus] meant the Spirit, whom those who believed in him were later to receive. Up to that time the Spirit had not been given, since Jesus had not yet been glorified.

When those individuals believed, the Holy Spirit would come on them just as it had come on all who had previously believed in the days of the Old Testament. But now the Holy Spirit would not come quietly and internally, for as Goodwin argued, 'He must have a coming in state, in a solemn and visible manner, accompanied with visible effects as well as Christ had on Calvary, and whereof all the Jews should be, and were, witnesses.'[5]

Therefore, just as the feast of Pentecost was tied to the Passover, coming 50 days later, so the coming of the Holy Spirit, in visible stateliness, was tied to the death of Christ and followed it 50 days later. Here was God's signal that the day that had been anticipated since the ministry of Joel (2.28-32) had now been inaugurated. God had begun to pour out his Spirit on all flesh, without regard to gender, age or race. Here now was the predicted baptism of the Holy Spirit whereby all who believed were incorporated into one body of Christ, his Church.

G. Smeaton comments on Jn 7.37ff. in this manner:

> But the apostle adds that 'the Spirit was not yet' because Christ's glorification had not yet arrived. He does not mean that the Spirit did not yet exist—for all Scripture attests His eternal pre-existence—nor that His regenerative efficacy was still unknown—for countless millions had been regenerated by His power since the first promise in Gen.—but that these

bridge, 1881; repr. Grand Rapids: Eerdmans, 1967), *ad. loc.*

5.   Quoted by G. Smeaton, *The Doctrine of the Holy Spirit* (London, 1958), p. 49 from T. Goodwin, *Works* (Edinburgh: T. & T. Clark, 1961), VI, p. 8.

operations of the Spirit had been but an anticipation of the atoning gift of Christ rather than a GIVING. The apostle speaks comparatively, not absolutely.[6]

Thus, the experience of believers in the days before Christ's first coming was as full an experience of the Holy Spirit as that experienced by the New Testament saints in every way except two—the Holy Spirit's visible coming in state and his act of incorporating believers into one body, the Church. Both eras of saints experienced the regenerating experience of new life, but there was another major difference.

After Pentecost, the New Testament writers began to link the Holy Spirit with Jesus in a special way. He is 'the Spirit of Christ' (Rom. 8.9), and 'the Spirit of [God's] Son' (Gal. 4.6). The Holy Spirit was now seeking to bring believers into conformity to the life and character of Jesus Christ (2 Cor. 3.18). As Geoffrey Grogan summarized the matter:

> Hence we may say that the *full* New Testament experience of the Spirit of Christ from Pentecost onwards is at one with that of the true saints of the Old Testament in that it was always a regenerating experience, bringing men to newness of life, but that there is an important difference. It is not simply that the Spirit now operates on the basis of the perfect character of Jesus. Presumably He had already done this in anticipation even in the Old Testament. Rather it is that He operates on the basis of that character *as now revealed historically* and so held before the minds of those who now experienced His activity in their hearts.[7]

5. *Distinctive Old Testament Passages on the Holy Spirit*

But what of the Old Testament itself? I have been arguing on the basis of the pre-crucifixion statements by Jesus that the Holy Spirit was certainly operative in an individual's life in giving new birth and the work of regeneration. But there were other works as well. Neh. 9.20 mentioned the goodness, or even the graciousness, of the Spirit when he came to instruct Israel through Moses: 'You gave your good Spirit to instruct them.' Even earlier in the Old Testament, the Holy Spirit is represented as coming mightily on Saul with enormous personal effects: 'The Spirit of the Lord will come upon you in power, and you will prophesy with them; and you will be changed into a different person' (or, as the Hebrew has it, 'turned him into another man'; 1 Sam. 10.6).

---

6.   Smeaton, *Doctrine*, p. 49.
7.   Grogan, 'Salvation', p. 17. The emphases are his.

As B.B. Warfield concluded,

> At all events this conception of a thorough ethical change characterizes the Old Testament idea of the inner work of the Spirit of Holiness, as He first comes to be called in the Psalms and Isaiah (Ps. li.11; Isa. lxiii.10, 11 only [*sic*]). The classical passage in this connection is the Fifty-first Psalm—David's cry of penitence and prayer for mercy after Nathan's probing of his sin with Bathsheba. He prays for the creation within him of a new heart and the renewal of a right spirit within him; and he represents that all his hopes of continuing power of new life rest on the continuance of God's holy Spirit, or the Spirit of God's holiness, with him.[8]

5.1 *Ezekiel 36.23-32: The Spirit and the New Covenant*

While many prefer to assign this prophecy to eschatological times, apparently they forget that the New Covenant, which many present day believers enjoy, had its inauguration in Jer. 31.31-34 with the people of Jeremiah's day and with the believers of the New Testament Church. Even though Ezekiel does not use the term 'New Covenant' as Jeremiah did, it is clear from the contents of his message that he is speaking of a covenant renewal—for example, Ezek. 36.28 promised: 'You will be my people and I will be your God.'

Here the Lord intended to prove his holiness by manifesting his power by restoring Israel to her land before all the nations. But that was not all that God would do; most importantly he would cleanse them from all their sins with clean water followed by the gift of the Holy Spirit and a new heart. As George T. Montague observed, this

> is unprecedented in the pneumatology of the Old Testament. The need for a washing clean had of course already been stressed by the prophets (cf. Is 4.4) but the *rûaḥ* or 'spirit' there was the agent of the cleansing itself. Here the new spirit appears as the positive life which *follows* the cleansing. The 'new spirit' (vs. 26) is the Lord's own spirit (vs. 27) and that is why it manifests itself in a willing observance of the Lord's mind for his people, the law (36.27).[9]

It is clear, of course, that Ezekiel, like Jeremiah, has a form of inaugurated eschatology which embodies a 'now' and a 'not yet' aspect of the Spirit's work. The cleansing with water is correctly associated with

---

8. B.B. Warfield, 'The Spirit of God in the Old Testament', in Samuel G. Craig (ed.), *Biblical and Theological Studies* (Philadelphia: Presbyterian and Reformed, 1952), p. 147.

9. G.T. Montague, *The Holy Spirit: Growth of a Biblical Tradition* (Peabody, MA: Hendrickson, 1994), pp. 46-47.

Christian baptism, and the new heart and the new spirit are likewise correctly connected to the Spirit's work in regeneration and the new birth.

But typical of the New Covenant and many of the prophecies of Scripture, the full impact of that work of God would not be completely realized until that final eschaton—in this case, until Israel was once again restored to her land in a day yet future to this present day. The full description of the rebirth of the nation Israel is given in Ezek. 37.1-14. That passage concludes in v. 14 by noting the threefold effect of the Spirit on the nation: it is the Spirit who gives life, who leads the people back to their homeland, and who also renews in them a conviction of the reality of the Lord.

5.2 *Joel and the Promise of the Holy Spirit*
Even though the immediate occasion for Joel's prophecy is a plague of locusts, Joel sees this event as a symbol of the coming 'day of the Lord'. If the four verbs in Joel 2.18 are correctly understood to be past tense verbs (Hebrew, *waw*-consecutives with the imperfect), then we may be assured that the people did repent as a result of Joel's preaching. What followed were the immediate results of that repentance (2.19-27) and mostly the distant or future and eschatological aspects of their repentance (2.28-32 [Heb. 3.1-5]).

As we have seen in the prophecies of the New Covenant in Jeremiah and Ezekiel, so Joel has the same inaugurated eschatology of a 'now' and a 'not-yet' inclusion within one and the same prophecy. In fact, Joel divides the effects of the people's repentance by referring to the return of the autumn and spring rains 'as before' (בראשׁון, 'in the first, beginning', Joel 2.23d; NIV, 'as before') and the downpour of the Holy Spirit that would come 'afterward' (אחרי־כ, 'after this', Joel 2.28 [Heb. 3.1]).[10]

The fact that Peter on the day of Pentecost assured those present that 'this is what was spoken by the prophet Joel' (Acts 2.16) shows that this prophecy, like the others about the Holy Spirit, was being fulfilled throughout history. What has not received any fulfillment whatsoever is Joel 2.30-31; the great cosmic effects that predict 'blood and fire and billows of smoke [in which] the sun will be turned into darkness and the

---

10. For a fuller discussion of this passage, see my discussion in *The Use of the Old Testament in the New* (Chicago: Moody, 1985), pp. 89-100, an article that originally appeared in 'The Promise of God and the Outpouring of the Holy Spirit', in M. Inch and R. Youngblood (eds.), *The Living and Active Word of God*, (Winona Lake, IN: Eisenbrauns, 1983), pp. 109-122.

moon into blood before the coming of the great and dreadful day of the Lord'. Thus what was to happen in the eschaton on a macro-level, was now being realized in the present on a micro-level. Men and women, both young and old, Jew and Gentile, were all receiving a tropical out-pouring of the Holy Spirit in the present age. Ezekiel (39.29) appeared to restrict this outpouring to 'the house of Israel', but Joel democratized it by having it come 'on all flesh', without favor to gender, age or race, just as Num. 11.25-29 had envisioned.

6. *Conclusion*

Very few writers have written on the Holy Spirit and the Old Testament. Among the better known are J.C.J. Waite,[11] Lloyd Neve,[12] Leon Wood,[13] John Rea[14] and Wilf Hildebrandt.[15] It is clear that much more work must be done before a clearer picture of the Holy Spirit's work in the life of the individual believer of the Old Testament fully comes to light. But for my part, I feel that the basic outlines have already been unfolded in the key passages discussed above.

The chief hurdle lies in recognizing that Ezekiel 36 is not exclusively eschatological, but it, along with the New Covenant, has both a present and a future application. That is what opens up the new doors on this fascinating topic.

11   *The Activity of the Holy Spirit within the Old Testament Period* (a 1961 London Bible College Annual Lecture).

12. *The Spirit of God in the Old Testament* (Tokyo: Seibunsha, 1972).

13. *The Holy Spirit in the Old Testament* (Grand Rapids: Zondervan, 1976).

14. 'The Personal Relationship of Old Testament Believers to the Holy Spirit (Psalm 51:11)', in P. Elbert (ed.), *Essays on Apostolic Themes*, (Peabody, MA: Hendrickson, 1985).

15. *An Old Testament Theology of the Spirit of God* (Peabody, MA: Hendrickson, 1995).

SPIRIT-BAPTISM AND SPIRITUAL GIFTS[*]

Robert P. Menzies

Since the earliest days of the modern Pentecostal revival, Pentecostals have advocated a baptism in the Holy Spirit distinct from conversion (Acts 1.5, 8; 2.4) and the present reality of spiritual gifts (1 Cor. 12.8-10). These twin themes of Spirit-baptism and spiritual gifts have decisively marked the movement. Yet surprisingly, the nature of the relationship between Spirit-baptism and the gifts of the Spirit has not received much attention. Early Pentecostal writers generally described baptism in the Holy Spirit as the 'door' or gateway to the gifts, but this position was stated or assumed rather than developed in a significant way.[1] More recent Pentecostal writings have shed little light on this subject, and the implicit assumptions of an earlier generation still appear to be determinative. Today, Pentecostals generally affirm that Spirit-baptism is the 'gateway' to the gifts, but a clear biblical rationale for this position has never been articulated.[2]

---

[*]   With a heart full of gratitude and fond memories, I present this essay to my Father—a man who has modeled for me what it means to 'walk in the Spirit'.

1.   Thus Myer Pearlman declares that the baptism in the Holy Spirit enables Christians to experience 'the charismatic operation of the Spirit' (*Knowing the Doctrines of the Bible* [Springfield, MO: Gospel Publishing House, 1937], p. 313). See also W. Cantelon, *The Baptism of the Holy Spirit* (Springfield, MO: Acme Printing, 1951), p. 15; E.S. Williams, *Systematic Theology* (3 vols.; Springfield, MO: Gospel Publishing House, 1953), III, pp. 63-75; R. Riggs, *We Believe* (Springfield, MO: Gospel Publishing House, 1954), p. 28; D. Gee, *Spiritual Gifts in the Work of the Ministry Today* (Springfield, MO: Gospel Publishing House, 1963), p. 18.

2.   See P.C. Nelson, *Bible Doctrines* (Springfield, MO: Gospel Publishing House, 1962), 78; S.M. Horton, *What the Bible Says about the Holy Spirit* (Springfield, MO: Gospel Publishing House, 1976), p. 261; and G.R. Carlson, *Our Faith and Fellowship* (Springfield, MO: Gospel Publishing House, 1977), pp. 65-67. Note also the Assemblies of God Statement of Fundamental Truths, 7, The Promise of the Father:

This understanding of Spirit-baptism as the gateway to the gifts was generally linked to an emphasis on the 'nine special gifts' of 1 Cor. 12.8-10.[3] Yet today few would speak of only nine gifts. Donald Gee reflects what is today a consensus among students of the Bible: 'I now think it is a mistake to always refer to the "nine gifts" as though the catalogue there [1 Cor. 12.8-10] is exhaustive'.[4] The recognition that there is a rich variety of spiritual gifts has led many charismatics to reject the 'gateway' position of Pentecostalism. H.I. Lederle states the matter directly: 'There is no biblical support for any particular crisis experience or event being the gateway to the functioning of the gifts of the Spirit...every Christian is, and should be increasingly, charismatic.'[5]

More recently the Pentecostal position has been challenged on another front. A large and rapidly growing group of non-Pentecostal Evangelicals are seeking after and experiencing spiritual gifts. This fresh emphasis on the charisms is remarkable in that it is occurring in evangelical circles which, in the past, had rejected the continuing validity of spiritual gifts. This new outpouring of charismatic vitality has been designated the 'third wave'. The term refers to an energizing work of the Spirit among evangelical Christians subsequent to the 'first wave' of renewal which birthed the classical Pentecostal denominations and the 'second wave' which impacted mainline denominations and ignited the charismatic movement. Third wavers consciously reject the Pentecostal understanding of Spirit-baptism, yet affirm the importance and availability of all of

All believers are entitled to and should expect and earnestly seek the promise of the Father, the baptism in the Holy Ghost and fire, according to the command of our Lord Jesus Christ. This was the normal experience of all in the early Christian Church. With it come the enduement of power for life and service, the bestowment of the gifts and their uses in the work of the ministry.

3. For a focus on the 'nine gifts' of 1 Cor. 12.8-10 see Pearlman, *Doctrines*, pp. 321-27; C. Brumback, *What Meaneth This?* (Springfield, MO: Gospel Publishing House, 1947), p. 153; Cantelon, *Baptism*, p. 15; Riggs, *We Believe*, pp. 28-29.

4. Gee, *Spiritual Gifts*, p. 5. Williams, *Systematic Theology*, III, pp. 75-82, and Horton, *Holy Spirit*, p. 209 also acknowledge that the 'nine gifts' of 1 Cor. 12.8-10 are suggestive.

5. H.I. Lederle, *Treasures Old and New: Interpretations of 'Spirit-Baptism' in the Charismatic Renewal Movement* (Peabody, MA: Hendrickson, 1988), pp. 218, 228. See also D. and R. Bennett, *The Holy Spirit and You* (Plainfield, NJ: Logos, 1971), p. 81, who argue that believers who have not been baptized in the Spirit may manifest seven of the nine gifts listed in 1 Cor. 12.8-10 (tongues and the interpretation of tongues are the exception).

the spiritual gifts listed in 1 Cor. 12.8-10.[6] The theology and experience
of these third wavers thus represent a significant challenge to the
Pentecostal 'gateway' position.

As a result of these developments, Pentecostals are being challenged
to reassess previous assumptions and to articulate more clearly the
biblical basis for their position. Indeed, the charismatic emphasis on the
diverse nature of the gifts coupled with the explosion of gifts among non-
Pentecostal Evangelicals raises crucial questions: Must one be baptized in
the Holy Spirit before one can experience any of the charisms? What is
the nature of the relationship between Spirit-baptism and the gifts of the
Spirit? I shall seek to answer these questions by first critiquing the
'gateway' position outlined above, and then suggesting an alternative
approach which does justice to the distinctive theological perspectives of
both Luke and Paul.

1. *Pentecost: Gateway to the Gifts?*

The Pentecostal position that the baptism in the Holy Spirit constitutes a
necessary prerequisite for the operation of the gifts (indeed, any gift)
faces three insurmountable obstacles. First, as noted above, the Pentecostal position was generally associated with an exclusive focus on the
'nine gifts' listed in 1 Cor. 12.8-10. Today, even in classical Pentecostal
circles, most would acknowledge that Paul's gift list in 1 Cor. 12.8-10 is
suggestive rather definitive. A comparison of the Pauline gift lists (1 Cor.
12.8-10; 12.28; 12.29-30; Rom. 12.6-8; Eph. 4.11), which describe a rich
variety of gifts, virtually demands such a conclusion. Stanley Horton, a
leading Pentecostal scholar, speaks for many when he concludes: 'It
seems better to take all of these lists [the lists in 1 Cor. 12.8-10; 12.28;
and 12.29-30] as merely giving samplings of the gifts and callings of the
Spirit, samplings taken from an infinite supply.'[7]

This judgment, however, represents a significant obstacle for the
'gateway' position. It is one thing to suggest that Spirit-baptism is the
'gateway' to specific gifts such as speaking in tongues or prophesy. Yet

---

6.   See for example G.S. Greig and K.N. Springer (eds.), *The Kingdom and the
Power* (Ventura, CA: Regal Books, 1993), p. 21; C.P. Wagner, *The Third Wave of
the Holy Spirit* (Ann Arbor, MI: Vine Books, 1988), pp. 18-19; J. Wimber and
K. Springer, *Power Points* (New York: HarperCollins, 1991), pp. 135-36 and *Power
Evangelism* (San Francisco: Harper & Row, 1991), p. 148.

7.   Horton, *Holy Spirit*, p. 209.

it is quite another to suggest that all the gifts, including gifts of 'administration' (1 Cor. 12.28), 'serving' (Rom. 12.7) or 'giving' (Rom. 12.8), necessarily flow from a prior Spirit-baptism. That is to say, if Paul were speaking only of a select group of gifts, perhaps it would be plausible to suggest that a baptism in the Spirit distinct from conversion functions as the 'gateway' to their operation. But Paul's emphasis on the rich variety of charisms encourages us to see his gift language as embracing the entire range of enablings which the Spirit grants to members of the Christian community for the common good. The rich diversity of the gifts then suggests that they cannot be described as the result of a specific experience distinct from conversion.

This leads us to the second obstacle. Paul not only highlights the diverse character of the charisms, he also declares that every Christian has a role to play. This conclusion is confirmed by Paul's words in 1 Cor. 12.11: 'All these are the work of one and the same Spirit, and he gives them to each one, just as he determines.'[8] In Paul's perspective then, every Christian is charismatic. And nowhere does Paul speak of a baptism in the Spirit distinct from conversion which might serve as a 'gateway' to the gifts. While Paul does encourage every Christian to 'be filled with the Spirit' (Eph. 5.18), this experience is related to Christian maturity rather than the operation of charisms, it centers on the fruit of the Spirit rather than the gifts.[9] Thus it is exceedingly difficult to argue that Paul viewed such an experience as a necessary precondition for entering into the charismatic dimension of the Spirit.

The third obstacle takes us to the very heart of the matter, for it explains why the 'gateway' position fails to understand Paul adequately. The 'gateway' position is based on a fundamental methodological error. It uncritically blends together theological concepts from Luke (Spirit-baptism) and Paul (spiritual gifts) with little regard for the context in which they are used by their respective authors. Thus, 'gateway' proponents have assumed that the Spirit-baptism distinct from conversion described by Luke (Acts 1.5, 8; 2.4) represents the 'gateway' to the Pauline gifts (1 Cor. 12.8-10; 12.28; 12.29-30; Rom. 12.6-8; Eph. 4.11). This is the case, although Paul never explicitly speaks of Luke's Spirit-baptism (i.e. the Pentecostal gift) and thus never relates it to spiritual gifts. The weakness of this approach is apparent. A framework alien to

8. All biblical quotations are taken from the NIV unless otherwise indicated.
9. Note the context, esp. Eph. 5.15: 'Be very careful, then, how you live—not as unwise but as wise.'

the perspective of the biblical authors has been imposed upon the biblical data producing a system which is essentially extra-biblical.

There is a better way. A truly biblical theology develops only when we treat 'each biblical author or book separately and...outline his or its particular theological emphases'. Only after we have 'set a text in the context of its author's thought and intention....only then can the biblical-theologian feel free to let that text interact with other texts from other books'.[10] Thus, in order to answer the question concerning the nature of the relationship between Spirit-baptism and spiritual gifts, we must first place these concepts within their proper Lukan and Pauline contexts. To this task I now turn.

2. *Two Trajectories: The Perspectives of Paul and Luke*

An analysis of the pneumatologies of Paul and Luke reveals a number of significant differences. Their pneumatologies appear to have distinct trajectories, each moving in a unique and significant direction. For this reason, it will be important to outline the basic characteristics of these distinctive trajectories. Then, against this backdrop, I shall seek to define the concepts of Spirit-baptism and spiritual gifts.

2.1 *The Pauline Trajectory*
At the outset, it is evident that Paul presents a fuller, larger picture of the Spirit's work than Luke. For Paul, the Christian life in its entirety is an outworking of the Spirit of God. The Spirit is the source of cleansing (1 Cor. 6.11; Rom. 15.16), righteousness (Gal. 5.5; Rom. 2.29; 8.1-17; 14.17; Gal. 5.16-26), intimate fellowship with (Gal. 4.6; Rom. 8.14-17) and knowledge of God (1 Cor. 2.6-16; 2 Cor. 3.3-18), and ultimately, eternal life through the resurrection (Rom. 8.11; 1 Cor. 15.44-49; Gal. 6.8). Thus, it is not surprising that Paul describes each believer's ability to contribute to the life of the community as a manifestation or gift of the Spirit (1 Cor. 12.8-10; 12.28; 12.29-30; Rom. 12.6-8; Eph. 4.11). More specifically, the rich variety of the gifts granted to each believer for the common good appears to be a natural extension of Paul's larger pneumatological perspective. Since from Paul's perspective the Christian life from the very outset is shaped by the Spirit of God, there is little reason to suggest that spiritual gifts are transmitted or actualized by some experience subsequent to conversion. It would appear that the gift

10. J.D.G. Dunn, *Baptism in the Holy Spirit* (London: SCM Press, 1970), p. 39.

of the Spirit which brings Christian life, also brings the ability to bless the community.

2.2 *The Lukan Trajectory*

Luke's perspective is considerably different from that of Paul. Unlike Paul, who frequently speaks of the soteriological dimension of the Spirit's work, Luke consistently portrays the Spirit as the source of prophetic inspiration. From the very outset of his two-volume work, Luke emphasizes the prophetic dimension of the Spirit's activity. The profusion of Spirit-inspired pronouncements in the infancy narratives herald the arrival of the era of fulfillment (Lk. 1.41-45, 67-79; 2.25-32). This era is marked by the prophetic activity of John, the ministry of Jesus, and the mission of his church, all of which are carried out in the power of the Spirit. Filled with the Spirit from his mother's womb (Lk. 1.15, 17), John anticipates the inauguration of Jesus' ministry. By carefully crafting his narrative, Luke ties his account of Jesus' pneumatic anointing (Lk. 3.22) together with Jesus' dramatic announcement at Nazareth (Lk. 4.18-21), and thus indicates that the Spirit came upon Jesus at the Jordan in order to equip him for his task as messianic herald. Literary parallels between the description of Jesus' anointing at the Jordan and that of the disciples at Pentecost suggest that Luke interpreted the latter event in light of the former: the Spirit came upon the disciples at Pentecost to equip them for their prophetic vocation. This judgment is supported by the Baptist's prophecy concerning the coming baptism of Spirit and fire (Lk. 3.16), for Luke interprets the sifting activity of the Spirit of which John prophesied as being accomplished in the Spirit-directed and Spirit-empowered mission of the Church (Acts 1.5, 8). It is confirmed by Luke's narration of the Pentecost event (Acts 2.1-13), his interpretation of this event in light of his slightly modified version of Joel 3.1-5a (LXX), and his subsequent description of the Church as a prophetic community empowered by the Spirit. Whether it be John in his mother's womb, Jesus at the Jordan, or the disciples at Pentecost, the Spirit comes upon them all as the source of prophetic inspiration, granting special insight and inspiring speech.

Thus, in Luke's perspective, the disciples receive the Spirit, not as the source of cleansing and a new ability to keep the law, nor as the essential bond by which they (each individual) are linked to God, not even as a foretaste of the salvation to come; rather, the disciples receive the Spirit as a prophetic anointing which enables them to participate effectively in the missionary enterprise of the Church.[11]

Several significant implications emerge from this survey of Lukan pneumatology. First, Pentecostals are right to speak of a baptism of the Holy Spirit 'distinct from and subsequent to the experience of new birth'.[12] This Pentecostal understanding of Spirit-baptism as distinct from conversion flows naturally from the conviction that the Spirit came upon the disciples at Pentecost and throughout the books of Acts, not as the source of new covenant existence, but rather as the source of prophetic inspiration.

Secondly, Luke describes the work of Spirit in a strikingly different— although ultimately complementary—manner from that of Paul. For Luke, the Spirit comes exclusively as the source of prophetic inspiration, granting special revelation and inspiring speech.

Thirdly, although Luke never uses key Pauline terms such as χάρισμα and πνευματικά, he does associate phenomena found in Paul's gift lists with the inspiration of the Spirit. Luke's narrative is filled with references to prophecy and speaking in tongues.

3. *Theological Synthesis*

I now press on to define more specifically the concepts of Spirit-baptism and spiritual gifts by placing them against the theological backdrop provided by my survey of the pneumatologies of Paul and Luke. The goal is to synthesize my findings into a coherent answer which does justice to the perspectives of both Paul and Luke. I shall begin by defining the concepts of Spirit-baptism and spiritual gifts, and then seek to describe the nature of their relationship.

3.1 *Spirit-Baptism*
We have seen that the concept of a baptism in the Spirit distinct from conversion flows from Luke's theology of the Spirit. According to

11. Note that Luke not only refrains from attributing soteriological functions to the Spirit in a manner analogous to Paul, his narrative presupposes a pneumatology which excludes this dimension (e.g. Lk. 11.13; Acts 8.4-17; 19.1-7). For detailed argumentation supporting this analysis of Luke's pneumatology see R.P. Menzies, *Empowered for Witness: The Spirit in Luke–Acts* (JPTSup, 6; Sheffield: Sheffield Academic Press, 1995).

12. *Minutes of the 44th Session of the General Council of the Assemblies of God* (Portland, OR, August 6-11, 1991), p. 129.

Luke, the Spirit comes upon the disciples as the source of prophetic inspiration rather than justification, cleansing, or a new sense of filial relationship to God. This indicates that the Lukan gift of the Spirit should not—indeed, cannot—be equated with the Pauline gift of the Spirit which forms the climax of the conversion experience and mediates the soteriological blessings of Christ (i.e. justification, cleansing, filial relationship) to the believer. Spirit-baptism in the Lukan sense (the gift of the Spirit or the Pentecostal gift) then must be distinguished from the gift of the Spirit which Paul associates with conversion.

This concept of a Spirit-baptism distinct from conversion, while not specifically articulated by Paul, is consistent with (and complementary to) his theological perspective. Paul frequently alludes to the power of the Spirit enabling his own ministry (Rom. 15.19; 1 Cor. 2.4; 1 Thess. 1.5). And he also refers to special anointings which energize the ministry of others (1 Tim. 4.14; 2 Tim. 1.6-7; cf. 1 Thess. 5.19). In view of the *ad hoc* nature of the Pauline epistles, it should not surprise us that Paul nowhere speaks of the Pentecostal gift. Paul has not set out to write a comprehensive theological treatise delineating the dynamics of spiritual life. Nevertheless, it is evident that Luke's emphasis on the significance of the Pentecostal gift for the vitality of the Church and the missionary enterprise (Acts 1.8; 2.17-18) resonates well with Paul's perspective.

If we ask more specifically concerning the impact of Spirit-baptism in Luke–Acts, we immediately note that Luke's perspective is quite similar to that of the Judaism of his day. First-century Jews identified the gift of the Spirit with prophetic inspiration.[13] Thus, for example, Isa. 44.3 ('I will pour out my Spirit on your offspring') was interpreted by the rabbis as a reference to the outpouring of the Spirit of prophecy upon Israel; and the transformation of the heart referred to in Ezek. 36.26-27 was viewed as a prerequisite for the eschatological bestowal of the Spirit, generally interpreted in light of Joel 2.28-32 as a restoration of the Spirit of prophecy.[14]

As the source of prophetic inspiration, the Spirit grants special revelation and inspired speech. These twin functions are exemplified by the

13. This view was dominant for the Judaism which gave birth to the early Church, with Wisdom of Solomon and the Hymns of Qumran providing the only exceptions. See R.P. Menzies, *The Development of Early Christian Pneumatology with Special Reference to Luke–Acts* (JSNTSup, 54; Sheffield: JSOT Press, 1991), pp. 52-112.

14. Menzies, *Development*, pp. 91-111.

many instances where the rabbis speak of 'seeing' or 'speaking in the Spirit'. One early citation (probably pre-Christian), *ARN* A.34, is also illustrative: 'By ten names was the Holy Spirit called, to wit: parable, metaphor, riddle, speech, saying, glory, command, burden, prophecy, vision.'[15] Notice here how the various 'names' identified with the Holy Spirit feature charismatic revelation ('prophecy', 'vision') and speech ('speech', 'saying', 'command').

Luke also presents the Spirit as the source of prophetic inspiration. This is apparent from the outset of his Gospel, which features outbursts of prophetic speech. It is highlighted in the programmatic accounts of Jesus' sermon at Nazareth (Lk. 4.18-19) and Peter's sermon on the day of Pentecost (Acts 2.17-18). Both accounts indicate that the Lukan gift of the Spirit is intimately connected to special revelation and inspired speech. Furthermore, references to charismatic revelation and speech punctuate Luke's two-volume work (e.g. Lk. 10.21; 12.10-12; Acts 4.31; 6.10; 7.55; 10.19; 13.2). Thus, Luke affirms that Spirit-baptism is intimately connected to the bestowal of charismatic wisdom and speech.

The connection to Paul's language and perspective is immediately apparent. In relation to the Pentecostal gift, Luke actually refers to specific gifts named by Paul: glossolalia and prophecy (e.g. Acts 2.4, 18; 10.46; 19.6). And, of course, Paul alludes to spiritual gifts which center on Spirit-inspired revelation and speech. To this significant fact we now turn.

3.2 *Spiritual Gifts*
Paul's gift language is, in reality, quite nuanced. In 1 Corinthians, Paul uses two terms to refer to gifts granted by the Spirit: χαρίσματα ('gifts')[16] and πνευματικά ('spiritual gifts').[17] The term πνευματικός ('spiritual man', 1 Cor. 2.15; or 'spiritually gifted', 1 Cor. 14.37) is also prominent. The significance of Paul's language at this point is debated.

Earl Ellis has argued that the term χαρίσματα has a broad range of meaning and can be used to refer to any or all of the gifts. The term

---

15. ET from J. Goldin, *The Fathers according to Rabbi Nathan* (Yale Judaica Series, 10; New Haven: Yale University Press, 1955). On the dating of *ARN* A.34, see Menzies, *Development*, pp. 97-99.

16. Normally the plural form of χάρισμα or 'gift' is used; see 1 Cor. 1.7; 7.7 (sg.); 12.4, 9, 28, 30, 31.

17. Plural forms appear in 1 Cor. 12.1 (probably neuter) and 14.1. In both instances the NIV translates 'spiritual gifts'.

πνευματικά, by way of contrast, refers to a more restricted grouping of spiritual gifts, the 'prophetic-type gifts'.[18] Ellis suggests that the terms πνευματικά and πνευματικός 'denote, respectively, gifts of inspired utterance or discernment and men who exercise such gifts'.[19] Several points suggest that Ellis's judgment may indeed be correct.

First, the way Paul alternates between πνευματικά (1 Cor. 12.1; 14.1) and χαρίσματα (1 Cor. 12.4; 12.31) in 1 Corinthians 12–14 suggests the former denotes a sub-category of the latter. The περὶ δὲ ('now concerning') construction of 12.1 indicates that the Corinthians, in their letter to Paul, have raised questions concerning the exercise of the πνευματικά. It would be natural for the Corinthians, enamored as they were with glossolalia, to focus on this more specific grouping of gifts. Paul, on the other hand, seeks to broaden the Corinthians' perspective by referring to the larger grouping of gifts, the χαρίσματα. The parallelism between 1 Cor. 12.31, 'eagerly desire the greater gifts (χαρίσματα)' and 1 Cor. 14.1, 'eagerly desire spiritual gifts (πνευματικά)' supports this reading of the text. Here the πνευματικά are identified as a sub-class of the χαρίσματα and closely linked to prophecy. The 'greater gifts' of 1 Cor. 12.31 are prophetic-type gifts which edify the body (and thus, as Paul emphasizes, they must communicate an intelligible message).

A second point in favor of Ellis's thesis emerges in 1 Cor. 14.37: 'If anybody thinks he is a prophet or spiritually gifted (πνευματικός)... ' This text identifies or closely associates those who possess the πνευματικά (i.e. the πνευματικός) with prophets.

Finally, the discernment characteristic of prophets is, in 1 Cor. 2.6-16, ascribed to the πνευματικός: 'The spiritual man (πνευματικός) makes judgments about all things, but he himself is not subject to any man's judgment' (1 Cor. 2.15). However, Gordon Fee challenges the notion that this passage distinguishes between a special group of pneumatics and believers in general. According to Fee, the contrast is between non-believers without the Spirit and believers, all of whom possess the Spirit of God.[20] Nevertheless, even if Fee's reading is accepted at this point,

18. E. Ellis, 'Prophecy in the New Testament Church—And Today', in J. Panagopoulos (ed.), *Prophetic Vocation in the New Testament and Today* (Leiden: Brill, 1977), p. 48.

19. E. Ellis, '"Spiritual" Gifts in the Pauline Community', *NTS* 20 (1973–74), p. 128.

20. G.D. Fee, *The First Epistle to the Corinthians* (NICNT; Grand Rapids: Eerdmans, 1987), pp. 97-120.

Ellis's thesis remains plausible as a description of Paul's language in 1 Corinthians 12–14.

Ellis's thesis is not without its critics,[21] but it does highlight significant texts which appear to link the πνευματικά with gifts of special revelation and inspired speech. If Ellis is correct, then the Pauline category of πνευματικά is strikingly similar in function to the Lukan gift of the Spirit.

Even if Ellis is wrong and the πνευματικά do not refer to a spe cial cluster of prophetic-type gifts, it is evident that Paul's lists in 1 Corinthians do contain a number of gifts that are prophetic in character. Gifts associated with special revelation and/or inspired speech include: 'a message of wisdom' (v. 8); 'a message of knowledge' (v. 8); 'prophecy' (v. 10); 'the ability to distinguish between spirits' (v. 10); [22] 'the ability to speak in different kinds of tongues' (v. 10); 'the interpretation of tongues' (v. 10).

We have already noted that Spirit-baptism in the Lukan sense also grants special revelation and inspired speech. Here, then, is the key intersection where the trajectories of Luke and Paul meet, the point of contact between Spirit-baptism in Luke–Acts and spiritual gifts in Paul. Although Paul does not explicitly refer to this Pentecostal gift, he does acknowledge that the Spirit functions in a similar manner. Paul's language and categories are different from those of Luke, but the overlap is apparent. The Lukan gift of the Spirit and the prophetic-type gifts (whether these be described as the πνευματικά or not) which Paul enumerates have virtually the same impact on their recipients.

4. *Conclusion*

We are now in a position to answer our question concerning the nature of the relationship between Spirit-baptism and spiritual gifts. While it cannot be maintained that Spirit-baptism is the 'gateway' to every spiritual gift, the biblical evidence suggests that Spirit-baptism is the

---

21. Note for example the objections raised to this perspective by D.A. Carson, *Showing the Spirit: A Theological Exposition of 1 Corinthians 12–14* (Grand Rapids: Baker, 1987), pp. 23-24; and S. Schatzmann, *A Pauline Theology of the Charismata* (Peabody, MA: Hendrickson, 1987), p. 7.

22. This is especially true if we see this gift closely linked to the weighing of prophecy described in 1 Cor. 14.29. Note the occurrence of διακρίνω in 1 Cor. 12.10 and 14.29.

'gateway' to a special cluster of gifts described by Paul, the prophetic-type gifts which are associated with special revelation and inspired speech. Certainly it is true that, in one sense, every Christian 'is, and should be increasingly, charismatic'.[23] Paul highlights this fact: every believer has something to contribute, everyone is enabled by the Spirit to contribute to the common good (1 Cor. 12.11). Yet it is also true that there is a dimension of the Spirit's enabling that one enters by virtue of a baptism in the Spirit distinct from conversion. This dimension might be properly called the prophetic dimension. In Luke's perspective, the community of faith is potentially a community of prophets; and, it is by reception of the Pentecostal gift (Spirit-baptism) that this potential is realized. It was Luke's expectation that this potential would indeed be realized in the Church of his day as it had been in the past (e.g. Lk. 3.16; 11.13; Acts 2.17-18). Paul's epistles reveal a similar sense of expectation, although it is frequently found in the guise of a challenge: 'eagerly desire spiritual gifts (πνευματικά), especially the gift of prophecy' (1 Cor. 12.31).

23. Lederle, *Treasures Old and New*, p. 228.

THE PROPHETHOOD OF ALL BELIEVERS:
A STUDY IN LUKE'S CHARISMATIC THEOLOGY

Roger Stronstad

1. *Introduction*

The Church is a community of prophets.[1] This is truer in potential than
it is in practice. Indeed prophets and prophesying among God's people
have had a checkered history. For example, Israel began as a priestly
nation rather than as a prophetic community. Nevertheless, as the centuries passed, and as the nation proved to be stubborn and rebellious,
God raised up prophets to be an alternative to a priesthood which was
often accommodating and compromising. During the intertestamental
period, however, the priesthood gained the ascendency, and prophecy
ceased in Israel. Nevertheless, with the coming of Jesus, prophecy was
once again restored in Israel, and, as a result of the subsequent outpouring of the Holy Spirit upon the disciples, the Church was constituted a nation of prophets.

As the history of the Church advanced, for the second time in the
history of God's people, the priesthood once again gained the ascendency over the prophets. Except for isolated and sporadic outbursts of
prophetic activity, such as was to be found among the Montanists,

---

1.   The following discussion returns to and develops the subject about which I
first wrote in the short, popular article, 'Prophets and Pentecost', in *The Pentecostal
Testimony* (March, 1976), p. 5. This discussion also presupposes that the reader will
be familiar with my monograph, *The Charismatic Theology of St. Luke* (Peabody,
MA: Hendrickson, 1984). The present study is based upon the Pentecostal lecture-
ship of the same name which I gave at Asia Pacific Theological Seminary, Baguio
City, Philippines, February 16-19, 1993. A revised version of this paper was given
as the Presidential Address at the 24th Meeting of the Society for Pentecostal Studies
under the title, "Affirming Diversity: God's People as a Community of Prophets".
This appeared in *Pneuma, the Journal of the Society for Pentecostal Studies 17*
(1995), pp. 145-57.

prophecy died out in the Church. Thus, by the mediaeval period the power to administer or withhold the sacraments lay in the hands of the priesthood. The Reformers rejected this, but instead of developing the New Testament doctrine of the Church as a prophethood of all believers, they developed the doctrine of the priesthood of all believers.

This sacerdotal ecclesiology espoused by the Reformers was a natural and understandable reaction to the Roman Catholic doctrine of the priesthood. Nevertheless, as a return to a biblical model of the people of God, it suffers from the severe limitation that New Testament Christianity knows nothing of a priesthood apart from Christ. There are disciples, apostles, brethren, evangelists, pastors, prophets, overseers, elders and deacons in the New Testament, but there are no priests. Thus, rather than developing the doctrine of the priesthood of all believers, the Reformers would have served the Church better, in their time and in ours, if they had chosen to shape the Church, not only theologically and functionally but also experientially, as the prophethood of all believers. This, in fact, is Luke's distinctive vision of the people of God. They are the eschatological community upon whom Jesus, the eschatological prophet, has poured out the Spirit of prophecy—for their own generation, for their children's generation, and for every succeeding generation.

The doctrine of the prophethood of all believers did not originate with Luke. It was first articulated when Moses expressed the earnest desire that all God's people would be prophets (Num. 11.25-29). It is then given biblical definition and delineation in an ancient oracle of the prophet Joel (2.28-32). Finally, it is inaugurated through the prophetic ministry of Jesus. In the discussion which follows, I will: 1) trace the doctrine of the prophethood of all believers in Moses' earnest desire; 2) demonstrate its inauguration in Luke–Acts; and 3) discuss its partial recovery in the Pentecostal revival in the twentieth century.

2. *Earnest Desire: A Nation of Prophets (Numbers 11.24-30)*

The concept of the prophethood of all believers is rooted in the beginnings of Israel as a nation. At Mt Sinai God covenanted with his people to make them: 'a kingdom of priests and a holy nation' (Exod. 19.6). While God was true to his commitments; Israel, especially the first generation of the Exodus, betrayed its commitments to its redeemer. Israel's leader, Moses, quickly discovered that not only were the people rebellious and disobedient to God, but they were impossible to lead. And so it was in a time of leadership crisis for Moses that God instructed Moses to delegate leadership responsibilities among the seventy elders of Israel. With this transfer of leadership there was also a complementary transfer of the empowering Spirit. This transfer happened at the Tabernacle and is reported in these words:

> He took of the Spirit who was upon him and placed *Him* upon the
> seventy elders. And it came about that when the Spirit rested upon
> them, they prophesied (Num. 11.25).

But two of the elders had remained in the camp, and they also prophesied. When this was reported to Moses, Joshua, his attendant, urged: 'Moses, my lord, restrain them' (Num. 11.28). With a wisdom born out of his struggles as a leader of a stubborn nation, Moses replied with the earnest desire: 'Would that all the Lord's people were prophets, that the Lord would put his Spirit upon them!' (Num. 11.29b). Thus, the ideal for Israel is that not only would it be a kingdom of priests but also that it would be a kingdom of prophets. Moses' earnest desire that Israel be a nation of prophets remained unfulfilled across the advancing centuries, until God himself raised up the eschatological prophet like Moses, who, in turn, became the fountainhead of a community of prophets

3. *Inauguration: The Restoration of Prophecy (Luke–Acts)*

A millennium and more passed before Moses' earnest desire that God's people would be a nation of prophets was fulfilled. It was fulfilled in the life and ministry of a Galilean peasant, Jesus of Nazareth.[2] Through the transfer of the Spirit of prophecy, it was extended from him to the small company of his followers.

3.1 *Jesus: The Anointed Prophet*
3.1.1 *The restoration of prophecy*. When Jesus was born to Mary, a young peasant woman from Nazareth in Galilee, Rome ruled Palestine with a grip of iron, the scribes and pharisees and the synagogue vied with the priesthood and the Temple for the religious affections of the

---

2.   The subject of Jesus and his disciples as prophets has recently received much scholarly attention. Important and readily available treatments include: P.S. Minear, *To Heal and to Reveal* (New York: Seabury, 1976); D. Hill, *New Testament Prophecy* (Atlanta: John Knox, 1976); and D.E. Aune, *Prophecy in Early Christianity and the Ancient Mediterranean World* (Grand Rapids: Eerdmans, 1983).

people, and, with a few exceptions,[3] the prophet and prophecy had been silent in Israel for four hundred years.[4] Into this environment God restored prophecy suddenly, dramatically, and unexpectedly. A young baby, who a generation later will appear among the people identified as John the Baptist, was, 'filled with the Holy Spirit, while yet in his mother's womb' (Lk. 1.15), and was, consequently, '(to) be called the prophet of the Most High' (Lk. 1.76). Even before he was born, his mother Elizabeth, was similarly, 'filled with the Holy Spirit' and broke out in a song of praise (Lk. 1.41-45). Not only this, but after John was born, Zacharias, his father, 'was filled with the Holy Spirit and prophesied' (Lk. 1.67-79). In addition Simeon, who had the Spirit upon him, who had revelations by the Spirit, and who was led by the Spirit, gave inspired, that is, prophetic praise when he discovered the baby Jesus in the Temple with his parents (Lk. 2.25-35). Further, an elderly prophetess, Anna, gave thanks to God, and continued to speak about Jesus (Lk. 2.36-38). Finally Mary, who conceived Jesus by submitting to the overshadowing power of the Spirit and who also sang a song of praise (1.35-38, 46-55), was, like John, Elizabeth, Zacharias, Simeon and Anna, a prophet.

This outburst of prophecy in Israel after four hundred years of silence was the ἀρραβών, that is, the promise or pledge of the fulfillment of Moses' earnest desire that all of God's people would be prophets. In other words, these six—John, Mary, Elizabeth, Zacharias, Simeon and Anna, anticipate the next generation of God's people—the daughters, the young men, the old men and the bondslaves, both men and women—upon whom the Lord will on the day of Pentecost pour out the Spirit so that they will prophecy. And so, in this outburst of prophecy, which was associated with the births of these two cousins, John and Jesus, the Spirit of prophecy came upon 'all flesh' in these six persons, who were anticipatory representatives of that nationwide, or universal, gift of prophecy which both transcends and negates all age, gender and social barriers among God's people. Thus, this dramatic outburst of prophecy presaged the dawning of the new age—the age of the Messiah and the subsequent complementary and unprecedented gift of prophecy among his followers.

3.   Josephus, *War*, 1.68-69; *Ant.* 13.311-13; 15.373-8; 17.345-8.
4.   The belief in the cessation of prophecy in Israel is explicit in the following texts: 2 Bar. 85.3, *Apion* 1.41, and *t. Sot.* 8.2. It is implicit in texts such as 1 Macc. 4.46; 14.44.

3.1.2 *Jesus: The anointed prophet.* About thirty years after God had restored prophecy in Israel, and at the time when the ministry of John the Baptist was at its height, Jesus came to the Jordan river to be baptized by his cousin. Luke reports:

> and while he (Jesus) was praying, heaven was opened, and the Holy Spirit descended upon him in bodily form like a dove, and a voice came out of heaven, 'Thou art my beloved Son, in thee I am well pleased' (Lk. 3.21b-22).

Subsequently, when Jesus returned to the synagogue in Nazareth one sabbath he explained the meaning of his baptismal experience in the language of the prophet Isaiah, who wrote:

> The Spirit of the Lord is upon me,
> Because he anointed me to preach the gospel to the poor.
> He has sent me to proclaim release to the captives,
> And recovery of sight to the blind,
> To set free those who are downtrodden,
> To proclaim the favourable year of the Lord (Lk. 4.18-19).

Next, he challenged the people to accept him as the Spirit-anointed prophet, solemnly affirming: 'Truly I say to you, no prophet is welcome in his home town' (Lk. 4.24). He continued by identifying his situation as a prophet in Nazareth with that of the two great charismatic prophets, Elijah and Elisha, who were both rejected by their own people, and subsequently ministered to strangers (Lk. 4.25-30). All of this means that Jesus, God's Son, is the Spirit-anointed prophet. In other words, Jesus is the Messiah, but after the prophetic pattern rather than after either the royal or the priestly patterns. Because it is the Son who is the Spirit-anointed prophet, one can say that through the incarnation God becomes his own prophet.[5]

The Gospels show that Jesus' ministry was meteoric. It began in a blaze of public popularity as the people wondered at his gracious words and witnessed his amazing miracles. But like the prophets, his predecessors, he quickly became the rejected prophet. As a result, within three years of his baptism by John at the Jordan he was crucified on a cross at the hands of godless men—both Jewish and Gentile. Three days after this brutal and fearful event, Jesus, now risen from the dead, joined a disillusioned Cleopas and companion as they were walking from

5.   M. Muggeridge, *Jesus: The Man Who Lives* (London: Collins, 1975).

Jerusalem to Emmaus (Lk. 24.13-20). He asked them what things they had been talking about. They replied:

> The things about Jesus the Nazarene, who was a prophet mighty in deed and word in the sight of God and all the people, and how the chief priests and our rulers delivered him up to the sentence of death, and crucified him (Lk. 24.19-20).

Here in this reply is the report of Jesus' status, namely, though he was a prophet in the sight of God and the people, he died as a rejected prophet. Further, his deeds, or his works, and his words were powerful. In other words, beginning with his baptism, all the works which Jesus performed were empowered by the Spirit. In the same way, all the words which he spoke were empowered, and, indeed, inspired by the Spirit (cf. Acts 1.2). Clearly, then, between Jesus' reception of the Spirit at the Jordan and his pouring forth of the Spirit on the day of Pentecost everything which he said and did was the work and words of a Spirit-anointed, Spirit-filled, Spirit-led and Spirit-empowered prophet (Lk. 3.22; 4.1, 14, 18).

This observation is fully born out by Luke's report about Jesus' ministry. For example, when Jesus raised the son of the widow of Nain from the dead the people exclaimed: "'A great prophet has risen among us!" and, "God has visited his people!"' (Lk. 7.16). Further, Simon the Pharisee rejected Jesus as a prophet because he apparently did not know that the woman who had just anointed his feet was a sinner (Lk. 7.39). In time even Herod the tetrarch heard about Jesus' reputation as a prophet—namely, as John raised from the dead, or as Elijah, or as one of the other prophets of old (Lk. 8.7-9; cf., 8.18-19). Also, Jesus rebuked the lawyers for killing and persecuting prophets and apostles, including himself (Lk. 11.45-52). Finally, Jesus not only journeyed to Jerusalem to die there as the rejected prophet (Lk. 13.31-35), but, after he was arrested, he was blindfolded, beaten and mocked as a prophet (Lk. 22.63-65).

Although Jesus, the eschatological Spirit-anointed prophet, died in Jerusalem as the rejected prophet, prophecy itself did not die out among God's people. To the contrary, on the day of Pentecost Jesus transferred the Spirit from himself to his disciples, thereby raising up a company of eschatological, Spirit-baptized, Spirit-empowered and Spirit-filled prophets who are, in turn, to witness about him to the ends of the earth.

3.2 *The Disciples: A Company of Spirit-Baptized Prophets*

After the contemporary pattern of a rabbi and his disciples, or after the earlier pattern of a prophet and the sons of the prophets, Jesus called to himself a company of disciples who, following his ascension to heaven, would be heirs and successors to his ministry (Lk. 5.1-12). To this end he taught them (Lk. 6), modelled the prophetic ministry (Lk. 7–8), and sent them out to minister (Lk. 9). But Jesus knew that if his disciples were to succeed him as a company of prophets, they would need more than instruction, role modeling and ministry experience. They would need to be empowered by the same Spirit as he was. Thus, anticipating the not too distant end to his earthly ministry Jesus began to promise the future outpouring of the Spirit upon them.

Luke reports that Jesus, in fact, made six direct or indirect promises about the future outpouring of the Spirit. He made three of these promises before his death and resurrection. First, in the context of encouraging his disciples to pray, he assured them that, '*your* heavenly Father (will) give the Holy Spirit to those who ask him' (Lk. 11.13). Secondly, Jesus promised the disciples that when they would be put on trial the Holy Spirit would teach them what to say (Lk. 12.11-12). Thirdly, he later assured his disciples that when they were persecuted he would give them an irresistible 'utterance and wisdom' (Lk. 21.15), fulfilled, for example, in Stephen's Spirit-inspired witness (Acts 6.10). These three pre-resurrection promises about the Spirit are matched by three post-resurrection promises. These specifically focus upon the outpouring of the Spirit on the day of Pentecost. First, Jesus commissioned his disciples to be his witnesses (Lk. 24.48), promising: 'And behold, I am sending out the promise of my Father upon you; but you are to stay in the city until you are clothed with power from on high' (Lk. 24.49). Secondly, Jesus renewed John the Baptist's earlier announcement that they would be, 'baptized with the Holy Spirit' not many days later (Acts 1.4-5). Finally, Jesus promised them: 'you shall receive power when the Holy Spirit has come upon you' (Acts 1.8). It was this inspiration of the Spirit, this being baptized with the Spirit, and this empowering of the Spirit which was to transform the followers of Jesus from mere disciples to dynamic prophets.

These promises of the Spirit and the transformation of his followers from disciples to prophets began to be fulfilled when Jesus poured out the Spirit on them on the day of Pentecost. In itself, this initial outpouring of the Spirit is part of a great theophany on the Temple Mount, where the disciples had gathered.[6] At that time

> suddenly there came from heaven a noise like a violent, rushing wind, and it filled the whole house where they were sitting. And there appeared to them tongues as of fire distributing themselves, and they rested on each one of them. And they were all filled with the Holy Spirit and began to speak with other tongues, as the Spirit was giving them utterance (Acts 2.2-4).

When Luke's report is compared with the two earlier theophanies at Mt Sinai, namely, when God made his covenant with Israel after he had redeemed them out of Egypt (Exod. 19.16-18), and later when He appeared to Elijah (Lk. 19.11-12), it is evident that the first two signs—the sound of the violent wind and the tongues as of fire—are signs of theophany. In other words, they are signs of God's manifest presence, but are not signs of the outpouring of the Spirit. It is the third sign alone, the tongues-speaking, which is the sign of the pouring forth of the Spirit. But what did it all mean?

This theophany and the complementary pouring forth of the Spirit is the promissory or programmatic beginning of the prophethood of all believers. This observation is confirmed by Peter's explanation of the signs, in which he quotes an ancient oracle of the prophet Joel:

> 'And it shall be in the last days', God says,
> 'That I will pour forth of my Spirit upon all mankind;
> And your sons and your daughters shall prophesy,
> And your young men shall see visions,
> And your old men shall dream dreams;
> Even upon my bondslaves, both men and women,
> I will in those days pour forth of my Spirit
> And they shall prophesy.
> 'And I will grant wonders in the sky above,
> And signs on the earth beneath,
> Blood, and fire, and vapour of smoke.
> 'The sun shall be turned into darkness,
> And the moon into blood,
> Before the great and glorious day of the Lord shall come.
> 'And it shall be that everyone who calls on the name of
> the Lord shall be saved (Acts 2.17-21).

Joel's oracle, with its announcement of wonders and signs, is an exact

---

6. For a detailed discussion of Luke's report about this theophany see my paper, 'Signs on the Earth Beneath', which was read at the twenty-first annual meeting of the Society for Pentecostal Studies (1991).

description of the two signs of the theophany and the sign of the pouring forth of the Spirit. More importantly, it carries a threefold theology. First, the pouring out of the Spirit is an eschatological event; that is, it is in the last days. In Jewish historiography, the period of the last days is the age of the messiah and the complementary age of the Spirit. Thus, the turning of the ages happened one generation prior to Pentecost, when not only the messiah was born, but also when the Spirit restored prophets and prophecy to Israel once again. And so, the pouring forth of the Spirit on the day of Pentecost is not the beginning of the last days, but, rather, it advances them one generation along. Secondly, the gift of the Spirit is (potentially) universal; that is, it is for 'all flesh' (Joel) or 'all humankind' (Peter). In other words, in contrast to the former days, when the activity of the Spirit was limited to isolated periods and select leaders; in the messianic age, the activity of the Spirit is unlimited by gender, age or social conditions. Specifically, it is for male and female, young and old and even for the disenfranchised (Acts 2.17b-18a). Furthermore, it is transgenerational; it is for the generation of Peter's audience, for their children, and for all those generations down through the ages who are afar off (Acts 2.39). Thirdly, the gift of the Spirit is prophetic: sons and daughters shall prophecy; visions and dreams are the ancient media of prophetic revelation (cf. Num. 12.6), and when the Spirit is poured forth all shall prophesy (Acts 2.17b-18). Since Peter has declared that the signs of Pentecost fulfill Joel's prophecy, then, by definition, speaking with other tongues is a type of eschatological prophecy. Thus, the pouring forth of the Spirit upon the disciples on the day of Pentecost is eschatological, universal and prophetic—the prophethood of all believers.

This pouring forth of the eschatological and universal gift of the Spirit of prophecy stands in a point–counterpoint relationship to the experience of Israel at Mt Sinai when God covenanted with his people. At that time he established them as a nation of priests. On the day of Pentecost he establishes his people of the new covenant to be a company of prophets. This, as we have already seen, was inaugurated at the restoration of prophecy which was associated with the births of John and Jesus. On the day of Pentecost, however, Moses' earnest desire that all God's people would be prophets took a quantum leap toward literal fulfillment. Soon, and for the first time in redemptive history, the Spirit would be poured out upon God's people as a young and small, but nevertheless real nation.

3.3 *A Nation of Prophets*

The outpouring of the Holy Spirit upon the disciples on the day of Pentecost programmatically, but not literally, fulfills the prophecy of Joel for a nationwide outpouring of the Spirit. In other words, the company of 120 disciples who are filled with the Holy Spirit on the day of Pentecost are not in themselves a nation. Nevertheless, because of the success of their Spirit-empowered witness, this company of Spirit-baptized prophets will soon grow to true nationhood.

Luke reports the rapid growth of the disciples toward nationhood in a series of quantitatively escalating terms. Luke opens his narrative in Acts reporting about the eleven apostles, who soon have a twelfth added to their number (Acts 1.2, 13, 26). He next reports the company of 120 persons, who have gathered together to await the promised Holy Spirit (1.14-15). On the day of Pentecost about 3,000 are added to that number (2.41). As the apostles continued to witness in Jerusalem the number of believers came to be about 5,000 men (4.4). At this point Luke stops counting and describes the believers simply as 'the multitude' (4.32). Finally, Luke describes the followers as 'the church' (τὴν ἐκκλησίαν, 5.11). This term first appears in scripture to describe Israel gathered together as a nation (Deut. 4.10; 9.10; 18.16 LXX; cf. Acts 7.38). Therefore, at this point in his narrative, Luke has borrowed a term from the Septuagint (LXX) to portray to his readers that the growing community has now reached the status of nationhood, akin to the nationhood of the first generation of the Exodus.

Not only have they become a nation which numbers over 5,000 men plus women and children, but, during a second theophany on the Temple Mount in Jerusalem, they have also become a nation of prophets. Luke reports:

> And when they had prayed, the place where they had gathered together was shaken, and they were all filled with the Holy Spirit, and began to speak the word of God with boldness (Acts 4.31).

In this text Luke briefly but clearly conveys the following information to his readers: 1) the disciples have gathered together on the Temple Mount, for the term 'place' (τόπος) in an adjacent context describes the Temple (Acts 6.13, 14); 2) the disciples who have gathered together are the 5,000 men reported in Acts 4.4;[7] 3) the disciples experience a

---

7.   Contra E. Haenchen, *The Acts of the Apostles: A Commentary* (trans.

theophany, for the earthquake is as typical a sign of theophany as the wind and fire were typical signs of theophany on the day of Pentecost (cf. Exod. 19.18, 1 Kgs 19.11); and 4) filled with the Holy Spirit, the disciples speak the word of God with boldness, that is, they prophesy.

These four facts lead to the inescapable conclusion that in this text (Acts 4.31) Luke is describing a corporate outburst of prophecy among all disciples/believers, who number in the thousands. Thus, Luke has reported more than the representative (Lk. 1–2) and more than the promissory or programmatic (Acts 2) universal outpouring of the Spirit of prophecy. In this second theophany there is the literal fulfillment of Moses' earnest desire that all the Lord's people would be prophets, for the Lord has put his Spirit on them; more specifically, the Lord has filled them all with his Spirit. Therefore, after and because of this massive outburst of prophecy it is appropriate for Luke to identify the disciples as 'the church' that is, 'the nation' (την ἐκκλησιαν) in a way that is not appropriate to describe the company of disciples on the day of Pentecost who prophesy. Here in Luke's narrative, and for the first time ever in the redemptive history of God's people, they truly function as a nation of prophets—the prophethood of all believers.

3.4 *Six Charismatic Prophets*
In the narrative of Luke–Acts, Luke first reports the three-stage representative, programmatic and literal fulfillment, respectively, of Moses' earnest desire that all God's people would be prophets (Lk. 1–2,

B. Noble and G. Shinn; Oxford: Basil Blackwell, 1971), p. 226, who, commenting on 4.23, writes:

> When Luke speaks of the community assembled for worship or deliberation, he sees in his mind's eye not the great numbers he used in 2.41 and 4.4 to illustrate the divine blessing that lay on the community, but the band of believers gathered in *one room* which he was accustomed to see around him in the services of his own congregation. (My emphasis).

Similarly, I.H. Marshall, *The Acts of the Apostles: An Introduction and Commentary* (TNTC; Grand Rapids: Eerdmans, 1980), p. 107, writes without explanation: 'The *room* in which the disciples were gathered shook as if an earthquake were taking place' (My emphasis). Both of these commentators negate the possibility that Luke is reporting a theophany on the Temple Mount accompanied by a nationwide pouring forth of the Spirit of prophecy. Restricting the disciples and place to a gathering in a room, as they do, not only ignores the parallels between this narrative and the Pentecost narrative but also ignores both the fact that the disciples met on the Temple Mount every day (Acts 2.46; 5.42), and that Luke uses the term 'place' (τόπος) to describe the Temple (Acts 6.13, 14), not some 'room'.

Acts 1.1–6.7). In the remaining three quarters of his narrative he reports about six charismatic prophets: Stephen, Philip, Barnabas, Agabus, Peter and Paul (Acts 6.8–28.31). These individual prophets typify and illustrate the ministry of the prophethood of all believers, witnessing in Jerusalem, Judea and Samaria and to the ends of the earth by works which were empowered by the Spirit and by words which were inspired by the Spirit.

Stephen is the first deacon[8] and the first of these six prophets about whom Luke will report. He had a fivefold experience of the Spirit: 1) along with the other deacons he was, 'full of the Holy Spirit and wisdom' (Acts 6.3); 2) he was also, 'a man full of faith and of the Holy Spirit' (6.5); 3) he was, 'full of grace and power' (6.8); 4) he spoke with wisdom and the Spirit (6.10); and 5) he was, 'full of the Holy Spirit', and had a vision of the risen Jesus (7.55). Clearly, his works—the great wonders and signs which he performed (6.8)—were empowered by the Spirit. Similarly, his words—not only his witness to the Synagogue of the Freedmen (6.9-10), but also his prophetic denunciation of the Sanhedrin (7.2-53)—were inspired by the Spirit. Therefore, what had earlier been reported about Jesus was also true of Stephen; namely, he was a prophet mighty in works and word in the sight of God and all the people and the chief priests and rulers put him to death.[9]

---

8. Of course, Luke does not actually use the Greek equivalent of deacon. Nevertheless, since the function of the seven is to 'serve tables' (διακονεῖν τραπέζαις) 'deacon' is a better title for this role than other titles, such as 'almoner' (for this term see F.F. Bruce, *Peter, Stephen, James and John: Studies in Early Non-Pauline Christianity* [Grand Rapids: Eerdmans, 1980], p. 51).

9. Luke's report about Stephen is a typical example of how the agenda and/or theology of interpreters are out of step with Luke's agenda and theology. In his brief report about Stephen, Luke gives four direct and one indirect reference to his experience of the Spirit—the highest concentration of references to a person's experience of the Spirit in Luke–Acts, apart from Luke's report of Jesus' experience of the Spirit. Yet in his chapter, 'Stephen and Other Hellenists', in *Peter, Stephen, James and John*, pp. 59ff., Bruce simply comments, 'Luke, at any rate, looks on all seven as Spirit-filled men, Stephen outstandingly so (Acts 6.3, 5)'. Similarly, G. Stanton, 'Stephen in Lucan Perspective', *Studia Biblica, 1978, III, Papers on Paul and Other New Testament Authors* (Sheffield: JSOT Press, 1980), p. 355, makes but one comment on Stephen's experience of the Spirit: 'Stephen's accusers oppose the Holy Spirit, but in stark contrast Stephen himself, full of the Holy Spirit, gazes into heaven and sees the glory of God and Jesus standing at the right hand of God (v. 55)'. Nowhere do these interpreters show any awareness that Luke portrays Stephen as a disciple whose works were empowered by the Spirit and whose words—that is, his

Philip is the second deacon and the second of the six prophets about whom Luke reports. Stephen witnessed in Jerusalem. In contrast, Philip witnessed in Samaria and Western Judea (Acts 8.4-40). Philip had a threefold experience of the Spirit: 1) like Stephen he was, 'full of the Holy Spirit and wisdom' (6.3); 2) he was led by the Spirit (8.29); and 3) he was supernaturally transported by the Spirit (8.39). He witnessed by works empowered by the Spirit. Specifically, he cast out unclean spirits and healed the sick (8.7). He also witnessed by words which were inspired by the Spirit, proclaiming Christ to the Samaritans (8.5) and preaching Jesus to the Ethiopian court official (8.35).

Whereas Luke portrays Stephen and Philip to be prophets by function, though he does not identify them as such, he does identify Barnabas, the third of the six, as a prophet (Acts 13.1). Luke reports that Barnabas had a threefold experience of the Spirit: 1) like Stephen he was, 'full of the Holy Spirit and of faith' (11.24; cf. 6.5); 2) he was led by the Spirit (13.1-4); and 3) along with the other disciples at Iconium he was, 'continually filled with joy and with the Holy Spirit' (13.52). Like all of the charismatic prophets who preceded him, Barnabas, in company with Paul, was a prophet who was powerful in work and word. Thus, at Pisidian Antioch he spoke out boldly (13.46), a mark of being filled with the Spirit (cf. 4.13, 31). Further, at Iconium he performed signs and wonders (14.3; 15.12; cf. 2.43; 5.12; 6.8; 8.16, 13).

The fourth charismatic prophet is Agabus. Along with other, anonymous prophets, he came down from Jerusalem to Antioch. There he 'indicated by the Spirit that there would certainly be a great famine all over the world' (Acts 11.28). He next reappears in the narrative when Luke reports about Paul's journey to Jerusalem at the end of this third missionary journey. Luke reports that when Paul arrived at Caesarea, 'a certain prophet named Agabus came down from Judea' (21.10). Agabus took 'Paul's belt and bound his own feet and hands' (21.11a). Adding voice to action he then said, 'this is what the Holy Spirit says: "In this way the Jews at Jerusalem will bind the man who owns this belt and deliver him into the hands of the Gentiles"' (21.11b). In each of these two episodes Agabus functioned as a prophet by speaking words which were inspired by the Spirit.

Peter is the fifth and, in many ways, the most important prophet

reply to the High Priest's question—were inspired by the Spirit. This neglect of a subject which is so prominent in Luke's narrative is deplorable. The other leaders, who are subjects of this section, suffer similarly at the hands of many interpreters.

about whom Luke reports. He had manifold experience of the Spirit. For example, in Jerusalem he was filled with the Spirit three times (Acts 2.4; 4.8, 31). Later, in Samaria he was used to bestow the Holy Spirit to the believers there (8.15-17). Finally, in Joppa he was instructed by the Holy Spirit to go to the home of Cornelius, a Gentile (10.19-20), who along with his household would be baptized with the Holy Spirit while Peter witnessed to them (10.44-48; 11.15-17). Along with the other apostles, Peter performed signs and wonders in Jerusalem (2.43; cf. 3.1-10; 5.12-16). He also performed signs and wonders in Western Judea, such as healing a cripple in Lydda (9.32-35), and raising the dead in Joppa (9.36-43). He not only witnessed by works empowered by the Spirit but he also witnessed by words inspired by the Spirit (2.4, 14-36; 4.8-12). Indeed, Peter personally fulfilled the programmatic outline of Spirit-empowered witness reported at the beginning of Acts (1.8). In geographic terms, he ministered in Jerusalem, then in Samaria, and, finally, in Judea. In racial terms he witnessed to Jews, Samaritans and Gentiles, respectively. In the light of this record, it is little wonder that Peter is so prominent in Luke's narrative about the origin and the witness of this prophetic community. It is little wonder, further, that Peter is the standard as apostle and prophet by which Luke will measure Paul as apostle and prophet.

Paul is the final, and, quantitatively, the most prominent prophet about whom Luke reports. Luke identifies him as a prophet at Antioch (Acts 13.1). He also had manifold experience of the Spirit. For example, like Peter he was filled with the Holy Spirit three times (9.17; 13.9, 52). He was also led by the Spirit (13.1-4; 16.6-8), and used to impart the Holy Spirit (19.6). Paul witnessed by signs and wonders (14.3; 15.12; 19.11). He also witnessed by words inspired by the Spirit (13.9). Clearly, Paul's charismatic apostleship and prophethood was the equal of Peter's—a fact that many in the church in Jerusalem may have questioned.

To sum up, this survey of Luke's narrative about the acts of these six charismatic prophets (Acts 6.8–28.31) has consistently shown examples of prophets whose works were empowered by the Spirit and whose words were inspired by the Spirit. In fact, Luke gives no other picture in this narrative, or, indeed, either earlier in Acts (1.1–6.7) or in his first account about Jesus, who was the Spirit-anointed prophet mighty in work and word. Thus, for example, in Luke's narrative Stephen and Philip were not the only charismatic deacons. The other five were as well (6.3). Similarly, Barnabas and Agabas were not the only prophets.

Rather, each represented groups of prophets (11.27; 13.1). Finally, Peter and Paul were not the only charismatic apostles. The other eleven were as well. Indeed, not only were these leaders all charismatic prophets in function, but, beginning with the outpouring of the Spirit on the day of Pentecost, all the disciples were (2.4; 4.31). This was as true for Samaritan believers (8.15-17) and for Gentile believers (10.44-48; 19.1-7), as it was for disciples in Jerusalem. So, the disciples generally were the prophethood of all believers. As Luke shows, their leaders, such as Stephen, Philip, Barnabas, Agabas, Peter and Paul, could be no less. Luke has shown that all the Lord's people were prophets, because he put his Spirit upon them. He did this by pouring out his Spirit upon sons and daughters, upon young men and old men, upon the slave and the free—representatively (Lk. 1–2), programmatically (Acts 2), and nationally (Acts 4.31). Thus, in its first generation the Church became a nation, or a community of prophets.

4. *Recovery: The Twentieth-Century Outpouring of the Holy Spirit*

Such is Luke's vision of the eschatological people of God. As heirs and successors to the former people of God, who were a nation of priests, the new people of God are a nation of prophets. This is how they functioned, more or less completely, during the first generation. But very quickly subsequent generations ceased to function as prophets, either individually or corporately. Identifying the reception of the Spirit with water baptism, institutionalizing the gifts of the Spirit, and reacting to perceived excesses in prophetic movements, such as the Montanists—these actions all contributed to the cessation of prophecy in the Church. But this was never a permanent condition. Among both individuals and renewal/pietistic groups, prophets and prophesying sporadically reappeared. Now, in the twentieth century, Luke's vision of the people of God as the prophethood of all believers has been permanently, though only partially, restored.

The outpouring of the Spirit and of the complementary gift of prophecy, such as Luke reported happening on the day of Pentecost, is being restored among God's people through the contemporary Pentecostal/charismatic movement. This restoration began on January 1, 1901, when Agnes Ozman, a student at Bethel Bible School, Topeka, Kansas, began to speak in other tongues. This fresh outpouring of the Spirit spread like prairie wildfire from Kansas and Missouri to Texas, on to California, and from there to the ends of the earth. By 1992 the total number of Pentecostals/charismatics was estimated to be 410 million.[10] This means that in this century to a greater or lesser extent Moses' earnest desire that God would put his Spirit on all his people is being realized.

This outpouring of the Spirit of prophecy in the contemporary Pentecostals/charismatic renewal restores important New Testament realities. For example, the baptizing/filling with the Holy Spirit restores the immediacy of God's presence to his people. In other words, the formerly transcendent God becomes immanent in the conscious experience of his people. As a corollary, worship gains a dynamism and a vitality that is often otherwise lacking. Further, there is a new hunger for the Word of God, and a new existential understanding of God's Word. Finally, and more directly related to the age-old purpose for the gift of the Spirit, the baptizing/filling with the Spirit restores the Spirit's empowering in witness. Thus, Pentecostals/charismatics witness as prophets by works which are empowered by the Spirit and by words which are inspired by the Spirit. Indeed, right from the start, Pentecostalism has been an evangelism and missionary movement.

Although it represents the restoration of prophecy in this century, the Pentecostal/charismatic movement does not fully measure up to the effectiveness of that first generation of prophets which Luke reports about. There are perhaps as many reasons for this as there are Pentecostals/charismatics. Nevertheless, there are several basic reasons for this which deserve comment. For example, Pentecostals, themselves, do not fully understand the meaning of the outpouring of the Spirit according to Luke's primary emphasis, namely, as the restoration of prophecy. Rather they are preoccupied with secondary terminology, namely, baptized with the Spirit, speaking with other tongues, and initial evidence. As a result they are not challenged to function in the Church and in society as Spirit-baptized, Spirit-empowered and Spirit-filled prophets. Consequently, though they have a zeal for missions and evangelism, their works are not always empowered by the Spirit, nor are their words always inspired by the Spirit.

As a further result of not understanding that their experience is

10. V. Synan, 'A Global Family: Size and Scope of the Movement', in *A Reader on the Holy Spirit: Anointing, Equipping and Empowering for Service* (A L.E.A.D. Text; Los Angeles: International Church of the Foursquare, 1993), p. 7.

prophetic—which is necessarily directed toward others—the Pentecostal's experience tends to be individualistic, self-centered and, even, narcissistic. In other words, the experience is sought as a private blessing, rather than as an empowering for ministry. Far too many Pentecostals receive the blessing of the Holy Spirit in the prayer room and have never been taught to take the empowering of that gift into the streets and market places of society.

In addition, the restoration of prophecy is often trivialized and/or commercialized. Christian bookstores and church libraries are filled with literature and tapes on prophecy whose contents all too often border on the credulous, the absurd, the blasphemous and the exploitative. To the authors and publishers of this material about prophecy, prophecy is about new revelations and novel and authoritative interpretations of the Bible, and about who to marry and when to have babies. It is also about material prosperity, and about careers, either sacred or secular. All over the world there are prophets who, like Balaam, prostitute the gift of prophecy for money and power and who grandstand the gift for prestige. This emphasis totally misses the first-century function of prophets and prophesying. At that time it was in terms of a local, regional and world-wide witness about Jesus. All too often it is now about revelation knowledge and health and wealth—all delivered for a Pentecostal handshake, a love offering or an honorarium.

Finally, the restoration of prophecy in this century is a splintered or fractured phenomenon. Independence and individualism characterize the Pentecostal movement. Split churches, independent churches, a multiplicity of denominations, and split-off denominations abound. Often absent is the unity, the all togetherness, the one accordness, which characterized the first-century prophets.

The antidote to these and other ills in the Pentecostal movement, as the restored community of prophets, is to recapture Luke's vision of God's people as the prophethood of all believers. This is to recapture the reality of the Church as a nation of prophets. It is to recapture the gift of the Spirit as the source of Spirit-empowered witness. It is also to recapture the divine seriousness of the gift in meeting eternal rather than merely temporal and material human needs. Finally, it is to recapture the unity of the Spirit. As the writer of Luke–Acts, Luke undoubtedly perceived himself to be a Spirit-inspired prophet, just as the anonymous writers of the former prophets were. Luke–Acts itself, then, is a prophetic word to the contemporary Church, exposing our narcissistic, divisive, trivial and commercial use of the Spirit; and, by giving us the example of the disciples as a prophetic community, it points the Church to how it should properly and effectively function as a nation of prophets—the eschatological prophethood of all believers.

Part II

THE THEOLOGICAL CONTEXT

The Language Game of Glossolalia, or Making Sense of the 'Initial Evidence'

Simon Chan

Historically, Pentecostals have distinguished themselves from their holiness and Wesleyan counterparts by their doctrine of baptism in the Holy Spirit 'witnessed by the initial physical evidence of speaking in tongues'.[1] But is the belief itself justified? If the essays in *Initial Evidence*, which is probably the most concerted reflection on the doctrine that we have thus far, are anything to go by, it would appear that the classical Pentecostal position is in tatters.[2] Except for Donald Johns's explicit apologetic, the other contributors, both Pentecostal and non-Pentecostal, have little to put up for its defense. Lederle, for instance, calls for 'a critical reinterpretation and reappropriation' of the doctrine but does not go further to show how it could be done.[3] There is no doubt that the Pentecostal doctrine needs refinement and reinterpretation, but Pentecostals have not been generally happy with what has been done for them so far, as when they are told to abandon the doctrine for the sake of the peace of the Church[4] or to accept it as one of the 'normal' manifestations of the Spirit without insisting on it as the 'norm'.[5] Pentecostals by and large may not be very theologically articulate, but they often manifest an unusually sharp instinct as the children of God.[6] They recognize that these well-intentioned bits of advice

1. The Assemblies of God Statement of Fundamental Truths, 8.
2. G.B. McGee (ed.), *Initial Evidence, Historical and Biblical Perspectives on the Pentecostal Doctrine of Spirit Baptism* (Peabody, MA: Hendrickson, 1991).
3. H.I. Lederle, 'Initial Evidence and the Charismatic Movement: An Ecumenical Appraisal', in McGee (ed.), *Initial Evidence*, p. 138.
4. For example, G. Osborne, 'A Truce Proposal for the Tongues Controversy', *Christianity Today* 16 (1971), pp. 6-9.
5. L.W. Hurtado, 'Normal But Not the Norm: Initial Evidence and the New Testament', in McGee (ed.), *Initial Evidence*, pp. 189-201.
6. The warning of Donald Gee not to give up tongues is perhaps representative

somehow do not ring true to their deepest experience, even if they are unable to say why. What has happened is that Pentecostals intuitively recognized the uniqueness of their experience of the Spirit but lacked the conceptual tools to express it in a precise manner. The Pentecostal doctrine can and must be reformulated, but any attempt to do so must maintain the integrity of Pentecostal experience.

In the meantime, charismatics who generally reject the classical formulation are no better off for it. Lederle interestingly notes that most charismatics who reject 'initial evidence' do experience tongues 'regularly' and even place this experience 'in a prominent position'.[7] Yet they do not have a theology which makes sense of this regularity and prominence in their experience. May they not have something like an 'initial evidence' *experience* even though the *doctrine* itself is denied? If this is the case, then it is imperative that both Pentecostals and charismatics alike seek to develop a doctrine which accurately reflects their particular kind of experience. We must not be satisfied with just having an experience of the Spirit without an undergirding theology. Without a theology, experience cannot be sustained for long. In this respect, Pentecostals are in a better position than the charismatics who are content with just their experience of tongues. For with at least a rudimentary theology of glossolalia the tradition of the Pentecostal experience of the Spirit can, in some measure, be ensured.

Still, what is required is a better theology of glossolalia. For a start, the question about the appropriateness of the term 'initial evidence' needs to be addressed. J. Ramsey Michaels, for instance, may well be right to question the biblical basis of the Pentecostal usage. For in those instances where Pentecostals have drawn their support (namely, Acts 2, 10, 19), the evidence is probably not tongues but the Spirit himself.[8] But Michaels's conclusion does not necessarily invalidate the doctrine of initial evidence; it has only invalidated the traditional basis for the doctrine. 'Evidence' may not be the best way to describe what Pentecostals really thought and felt. But what that term seeks to encapsulate is a distinct sort of experience in which the powerful presence of the Spirit bears a unique relationship to speaking in tongues. It is to exploring this unique relationship that the rest of this essay is devoted.

of such an awareness (noted by Lederle, 'Initial Evidence', p. 132).

7. Lederle, 'Initial Evidence', p. 132.

8. J.R. Michaels, 'Evidences of the Spirit, or the Spirit of Evidence? Some Non-Pentecostal Reflections', in McGee (ed.), *Initial Evidence*, pp. 204-205.

But before doing that, a word must be said about the recent Pentecostal apologetics implied in the works of scholars like Roger Stronstad, Robert Menzies[9] and summed up in Johns's essay. Their argument, briefly stated, is that Luke's narrative is intended to teach theology. Historical patterns in Luke–Acts are not merely journalistic reports of what happened but belong to a literary genre in which normative truth is conveyed differently. The means to bring out the Lukan theology is mainly through narrative and redactional criticism. The main difficulty with their approach, as with any attempt at interpreting a narrative or story, is that one is usually left with as many interpretations as interpreters. A recent symposium on the children's story, 'The Giving Tree', by Shel Silverstein is a good case in point.[10] It is hardly surprising that twelve interpreters should understand the story in twelve slightly to very different ways; what is surprising is that each viewpoint could be backed by very sound and compelling explanations! The point is already illustrated in the differing readings by Donald Johns and Larry Hurtado concerning the purpose of Acts.[11] The most that can be said about the fine works of Stronstad and Menzies is that their interpretation represents one significant level of reading Luke. But it does not constitute a strong enough foundation on which a Pentecostal theology can be built or vindicated.[12] If Pentecostals are to make a case for their 'initial

9. R. Stronstad, *The Charismatic Theology of St Luke* (Peabody, MA: Hendrickson, 1984); R.P. Menzies, *The Development of Early Christian Pneumatology with Special Reference to Luke–Acts* (JSNTSup, 54; Sheffield: JSOT Press, 1991).

10. S. Silverstein, 'The Giving Tree: A Symposium', *First Things* 49 (1995), pp. 22-45.

11. D.A. Johns, 'Some New Directions in the Hermeneutics of Classical Pentecostalism's Doctrine of Initial Evidence', in Mcgee (ed.), *Initial Evidence*, pp. 145-67; Hurtado, 'Normal, but Not the Norm', pp. 193-95.

12. Menzies' more recent book *Empowered for Witness: The Spirit in Luke–Acts* (JPTSup, 6; Sheffield: Sheffield Academic Press, 1994) includes two chapters which attempt to bring his basic thesis of a distinct Lukan pneumatology to bear on the doctrine of subsequence and initial evidence. The attempt, however, entails methodological difficulties. Granted that Luke's prophetic understanding of the Spirit is 'logically distinct' from Paul's soteriological emphasis, the question is, in what sense can we speak of the difference as theological? What does Menzies mean by saying that Luke is 'a theologian in his own right'? And if Luke and Paul are also complementary how are they so? To answer these questions involves second level theological reflection which Menzies has not done. The closest that he has come to answering them is to say that Paul had a more developed pneumatology that includes

evidence' doctrine they must move beyond the Acts patterns as its ultimate justification. This does not mean that we must fall back on the hermeneutic of 'original intention' of the mainline evangelicals.[13] Rather, if the doctrine is to be validated, it has to be seen as part of a larger coherent theology. That is to say, if the 'initial evidence' doctrine is to commend itself as serious theology, glossolalia must be brought into a meaningful relationship to other significant theological symbols.

the charismatic dimensions while Luke 'bears witness solely to the prophetic dimension of the Spirit's work and thus he gives us a glimpse of only a part of Paul's fuller view' (p. 241). Perhaps as a biblical theologian he is not expected to answer such questions. But if he is seeking to show that Lukan pneumatology justifies the traditional Pentecostal doctrine of subsequence, he needs to move beyond mere affirmation of distinction to a more systematic relation of the Lukan and Pauline pneumatologies. It is at this level that Fee comes in by showing that Luke's pneumatology can best be understood in the light of Paul's precisely because the latter includes a charismatic dimension within its soteriological framework. The difference between Menzies and Fee here lies in the fact that Menzies has not quite moved beyond the first level of exegetical reflection and therefore confuses the phenomenological and the theological. I would like to suggest that Luke's pneumatology is basically phenomenological (for which there might well be theological reasons) whereas Paul, by contrast, was the theologian proper by his understanding the prophetic dimension of the Spirit within a larger soteriological framework. Such an understanding provides a better basis for maintaining complementarity as well as difference between Luke and Paul. On the issue of initial evidence Menzies is correct to say that it is a question of systematic theology (*Empowered for Witness*, p. 250), but the Pentecostal doctrine as it stands cannot be answered even at the level of systematic theology. Even granting Menzies' understanding of Lukan pneumatology, I find it difficult to see how 'the *normative* character of evidential tongues' could be inferred (p. 252, emphasis added). Given the preponderance of prophetic utterances in Luke–Acts, it would seem equally, if not more, plausible to infer prophecy as initial evidence. Menzies' preference for tongues because of its 'unusual' character (p. 251) seems to be going beyond legitimate inference. In sum, while the works of Stronstad and Menzies do not sufficiently vindicate Pentecostal beliefs, they show that the Pentecostal distinctives are not contrary to Scripture either. But for an adequate Pentecostal apologetic to be developed it has to move beyond biblical and systematic theology to larger philosophical considerations which integrate Pentecostal doctrine with Pentecostal religious experience.

13. As exemplified by G.D. Fee, 'Hermeneutics and Historical Precedent—A Major Problem in Pentecostal Hermeneutics', in R.B. Spittler (ed.), *Perspectives of the New Pentecostalism* (Grand Rapids: Baker, 1976); and M. Erickson, *Christian Theology* (Grand Rapids: Baker, 1985), pp. 79-80.

1. *The Logic of Glossolalia*

One way to do this is to understand glossolalia in terms of what linguistic philosophers called its 'logical function'. That is to say, in what logical context or universe of discourse can this phenomenon best be understood? The fact that tongues-speaking involves the use of language (leaving aside, for the time being, the question of what kind of language it is) suggests that its logical function must be located within the context of personal relationship. Tongues, of course, could be explained in other ways, depending on the perspective with which one approaches it: for example, from a socio-psychological perspective, in which case the focus is on the psychological state of the glossolaliacs or their social dynamics.[14] But *theologically* tongues are best understood as denoting a certain *kind* of personal relationship that believers have with God.

Baptism in the Spirit, to which glossolalia points, has always been understood as the coming of God's Spirit into the believer's life in a very focused way. This is the subject of a recent article by Frank Macchia.[15] Macchia discusses a number of views regarding the significance of tongues which highlight important aspects of the Christian life. But essentially, to summarize Macchia, tongues are attempts to express the inexpressible[16] and what this means is that the Christian has encountered a 'theophany' which 'included the transformation of language into a channel of the divine self-disclosure' in which the Holy Spirit 'encounter[s] us in dramatic and unforeseen ways that change our outlook and broaden our horizons'.[17] Tongues opens up the believer to realities way beyond him or herself: the eschatological, Christological and communal, which includes sympathetic identification with suffering *(theologia crucis)*. It is interesting to note that in a penetrating study of Christian spirituality Rowan Williams says very much the same thing about the nature of the contemplative tradition. Far from being individualistic and world-denying, it seeks for the most intimate union with God through Christ in the world with all its sufferings, temptations and weaknesses. In Williams's words, 'the state of union involves

14. See, for example, Pts 4 and 5 of W.E. Mills (ed.), *Speaking in Tongues: A Guide to Research in Glossolalia* (Grand Rapids: Eerdmans, 1986).

15. F. Macchia, 'Sighs Too Deep for Words: Toward a Theology of Glossolalia', *Journal of Pentecostal Theology* 1 (1992), pp. 47-73.

16. Macchia, 'Sighs Too Deep for Words', p. 61.

17. Macchia, 'Sighs Too Deep for Words', p. 57.

a re-conversion to creatures'.[18] Both the contemplative and the Pentecostal may be traveling by different paths to the same goal: an intimacy with God that breaks through the bounds of self-centered isolation into the world where God is to be found in suffering and death.

Leaving aside the social implications of Spirit-baptism, the experience, unfortunately, was later encapsulated in a doctrine that narrowly defines it in terms of power for service.[19] But it does not alter the fact that Spirit-baptism was experienced as something much more. Peter Hocken has shown that in the many less formal statements and testimonies of early Pentecostals, Spirit-baptism was more a 'revelation' in which the 'distinctive roles of the three Divine Persons are seen in their saving vivifying action upon the believers'. They testified, among other things, to the nearness of Jesus and of the 'revelation of the triune God in me'.[20] The testimony of one Pentecostal who recounted a visit to a Pentecostal church for the first time is perhaps representative:

> I had never heard such praise, such love and adoration to the Lord Jesus. Indeed 'tongues' were largely an expression, an overflow, of the worship…there was an intense recognition of the Lordship of Christ, and of His absolute rights over their lives (1 Cor. 12.3), a deep gratitude for His precious blood, shed for their sin on Calvary's Cross, a yearning for His return.[21]

It is in order to capture the depth of such personal intimacy that glossolalia was set forth as the 'initial physical evidence'. In other words, the initial evidence doctrine makes the best sense only in the context of such intimacy. I would like to explore their relationship further by means of two analogies. The first is that of intimate lovers whose depth of intimacy is sometimes expressed in an 'idiolect'[22] known only to themselves: we

18. R. Williams, *The Wound of Knowledge* (Cambridge, MA: Cowley Publications, rev. edn, 1991), p. 179

19. Statement of Fundamental Truths, 7. The statement actually refers to 'the inducement of power for *life* and service, the bestowment of the gifts and their uses in the work of the ministry'. While the relationship of Spirit-baptism to life is recognized, the emphasis falls more heavily on service.

20. P. Hocken, 'The Meaning and Purpose of Spirit-Baptism', *Pneuma* 7 (1985), pp. 130, 133.

21. Hocken, 'Meaning and Purpose', p. 133.

22. The term is used by Ernest Best to refer to glossolalia. But Best attributes the presence of the Pentecostal idiolect to certain social conditions that obtain in our times. ('The Interpretation of Tongues', in Mills [ed.], *Speaking in Tongues*, see esp. pp. 306-308)

call it 'lovers' talk' or 'sweet nothings'. Even if such talk means nothing to an observer, who is to say that it is not profoundly meaningful to the lovers themselves? In this context, Paul's point that 'the one who speaks in an unknown tongue edifies himself' certainly makes good sense. But the lover analogy must be complemented by another picture, that of a child bombarding its parent with a stream of 'meaningless' prattle. Here is a different kind of intimacy. We may call it an intimacy of familiarity. The child–parent analogy helps us to understand that glossolaliacs may not always be the most spiritually mature, yet within their limited knowledge they are able to enter into a deeply meaningful level of personal engagement with their heavenly Father, which, as history has shown, gives them an extraordinary boldness to venture 'by faith' (that is, without much theological training or financial support) into the far-flung mission fields.[23]

Now, if glossolalia is understood as a sign of one's intimacy with God, can we then establish the link as a necessary one, in other words, not only as one of many possible signs but *the* sign of Spirit-baptism? I believe that a case can be made for such a link at a number of related levels.

First, in a general way, a connection can be made between tongues as a sign and the presence of the Spirit as the thing signified from a sacramental perspective. This has been done in another article by Macchia.[24] Building on the sacramental theology of contemporary Catholic theologians like Rahner and Schillebeeckx, Macchia sees the spiritual reality (Spirit-baptism) as something present in and experienced through the visible sign (tongues) 'in the process of signification'.[25] But the link is a general one; in other words, the physical sign does not have to be speaking in tongues. While the Acts pattern gives some basis for Pentecostals' making the link, Macchia, as a matter of fact, cautions that it should not be developed into a fixed law. That being the case, Macchia would rather not use the term 'evidence' since it connotes a too scientific connection.[26]

---

23. The beginning of the Assemblies of God in Brazil by two Swedish immigrant workers is one of many such instances. See W. Hollenweger, *The Pentecostals* (London: SCM Press, 1972), pp. 75ff.

24. F. Macchia, 'Tongues as a Sign: Towards a Sacramental Understanding of Pentecostal Experience', *Pneuma* 5 (1993), pp. 61-76.

25. Macchia, 'Tongues as a Sign', p. 62.

26. Macchia, 'Tongues as a Sign', pp. 66, 68.

Macchia's sacramental understanding of tongues has important implications for Pentecostal spirituality by helping to locate glossolalia within
a broader ascetical framework which is essential for any enduring spirituality. It is a spirituality that does not demean nature or set grace and
nature in opposition but sees nature as a means of grace. Its Thomistic
watchword is: *Gratia non tollit sed attolit naturam* (Grace does not
destroy nature but lifts nature up). But the sacramental understanding
still does not fully explain the distinctive role that Pentecostals give to
tongues. One reason is that the Pentecostal experience of tongues *as* evidence includes another essential component which a sacramental model
does not encompass. We may call this the enthusiastic component, to use
a traditional term. One of the main characteristics of enthusiasm is that
the subject of a powerful spiritual experience feels impinged upon by the
direct action of God in such an overwhelming way that the only appropriate response is open receptivity. This phenomenon can be found, perhaps in rather exaggerated forms, among the early Quakers.[27] But it can
also be seen in the contemplative tradition where it is usually identified
with the higher degrees of prayer known as 'passive' or 'infused' contemplation. In St. Teresa of Avila's seven-grade scale of prayer, infused
contemplation begins at the 'fourth mansions'. It is associated with the
'prayer of quiet' which bathes the whole being with 'sweetness and
consolation'. Interestingly, Teresa uses the picture of a river that pours
directly from God into a basin (the soul). It begins in the deepest part of
the soul beyond the faculties ('I cannot say where it arises or how'),
overflows into the faculties and eventually submerges the whole 'outer
man'.[28] The early Pentecostals seemed to experience something struc-
turally very similar. Tongues, for them, were not the means of grace but
the *fruit* of grace, the spontaneous response to the *prior* action of God
in their innermost being. It is primarily in this aspect of Pentecostal experience that tongues functions as 'evidence' rather than as sacramental
sign. This is how one early Pentecostal leader explained the nature of
baptism in the Spirit.

> The Baptism [in the Spirit] is the submerging of the whole being including
> the mind, and tongues proves the submerging of the mind. Speaking a

27. G.F. Nuttall, *Studies in Christian Enthusiam* (Wallington, PA: Pendle Hill,
1948).
28. *The Interior Castle* (trans. and ed. E. Allison Peers; Garden City, NY: Image
Books, 1961), pp. 80-81. Cf. n. 44 below.

language unknown to the mind shows that the mind and the whole being are, at the moment, subjected to God.[29]

The speaking in tongues is associated with the 'submerging of the mind', that is, the momentary suspension in whole or in part of the ordinary rational processes. This is the typical language of the enthusiast. It should also be noted that this state is not carried over into the rest of life. It occurs 'at the moment' of Spirit-baptism. In this respect, the Pentecostals differ markedly from the Quakers, whose inner light ('the Christ within') was a perpetual source of guidance and dramatic actions.[30]

Another Pentecostal, W.T. Gaston, one-time general-superintendent of the Assemblies of God, USA, distinguished tongues as evidence from the gift of tongues in this way:

> The yielded human vessel is controlled entirely by the divine Spirit—hence unlimited and unrestrained. And as a gift in the established assembly as at Corinth, where the manifestation is under the control of the anointed human mind, its exercise is limited and prescribed.[31]

The distinction between tongues as evidence and as gift in the assembly is very much a part of the Pentecostal 'tenets of faith'. But what is important is that the two functions bear substantially different relations to the Spirit. In Spirit-baptism the Spirit is in complete control (evidenced by tongues), whereas in the gift of tongues no such entire control is assumed. On the contrary, one may safely assume that its regulation in the public assembly suggests a high degree of human control.

It would appear, therefore, that Macchia's sacramental understanding of tongues could be better applied to the second function of tongues. For here, Pentecostals often speak of the gift of tongues for self-edification as a 'prayer language' which the Spirit-filled believer is encouraged to exercise. This is usually linked to Rom. 8.26. It is a learned behavior and functions as a means of grace. The believer in the very act of speaking may be said to realize sacramentally the presence of God.[32]

29. Quoted by G.B. McGee, 'Popular Expositions of Initial Evidence', in *idem* (ed.), *Initial Evidence*, p. 123.

30. One could not help but be impressed by how they were 'moved', 'commanded', 'compelled' by the power of God as a matter of course. The ensuing actions were sometimes quite ennobling, but at other times quite macabre as reported by friends and foes alike. See Nuttall, *Studies*, pp. 29-33, 59-61.

31. Cited by McGee, 'Popular Exposition', in *idem* (ed.), *Initial Evidence*, p. 128.

32. The dynamic between sign and thing signified is greatly illuminated in C.S. Lewis's theory of transposition. When a higher medium (the spiritual) transposes

Earlier on, I spoke of tongues as occurring in the context of personal intimacy using the analogies of lovers and parent–child. The link is a natural one because language is the most basic way in which personal relationship finds its fulfillment. Theologically, the essential link between language and personhood can be stated in terms of the doctrine of the Trinity. The eternal relationship between the Father and the Son is one in which the Father eternally speaks the Word and in the speaking, the personal identities of Father and Son are realized.[33] One could even state, as a general rule, that the more intimate the relationship the more idiosyncratic the language. In very casual relationships we tend to use the most conventional, 'diplomatic' form of language. Among friends we might perhaps revert to a dialectic variation; between lovers, an idiolect. Is it not possible, then, that in a relationship involving the soul[34] and its God, at the deepest level of personal engagement in which the soul surrenders totally to the one who is all in all, a highly personalized kind of idiolect becomes not just one of the possible forms of expressions but the only appropriate form there is?[35] Given the Pentecostal

itself into a lower medium (the physical) the only way in which it could express itself is in characteristics associated strictly with the lower. Thus tongues will always sound no more than 'gibberish' to those who approach it from a human point of view (C.S. Lewis, *Transposition and Other Addresses* [London: Geoffrey Bles, 1949], pp. 9-20).

33. For a classic formulation of this concept see Thomas Aquinas, *Summa Theologiae* 1a, Q.43 (London: Eyre & Spottiswoode, 1976), esp. pp. 27-37. One of the most illuminating discussions of this trinitarian dynamic can be found in D.L. Sayers, 'Towards a Christian Aesthetic', in *idem, Christian Letters to a Post-Christian World* (Grand Rapids: Eerdmans, 1969), pp. 69ff. Sayers sees the creative work of the poet involving experience, *expression* and recognition as imaging the creative trinitarian life. Within the contemplative tradition, language has the same logical function but expressed differently: in wordless language rather than unknown language. Cf. St John of the Cross: 'God has only spoken One Word which is His Son and he has spoken It in eternal silence' (quoted in the Preface of Teresa of Avila, *Interior Castle* [New York: Paulist, 1979], xvii).

34. I have used the word 'soul' here not in contrast to the body but in keeping with traditional spiritual writers' usage where soul refers to the innermost being of the person.

35. Traditionally two variations of the same idiolect have been the usual response: one either is struck dumb or breaks out in tongues. The first is usually associated with the contemplative tradition and the Quakers, the second with the Pentecostals. Silence and glossolalia in this instance share the same logical status. Both are extraordinary language expressing the inexpressible. But why tongues for the Pentecostals

understanding of Spirit-baptism as an overpowering 'theophany', the insistence on tongues as *the* evidence is not as far-fetched after all. Still, the question is, could the lover or the child not respond in any other appropriate way? I suppose they could, but would they? Perhaps another analogy might help. I often put this question to my students whenever the issue of the evidential nature of tongues is raised: What happens when one is sad? Invariably, the spontaneous answer is, one sheds tears or cries. The relationship between glossolalia and baptism in the Spirit is very similar. Glossolalia may be compared to the 'gift of tears'.[36] The questions to ask, therefore, are not, are there not other signs of sadness that we can look for? Or worse, must one cry in order to be sad? (cf. a similar, equally misplaced question: Must I speak in tongues in order to be filled with the Spirit?) Rather, one simply *recognizes* a 'necessary' relationship between tears and sadness. They are concomitant to each other, or, if we prefer, tears evidence sadness in a unique way that perhaps nothing else does. In brief, if the *initial* baptism in the Spirit is understood as essentially denoting an experience of deep personal intimacy with the triune God in which the Spirit exercises full control, then it would in fact be quite accurate to see tongues as its natural concomitance or evidence.

2. *The Issue of Separability and Subsequence*

If the preceding explanation of the logical function of tongues is accepted it would seem that some kind of doctrine of 'subsequence' follows. But first, it needs to be pointed out that perhaps the primary concern of classical Pentecostals is not so much to establish the chronological order of salvation and Spirit-baptism but to stress the distinctiveness of the latter. It is unfortunate that discussion of this issue is often schematized into a 'doctrine of subsequence' when the chief concern is actually with its being '*distinct from* and subsequent to the new birth' (Assemblies of

and silence for the contemplative and Quaker? An adequate answer to this question would require discussions on the complex relationship between an experiential reality and the theological framework which shapes it and which in turn is shaped by it. In brief, Pentecostals had already inherited a framework which inevitably led them to support their experience from historical precedents in Acts.

36. The comparison is made by Francis Sullivan, although the point of his analogy is to highlight tongues as a natural event with 'quasi-sacramental' efficacy (*Charisms and the Charismatic Renewal* [Ann Arbor: Servant Books, 1982], pp. 145-46).

God Tenets of Faith, 7). That subsequence is not the primary consideration is indicated by the fact that Pentecostals, following the Acts 10
pattern, generally hold that Spirit-baptism could occur simultaneously
with conversion. But what they would insist on is its being a distinct
experience.[37] The problem with the classical Pentecostal explanation
here is that it fails to distinguish between a phenomenological reality and
a theological reality. What is phenomenologically different may yet be
theologically one as Gordon Fee has pointed out.[38] This is in fact the
standard position of most Roman Catholic charismatics today. Spirit-
baptism and conversion are parallel to the sacraments of confirmation
and baptism respectively but these two, while distinct experientially, are
one theological reality, one great work of Christian initiation.[39] The
problem with Pentecostals here does not lie in their understanding of
Spirit-baptism but in their inadequate understanding of conversion. They
have tended to adopt the popular evangelical position of explaining conversion as a single crisis experience, so that whatever experience comes
subsequent to it is taken to be theologically distinct.

Pentecostals are on much more solid ground, however, when the distinctive experience is understood within the logical context of tongues as
the initial evidence. The spontaneous outburst of tongues itself signifies
an experience of an overwhelming nature: it is nothing less than a basic
paradigm shift, a theophany. Perhaps another illustration might help.
Tolkien aficionados may recall one of the most critical moments for
Frodo and Sam Gamgee as they made their journey to Mount Doom to
fulfill their appointed task. In their desperation to find a way into Mordor
they were forced to take the path that led them into the foul habitation
of the spidery monster, Shelob. Their encounter with her left Frodo
stung and Sam in a swoon. Here was the critical moment:

37. The secondary importance of subsequence has been argued by Russell
Spittler who thinks that the primary intent of the doctrinal formulation is to show that
'glossolalic encounter with the Holy Spirit is a desirable experience for believers'
(R.P. Spittler, 'The Pentecostal Tradition', *Agora* 1.1 (Summer, 1977), pp. 10-11.

38. G.D. Fee, 'Baptism in the Spirit: The Issue of Separability and Subsequence',
Pneuma 7 (1985), pp. 87-99 (90-91).

39. For a summary of various Catholic charismatic views, see H.I. Lederle,
*Treasures Old and New: Interpretations of 'Spirit-Baptism' in the Charismatic
Renewal* (Peabody, MA: Hendrickson, 1988), pp. 104-38. A more recent restatement
of the Catholic sacramental view can be found in K. McDonnell and G. Montague,
*Christian Initiation and Baptism in the Holy Spirit: Evidence from the First Eight
Centuries* (Collegeville, MN: Liturgical Press, 1991).

Even as Sam himself crouched, looking at her, seeing death in her eyes, a thought came to him, as if some remote voice had spoken, and he fumbled in his breast with his left hand, and found what he sought: cold and hard and solid it seemed to his touch in a phantom world of horror, the Phial of Galadriel.

'Galadriel', he said faintly, and then he heard voices far off but clear: the crying of the Elves as they walked under the stars in the beloved shadows of the Shire, and the music of the Elves as it came through his sleep in the Hall of Fire in the house of Elrond.

> *Gilthoniel O Elbereth!*

And then his tongue was loosed and his voice cried in a language which he did not know:

> *O Elbereth Gilthoniel*
> *O menel palan—diriel*
> *le nallan sí di'nguruthos*
> *A tíro nin, Fanuilos.*

And with that he staggered to his feet and was Samwise the hobbit, Hamfast's son, again.[40]

At the critical moment when Sam broke out in the elvish tongue, he crossed the threshold, as it were, in a manner which would not be too far different from the Pentecostals' own experience, an experience which, upon later reflection, they would have felt entirely justified to describe using the language of separability and subsequence. In short, the stress on distinctiveness is apparently the Pentecostal way of schematizing what must have been for them a major spiritual transition, perhaps even a quantum leap in their religious consciousness. It further qualifies their experience of Spirit-baptism as not only the experience of deep intimacy and total surrender but also one that dramatically heightens their spiritual awareness.

---

40. J.R.R. Tolkien, *The Two Towers* (Cambridge, MA: Houghton Mifflin, n.d.), pp. 338-39. The idea of using Tolkien was first gleaned from Ernest Best, 'The Interpretation of Tongues', in W.E. Mills (ed.), *Speaking in Tongues: A Sample of Research on Glossolalia* (Grand Rapids: Eerdmans, 1986), pp. 295-312, but for him the 'idiolect' is explained in socio-psychological terms.

3. *Towards a Reinterpretation of Baptism in the Spirit*

It is certainly not possible within the scope of an essay to attempt a reinterpretation or reappropriation of the doctrine of baptism in the Spirit. What I would like to propose are two directions that must be taken into consideration in such an undertaking.

If the Pentecostal experience of baptism in the Spirit is understood as essentially an experience of an overwhelming divine presence to which the subject can only respond with total receptivity, then the doctrine of 'initial evidence' is a generally accurate schematization of it. The problem, therefore, does not lie with this part of the traditional formulation; rather, it is in the way the nature and purpose of Spirit-baptism have been traditionally defined. What is needed, therefore, is to enlarge the understanding of the experience in order to make better sense of the doctrine of initial evidence rather than revise the doctrine to fit the current definition of Spirit-baptism (which is what many non-Pentecostals would like to see done—and what some Pentecostals are tempted to do). Most of the classical Pentecostal denominations have tended to associate it too narrowly with power for service. This, as we have noted from Hocken, is manifestly inadequate as it does not encompass the *actual* experience of Pentecostals themselves. Some recent Pentecostal scholars, however, have argued that this traditional understanding was in fact an exclusive Lukan concern.[41] If indeed this was so, the early Pentecostal experience was surely much larger than Lukan pneumatology. But I am more inclined to think that what they experienced was simply biblical pneumatology, and that their explanation was probably constricted by their too literalistic reading of Luke.[42] Being biblicists they had to find some direct scriptural justification for their experience. In short, if there is to be any reinterpretation of Pentecostal theology, it should begin with the issue of the nature and purpose of Spirit-baptism rather than the 'initial evidence'. If this is done, Pentecostals today will be able to reappropriate a vital component of their spiritual heritage which their

---

41. For example, R.P. Menzies, *Development of Early Christian Pneumatology*, pp. 278-79; and *idem*, 'Luke and the Spirit: A Reply to James Dunn', *Journal of Pentecostal Theology* 4 (1994), pp. 115-38 (137-38).

42. Most New Testament scholars, however, would agree with Dunn's assessment that although Luke has his own distinctive emphasis, the framework of his pneumatology is similar to Paul's (J.D.G. Dunn, *Baptism in the Holy Spirit* [London: SCM Press, 1970]).

forebears instinctively understood when they described their own Spirit-baptism as a 'revelation of the triune God in me'.

Further, for an adequate Pentecostal theology to be developed, the two functions of tongues (tongues as evidence and tongues as prayer) must be clearly distinguished. I believe that part of the confusion in current scholarship with regard to the initial evidence and its corollary, the doctrine of separability, is due to the failure to distinguish between these functions. The tendency is to treat glossolalia as a single phenomenon. The result of this conflation is that while the theological (not to mention the socio-psychological) significance of glossolalia *qua* glossolalia has now been fairly well explored, the distinctive experience embodied in the first function has largely been lost. In fact, by maintaining the two functions of tongues, Pentecostal theology could well provide a framework for a spirituality broad enough to encompass both the enthusiastic and ascetical dimensions of the spiritual life. This is claiming a lot for Pentecostal theology, considering that historically both the enthusiastic and ascetical camps had hardly been on speaking terms with each other. The former had been treated with suspicion and marginalized by both Catholics and Protestants alike,[43] and it is only in recent years that it has begun to gain some measure of acceptance—but not without careful qualifications—in the mainline churches. Simply put, the first function of tongues as initial evidence captures the enthusiastic dimension of Pentecostal spirituality, while the second, as a 'prayer language' or 'sacrament' of the Spirit's presence, brings out its ascetical dimension. Pentecostal theology, grounded in a proper understanding of the dual function of tongues, could well point the way forward to a better integration of these two components of the spiritual life. Within this integrated spirituality, the Pentecostal experience of personal intimacy could be freely explored without the usual dangers attendant on an unrestrained enthusiasm. If this is done we will discover something which is not quite unlike the experience of intimacy embodied in the Church's mystical tradition,[44] but with perhaps

---

43. A good example is R.A. Knox's famous study, *Enthusiasm: A Chapter in the History of Religion* (Oxford: Clarendon Press, 1959).

44. The structural similarity between glossolalia and Teresa of Avila's 'fourth mansion' which marks the beginning of infused contemplation merits closer examination. The soul's movement from activity (represented by the first three mansions) to receptivity is achieved by the 'prayer of recollection' (*Interior Castle*, chapter 3) of which Rowan Williams gives this succinct summary:

one notable difference. In the mystical tradition (such as we see in St Bernard of Clairvaux) the image of the lover predominates, whereas Pentecostal spirituality could be chiefly characterized as the spirituality of the child,[45] whose faith in the heavenly Father is so implicit that it dares to take incalculable risks for the sake of the kingdom of God. In short, an integrated Pentecostal spirituality embodies the spirit of adventure without losing itself in reckless ventures.

'Recollection' is the state in which the inner gaze of the soul is becoming more and more steadily fixed on God's self-giving, and that steady regard finds expression in simple patterns of words; as this deepens and simplifies, God's activity engages us with greater completeness, and our deepest 'mental' activities are reduced to silence ... (*Teresa of Avila* [Harrisburg, PA: Moorehouse Publishing, 1991], pp. 125-26).

Both glossolalia and the prayer of recollection share a similar moment of transition from the natural to a more supernatural state.

45. The child analogy, however, is not entirely absent in the larger spiritual tradition. One of its usages which comes very close to our characterization of Pentecostal spirituality can be found in the prayer of François Fénelon:

I desire to find in the most secret place of my heart, an intimate familiarity with thee, through thy son Jesus, who is thy wisdom and thy eternal mind, become a child to humble our vain and foolish wisdom by his childhood and the folly of his cross. It is there that I wish, whatever it costs me, in spite of my foresight and my reflections, to become little, senseless, even more contemptible in my own eyes than in those of all the falsely-wise. It is there that I wish to become inebriate of Holy Spirit, as the Apostles were, and to be willing as they were to be the laughing stock of the world (*Christian Perfection* [New York: Harper & Brothers, 1947], p. 123).

Peter D. Hocken

In this contribution to the Festschrift for William W. Menzies, I want to
reflect on the specificity of the Pentecostal-charismatic phenomenon
of the twentieth century, and in particular on the relationship between
Pentecostalism and Evangelicalism. I propose to do so by way of chronicling the evolution of my own understanding. I am approaching this
theological topic in such a personal way for two connected reasons:
1) my own understanding has developed—and I hope deepened—
through the interaction of my personal commitment within the body
of Christ and my historical-theological reflection and writing; and
2) because testimony is a distinctively Pentecostal-charismatic literary
form, that does not have to be excluded from the sphere of theological
reflection.[1] As such, I hope that it may be a fitting tribute to Bill
Menzies, who has always sought to integrate his Pentecostal faith and his
scholarly work.

I approach the distinctiveness of Pentecostalism as a Roman Catholic,
and as a charismatic. As a Roman Catholic, I approach Pentecostalism
from a non-evangelical background; as a charismatic, I share in the foundational Pentecostal-charismatic experience of being baptized in the Holy
Spirit. Chronicling my own developing understanding in the context of
my own background and presuppositions may help readers from other
backgrounds to greater clarity concerning the connection between their

---

1.   I must also confess a related motive for chronicling the development of my
thinking. The presentations of my understanding of baptism in the Spirit by other
scholars are, despite their best intentions, not wholly accurate. This is partly because
my thinking on this new and challenging subject changed and evolved more than on
most theological questions, partly because my writings on this subject have mostly
been occasional rather than systematic treatments. This article presents an opportunity
to provide some clarification. See subsequent footnotes for further references.

theological convictions and their Christian contexts.[2]

1. *First Impressions*

Before my introduction to charismatic renewal, I had virtually no know-ledge of Pentecostals. As a child and as a young man, I had seen an Elim Pentecostal chapel not far from my home, but I had no idea who these people were or how they differed from other 'sects'. All I knew from my middle-class background was that they belonged to the 'other side of the street' in a working-class area. In the mid-1960s as a young priest, active in a local Ministers' Fraternal in England, I met an Assemblies of God pastor, who participated quite regularly, and whom I regarded as being on the 'fringe'. I had no idea that he might be taking a risk in coming to such an ecumenical body.

My first real fellowship with Pentecostals occurred within days of my being baptized in the Spirit. The Catholics I had met, who moved in the realm of the Spirit and the Spirit's gifts, had been impacted by the Lord, not through contact with Catholic charismatics, but through the preaching and ministry of some English Pentecostals (in Oxford and Birmingham).[3] They quickly took me to Hockley Pentecostal Church in Birmingham.[4]

At Hockley, I immediately saw that there was something different about these Christians and their ways from all the patterns of Christianity that I had previously met. I had some familiarity with Evangelicalism, partly through having a devout evangelical grandmother, and being sent to an evangelical Sunday School as a boy, partly from living in a Baptist home when I began work in London at the age of 17. I knew instinctively that this Pentecostal expression of Christian faith was significantly different from the evangelical patterns that I had seen.

What did I see that produced these clear initial impressions? I noticed the following:

2.   See G.D. Fee, 'Exegesis and the Role of Tradition in Evangelical Hermeneutics', *Evangelical Review of Theology* 17 (1993), pp. 421-36.

3.   This story does not appear as yet in any historical studies on the charismatic movement in Britain. Some of my own research and experience is reflected in a popular article: 'Joan Steele and the Denton Prayer Meeting', *Renewal* 199 (Dec., 1992), pp. 39-40.

4.   The story of Hockley Pentecostal Church has been told in H. Fisher and O. Reeve, *Still It Flows* (Birmingham: Hockley Pentecostal Church, n.d.).

1. A directness of relationship to God with corresponding expectations of divine revelation, divine acts in ministry.
2. A genuinely participatory pattern of worship not dominated by priest or preacher.
3. A different configuration between the roles of Scripture, tradition and experience to either modern Roman Catholicism, liberal Protestantism or evangelical Protestantism.
4. A practice that was less rationalist and less cerebral than Evangelicalism, in which there was a greater physical element than other Protestant patterns and a greater integration between the physical and the spiritual.
5. A use of Scripture and a style of preaching and ministry that was more anecdotal and narrative than schematic and doctrinal.[5]

I was much more impressed by Pentecostal practice than by Pentecostal theory.[6] Whenever I went to Hockley, I found myself operating a kind of instant sifting between the practice and the explanation, between the primary and the secondary. Thus I was much more impressed by the use of Scripture in prophetic utterance and in narrative-type sermons than in the doctrinal expositions found in some Pentecostal literature.

Some others who have noted the same point have said that Pentecostalism (and charismatic renewal) is an experience in search of a theology. This seems to be a less felicitous formulation. First of all, the strong points of Pentecostalism are not adequately expressed by the term 'experience'; practice is wider than experience. Secondly, the language of experience suggests a subjectivist focus, in which there is an indifference to the content of the experience. Such a judgment is not warranted. No sane Pentecostal or charismatic Christian would regard baptism in the Spirit as a kind of generic experience into which any kind or a wide range of types of contents could be fitted.

---

5.   These convictions concerning the distinctive features of Pentecostalism are expressed in my contribution 'The Significance and Potential of Pentecostalism' in P. Hocken *et al.*, *New Heaven? New Earth?* (Springfield, IL: Templegate, 1977), pp. 16-67.

6.   I was convinced of this before I met and began to read the writings of Professor Walter J. Hollenweger, who has long argued this position: 'the questions posed for traditional churches by the spread of the Pentecostal movement are more important than the answers given by Pentecostalism' (*The Pentecostals* [Minneapolis: Augsburg, 1972], p. 507).

Thus my first impressions encouraged me to emphasize the differences between Pentecostalism and Evangelicalism. These impressions were reinforced by my reading of the writings of Walter Hollenweger and by a growing sense that the charismatic movement needed to affirm its kinship with Pentecostalism, but not copy its theology, if it was to retain its dynamic power and impact.

Being more impressed by Pentecostal practice than Pentecostal theory, I was more struck by the spiritual reality of 'Pentecost' than by the Pentecostal doctrine of baptism in the Holy Spirit. I went through a phase of strong affirmation of the reality, while questioning the terminology of baptism in the Spirit.[7] I was initially led back to greater sympathy for the Pentecostal terminology by the pragmatic observation that there was a positive correlation between use of this language and people being led into the reality.

2. *Closer Knowledge*

My moving to the United States to join the Mother of God Community in Gaithersburg, Maryland, in 1976, was a water-shed for several reasons. First, I was coming into a community that had a clarity about the gospel, and that clearly preached repentance for sin and the power of the blood and the cross of Jesus Christ. I realized over time that this rootedness in the gospel, what we may call its evangelical character, grounded the solidity of the Community's spiritual foundations and its clear sense of direction. This new appreciation for the gospel message opened the door for a more positive appreciation of Evangelicalism—and to move beyond the paradoxical position of approving Pentecostalism (its practice rather than its theology) while continuing to see Evangelicalism in rather negative terms.

Secondly, the Mother of God Community had a strong commitment to baptism in the Spirit, both to the reality and to the terminology. By this time, many Catholic commentators had expressed serious reservations about the terminology of baptism in the Spirit. In the English-speaking world, these hesitations had little effect on Catholic charismatic usage; in France, Germany, Italy and Poland, however, the theological objections generally led to the use of another term.[8] The Community's

7.   It was at this point that I wrote the articles, 'Catholic Pentecostalism: Some Key Questions', *HeyJ* (1974), I: 15.2, pp. 131-43; II: 15.3, pp. 271-84.

8.   Thus the preferred terms have been *effusion de l'Esprit* (French),

insistence on the language of baptism in the Spirit reflected several instincts: the affirmation of a sovereign act of God in our day; its association with Pentecost; the total character of this immersion in the Spirit; a pastoral sense that people had needed conversion to Jesus before introduction to the realm of spiritual gifts.[9]

This commitment to baptism in the Spirit was associated with a genuine reverence for the work of the Spirit among Pentecostals. This emphasis harmonized fully with my earlier involvement with Pentecostals.[10] Thus in 1977, I attended the Society for Pentecostal Studies conference for the first time. Being convinced that the Pentecostal and charismatic movements are two strands of one and the same work of God, I sensed that I should participate regularly in the Society, whether or not I was presenting a paper.[11]

The Catholic influence on the Community's commitment to baptism in the Spirit has been most manifest in its contemplative approach, insisting on the constant need for deeper prayer and reflection if we are to penetrate and build on such a work of God. This stance involves a growing reverence for such a wonderful gift of the Lord, an awareness that the works of the Most High are not easily understood by human minds, and that the significance of this Pentecostal grace of baptism in the Holy Spirit is not simply obvious to any participant, but must be sought out in prayer and study of the Word in mutual sharing. This conviction led the Community members to grow in an awareness of the centrality in the 'baptism' of the revelation of Our Lord Jesus Christ in his fullness. At the same time, it led me in my reading of early Pentecostal literature to notice how the testimonies to baptism in the Spirit contained much more than the emerging Pentecostal doctrine affirmed.

Tauferneuerung, that is renewal of Baptism (German) and *effusione dello Spirito* (Italian). Interestingly, the Polish term literally means 're-birth'.

9. This last emphasis, that could be called a form of 'pastoral subsequentialism', influenced my writings and no doubt led Henry Lederle to classify my position as 'neo-Pentecostal' in *Treasures Old and New: Interpretations of 'Spirit baptism' in the Charismatic Revival* (Peabody, MA: Hendrickson, 1988), pp. 85-90.

10. This affinity was one of the reasons that led the Community leaders to invite me for a visit after reading my series of articles 'Pentecostals on Paper', *Clergy Review* 59 (1974), pp. 750-67; 60 (1975), pp. 161-83; 60 (1975), pp. 344-68.

11. I think the paucity of other regular Catholic members in the Society for Pentecostal Studies over the years suggests that not many Catholic Charismatics have had this conviction.

In 1979 I began my studies for a PhD at the University of Birmingham under Professor Hollenweger. I spent almost two years studying
Pentecostal and charismatic origins, with a view to doing a dissertation
comparing and contrasting the two. Now, for the first time, I began to
have close acquaintance with the pioneers of the Pentecostal movement.
I saw the affinity between the pioneers and the vital features at Hockley
Pentecostal Church. I found in the pioneers something richer than I
found among most of the white Pentecostals that I met in Britain and
North America (Hockley was blessedly untypical). I could see that the
Pentecostal movement went through phases: first, a wildfire phase,
marked by dramatic events, dynamic testimonies, enthusiastic preaching
and minimal organization. Secondly, the formation of denominations, initially often to counter the problems of disorganization and to coordinate
missionary work; this phase necessitated the formulation of official statements of Pentecostal doctrine and later led naturally to the development
of institutions for education and training. A third phase followed of
denominational expansion, with an increasing development of a whole
denominational ethos, and the growing influence of church departments
and college-trained ministers; in this third phase, the doctrinal bare-bones
of the Statements of Faith were developed into a more full-fledged
theology.

It was clear that the differences between Pentecostals and Evangelicals
were most marked in the first phase and least in the third. A major
reason for this evangelicalization was that the Pentecostals were evangelists and missionaries, not scholars; and that when they needed to
formulate their doctrine, they fell back on evangelical formulations. What
I am calling the 'evangelicalization' of Pentecostal faith was not the only
way that the formulation of Pentecostal convictions did not do full justice
to the richness of their foundational experience. The formulation of the
doctrine of baptism in the Spirit owed more to contemporary disputes
than it did to serious reflection on this work of the Spirit and on the
content of their personal and corporate experience.[12]

Although my doctoral dissertation had eventually to be confined to a
more manageable topic,[13] the research that I had done on the origins of

12. See P. Hocken, 'Jesus Christ and the Gifts of the Spirit', *Pneuma* 5 (1983),
pp. 1-16; and *idem*, 'The Meaning and Purpose of "Baptism in the Spirit"', *Pneuma*
7 (1985), pp. 125-33.

13. The origins and development of the charismatic movement in Great Britain,

Pentecostalism sharpened my sense of its differences from Evangelical-ism. A few times in the late 1970s and early 1980s I began to write an article on whether Pentecostalism was a sub-division of Evangelicalism, with the aim of demonstrating that the answer was 'no'. In the light of later developments, the non-completion of this article was providential.

At this time, I would have said that Pentecostalism was not simply a sub-division of Evangelicalism. I resonated most with the analyses of people like Bishop Lesslie Newbigin, whose seminal book *The Household of God* grasped the distinctiveness of the Pentecostal *gestalt*.[14]

3. *Grounds for Rethinking*

My study of Pentecostal origins made it clear that the first Pentecostals understood themselves as part of a revival movement, but a revival movement with a difference. As a revival movement, the Pentecostal revival followed in a historical sequence from the revivals that had shaped Evangelicalism. But as a revival with a difference, it was a revival *plus*.[15] The 'plus' factor was expressed in such phrases as 'The Full Gospel', 'The Apostolic Faith', 'The Latter Rain'. While this accounts for the restorationist character of Pentecostalism, with its self-understanding as a full restoration of the level of New Testament blessing and power, I do not think that 'restorationism' by itself adequately accounts for the distinctiveness of Pentecostalism. It does not do sufficient justice to the eschatological character of the Pentecostal-charismatic outpouring.[16]

Although I have been classified among 'neo-Pentecostals' in terms of my understanding of baptism in the Spirit,[17] my support since the late 1970s for a 'two-stage' understanding of conversion-regeneration and Spirit-baptism has always been more pastoral than theological. I have

published under the title *Streams of Renewal* (Exeter: Paternoster; Gaithersburg, MD: Word Among Us, 1986).

14. (London: SCM Press, 1953). It should be noted that Newbigin's use of the term 'Pentecostal' is wider than the Pentecostal movement, and also includes other Christian groupings emphasizing the illumination and guidance of the Holy Spirit, such as the Quakers.

15. This was the consistent position of Donald Gee. Gee wrote: 'It is possible to live as a denomination and die as a Revival' ('Movement or Message?', *Pentecost* 37 [Sept., 1956], inside of back cover).

16. I develop this point more fully in *The Glory and the Shame* (Guildford, UK: Eagle & Wheaton; Illinois: Harold Shaw, 1994), esp. in chs. 5–7.

17. See Lederle, *Treasures Old and New*, pp. 85-90.

never been persuaded that a 'two-stage' understanding can be justified as a doctrine from the New Testament. The Pentecostal attempts to justify such a doctrine biblically seem to belong to a restorationist framework. It was only as my understanding of New Testament eschatology developed that I came to see the eschatological context of the New Testament references to 'baptizing with Spirit', and the applications to Pentecost and the outpouring on the Gentiles at Caesarea as prophetic interpretations of the acts of God.[18] In other words, I have slowly been working toward an eschatological rather than a merely restorationist understanding of the whole Pentecostal-charismatic phenomenon.

The view that Pentecostalism is a revival with a difference leaves open to some degree the relationship with evangelicalism. For the plus factor can be understood as simply an intensification of evangelicalism, but an intensification that respects and retains all its classical elements. In that case, Pentecostalism is rightly seen as a sub-division of evangelicalism: a sub-division differently interpreted by Pentecostals and non-charismatic Evangelicals.

On the other hand, the plus factor can be understood as a transforming element that acts upon the common evangelical heritage, changing it into something that no longer falls simply under the generic evangelical heading. I believe this latter to be the case, primarily because the Pentecostal faith-life in its full originality understands differently the relationships between God, Jesus, the Word, the Spirit, the Church and the Christian. At the level of historical influences, the most obvious 'new' factor in Pentecostalism, that is clearly not of evangelical provenance, is the African-American component that entered at Azusa Street.[19] Thus, it is no coincidence that the most articulate proponents of Pentecostalism as a distinctive Christian *gestalt*, not capable of being submerged under the evangelical heading, have been the upholders of Azusa Street as the crucial event in its origins and of the inter-racial nature of the movement as essential to its character.[20]

18. This position is developed in Hocken, *The Glory and the Shame*, ch. 5, pp. 39-50.

19. See P. Hocken, *Le Réveil de l'Esprit* (Montreal: Fides, 1994), pp. 58-64.

20. Obviously Walter J. Hollenweger is the foremost advocate for this position.

4. *Rethinking Evangelical History*

As I developed a greater sympathy for Evangelicalism—an important phase in ecumenical maturity—I began to read more widely in evangelical literature and history. As I did this, I began to see the necessity of applying to Evangelicals the same distinction I had used for years in relation to the Pentecostals: namely between their practice and their theology. What then is the relationship between evangelical revivals and evangelical doctrine (both in preaching and in systematic theology)?

It is evident that Evangelicalism as a recognizable movement in the Protestant world has had a strong doctrinal component from its earliest days. The preaching of evangelical doctrines on the gospel, on sin and salvation, on the atonement and the blood once shed, on the authority of the Bible as the Word of God, all these have contributed strongly to evangelical vitality and impact. The Pentecostal challenge raises the question as to the extent to which evangelical theology has done justice both to the spiritual reality in the evangelical revivals and to their basic biblical convictions.

Any Pentecostal or charismatic Christian reading the accounts of evangelical revivals is struck by the occurrence of phenomena that are more common in the Pentecostal-charismatic world. We read of healings, of physical manifestations accompanying conviction and conversion, of people having visions or hearing words from the Lord. But much evangelical theology, particularly of the cessationist type, has either disapproved or excluded any spiritual significance being attached to these phenomena. Such theological suspicion no doubt colored the historical accounts that have come down to us. A charismatic pastor in Scotland, whom I know, grew up on the island of Lewis during the Revival of 1949.[21] He told me that the Lewis revival had a strong charismatic dimension in its origins that was subsequently erased from the published accounts.[22]

---

21. For an account of the Lewis Revival, see D. Campbell, *The Lewis Awakening 1949–1953* (Edinburgh: Faith Mission, 1954).

22. It is interesting that the short popular biography of the founders of the Apostolic Church, a Pentecostal denomination with its headquarters in Wales, says of the beginnings of the Welsh Revival in 1904–1905: 'Many were at this time heard speaking with tongues and prophesying' (T.N. Turnbull, *Brothers in Arms* [Bradford: Puritan Press, 1963], p. 23). Is this Pentecostal exaggeration on the part of Turnbull or does it represent a downplaying of the spiritual gifts in evangelical accounts of the Welsh Revival?

Several students of Evangelicalism have commented on the contemporaneity of evangelical beginnings and the Enlightenment.[23] Any Catholic theologian, not too infected by the spirit of the age, can hardly avoid sensing the rationalism that pervades much evangelical exegesis and preaching. It shows up in all forms of literalism, in a quasi-scientific model for truth, in the assumption that statements have only one level of meaning obvious to anyone who knows the meaning of the words, in the tendency to reduce spirituality to morality, in its individualism. These statements are more obviously applicable to evangelical theology and thought patterns, and less immediately applicable to basic biblical convictions. But where these rationalist patterns are operative in the realm of theology, they cannot help but be reductionist in their effects—taking a richer reality and filtering it through a theological grid that eliminates non-rational, non-logical elements, even though at the same time it is protesting vigorously against those who utilize the same *Zeitgeist* in more blatantly unbelieving ways.

The picture I am painting is one that sees Evangelicalism as at one and the same time a wonderful proponent of essential biblical truths that safeguard the vitality of Christian preaching and mission and a thought-world that despite the best intentions undermines its supernatural power and its outward expression by its rationalist spirit.

In this light, it may be that the history of Evangelicalism is in some way the struggle—the Divine struggle—for Pentecost to break out. The African-American element in the origins of Pentecostalism would then represent the insertion of a world-view and a practice largely unaffected by post-Enlightenment rationalism and individualism. If this interpretation is on the right lines, the Evangelicalization of Pentecostalism, as it has been called, represents at one and the same time contradictory tendencies: on the one hand, the acceptance of fundamental biblical principles that are essential for authentic spiritual growth, and on the other hand, yet another attempt to curb and constrain the divine *largesse* into restricted theological categories. The charismatic renewal, with the gift of Pentecost being poured out on non-evangelical Christians, would then represent another God-given opportunity to escape from our ideological boxes and to expand our human thinking and theology to the larger and

23. See D.W. Bebbington, 'Revival and Enlightenment in Eighteenth-Century England', in E.L. Blumhofer and R. Balmer (eds.), *Modern Christian Revivals* (Urbana: University of Illinois Press, 1993), pp. 17-41.

extraordinary scope of God's purposes. However, charismatic theologians in general have not risen to this challenge, and often manifest different ways of subordinating the divine gift to a human system of thought.[24]

5. *The Need for an 'Ecumenical', Charismatic and Reverent Theology*

As all Pentecostal readers will well know, evangelical critics have accused Pentecostalism of being essentially subjectivist, involving an appeal to present experience in a way that subverts the objectivity of the Scriptures. Pentecostal preference for biblical narrative is seen as a sign of inadequate rooting in the biblical doctrine of the New Testament epistles.

I had begun my own charismatic involvement with first-hand experience of the spiritual weakness of a charismatic renewal that was not properly grounded in the gospel. The whole Church, including its Pentecostal and charismatic elements, needs the authentic biblical witness of the Evangelicals. We need a theology that reverently opens up and safeguards the full richness of the Holy Spirit's work in our day. Can Pentecostals produce such a theology? I do not believe that they can do it on their own, even if most Pentecostal scholars come to agree on the need. I am convinced that only when we come together and utilize the resources and wisdom of all the major Christian traditions—Pentecostal, Evangelical, Reformation (radical and mainline), Orthodox and Catholic— will such a theology become possible. For the reverent reflection of Spirit-filled scholars must be as wide and as far-ranging as the extent of the Spirit's outpouring in this century.[25]

---

24. I have protested against this tendency in many writings.

25. For further development of this point, see P. Hocken, *One Lord One Spirit One Body*, ch. 11, 'Ecumenical Grace Requires Ecumenical Theology'; and *idem*, *The Glory and the Shame*, ch. 20, 'Reconciliation and Reintegration in Christ'.

THE ASSEMBLIES OF GOD AND ECUMENICAL COOPERATION:
1920–1965

Cecil M. Robeck, Jr

The relationship between the Assemblies of God and the larger ecumenical world is an area which has been little explored in the histories of the fellowship. In 1961 Klaude Kendrick announced as a matter of fact that 'Pentecostals have avoided participation both in the World Council of Churches and in the National Council of Churches'. He went on to suggest two reasons for this apparent choice. 'Partly this is because the older denominations seem to regard the Pentecostal sects as "not yet qualified for recognition" in the family of churches, but mainly it is because Pentecostals themselves entertain serious objections to the Councils as presently constituted.'[1] Neither the history of the Assemblies of God published two years earlier, the work of a professional journalist who collaborated with the executive officers of the Assemblies of God, nor the authorized history of the Assemblies of God authored by Carl Brumback and published simultaneously with Kendrick's work even mentioned the subject.[2]

With the publication of William W. Menzies's *Anointed to Serve*[3] a decade later the subject of the Assemblies of God and the larger church

1.   K. Kendrick, *The Promise Fulfilled: A History of the Modern Pentecostal Movement* (Springfield, MO: Gospel Publishing House, 1961), pp. 203-204. As to the 'nature and extent' of these objections, Kendrick allowed the National Association of Evangelicals to speak for the Assemblies of God by reprinting a ten-point critique of the World Council of Churches which had been published several years earlier in the National Association of Evangelicals' house organ. Kendrick, *Promise Fulfilled*, pp. 204-205.

2.   I. Winehouse, *The Assemblies of God: A Popular Survey* (New York: Vantage Press, 1959); C. Brumback, *Suddenly...from Heaven: A History of the Assemblies of God* (Springfield, MO: Gospel Publishing House, 1961).

3.   W.W. Menzies, *Anointed to Serve: The Story of the Assemblies of God* (Springfield, MO: Gospel Publishing House, 1971).

world received some additional scrutiny. It came in a chapter titled
'Cooperation: From Isolation to Evangelical Identification', which included a two-page section titled 'Opposition to Ecumenism'.[4] Menzies's
treatment of the relationship of the Assemblies of God with many of the
historic churches between the years 1914–63 was sketched in such a
way as to tantalize his readers. Largely because he was not given access
to the materials he might need to paint the full picture, Menzies chose
instead to emphasize the entry of the Assemblies of God into the
National Association of Evangelicals.

Menzies would set the agenda for historians who followed him. Yet,
his description held several facts which had not appeared in any history
before his. First, the Assemblies of God had participated, as he put it,
'on an unofficial basis' with several agencies which ultimately found
their way into the National Council of Churches. Secondly, the Assemblies
of God had participated in the National Council's stewardship seminars
during the 1950s. Thirdly, Robert C. Cunningham, in an extensive editorial titled, 'Unity—False and True', published in the *Pentecostal Evangel*
in 1950, had raised questions about the legitimacy of the National
Council of Churches and its agenda. Fourthly, he noted that there was a
rising fear among Pentecostals 'that the Ecumenical Movement posed a
threat to their unrestricted freedom'.[5] Subsequent histories of the
Assemblies of God by Edith Blumhofer have developed more fully the
factors surrounding the entry of the Assemblies of God into the National
Association of Evangelicals,[6] but like previous histories, have added little
to our knowledge about the involvement of the Assemblies of God and
its leaders with the wider ecumenical world.

Brumback was nearly euphoric in his treatment of the role which the
National Association of Evangelicals played in the life of the Assemblies
of God and the role which the Assemblies of God would play in the life
of the National Association of Evangelicals. Brumback sketched one
man's call to ministry, in spite of a promising career in another field,

---

4.   Menzies, *Anointed to Serve*, pp. 220-21.
5.   Menzies, *Anointed to Serve*, p. 221.
6.   E.W. Blumhofer, *The Assemblies of God: A Popular History* (Springfield,
MO: Radiant Books/Gospel Publishing House, 1985); E.L. Blumhofer, *The
Assemblies of God: A Chapter in the Story of American Pentecostalism* (2 vols.;
Springfield, MO: Gospel Publishing House, 1989), II, pp. 13-49; E.L. Blumhofer,
Restoring the Faith: The Assemblies of God, Pentecostalism, and American Culture
(Urbana, IL: University of Illinois Press, 1993), pp. 158-60, 180-96.

then triumphantly announced, 'Instead of "winding up in the sticks", he has become the ninth General Superintendent of the Assemblies of God and the current President of the National Association of Evangelicals— *Thomas F. Zimmerman*!'[7] From Brumback's perspective, the entry of the Assemblies of God into the larger church world through the National Association of Evangelicals was a rags to riches story, and Thomas F. Zimmerman was a Pentecostal Horatio Alger. Brumback went on to describe the National Association of Evangelicals in glowing terms as a 'splendid agency of Evangelical Christianity [which] practices "cooperation without contumely"'.[8]

Kendrick was more guarded in his assessment of the National Association of Evangelicals which he described as an 'outstanding' example of 'organizations whose positions' were more in keeping with those of Pentecostalism. He went on to conclude that the organization's Statement of Faith was such 'that all fundamental, evangelical Christians can enter it without reservations'.[9]

It is Menzies and Blumhofer, however, who tell the best story about the emergence of the National Association of Evangelicals in 1942 and 1943, its relationship to fundamentalism, and the entry of the Assemblies of God into this new, but carefully defined relationship. Entry by the Assemblies of God into the National Association of Evangelicals was by no means painless. Both Menzies and Blumhofer describe the blistering attacks which fundamentalist preacher Carl McIntire and his American Council of Christian Churches (ACCC) made on both institutions.[10] Kendrick and Blumhofer note that everyone in the Assemblies of God was not satisfied with entry of the fellowship into this new organization either. Kendrick notes that in 1949, a half dozen years after the Assemblies of God entered the National Association of Evangelicals, a number of ministers asked for a discussion of the relationship. As a result, a motion was received and discussed at the 1949 General Council resolving that the General Council re-affirm the relationship.[11] This, of course, allowed for the discussion to take place. Blumhofer has pointed out that some of the concern raised within the fellowship revolved

7. Brumback, *Suddenly*, pp. 309-310.
8. Brumback, *Suddenly*, p. 315.
9. Kendrick, *Promise Fulfilled*, p. 205.
10. Menzies, p. 183; Blumhofer, *The Assemblies of God*, II, pp. 22-28; Blumhofer, *Restoring the Faith*, pp. 183-87.
11. Kendrick, *Promise Fulfilled*, p. 206.

around the fear that by participating as 'Evangelicals' in a National Association of Evangelicals, Pentecostals were betraying their own identity as 'Pentecostals'.[12]

Officially, the Assemblies of God aligned itself with the National Association of Evangelicals. Officially, it spurned the National and World Councils of Churches. Officially, the fears expressed in the 1949 General Council that the Assemblies of God would betray some of the essence of what it was to be Pentecostal in order to be identified with the Evangelicals, were groundless. But were they? Menzies provides hints that help us understand that before the Assemblies of God entered fully into the National Association of Evangelicals it had established long-standing relationships with the larger church world. It had found these relationships beneficial to its own mission and it tried to continue to maintain those relationships until so much pressure, both external and internal, was brought to bear upon it that it made the decision to conform officially to the demands of the fundamentalist and evangelical worlds by breaking off long-standing and beneficial relations with the larger church world. In order for us to understand the larger picture, it is necessary to begin the story with the Foreign Missions Conference of North America in 1920.

1. *The Assemblies of God Joins the FMCNA*

The Assemblies of God joined the Foreign Missions Conference of North America in 1920.[13] The Assemblies of God was only six years old at the time. What is clear is that this membership was thought to serve some purpose deemed important by the Assemblies of God, for it would keep its membership in the Council for the next thirty years, and even later, it kept up a cooperative relationship with several Conference constituents. But who made up the Foreign Missions Conference of North America in 1920, and what were its purposes?

12.   Blumhofer, *The Assemblies of God*, II, pp. 28-29; Blumhofer, *Restoring the Faith*, p. 187.

13.   The 1920 proceedings of the annual conference mention no Pentecostal participation, but J. Roswell Flower, then serving as Foreign Missions Secretary for the Assemblies of God, is listed among the personnel who attended the January 18-20, 1921 meeting in Garden City, Long Island, New York in his official capacity of 'corresponding member' of the Conference. See, F.P. Turner (ed.), *Foreign Missions Conference of North America: 1921* (New York: Foreign Missions Conference, 1921), p. 312.

The Foreign Missions Conference of North America was founded in 1893 in order to provide the various foreign mission boards of the United States and Canada with: 1) an annual conference; 2) a series of committees designed 'to investigate and study missionary problems'; 3) encouragement toward the promotion of missiology as a science; and 4) the ability to participate together in work of common interest.[14] Its tasks were clear and narrowly defined, and, perhaps of equal importance, the *Constitution of the Foreign Missions Conference* made it clear that 'questions of ecclesiastical faith and order' which represented 'denominational differences' were explicitly excluded from the purview of the group.[15] In short, its agenda was more pragmatic and activistic than theologically reflective.

The fact that doctrinal (faith) and polity (order) issues were essentially off limits to the Conference meant that groups which represented diverse theological positions or disparate ideological perspectives could participate together in an area which concerned them all, foreign missions work. As a result, when J.R. Flower, General Secretary of the Assemblies of God, attended his first conference in January, 1921, he found himself among a very diverse collection of Christians. There were representatives from such international mission organizations as the London Missionary Society, the Inland South America Missionary Union, the Canton Medical Missionary Society, and the Sudan United Mission.

A large number of historic Protestant groups such as the Congregationalists, Presbyterian USA, Reformed Church in the US and Reformed Church in America, American Baptists, Disciples, Methodist Episcopal and Methodist Episcopal (South), as well as a range of Lutheran groups dominated the membership. The Federal Council of Churches of Christ in the USA, forerunner to the National Council of the Churches of Christ in the USA, was a member of the Council. But other, smaller groups were full members as well. The Moravians, Christian Churches, Augustana, Missouri and Norwegian Lutherans, Church of the Brethren,

---

14. For a copy of the Constitution and Bylaws of this organization in 1921 see Turner (ed.), *Foreign Missions Conference of North America: 1921*, pp. 316-22.

15. 'The Constitution of the Foreign Missions Conference of North America', Article II, Functions, in Turner (ed.), *Foreign Missions Conference of North America: 1921*, p. 316. Under Article XI, Resolutions, the Council agreed that 'No restriction shall be considered which deals with theological or ecclesiastical questions that represent denominational differences, and if such resolutions are presented, the Chairman shall rule them out of order' (p. 319).

Brethren in Christ, United Evangelical, Reformed Presbyterians, African Methodist Episcopal, and Christian Reformed Churches were all members in good standing. Even the Universalists, who would later merge with the Unitarians, held membership in the Council.

A number of other denominations, who would come to join the Council over the next five years, sent participants in 1921 as well. Among them were the Wesleyan Methodists, Free Methodists, Church of the Nazarene, Christian and Missionary Alliance, Seventh Day Baptist and the Seventh Day Adventists.[16] What the Foreign Missions Conference of North America did, then, was to provide a missionary forum which was very inclusive in its membership. It embraced a wide theological spectrum.

In spite of such diversity, the Assemblies of God leadership was apparently quite at home participating regularly in the Council. While J.R. Flower was alone at the 1921 meeting, on January 11-13, 1922, Eudorus N. Bell, Chairman of the General Council of the Assemblies of God, accompanied Flower to the annual meeting in Atlantic City, New Jersey.[17] Some '328 delegates and corresponding members representing sixty-two Boards and Societies' attended this meeting at which the primary topic was 'the rising tide of Nationalism and its effect on the work of the Church in the foreign mission fields'.[18]

The following year, William M. Faux was elected to serve as the Foreign Missions Secretary for the Assemblies of God, a position he would hold until late 1926. In 1924 he and Ernest S. Williams, then pastor of Highway Mission Tabernacle in Philadelphia and an executive presbyter of the Assemblies of God, attended the Conference, held once again in Atlantic City, New Jersey.[19] John W. Welch, who had served as Chairman of the General Council from October, 1915–September, 1920 and who was re-elected to that position in September, 1923 for an additional term, attended the 1925 meeting in Washington DC.[20] The meeting

16.   Turner (ed.), *The Foreign Missions Conference of North America: 1921*, pp. 311-15.

17.   F.P. Turner and F.K. Sanders (eds.), *The Foreign Missions Conference of North America: 1922* (New York: Foreign Missions Conference, 1922), p. 301.

18.   E.N. Bell, 'Introductory Note', in Turner and Sanders (eds.), *The Foreign Missions Conference of North America: 1922*, p. 5.

19.   F.P. Turner and F.K. Sanders (eds.), *The Foreign Missions Conference of North America: 1924* (New York: Foreign Missions Conference, 1924), pp. 362, 365.

20.   J.W. Welch, 'The Present Great World Crisis', *The Pentecostal Evangel*

in Washington DC was much larger than normal. According to the official record some 4790 persons had registered for the Conference.[21] The size of the meeting was probably due to its venue in Washington DC as well as the fact that the President of the United States, Calvin Coolidge, was on the program. In any case, the Conference broke with its regular practice in 1925 and did not publish the names of those who attended.

John W. Welch's personal reflections on the meeting, apparently delivered as an address in Springfield, Missouri in early 1925 and subsequently published in the *Pentecostal Evangel*, make it clear that he attended the Washington meeting. But his reflections make it equally clear that he did not either fully understand nor appreciate all that he heard. 'All that I have been able to see in connection with the great Missionary Convention and all of the lessons that have to me grown out of it', he complained, 'reflect the condition of the world and the church, and have a distinct bearing on the coming again of Christ'.[22] Welch revealed much about his own personal mindset as he went on to criticize the call to accept the missionary agencies from all nations of the world as equal partners, and the call to be sensitive to the integrity of existing cultures wherever possible. He would have none of it.[23] He had an equally virulent disdain for setting aside those things which called attention to denominational distinctiveness. To him it was total compromise. 'The various denominations were represented at that conference and great care was taken in avoiding all things that would in any wise suggest denominationalism', he noted. But Welch went on in a leap of logic to contend that 'When they lay aside all of the Methodist doctrine, and the Baptist and Presbyterian, etc., so that there will be no friction,

590 (March 28, 1925), pp. 2-3, 8-9. Cf. G.B. McGee, *The Gospel Shall Be Preached: A History and Theology of Assemblies of God Foreign Missions to 1959* (2 vols.; Springfield, MO: Gospel Publishing House, 1986), I, pp. 120-21.

21.   F.P. Turner and F.K. Sanders (eds.), *The Foreign Missions Convention at Washington: 1925* (New York: Foreign Missions Conference of North America/ Fleming H. Revell, 1925), p. 410.

22.   Welch, 'World Crisis', p. 2.

23.   In a parody on inviting input from Christians in those newer countries who were rising as a result of increased nationalism he wrote, 'Pagan nation, come in and bring all your paganism, and we are going to try to mix it all up and put it all together; and we hope it will not poison us, and somehow we will be able to avoid these awful things we see in the air'. He appears to have totally misunderstood the nature of the conversation on this topic. Welch, 'World Crisis', p. 2.

there is nothing left much but a name'.[24] He seemed to miss the point that they had agreed to concentrate on what they held in common and not cause division with their points of disagreement.

Admittedly the period of the Conference which Welch attended was pregnant with the emotions, language and pain of the conservative–liberal debates of its day. These were not the wars of Pentecostals, but of the fundamentalists in mainline churches. Welch, however, was pointedly opposed to what he termed the 'get-together' idea. 'Satan's super-man is on the way', he warned, 'the modern church along with the nations, unconscious of what they are doing are leading their efforts directly to the establishment of conditions for the antichrist to take supreme control. This "get-together" idea', he concluded, 'is nothing other than that'.[25] It was ultimately based on the faulty concept of a universal 'brotherhood of man'.

For Welch to take this position is understandable in light of his eschatological commitments; the second coming was imminent and the gospel as he understood it needed to be preached in all of its untarnished glory. One did not need a super organization to do this. But Welch's criticism was not unanimously shared by all his sisters and brothers in the Assemblies of God. The 1921 General Council of the Assemblies of God had authorized formation of a committee, chaired by F.A. Hale, a General Presbyter from San Antonio, Texas, to explore greater cooperation between various Pentecostal groups.[26] Furthermore, Executive Presbyter Warren F. Carothers led a movement beginning in 1922 to form a coalition of denominations which was committed to the 'Scriptural Unity of the People of God in One Body'.[27] The first national meeting, although small, was held in St Louis, Missouri, October 24, 1922. It was followed by a second, larger meeting on November 11, 1923 in Chicago and a third in mid-July, 1924 at Owensboro, Kentucky.

In June, 1925, just three months after Welch's reflections were published in *The Pentecostal Evangel*, Carothers published a 'Prayer for the Peace and Unity of the Church' which he had taken from materials published at the recent World Conference on Faith and Order with a

24.   Welch, 'World Crisis', p. 3.
25.   Welch, 'World Crisis', p. 2.
26.   *Minutes of the General Council Held at St Louis, Missouri, September 13–18, 1923*, p. 61. Cf. McGee, *The Gospel Shall Be Preached*, I, p. 121.
27.   'Scriptural Unity of the People of God in One Body', *The Herald of the Church* 1:3 (June, 1925), p. 1.

complete rationale for doing so and he sent his periodical *The Herald of the Church* to leaders of historic churches throughout the country. Carothers's work toward Christian Unity would continue through May, 1934.[28]

Welch also criticized the bearing and attire of various delegates. Watching from the sideline as the delegates entered the auditorium, Welch sized them up as 'intelligent-looking, well-dressed, sufficient in themselves'. They looked self-assured on the outside, he claimed, but when he made conversation with them, they were not assured at all. 'All these things have come about', he judged 'because the church has lost her anointing'.[29] One can well imagine that Welch, himself, felt very ill at ease in this company of missionaries and church leaders. 'They are spending other people's money very lavishly and are glad to have the reputation of doing a great work in the ends of the world', he criticized. 'I saw a lot of missionaries', he said knowingly, 'but none of them seemed to show any evidence that they were willing to sacrifice'.[30] So frustrated did he become with things he heard at the conference that at one point he had to force himself to sit still. 'I came awfully near jumping to my feet and saying, "For God's sake, man, why don't you hit it square?"' Then he went zealously on with 'I would have given ten years of my life, I believe, for twenty minutes on that platform to force home to their hearts that the coming of the Lord draweth nigh'.[31]

With such strong feelings about the Conference by the Chairman of the Assemblies of God, one might have expected Welch to return to Springfield and instruct Flower or Faux to withdraw the Assemblies of God from its membership. But he did not. There was clearly more at stake than met the eye. There was something to be gained by holding membership in the Conference even if it was more popular to preach that there was not.

Membership in the Foreign Missions Conference brought with it a number of benefits. It provided access to many of the leading missiological thinkers of the day. John R. Mott, who had given his life to the missionary enterprise because of the impact of Dwight L. Moody and

28. W.F. Carothers, 'Truths Considered at Third General Unity Conference, Owensboro, Kentucky, July 11-14, 1924', *The Herald of the Church* 1:3 (June, 1925), p. 2; *idem*, 'Our Frontispiece', *The Herald of the Church* 1:3 (June, 1925), p. 6.
29. Welch, 'World Crisis', p. 3.
30. Welch, 'World Crisis', p. 9.
31. Welch, 'World Crisis', p. 9.

C.T. Studd, and who had chaired the famous World Missions Conference in Edinburgh, Scotland in 1910, played a significant and ongoing role in the organization. In 1922, for instance, he had delivered a plenary address on 'The Price Which Has to Be Paid to Ensure Truthful International Missionary Cooperation'.[32] Joseph Oldham, editor of the *International Review of Missions*, Samuel Zwemer, long-term missionary to the Middle East, Frank Mason North, President of the Federal Council of Churches, E. Stanley Jones, life-long missionary to India, Jonathan Goforth, missionary to China, James L. Barton, former missionary to Turkey and Foreign Secretary of the American Board are but a few of the names which show up among the participants in the 1920s. The ability to network with these and hundreds of other leaders was important to a relatively new but expanding missionary enterprise.

The Foreign Missions Conference elected in 1921 to become a charter member of the International Missionary Council.[33] Membership in this group which in 1961 would become the Commission on World Mission and Evangelism of the World Council of Churches, meant that in addition to having the potential for North American partners in the missiological enterprise, the Assemblies of God and its other partners in the Conference now also had the potential for international partners, that is, with Protestant missionary partners originating from Africa, Latin America and Asia. To what extent the Assemblies of God made use of this potential is not yet fully known, but membership in the Foreign Missions Conference and with it in the International Missionary Council made it possible for the Assemblies of God to interact with church leaders from around the world who were also involved in missionary work.

The Foreign Mission Conference also ran a Missionary Research Library which it had begun in 1914. By 1922 it boasted some 14,286 books, another 7404 bound volumes, and another 6574 pamphlets. It held paid or free subscriptions to 310 current periodicals around the

32. Turner and Sanders (eds.), *The Foreign Missions Conference of North America: 1922*, pp. 23, 65-73. On the life of Mott, see C.H. Hopkins, *John R. Mott, 1865-1955: A Biography* (Geneva: World Council of Churches, 1979).

33. The Motion to establish an International Missionary Committee of 20 representatives of the Foreign Missions Convention to be delegates at the meetings of the International Missionary Council was made by Dr Robert E. Speer on January 20, 1921. It was adopted by the Conference in Turner (ed.), *Foreign Missions Conference of North America: 1921*, p. 25. Cf., also pp. 42-47.

world.[34] By 1944 it had grown to 75,000 volumes and since 1929 had been housed in the Brown Memorial Tower at Union Theological Seminary, 3041 Broadway, New York City. Among its services to its constituents were interlibrary loan privileges, research assistants, bibliographic publications on topics about which questions were being raised, occasional 'Bulletins' on so-called 'live topics' and use by missionary personnel and researchers.[35] In return, the Assemblies of God, like other user groups donated funds on an ongoing basis for use of this cooperative library.

The Foreign Missions Conference also had a standing committee dedicated to the subject of Missions and Governments. The work of this committee on behalf of all constituents in the Conference, including the Assemblies of God, was undoubtedly very significant. It attempted to work with the United States Department of State to obtain passports and visas, to facilitate the transfer of missionary supplies, and to keep its constituents up to date on international developments, including areas of conflict and areas which were newly open for missionary expansion.

In 1922 this committee reported that the previous year it had held a conference on 'new conditions in the Far East'. It had met with the Secretary of State to lobby for the appointment of people to a variety of consular and diplomatic posts around the world who were sympathetic to missionary work. It had lobbied for a bill for the control of opium traffic, had intervened to help missionaries gain easier access to New Guinea, Mexico and Portuguese East Africa, had provided timely new information to constituent mission boards on passport and visa issues, had worked to bring government officials into contact with various Mission Boards, and facilitated approval of a list of Mission Boards which were now 'recognized' by the British Government. That year the General Council of the Assemblies of God, Inc., was placed on the 'recognized' list.[36]

The Foreign Missions Conference included a variety of other ongoing

34. Turner and Sanders (eds.), *The Foreign Missions Conference of North America: 1922*, pp. 61-62.

35. For a brief history of the Missionary Research Library see *Foreign Missions Conference of North America, January, 1944*, no editor named (New York City: Foreign Missions Conference of North America, 1944), pp. 200-202.

36. Turner and Sanders (eds.), *The Foreign Missions Conference of North America: 1922*, pp. 42-47 includes a full report of the Missions and Governments Committee's work in 1921.

programs and committees. There were a series of committees that
focused on specific geographic regions on which representatives from
the Assemblies of God served. The Church Committee for Relief in Asia
was one of these.[37] When on May 1, 1946 this committee merged with
the Committee for World Council Service and the Church Committee
on Overseas Relief and Reconstruction, to form the Church World
Service, Inc., the Assemblies of God became a member of this new
organization as well.[38]

Another group affiliated with the Foreign Missions Conference was
the Board of the United Council of Church Women. The Assemblies of
God would ultimately cooperate with this organization, especially at the
local level in later years, even after it became affiliated with the National
Council of Churches.[39] What this brief survey of services suggests is that
in spite of what the Chairman of the General Council might have
thought about the organization in 1925, it was clear that the Assemblies
of God was in their debt.

In January, 1926, William M. Faux, this time accompanied by his wife,
Bertha L. Faux, attended the Conference meeting in Atlantic City.[40]
Later that year Faux resigned from the Assemblies of God amid charges
of mismanaged mission funds.[41] He was succeeded by Noel Perkin as
the Secretary of the Foreign Missions Department.

Noel Perkin's tenure as Secretary of the Foreign Missions Department
spanned more than three decades (1927–59). From 1928 onward he
was listed as the corresponding member between the Assemblies of God
and the Foreign Missions Conference of North America.[42] That same

37.   Known more popularly as the China Relief Committee, Assemblies of
God membership is repeatedly acknowledged. See, for instance, R.T. McGlasson to
Reverend J.C. Burks, 24 January, 1961, 1. All letters cited in this article are housed
at the Assemblies of God Archive in Springfield, MO.

38.   *Foreign Missions Conference of North America: 1947* (New York: Foreign
Missions Conference of North America, 1947), pp. 60-61.

39.   Cf. Mrs. C.R. Love to Reverend Thomas F. Zimmerman, 18 May, 1963;
Thomas F. Zimmerman to Mrs. C.R. Love, 16 July, 1963; Barbara Leib to Brother
Zimmerman, 21 January, 1964; Thomas F. Zimmerman to Mrs. James Leib, 24
January, 1964; *Foreign Missions Conference of North America: 1947*, p. 117.

40.   F.P. Turner and F.K. Sanders (eds.), *The Foreign Missions Conference of
North America: 1926* (New York: Foreign Missions Conference, 1926), p. 420.

41.   Brumback, *Suddenly*, p. 298.

42.   L.B. Moss (ed.), *The Foreign Missions Conference of North America:
1928* (New York: Foreign Missions Conference of North America, 1928), p. 184.

year, 1928, the Assemblies of God was joined by another Pentecostal group, the United Holy Church in America, in a relationship with the Conference. Whereas the Assemblies of God held constitutional membership in the Conference, the African-American group known as the United Holy Church in America, Inc., was listed among the 'Boards and Societies which contribute to the support of the Conference but are not constitutional members'.[43] Elder E.B. Nichols, who served as the Foreign Secretary of the Missionary Department for the United Holy Church of America, Inc., until his untimely death while visiting missionary stations in Liberia in 1936, served as their correspondent.[44]

During his first decade as Secretary of the Foreign Missions Department of the Assemblies of God, Noel Perkin never attended a meeting of the Foreign Missions Conference of North America. One reason may have been that he, like John W. Welch, thought there was little to be gained from such a Conference. More than likely, however, he soon found himself to be too busy, keeping up with an expanding missionary program worldwide. Although he did not attend nor did he sponsor anyone else to attend the annual meetings of the Council, he continued the membership of the Assemblies of God in the Council, and from 1929 onward he cooperated with the Council by providing it with an annual set of statistics on income and expenditures in foreign missionary activity around the world.[45]

With the specter of a European war on the horizon, Noel Perkin

43.   Moss (ed.), *The Foreign Missions Conference of North America: 1928*, p. 191.

44.   On Elder E.B. Nichols's contribution to the United Holy Church of America, Inc., see C.W. Gregory, *The History of the United Holy Church of America, Inc. 1886–1986* (Baltimore, MD: Gateway Press, 1986), pp. 40, 55, 57, 192, 195, 197. E.B. Nichols and the United Holy Church of America continue to be listed through 1940, suggesting that this record had not been kept up to date following his death.

45.   In 1928 the report noted only that the Assemblies of God had received $216,797.17 from Living Donors who gave to missions (exclusive of Latin America) and spent $198,026.08 on the missionary enterprise. *The Foreign Missions Conference of North America: 1928*, p. 269. By 1938, total income was listed at $305,675, with expenses totaling $281,957 on the following fields: Africa $51,324; Near East and North Africa $20,324; India, Burma and Ceylon $74,564; China $70,948; Japan $11,728; the Philippines, Formosa and the Malay States $883; Latin America $38,982; and Europe and miscellaneous fields $13,206. See L.B. Moss and M.H. Brown (eds.), *Foreign Missions Conference of North America 1938* (New York: Foreign Missions Conference of North America, 1938), p. 159.

attended his first Council meeting January 4-6, 1938. It was convened at the Royal York Hotel in Toronto, Ontario, Canada. He was joined there by the Reverend A.G. Ward who that year would complete his six-year tenure as the Secretary–Treasurer of the Pentecostal Assemblies of Canada. Both Perkin and Ward registered as delegates from the Assemblies of God.[46] Undoubtedly Ward was Perkin's guest since the Pentecostal Assemblies of Canada had no relationship with the Council and according to the Constitution of the Council any member church whose missionary income exceeded $300,000, as did that of the Assemblies of God, was entitled to up to five delegates.[47]

While no one from the Assemblies of God attended the meeting of the Council in 1939 or 1942, the Assemblies of God was well represented at most of the annual meetings in the remaining years between 1940 and 1949. Perkin attended the meeting in 1940 and again with J.R. Flower, General Secretary of the Assemblies of God, in January, 1942. In 1944, Henry B. Garlock, Missions Field Secretary for Africa (1943–54) and E.C. Sumrall attended. As the end of World War II approached, Noel Perkin led a substantial delegation—including H.B. Garlock, Maynard Ketcham, missionary to India and later Field Secretary for Southern Asia, and George R. Upton—to the January 5-8, 1945 meeting convened once again in Toronto. No lists of attendees were published in 1946 or 1947, but again in 1948 Noel Perkin could be found among those who attended the Conference, taking with him Robert T. McGlasson, who now served as the Eastern Secretary for the Foreign Missions Department. The following year, 1949, Robert W. Cummings, recently returned from the mission field where he had served from 1946 to 1948 as Field Secretary for Southern Asia, represented the Assemblies of God at the Buck Hill Falls, Pennsylvania meeting.[48] Apparently Noel Perkin had determined that there was value in establishing closer relations with many of those who attended the meetings, if not with the Foreign Missions Conference of North America itself.

46.   Moss and Brown (eds.), *The Foreign Missions Conference of North America: 1938*, pp. 168-69.

47.   Moss (ed.), *The Foreign Missions Conference of North America: 1928*, Article V, p. 197.

48.   The lists of representatives who attended the annual meetings sketched out above may be found in the listing of 'Personnel' at the end of each annual report of the Conference.

2. *A New York Office Is Established*

As time passed, it became more apparent to the Foreign Missions Department of the Assemblies of God that their work could be facilitated by opening an office in New York City. New York City was important to the Assemblies of God from the beginning. It was, after all, the port through which scores of missionaries traveled when they went to Europe, Africa, the Middle East and elsewhere. Following World War II, the Foreign Missions Department thought it advisable to open an office there to facilitate its work. As a result, it opened a New York office in February, 1946. Directed by Robert T. McGlasson, aided by Emma D'Apice as secretary, Stephen Walegir, and David J. Allan, Export Manager, it was the task of the New York Office to help with the 'purchase of equipment and supplies, the procurement of visas, government contacts, and travel arrangements'.[49]

The office was relocated several times through the years beginning at 233 53rd Street in Brooklyn. In 1953 it could be found at 257 East 10th Street in New York, and from 1957–60 it occupied two different offices (Rooms 604 and 806) at 160 West Fifth Avenue in New York City. What is clear from the change of address each time is the apparent interest which the Foreign Missions Department of the Assemblies of God had in gaining proximity to other agencies with similar interests, regardless of their denominational affiliation.

The Foreign Missions Conference of North America was housed at 25 Madison Avenue from 1921–26, at 419 Fourth Avenue from 1927–34, and at 156 West Fifth Avenue from 1935–50. In 1950 the Foreign Missions Conference was absorbed by the National Council of Churches for whom it became the Department of Foreign Missions. Thus, it functioned as the Department of Foreign Missions at the same address until October 1960 when the National Council of Churches' offices were moved to The Interchurch Center, 475 Riverside Drive.[50]

When in 1955 the Foreign Missions Department of the Assemblies of

---

49.   McGee, *The Gospel Shall Be Preached*, II, p. 175. Cf. 'Missionaries Visit New York Office', *The Missionary Challenge* (August, 1949), pp. 16-17; [R.T. McGlasson], 'The New York Office', *The Missionary Forum* 14 (no date, but late December 1951 or January 1952), pp. 3-4.

50.   'Our Happy Cooperations', *The Christian Century* 77.24 (June 15, 1960), pp. 715-16; '475 Riverside Drive', *Christianity Today* 4:19 (June 20, 1960), pp. 32-33.

God established its Eastern or New York Office at 160 West Fifth
Avenue, it had clearly made a choice to move next door to the Foreign
Missions Department of the National Council of Churches. When in
January, 1960 the National Council of Churches moved into The Inter-
church Center, the Foreign Missions Department of the Assemblies of
God moved there as well. It leased and occupied Room 1928 and housed
at that location what was known as the Foreign Service Committee.

Such choices were not accidental. They were carefully and thoughtfully planned, and from all accounts they functioned well for the Foreign
Missions Department of the Assemblies of God. Even with the transition
of power from Noel Perkin to J. Philip Hogan in 1959, little changed in
the department with respect to the New York Office. Hogan tapped
Robert McGlasson to become his chief Secretary in the Springfield
office and Stephen Walegir, who had worked with McGlasson, was
named Eastern Secretary. Gustave Kinderman, who since 1945 had
served as Secretary for Relief and Rehabilitation, continued to work with
Walegir in New York and McGlasson in Springfield, Missouri.

When the Assemblies of God joined the National Association of
Evangelicals in 1943, it was important for the fellowship to engage in
cooperative efforts with the Association. As early as 1945, *The
Pentecostal Evangel* ran short articles which helped to paint the needs
for clothing and, later, for food which were essential to the recovery of
post-war Europe. These articles spoke specifically about the efforts being
made by the National Association of Evangelicals to address these needs.
Those with interest in providing clothes to Europe were urged to ship
them to The War Relief Commission, N.A.E., 536 West 46th Street, New
York 19, NY. In addition, donors were instructed to write the words
'Assemblies of God' beneath the return address, so that participation by
Assemblies of God people could be measured.[51]

Such notices became regular fare for *Evangel* readers. In March,
1947 J.R. Flower wrote an article for the *Evangel* explaining why the

---

51.   'Clothing for Europe', *The Pentecostal Evangel* 1618 (May 12, 1945), p.
6; 'Clothing for Distressed Believers in Europe', *The Pentecostal Evangel* 1631
(August 11, 1945), p. 9; 'Holland's Needy Saints', *The Pentecostal Evangel* 1649
(December 15, 1945), p. 11; 'A Word of Thanks from Belgium', *The Pentecostal
Evangel* 1654 (January 19, 1946), p. 9; R.C. Cunningham, 'Food for Body and
Soul', *The Pentecostal Evangel* 1708 (February 1, 1947), p. 10. From the perspec-
tive of the N.A.E. see J.E. Wright, 'Frank D. Lombar, O.C.D. ("Doctor of Old
Clothes")', *United Evangelical Action* 4:23 (January 15, 1956), p. 56.

Assemblies of God had joined the National Association of Evangelicals. Describing the N.A.E. as primarily being a 'service organization', he wrote enthusiastically about one of its 'greatest services'. It had to do with War Relief.[52] The next month the *Evangel* carried a full article which encouraged its readers to invest in C.A.R.E. (Cooperative for American Remittances to Europe, Inc.) packages to help the hungry in Europe.[53] Money for C.A.R.E. packages was to be sent to the World Missions Department in Springfield, MO, but clothing was to continue to be routed to the N.A.E.'s War Relief Commission.

Several things are striking about this strategy. First, the Assemblies of God had named missionary Gustave Kinderman its European Field Secretary, to head up its own relief efforts in 1945. Secondly, it had opened its New York Office in February, 1946 to facilitate such efforts as well as to aid Assemblies of God missionaries. Thirdly, while it continued to relate to the Foreign Missions Conference of North America behind the scenes through some of its senior missions personnel, it chose never to mention in a public forum that it had any such relationship. Indeed, Kinderman's own report as it was summarized in the 1947 General Council meeting mentions only the War Relief Commission of the National Association of Evangelicals;[54] but Kinderman had worked frequently with other church leaders.

On November 14, 1946, Gustave Kinderman met with J.R. Flower and Noel Perkin to fill them in on what was happening among European Pentecostals.[55] Kinderman reported that he had told various European Pentecostals how the National Association of Evangelicals worked and encouraged them toward greater cooperation. Kinderman told his supervisors, 'I encourage our people throughout Europe to form a relationship

52.   J.R. Flower, 'Why We Joined the N.A.E.', *The Pentecostal Evangel* 1716 (March 29, 1947), p. 12.

53.   'Helping Europe's Hungry', *The Pentecostal Evangel* 1728 (April 12, 1947), p. 11. See also H.D. Bollinger, 'This Is Mass Starvation', *The Christian Century* 63 (October 30, 1946), pp. 1310-11 which informed its readers of C.A.R.E.

54.   G. Kinderman, 'Relief and Gospel Work to Continue in Europe', *The Pentecostal Evangel* 1748 (November 8, 1947).

55.   An eight-page, typed, single-space manuscript of this conversation is available from the Assemblies of God Archive under the title 'Europe-Gustav [sic.] Kinderman-11-14-46'. It was transcribed from (recording?) disks found in Kinderman's files. On the jacket of the discs, in Noel Perkin's handwriting were the words 'Conference with G. Kinderman covering conditions in Europe. Noel Perkin and J. Roswell Flower were present at this conference.'

with the different organizations, not organically, but to unite with them before the government'. The reason for his advice was that most frequently they had to work with what he called a 'Roman Catholic Government'. As a result, he believed that ecumenical cooperation was critical for the survival and growth of the Pentecostal Movement specifically and Protestants in general, 'at least before the government'.[56] Fifteen years later (May, 1961) R.T. McGlasson would report that this basic policy was still intact, although with an important nuance not present in the Kinderman policy. 'We have advised our missionaries in different areas', wrote McGlasson, 'that for the sake of unity and mutual accomplishment it would be proper to join local Christian councils if and when those national councils were not tied to the World Council of Churches'.[57]

Kinderman found that the Polish Church of Evangelical Christians and Baptists had received but refused to share with Polish Pentecostals any of one hundred bales of clothing which had been sent by the National Association of Evangelicals. Kinderman cabled a Brother Nikoloff, most probably Nicholas Nikoloff, longtime missionary in Eastern Europe who had served as principal of the Gdanska Institute of the Bible from 1935–38 before going on to do evangelism in Bulgaria.[58] Now, in 1946, he was president of the Metropolitan Bible Institute in New Jersey. Nikoloff knew the Polish situation well and before long six bales were released to the Pentecostals. Still, at least in Poland, the relationship was not working well. Kinderman was clearly not satisfied with the six bales.[59]

Kinderman did not work only with the National Association of Evangelicals, he also established contacts in Europe with leaders of historic 'mainline' churches. One such contact was the Superintendent of the Methodist work in Poland, Konstanty Najder. Najder and Kinderman met at a consultation sponsored in Geneva, Switzerland, most likely in March, 1946 at the headquarters of the Provisional Committee of the World Council of Churches which had been formed August 29–

56. Kinderman, 'Europe', p. 8.
57. R.T. McGlasson to David T. Scott, 3 May, 1961.
58. G.B. McGee, 'Nicholas Nikoloff', in S.M. Burgess and G.B. McGee (ed.), *Dictionary of Pentecostal and Charismatic Movements* (Grand Rapids: Regency Reference Library, 1988), pp. 637-38; T. Salzer, 'The Danzig Gdanska Institute of the Bible', Assemblies of God *Heritage* 8:3 (1988), pp. 8-11, 18-19 (Part I), and *Heritage* 8:4 (1988–89), pp. 10-12, 17-18 (Part II).
59. Kinderman, 'Europe', p. 5.

September 1, 1938.[60] It would be another decade before the First Assembly of the World Council of Churches in Amsterdam begin ning August 22, 1948, largely because of the war. But the Committee obtained land at 17 Route de Malagnor in Geneva, and continued to plan for the First Assembly under the name of the World Council of Churches.

Many were the church leaders who visited the World Council's work in Geneva. Konstanty Najder was one and Gustave Kinderman was another.[61] Najder was very sympathetic to the Polish Pentecostals and he allowed churchless Pentecostals to use Methodist facilities so long as they could back their actions with Scripture. He would not tolerate any 'fanaticism'. Kinderman was also aided by Najder who, working with the World Council of Churches, obtained visas for Kinderman within two hours, visas which normally required a two to three month wait. Najder also helped Kinderman to obtain extremely favorably exchange rates for US dollars as he traveled in Eastern Europe.

Kinderman's initiation into a circle of friends who were working at or with the World Council in Geneva made it possible for him to hear, first hand, without traveling all over Europe, just what the conditions were. 'It was very interesting to hear the reports of different ones from Germany and elsewhere', Kinderman reported.[62]

Kinderman's view of the World Council of Churches was quite posi- tive. 'Many people look on the World Council of Churches as a mod- ernistic organization', he observed. 'It is true that it includes a number of modernistic organizations, but many among them are fine Christian

60.   W.A. Visser 't Hooft, 'The Genesis of the World Council of Churches', in R. Rouse and S.C. Neill (eds.), *A History of the Ecumenical Movement 1517–1948* (Philadelphia: Westminster Press, 1954), pp. 705-706. On the February meeting see R. Root, 'World Council Meets in Geneva', *The Christian Century* 63 (March 27, 1946), pp. 402-403; 'Choose Life, Not Death!', *The Christian Century* 63 (March 27, 1946), pp. 396-97. For two reports on its relief work contemporaneous to that of the Assemblies of God see R. Root, 'Permit Relief to Go into Germany', *The Christian Century* 63 (February 27, 1946), pp. 276-77; and R. Root, 'Survey European Church Relief', *The Christian Century* 63 (April 24, 1946), p. 531 which highlight the reports made at the Geneva meeting on relief and reconstruction held in March, 1946.

61.   See, for example, Paul Hutchinson, 'Men of Geneva', *The Christian Century* 63 (October 2, 1946), pp. 1175-77.

62.   Kinderman, 'Europe', p. 8.

leaders.'[63] Kinderman saw that the Council had limitations as it was then constituted, and he seemed disappointed to see representatives talk the language of unity when they were together only to fall back into their old ways once they returned home:

> Although they may talk about cooperation and working together, the very minute they go to different countries, they stick with their own. For this reason there is not this cooperation in the World Council of Churches that some people may think there is.[64]

In spite of this weakness, Kinderman worked pragmatically with the Council. He provided information to the World Council of Churches on inexpensive food parcels available in Denmark. He also gave them further information on the Polish scene. As a result, the World Council of Churches, through its representatives in Warsaw, gave Kinderman an endorsement for his work. The World Council also aided the Pentecostal work in Hungary. In Kinderman's words:

> The World Council of Churches has done quite a lot for us. I personally think that as long as we can get something out of it, and we do not have to unite with them officially, why not? We are not compromising or letting down our testimony. They appreciate us.[65]

The years 1947 through 1950 were critical for ecumenical discussions worldwide. The First Assembly of the World Council of Churches was convened in Amsterdam August 22–September 4, 1948. The World Council of Churches as we know it was formally constituted on August 23. In the United States, the Federal Council of the Churches of Christ in the USA was in its final days, and November 28–December 1, 1950 the constituting convention of the National Council of Churches was held in Cleveland, Ohio.[66] It is not surprising to find within these years an

---

63.   Kinderman, 'Europe', p. 8. This fact was even acknowledged by the National Association of Evangelicals in 'Ecumenical Rift?', *United Evangelical Action* 4:13 (August 1, 1945), p. 21.

64.   Kinderman, 'Europe', p. 8.

65.   Kinderman, 'Europe', p. 8.

66.   For the full story of the emergence of the National Council see the *Work Book for the Constituting Convention* (New York: Planning Committee for the National Council of Churches, no date), esp. pp. 1-10. It was at this time that the Federal Council of Churches, the Foreign Missions Conference of North America, the United Council of Church Women, the United Stewardship Council, and four other agencies came together as the National Council of the Churches of Christ in the USA.

increase of rhetoric aimed at the National and World Councils of Churches by those who opposed them. The National Association of Evangelicals was among the most vocal of its critics. The Reverend Carl McIntire gave voice to especially abrasive criticisms in *The Christian Beacon* and his radio program, 'The Twentieth Century Reformation Hour'.

The Assemblies of God criticized such moves toward greater visible Christian unity, led in large part by Robert C. Cunningham. Cunningham had been Associate Editor of *The Pentecostal Evangel* since 1943 and compiled a regular feature called, 'The Passing and the Permanent', in which he took short news items and added personal comment. As soon as the World Council of Churches had been officially constituted, Cunningham began a campaign of criticism. His initial article informed Assemblies of God readers that 'Member denominations, for the most part, are spiritually cold and formal. They have little concern for true evangelization.' His readers were advised that they should, therefore, 'come together for co-operative effort in doing what the big denominations, with all their strength and organizations, are failing to do—going into all the world and preaching the simple gospel of Christ to every creature'.[67] The following month he produced a similarly judgmental evaluation of the call to unity made by Bishop G. Bromiley Oxnam of the Methodist Church, labeling Oxnam a modernist and claiming that the call to unity was simply the means to add 'floods of unsaved church members to a merely man-made organization'.[68]

The attack continued in March, 1949 when Cunningham, commenting upon a *New York Times* article and quoting from evangelical prophecy teacher Dr Wilbur Smith, suggested that the World Council was moving the Church toward the inevitable 'apostate federation under the world state' in which everyone would ultimately worship the Beast of Revelation 13.8.[69] Throughout the remainder of the year Cunningham kept up his rhetorical campaign against the World Council of Churches.[70]

67. R.C. Cunningham, compiler, 'A World Council of Churches', *The Pentecostal Evangel* 1802 (November 20, 1948), p. 15.

68. R.C. Cunningham, 'Church Union', *The Pentecostal Evangel* 1803 (November 27, 1948), p. 15.

69. R.C. Cunningham, 'The "World Church" Movement', *The Pentecostal Evangel* 1820 (March 26, 1949), p. 10.

70. R.C. Cunningham, 'To Create A Superchurch?', *The Pentecostal Evangel* 1857 (December 10, 1949), pp. 8-9 in which the points that 'Evangelicals are opposed...', 'Evangelicals are not willing...' and 'Evangelicals could not...', seem to suggest that his Pentecostal readers are merely to identify themselves as

Similarly, when the National Council of Churches was constituted in November, 1950, Cunningham, now editor of *The Pentecostal Evangel,* was quick to raise criticism in his editorial 'Unity—False and True'. In his very public condemnation of the National Council he reiterated some of his criticism of the World Council of Churches. Its leaders were 'modernists' who would see to it that social work would replace soul-winning, medical missions would replace 'missionaries of the Cross', secular educators would replace Bible teachers, and they would 'seek to broaden the way to life, which Jesus said was narrow'. He could not help but draw parallels between the National and World Councils of Churches and between these Councils and the 'ecclesiastical union' predicted in Revelation 17 and 18. By way of contrast, he saw the 'World Pentecostal Conference' as something quite different, a group based upon spiritual rather than organizational unity.[71]

To be sure, there were Pentecostals who would fault Cunningham's logic as not sufficiently reactionary. A number of independent Pentecostals, even some Assemblies of God ministers, had criticized the formation of the Pentecostal World Conference (formed May 4-9, 1947) and the Pentecostal Fellowship of North America (formed May 26-28, 1948). They viewed these cooperative efforts as equally problematic as they viewed the National and World Councils of Churches.[72] But there were also Assemblies of God leaders who disagreed with Cunningham. Donald Gee of the British Assemblies of God had lamented the absence of Pentecostals at the Amsterdam Assembly of the World Council of

'Evangelicals'. Cf. R.C. Cunningham, 'The World Council of Churches', *The Pentecostal Evangel* 1865 (February 4, 1950), p. 9.

71.   R.C. Cunningham, 'Unity—False and True', *The Pentecostal Evangel* 1910 (December 17, 1950), pp. 11-12.

72.   'No Pentecostal World Organization', *Herald of Faith* 12:7 (July, 1947), p. 4; L. Pethrus, 'No Pentecostal World Organization', *Herald of Faith* 12:7 (July, 1947), p. 7; J. Mattson, 'Shall Pentecostal Bodies Consolidate?', *Herald of Faith* 13:10 (October, 1948), p. 7; 'Shall Pentecostal Bodies Consolidate: A Correction', *Herald of Faith* 13:11 (November, 1948), 4; J. Mattson Boze, 'Human Organization or Divine Administration', *Herald of Faith* 14:2 (February, 1949), pp. 4-5; 'Is There a National or World Organization to Be Found in Acts 15?', *Herald of Faith* 14:3 (March, 1949), pp. 4-6; 'Can There Be Real Unity in the Pentecostal Movement in the United States? Some Suggestions', *Herald of Faith* 14:5 (May, 1949), pp. 2-3, 11; 'Denominational Organization', *Herald of Faith* 15:2 (February, 1950), pp. 5-6, 14.

Churches.[73] But even in Springfield, Missouri there were those among the executives who appear to have questioned all the negative rhetoric and its fear-spawning consequences.

The 1950 consolidation of the Foreign Missions Conference of North America into the National Council of Churches meant, at least for the sake of its public image, that the Assemblies of God's relationship to the organization would have to be redefined. No longer would Noel Perkin be listed as the official correspondent representing the Assemblies of God as one of the Boards and Societies which enjoyed full membership. Beginning with the November 27-29, 1950 Conference, the Assemblies of God was listed as one of a number of 'Consultant Agencies', and Noel Perkin continued as the Assemblies of God correspondent.[74] With that issue, the annual minutes to the Conference ceased publication.

During the 1950s *The Pentecostal Evangel* continued to portray the National and World Councils in a negative light. Still, the Assemblies of God continued to work with both the National Council of Churches and the World Council of Churches. Most of this interaction was kept quiet, but it involved a number of people at the top level of leadership. On August 15-31, 1954, for instance, the Second Assembly of the World Council of Churches was held in Evanston, Illinois. The Reverend David J. du Plessis served as World Council of Churches staff person at the personal invitation of W.A. Visser 't Hooft, the General Secretary of the Council. Du Plessis had held the office of General Secretary in the Apostolic Faith Mission of South Africa and later as Secretary of the Pentecostal World Conference. At Evanston he coordinated 'non-English speaking delegates for radio and television press conferences'.[75] He would transfer his ordination into the Assemblies of God the following year.

More significantly, however, is the fact that J.R. Flower, both General Secretary of the Assemblies of God and acting Secretary for the 1955 meeting of the Pentecostal World Conference, served as an 'official observer' in Evanston, participating fully for a week in Section II, Group

73. D. Gee, 'Amsterdam and Pentecost', *Pentecost* 6 (December, 1948), Inside back cover.

74. *Foreign Missions Conference of North America: 1950* (New York: Division of Foreign Missions, National Council of the Churches of Christ in the USA, 1950), p. 161.

75. D.J. du Plessis with B. Slosser, *A Man Called Mr Pentecost* (Plainfield, NJ: Logos, 1977), p. 178.

5 whose task it was to speak to the topic of evangelism among the 'non-Christian faiths'.[76] Flower detailed his impressions of the Assembly which were quite positive. He noted that the ecumenical movement was becoming a force to be reckoned with. He was encouraged by the ability of the participants of this Assembly to share their convictions in an irenic fashion. He was impressed with what he termed the 'democratic nature of the Council', with the lack of apparent racial prejudice, with the predominance of 'conservative' theology, with its affirmation of the basic claims of the historic creeds, with its truly international character, with its organization and pageantry, its concern for the Word, for its worship, and finally with its potential for good. Almost echoing the sentiments of Gustave Kinderman eight years earlier he wrote,

> The question remains, after seeing all these bodies of Protestant faith here in one Council, if the Conservatives should abandon the W.C.C. to the Liberals, or whether they should take part in it, and dominate it for Christ and the Bible. They can dominate it if they have a mind to.[77]

When two months later Roy G. Ross, General Secretary of the National Council of the Churches of Christ invited Ralph M. Riggs, General Superintendent of the Assemblies of God, to attend the upcoming General Assembly or to name a 'fraternal delegate' to the meeting,[78] his request was taken seriously. Riggs reported that he had shared the letter with the Executive Presbytery, that all calendars were full, and sent his regrets for declining what he termed Ross's 'gracious invitation'.[79] When the next year Jordan L. Larson, Chair of the Committee on Religion and Public Education of the Commission on General Christian Education for the National Council of Churches, invited Riggs

---

76.   W.A. Visser 't Hooft (ed.), *The Evanston Report: The Second Assembly of the World Council of Churches: 1954* (New York: Harper & Brothers Publishers 1955), p. 284; D.J. du Plessis, 'The World Council of Churches', *Pentecost* 30 (December, 1954), p. 10; D. Gee, 'Pentecost and Evanston', *Pentecost* 30 (December, 1954), p. 17. Cf. also C.M. Robeck, 'A Pentecostal Looks at the World Council of Churches', *The Ecumenical Review* 47:1 (1995), pp. 60-69, especially pp. 60-63 for an overview of Pentecostal participation in and coverage of the Evanston Assembly.

77.   J.R. Flower, 'A Report Covering the First Week of the Second Meeting of the World Council of Churches, Convened at Northwestern University at Evanston, Illinois, August 14–31, 1954', typescript, p. 6. This manuscript is housed in the Assemblies of God Archive in Springfield, Missouri.

78.   Roy G. Ross to Ralph M. Riggs, 27 October, 1954.

79.   Ralph M. Riggs to Roy G. Ross, 6 November, 1954.

or another representative to attend a National Conference on Religion and Public Education in St Louis, Missouri, Riggs's secretary responded to the invitation in Riggs's absence from Springfield, suggesting that a delegate would 'very likely' be sent.[80]

In June, 1956 Ralph Riggs received an invitation to attend the North American Study Conference on 'The Nature of the Unity We Seek' sponsored by the US Conference of the World Council of Churches, the National Council of the Churches of Christ in the USA, and the Canadian Council of Churches. He was assured that he could participate 'on any basis, official or unofficial', which commended itself to him. In his initial response, Riggs noted the affiliation of the Assemblies of God with the National Association of Evangelicals, but promised that the Executive Presbytery would consider the request.[81] The Executive Presbytery met in early August and J.R. Flower responded on their behalf that they had agreed 'to appoint the Reverend Ralph M. Riggs as an observer' to the meeting scheduled for September 3–10, 1957 at Oberlin, Ohio. Flower went on to tell of his own experience at the Evanston Assembly. 'There was definite benefit gained from the World Council', he informed them, 'and we trust that the one chosen to represent the Assemblies of God at the Study Conference may be able to add something to the thinking of the delegates as well as receive benefit himself'.[82] Cavert responded enthusiastically, and Paul Minear and Cavert both sent Riggs some conference materials which he acknowledged, but in the end due to 'last moment circumstances' Riggs had to miss the meeting.[83]

80. Jordan L. Larson and R.L. Hunt to Mr Ralph M. Riggs, 22 September, 1955; Secretary to R.M. Riggs [G.C.] to Dr Jordan L. Larson, 5 October, 1955.

81. Henry Knox Sherrill, Chairman and Samuel McCrea Cavert, Executive Secretary, to Rev. Ralph M. Riggs, General Superintendent, 26 June, 1956; Ralph M. Riggs to Dr Henry Knox Sherrill, Chairman, and Dr Samuel McCrea Cavert, Executive Secretary, 11 July, 1956.

82. J.R. Flower to Dr Henry Knox Sherrill and Dr Samuel McCrea Cavert, 8 August, 1956.

83. For the complete exchange of correspondence see Samuel McCrea Cavert to Rev. Ralph M. Riggs, 9 October, 1956; Paul S. Minear to Rev. Ralph M. Riggs, 21 January, 1957; Ralph M. Riggs to Dr Paul S. Minear, 28 January, 1957; Samuel McCrea Cavert to Dr Riggs, 18 June, 1957; Ralph M. Riggs to Dr Samuel McCrea Cavert, 21 June, 1957; Frances Maeda to Dear Friend, 1 July, 1957; A. Greig Ritchie to Rev. Ralph Riggs, 23 September, 1957; and Ralph M. Riggs to Reverend A. Greig Ritchie, 26 September, 1957.

Whatever these circumstances were, they were not based upon lack of permission, personal unwillingness or ideological animosity. When in October, 1958 Riggs received an invitation to send a delegate to a meeting billed as 'Christian Responsibility on a Changing Planet' in a Fifth World Order Study Conference at Cleveland, Ohio for November 18-21, 1958 sponsored by the Department of International Affairs of the National Council of Churches, J.R. Flower enthusiastically recommended that Riggs attend the Conference. Riggs agreed to attend as an 'unofficial observer', and he did attend the conference.[84]

3. *Criticism from Fundamentalists and Evangelicals*

Several new factors converged beginning in 1959. First the General Council of the Assemblies of God was held August 26–September 1, 1959 in San Antonio, Texas, and it was marked by unprecedented change. Thomas F. Zimmerman was elected General Superintendent at that General Council, replacing Ralph M. Riggs. The Reverend J.R. Flower retired as General Secretary and was succeeded by Bartlett Peterson. Noel Perkin retired from the position of Director of Foreign Missions and was succeeded by J. Philip Hogan. In addition, the position of Director of Foreign Missions was given the title 'Assistant Superintendent, carrying the portfolio of Foreign Missions'.[85]

Secondly, the National Association of Evangelicals and *Christianity Today* began to pay more attention to the Assemblies of God. For some, such as Robert C. Cunningham, this may have seemed to be overdue.

---

84.   The exchange of correspondence includes J.R. Flower's typed and signed endorsement on the envelope of the first letter. He wrote, 'I would recommend that you accept this invitation, if at all possible. Attendance at these meetings is very stimulating and we get impressions that are very helpful—in spite of the fact some of the speakers go far from conservative principles'. The correspondence includes Edwin T. Dahlberg to Mr Ralph M. Riggs, 3 October, 1958; Secretary to Brother Riggs to Dr Edwin T. Dahlberg, 8 October, 1958; Ralph M. Riggs to Mr Edwin T. Dahlberg, 10 November, 1958; Kenneth L. Maxwell to the Rev. R.N. [*sic*] Riggs, 13 November, 1958. Riggs's conference name badge, a typescript 'Call' from Eugene Carson Blake dated 30 November, 1957, the Program with the notations of Ralph M. Riggs, a one-page typescript outlining 'A Nationwide Program of Education and Action for Peace June 1959–June 1960', and a four-page typescript of 'Conference Action on Recommendations' from Section Four with marks by Riggs: all are available from the Assemblies of God Archive.

85.   Menzies, *Anointed to Serve*, p. 398.

Throughout the 1950s he had continued to publish items which were unfavorable to the National and World Council of Churches. He also published items which were favorable to the National Association of Evangelicals. As editor of *The Pentecostal Evangel* he was single-handedly attempting to move the Assemblies of God along in its journey toward Evangelicalism.

On January 1, 1956, *The Pentecostal Evangel* began to print a new statement of Faith, titled 'We Believe', on the inside of the front cover.[86] It was not the Statement of Fundamental Truths adopted by the Assemblies of God, nor was it an abbreviated form of the Statement. Instead, Cunningham had been impressed with the statement 'This We Believe' published regularly in the National Association of Evangelicals' *United Evangelical Action*, and in consultation with J.R. Flower, had authored his own statement, patterned 'on that of the N.A.E. magazine' even to the extent of 'using the same phraseology' in most of the statement. To this he added a statement on the baptism of the Holy Spirit and one on the redemptive work of Christ. Later he amended the text further with a statement on the blessed hope. Thus, Cunningham published, without explanation, as though it were an official statement of Assemblies of God belief, his own stylized version of an Evangelical statement designed to serve Pentecostal needs.[87]

In spite of the process of evangelicalization which was going on in the Assemblies of God, not all Evangelicals were satisfied that it was sufficient. The result was a new level of attention given to the Assemblies of God. Not all of this scrutiny or attention was particularly welcome.

In July, 1959, Noel Perkin sent an internal memo to Ralph M. Riggs for discussion with the Executive Presbytery. In this memo he noted that for some years the Foreign Missions Department had conducted its relief program through Gustave Kinderman and the New York Office. They had tried to coordinate their efforts with those of the World Relief Organization of the National Association of Evangelicals. But Robert McGlasson, the current director of the New York Office, and Kinderman had also been working with the Church World Service on some important projects.

Formed in May, 1946, as an interagency committee shared by the Federal Council of Churches, the World Council of Churches, and the

---

86. 'We Believe', *The Pentecostal Evangel* 2173 (January 1, 1956), p. 2.

87. R.C. Cunningham, 'We Believe', Assemblies of God *Heritage* 15:3 (Fall, 1995), p. 15.

Foreign Missions Conference of North America, the Church World Service was designed to be an agency through which the participating churches themselves would work together. The Assemblies of God had attempted to work with the N.A.E., but by 1959 it was evident that to do so was not cost-effective. The Church World Service was clearly more efficient, and based upon the fact that the Assemblies of God was shipping between 500 and 600 tons of food, clothing and other goods overseas each year, Robert McGlasson made the recommendation to move out of the World Relief Organization and into greater cooperation with Church World Service.[88] By cooperating more fully with Church World Service, McGlasson and Perkin believed that the financial savings might offset any potential problem in public relations. To be on the safe side, however, Perkin asked Riggs to have the matter discussed by the Executive Presbytery.[89]

Before the issue could be resolved an editorial appeared in *Christianity Today* which made the startling revelation that the Assemblies of God maintained an associate membership in the National Council of Churches along with its National Association of Evangelicals affiliation. Furthermore, it reported, the Assemblies of God was renting space at the Interchurch Building at 475 Riverside Drive in New York.[90]

At the August General Presbytery meeting, a question of clarification was raised from the floor. It was explained that the Foreign Missions Department had only a 'consultative relationship to the Foreign Missions branch of the NCCC and was not an associate member of the NCCC'. Furthermore, the General Presbytery was informed that the Foreign Missions Department had worked with the Church World Service, 'in some cases for the distribution of food and supplies to the needy in foreign lands', and it was reported that the Church World Service had aided the Assemblies of God in 'getting Christian [Pentecostal] Russian refugees out of Communist held countries'. It was also noted that

88.   Evidence that the Assemblies of God was a participant in some Church World Service activities already can be seen in the pamphlet 'Pastors and Leaders Guide: The United Clothing Appeal of the Churches' (New York: Church World Service, 1958) with its 'Call to the Churches' issued February 6, 1958. On p. 4 it lists the Assemblies of God as one of the 'Denominations Participating in the Appeal'. McGlasson's primary motivation appears to have been one of good stewardship.

89.   Memo from Noel Perkin to Ralph M. Riggs, 20 July, 1959. Two pages, typed, double-spaced.

90.   'Theology for Evangelism', *Christianity Today* 3.22 (August 3, 1959), p. 22.

the relationship was economical, efficient and non-binding. Finally, the Foreign Missions Department reported that it had only been considering the use of office space in the Interchurch Center. The change of address was being considered in light of space needs and economy.[91]

Following the General Council meeting, the Executive Presbytery met to discuss how to resolve their concerns. A resolution was presented and apparently enacted which reads as follows:

> *Whereas*, the implication of any published relationship of the Assemblies of God with the National Council of the Churches of Christ or any of its subsidiary committees causes question from some of our Assemblies of God constituents, and
>
> *Whereas*, we are now listed as a consultant group in relation to the Foreign Missions Division of the National Council of the Churches of Christ and are also members of some of the regional and geographic sub-committees of the Foreign Missions Division, therefore be it
>
> *Resolved*, that all official relationship with the aforementioned group shall be discontinued but that benefits derived from the Missionary Research Library and Church World Service and any other service unto be conserved on a contribution basis, if consistent with the provisions of this resolution.[92]

Damage control began as soon as the General Council had ended. Riggs wrote to Carl F.H. Henry, editor of *Christianity Today*, complaining about the 'surprise, dismay, and a measure of resentment' he had felt as a result of the editorial. What was worse, Riggs went on to say, was that 'This occurred just before the opening of our General Council session in San Antonio which completely occupied us all for quite a number of days'. Riggs continued by arguing that the Assemblies of God was one of the 'most strictest sect[s] of the fundamental[ist]s today'. Furthermore, Riggs argued, 'If there is any church in America that is distinctly and utterly separate from the National Council of Churches it is the Assemblies of God'. Riggs asked that a full withdrawal of the statement regarding the relationship between the Assemblies of God and the National Council of Churches be published in the next issue of *Christianity Today*.[93]

91.　General Presbytery Minutes (August, 1959), p. 23. This fact is corroborated in Ralph M. Riggs to Dr Carl F.H. Henry, 25 September, 1959, pp. 1-2.

92.　Executive Presbytery Minutes (September, 1959), p. 1694.

93.　Ralph M. Riggs to Dr Carl F.H. Henry, 25 September, 1959, p. 1.

James DeForest Murch, managing editor of *Christianity Today*, responded to Riggs's complaint by offering that he had been absent when the editorial was written, but went on to say that the unnamed author of the editorial had checked with the Missionary Research Library's North America listing and had determined that the Foreign Missions Department was, in fact, listed as an associate member of the NCC Foreign Mission unit. 'Evidently', Murch maintained, 'the N.A.E. office was not aware of the fact that this liaison relationship had been recently concluded'. He offered to print a retraction. It appeared as an excerpt from Riggs's letter under the title 'Unrelated to NCC' in the October 26, 1959 issue.[94]

Technically, Riggs was correct. The Assemblies of God was not an associate member of the National Council of Churches. But its history of participation in Church World Service and a variety of other Committees had left it vulnerable to criticism for doing what it believed was good for its mission program involving the operation of a major social program including food, clothing and relocation as part of its overall evangelism program. In a sense, however, this arrangement violated the requirement of the National Association of Evangelicals that its members disengage and if necessary repudiate any connection with the National Council of Churches.[95] Still, Murch was left with the impression that the Assemblies of God had previously disengaged from the Council.

Noel Perkin wrote to Luther Gotwald, Executive Secretary of the National Council of Churches at the same time as Riggs wrote to Carl Henry. Perkin reminded Gotwald that on August 11, two weeks before the General Council, Perkin had made certain financial commitments toward 'the budget of the Division of Foreign Missions' of the National Council of Churches and to 'several of the area committees'. Now, he informed Gotwald, the 'Board of Directors of the General Council of the Assemblies of God' had felt that it was advisable to sever its official relationship 'with the National Council of Churches of Christ and the Foreign Missions Division'. This action, of course, would mean that the financial commitment for 1960 was now canceled and the National

94.   James DeForest Murch to Dr R.M. Riggs, 1 October, 1959; Murch is careful not to identify the author of the editorial. R.M. Riggs to Dr James DeForest Murch, 5 October, 1959; Ralph M. Riggs, 'Unrelated to NCC', *Christianity Today* Vol. 4.2 (October 26, 1959), 24; James DeForest Murch to Dr R.M. Riggs, 16 November, 1959.
95.   George L. Ford to Rev. Raymond R. Hicks, 11 July, 1961.

Council should remove the name of the Assemblies of God from its official records. Perkin went out of his way to let Gotwald know that this move was not 'due to any dissatisfaction' with the relationship which he described as courteous and pleasant. And he held out the possibility that 'by making some financial contribution' the Assemblies of God might still be able to use the services of such agencies as the Missionary Research Library and other 'distinctly service units of the National Council'.[96]

Gotwald was understandably surprised by the letter and he told Perkin that he regretted it because it meant the 'severance of fraternal association which, over the years' had been enjoyed. 'Also we are happy to note that our relations will not be completely severed', Gotwald continued, because of Perkin's interest in the Missionary Research Library and other service units. Gotwald suggested that Perkin might, after all, be interested in the Radio, Visual Education and Mass Communications Committee (RAVEMCCO) as well as the Committee on World Literacy and Christian Literature. Finally, Gotwald told Noel Perkin that he had met Maynard Ketcham, Assemblies of God Field Secretary for Southern Asia, within the previous month at a RAVEMCCO Consultation. He had talked with Ketcham about the new change in policy by the Assemblies of God, and he noted that Ketcham had been surprised.[97]

What seems clear from the decision of the Executive Presbytery and the correspondence with Carl F.H. Henry and Luther Gotwald, is that the Assemblies of God had been publicly embarrassed. Their evangelical partners had made public what had been a long-standing policy of the Assemblies of God. The denomination was, in spite of holding an unofficial position, deeply involved with a range of National Council units and committees. While it is doubtful that Riggs was not re-elected because of this issue, the very fact that it had to be handled at the time of the General Council meant that Thomas F. Zimmerman might well benefit from this revelation. Zimmerman was next in line for the presidency of the National Association of Evangelicals, and at the 1959 General Council he was voted into office as General Superintendent of the Assemblies of God.

When Thomas F. Zimmerman became General Superintendent, it fell to him to respond to critics of and queries regarding the Assemblies of

96.   Noel Perkin to L.A. Gotwald, 24 September, 1959.
97.   Luther A. Gotwald to Dr Perkin, 21 October, 1959.

God. In March, 1960, he received a letter from an Assemblies of God minister in Oklahoma who had only recently read the troublesome editorial in *Christianity Today*. Deeply concerned by the possibility that the Assemblies of God might have entered into an associate membership with what he described as this 'crooked bunch' of smoking and drinking 'modern and pro-Communist' leaders, he asked Zimmerman to tell him the truth. Did the Assemblies of God hold an associate membership in the Council and did it rent space in the 'ecumenical building in New York'?[98]

Zimmerman responded quickly. He acknowledged that as of January, 1960 the Foreign Missions Department had, indeed, moved its New York Office into the Interchurch Center at 475 Riverside Drive. But he explained, the New York Office, like the National Council of Churches, was merely a tenant of the same building which was actually run by another non-profit corporation. The fact that the New York Office of the Foreign Missions Department and the National Council of Churches occupied space in the same building should not imply any membership or organic ties.

Zimmerman went on to explain that the claim that the Assemblies of God held associate membership in the National Council was simply untrue. 'We do maintain liaison *and membership* in the Church World Service which is one of their departments', he went on, and he noted that the Assemblies of God was invited to serve as 'associates and observers' in 'many' of the National Council's meetings.[99]

Zimmerman was elected president of the National Association of Evangelicals in 1960. The report which appeared in *The Pentecostal Evangel* noted with some pride that although the Assemblies of God had participated in the National Association of Evangelicals from the beginning 'this is the first time a man of Pentecostal persuasion has headed the interchurch group'.[100] Zimmerman's term as President of the N.A.E., however, did not mean the end to questions about the relationship of the Assemblies of God to the National Council. If anything, it only increased concerns, spurred on by the fundamentalist gadfly, the Reverend Carl McIntire and his newspaper, *The Christian Beacon*.

98.   Guinn Brown to Thomas F. Zimmerman, 10 March, 1960.

99.   Thomas F. Zimmerman to Reverend Guinn Brown, 16 March, 1960, p. 1. Italics mine.

100.   'Assemblies Superintendent Named NAE Head', *The Pentecostal Evangel* No. 2409 (July 10, 1960), p. 14.

Carl McIntire was never a friend of the Pentecostal Movement. In spite of this fact, many Pentecostals seem to have subscribed to *The Christian Beacon* or were regular listeners to his radio program, 'The Twentieth Century Reformation Hour'. Founder of the fundamentalist predecessor and alternative to the National Association of Evangelicals known as the American Council of Christian Churches (ACCC), McIntire was deeply opposed to the National Council of Churches and its predecessor the Federal Council, but without any 'constructive ideas'.[101] The National Association of Evangelicals was more positive in its criticism of the Federal Council of Churches. It had refused to offer a blanket condemnation of this organization or its successor, the National Council of Churches. Carl McIntire made strong statements condemning the FCCC and the NCC, but had held out the possibility that he might merge with the National Association of Evangelicals if the National Association of Evangelicals would, among other things 'get rid of the radical Holiness, tongues groups'.[102] Sixteen years later, in 1961, McIntire was still, in the words of Robert McGlasson, 'rabidly anti-Pentecostal'.[103]

In mid-January, 1961 while Thomas Zimmerman was out of town, several letters, apparently spawned by something which McIntire said on his radio program, arrived in Springfield, Missouri. R.T. McGlasson, who now served as Foreign Missions Secretary in Springfield for J. Philip Hogan, was asked to respond in Zimmerman's absence. On January 24, 1961 he responded to two such inquiries, explaining the situation. To the Reverend J.W. Woolbridge of Meridian, Mississippi he noted:

> Carl McIntire is an enemy of the Pentecostal people, and he is clearly on record in opposition to us. His technique now in using this remote connection with an agency of the National Council of Churches is intended not only to harm and attack that organization but to harm the Assemblies of God and divide our ranks which heretofore he has been unsuccessful in attempting.[104]

What was the 'remote connection' to which McGlasson made reference and how did it serve the interests of the Assemblies of God? These

101. J.D. Murch, *Cooperation without Compromise: A History of the National Association of Evangelicals* (Grand Rapids: Eerdmans, 1956), pp. 52-53.
102. W.O.H. Garman, 'Analysis of National Association Convention and Constituency', *The Christian Beacon* 9:12 (April 27, 1944), pp. 1-2, esp. p. 2.
103. R.T. McGlasson to Reverend J. C. Burks, 24 January, 1961, p. 1.
104. R.T. McGlasson to Reverend J.W. Woolbridge, 24 January, 1961.

questions are best answered in his letter to J.C. Burks, then District Superintendent of the Assemblies of God in Mississippi. Once again the connection was described in terms that the Assemblies of God 'is a member of Church World Service' which in turn is 'a department of the National Council...' and it had expertise and experts which the Assemblies of God did not have. 'We have been members of this agency and its predecessor [the China Relief Committee of the Foreign Missions Conference of North America] for many years and have not canceled [sic.] this association', he wrote, since it had aided the Assemblies of God to transport and resettle in North and South America, Australia and elsewhere between 8000 and 9000 refugees, including some 'two thousand Pentecostal white Russian refugees out of China. The story is a thrilling one', McGlasson added, and 'We have continued to feel that this association had value sufficient for us to maintain it'. In a rare but strong show of support for the Church World Service and the National Council of Churches, McGlasson concluded by recounting 'the warmest of relations with the godly, born again men in this association', many of whom he claimed had recently 'received the baptism of the Holy Ghost just as we [have]'.[105]

Thomas Zimmerman developed a form letter response to the questions posed by others which declared that any suggestion that there was any relationship between the National Council and the Assemblies of God was merely rumor, that while the Assemblies had an office at 475 Riverside Drive (the probable cause of the rumor according to Zimmerman), proximity to the National Council did not imply membership, that the Foreign Missions Department of the Assemblies of God had a relationship with the Church World Service which predated the existence of the National Council, and that this relationship was still 'the best way to help our own Pentecostal brethren'. 'Our very association with the National Association of Evangelicals, of which I am

105. R.T. McGlasson to Reverend J.C. Burks, 24 January, 1961, pp. 1-2. Other letters reveal that the Church World Service also provided for refugee housing (Cf. Thos. F. Zimmerman to Reverend James D. Gast, 3 April, 1961), and for the shipping of missionary vehicles overseas. See William C. Senn to David Scott, 20 April, 1961; David T. Scott to Rev. Thomas F. Zimmerman, 26 April, 1961, who notes (p. 1) that 'Up until now the help has been given directly through Church World Service'; R.T. McGlasson to Reverend David T. Scott, 3 May, 1961.

president', concluded Zimmerman, 'indicates our choice of organizations'.[106]

While Zimmerman was busy explaining the relationship, Carl McIntire was busy collecting evidence for an exposé. It came in an article titled 'Assemblies of God and NCC', which appeared in the March 23, 1961 issue of *The Christian Beacon*. Apparently a woman who listened to McIntire's radio program had written to Zimmerman and received his form letter. Now it was photographically reproduced in McIntire's paper with certain words and phrases underscored. 'This letter is a splendid example of how Christian leaders are seeking to justify, rationalize, and explain their relationship to the National Council of the Churches of Christ in the U.S.A., and the power which the NCC has', the article stated. It went on to accuse Zimmerman of misrepresenting the position of the Church World Service with the National Council, of basing involvement with the Church World Service on expedience, and of compromising the Assemblies of God by relating to 'ecumenical apostasy'. The National Association of Evangelicals was excoriated for not being decisively separate from the National Council and the Pentecostal Movement was revealed as the weak link in any resolve, which the N.A.E. might have had to do so. One only needed to note that the World Council of Churches had just admitted a Pentecostal church from Chile into membership to see the handwriting on the wall. Church World Service was inducing Pentecostal compromise and now was the time for 'God-fearing, Bible-believing Pentecostals' to take a stand against 'the ecumenical movement, with its modernism...its Communist direction and control...[and] its drive to build the one-world church and one-world government...'[107] Needless to say, this article only produced more letters from fear-filled Pentecostals asking for the facts.

As a result of this increased pressure caused by Carl McIntire's attacks, Zimmerman was in a difficult position. He was not helped by the revelation that the National Council of Churches continued to list the

106. Cf. Thomas F. Zimmerman to Reverend Erling Saxelid, 6 February, 1961 in response to Erling Saxelid and Harold E. Daniel to Reverend Thomas F. Zimmerman, 31 January, 1961; Thomas F. Zimmerman to Reverend Willis E. Berry, Secretary-Treasurer, South Texas Assemblies of God, 14 February, 1961 in response to Willis E. Berry to Reverend Thomas F. Zimmerman, 9 February, 1961, and others.

107. 'Assemblies of God and NCC', *The Christian Beacon* 26:6 (March 23, 1961), p. 8.

Assemblies of God as an 'associate member', and the 'Executive brethren' were now beginning to raise questions about possibly cutting off any relationship with Church World Service.[108]

A meeting to determine whether or not to take that step as well as to close the New York Office was held in the New York office on April 26, 1961. Present at the meeting were Thomas F. Zimmerman, General Superintendent, J. Philip Hogan, Executive Director of the Foreign Missions Department, Gustave Kinderman, Secretary for Relief and Rehabilitation, now mostly retired, Robert T. McGlasson, former Eastern Secretary for the New York Office, now Foreign Missions Secretary in Springfield, Missouri, and Stephen Walegir, current Eastern Secretary. No final decision was reached during that meeting, but Kinderman was fairly certain that Zimmerman and Hogan 'would prefer not to associate or work through Church World Service' and that the New York staff, Walegir and Kinderman, should not be identified with 'CWS or associate organizations'.[109]

In his follow-up letter to McGlasson, Kinderman outlined his own missionary career. His primary purpose, however, was to determine what decision, if any, had finally been reached, and to explain why he needed that information. He was concerned about the ongoing 'Rehabilitation program among Russian Pentecostal believers in China and Hong Kong' in which the Assemblies of God Foreign Missions Department was engaged. The reason was that the Church World Service and the World Council of Churches were partners with the Assemblies of God in this relocation program.

> I should like to draw the attention of all concerned, that the High Commissioner for Refugees with United Nations as well as U.S. government representatives in Miami relating to Cuban Refugees, deal *not* with individual Denominations but rather with representatives of collective groups. The CWS represent ALL Evangelical groups in Miami, while the World Council of Churches of Geneva represents the Evangelical groups (rather Denominations) when dealing with the High Commissioner for Refugees.

As for the general relief program of the Assemblies of God, that still lay

---

108.   Cf. Thomas F. Zimmerman to Reverend James D. Gast, 3 April, 1961 in response to James D. Gast to Rev. Thomas F. Zimmerman, undated letter.

109.   G. Kinderman to Rev. Robert T. McGlasson, 7 June, 1961, p. 1.

with the World Relief Commission of the National Association of Evangelicals.[110]

McGlasson responded to Kinderman that the final decision was not yet made and would not be forthcoming for some time. He advised Kinderman that regardless of the final decision it would not be a simple matter to disengage from these things and that Kinderman should plan to continue things as they were presently 'for at least a year through June of 1962'.[111]

Thomas Zimmerman was preoccupied with other things on both sides of the Atlantic. As General Superintendent of the Assemblies of God, he would continue to respond to questions and provide leadership to the Fellowship. As the newly elected president of the National Association of Evangelicals he was having to measure up to Evangelical expectations in a group where questions continued to surface regarding the ecumenical commitments of the Assemblies of God.

In August, 1960 British Assemblies of God minister Donald Gee, as well as David du Plessis, had attended two sessions of the Faith and Order Commission of the World Council of Churches in St Andrews, Scotland. Gee wrote an editorial about his experience in *Pentecost*, the organ of the Pentecostal World Conference. He argued that Pentecostals need not be viewed as compromisers merely because they worked with Christians with whom they might have deep theological differences.[112] Besides, he argued, such people did not want compromise from Pentecostals in any case, but 'more of the Holy Spirit'.

Both Gee and du Plessis were invited to attend the third Assembly of the World Council of Churches in New Delhi (November 19–December 5, 1961). That fact raised questions once again. Pressure was focused on Donald Gee to decline.[113] Zimmerman applied great pressure to Gee when in May, 1961 he delivered a keynote address to the Pentecostal

110. G. Kinderman to Rev. Robert T. McGlasson, 7 June, 1961, pp. 1-2.
111. R.T. McGlasson to Rev. G. Kinderman, 12 June, 1961
112. D. Gee, 'Contact Is Not Compromise', *Pentecost* 53 (September–November, 1960), inside back cover.
113. Cf. B. Ross, 'Donald Gee: Sectarian in Search of A Church', *Evangelical Quarterly* 50 (1978), p. 101. See also A.W. Edsor (Editor of *The Pattern*, the organ of The Bible-Pattern Church Fellowship) to Rev. Thomas Zimmerman, 4 July, 1961, who promised that he intended to challenge in *The Pattern* those 'Pentecostal leaders who have intimated that they hope to be present at the next Assembly of the World Council of Churches at New Delhi later this year'. Gee and du Plessis were clearly in mind.

World Conference meeting in Jerusalem. He contended that those persons who 'join hands with those who do compromise are being unwittingly used as tools against us, not for us'.[114] Obviously Zimmerman was concerned about Gee's editorial, but Gee continued to press his point. He was concerned about the pressure which he saw being applied to Zimmerman, pressure from Zimmerman's evangelical and fundamentalist critics. Many people who are 'faithful to the Fundamentals of the faith', Gee reminded his readers, 'have been the bitterest opponents of the Pentecostal Movement'. They ought not to set the Pentecostal agenda of those with whom it should have contact.[115] Ultimately Gee did not attend the New Delhi meeting, but David du Plessis did.

David du Plessis was reaching the height of his ecumenical career in 1961. He was highly visible and frequently used in charismatic circles. Already he was known widely as 'Mr Pentecost', yet because he was an Assemblies of God minister he was subject, in one sense, to Thomas F. Zimmerman, his General Superintendent. Once again, the National Association of Evangelicals entered the picture. W. Stanley Mooneyham had been watching David du Plessis who was often being featured in the news media as a spokesperson for Pentecostalism and an ecumenical enthusiast. He took it upon himself to conduct a poll including selected Pentecostal leaders from among the Pentecostal Fellowship of North America. The results were published in June 1961 in the organ of the National Association of Evangelicals, *United Evangelical Action*, a month after Zimmerman had spoken out against ecumenism. 'Mr du Plessis doesn't speak for any of their movements and he has no constituency of his own', concluded Mooneyham.[116] But once again Zimmerman was in a difficult situation. He was, after all, du Plessis's General Superintendent as well as President of the National Association of Evangelicals.

By August the Assemblies of God had made its decision. It would break off its relationship with the Church World Service. Robert McGlasson was drafted to inform them of this decision. On August 9 he wrote to Bishop Frederick Newell, Executive Director of Church World

114. *Addresses Presented at the Sixth Pentecostal World Conference, Jerusalem, Israel, May 19th to 21st, 1961* (Toronto: Testimony Press, 1961), p. 55.

115. D. Gee, 'What Manner of Spirit?', *Pentecost* 57 (September–November, 1961), inside back cover.

116. W.S. Mooneyham, 'Pentecostals and the W.C.C.', *United Evangelical Action* 20:4 (June, 1961), pp. 28-29.

Service and informed him that 'with the deepest regret...we advise you
of our decision to withdraw our membership in Church World Service
and tender to you this official letter of resignation'. McGlasson gave no
reasons for the decision, but was gracious in his thanks for the gen-
erosity of the National Council of Churches. He assured Bishop Newell
of a desire for continued cooperation in the area of resettlement and
promised a smooth transition in the closure of this relationship.[117]

That was not the end of the story, however, for McGlasson also sent
a confidential personal letter to Bishop Newell and the Executive
Committee of the Church World Service with a much fuller explanation.
The decision for the Assemblies of God to leave Church World Service
was a very painful one. It was especially difficult for McGlasson because
he was, himself, 'a member of the Executive Committee' of Church
World Service in whose absence Stephen Walegir served as proxy. But
the Assemblies of God, 'representing not only its own membership but
in reality all other Pentecostal bodies' had acted as a lightening rod long
enough.

McGlasson informed the Committee that in recent years the Assemblies
of God had 'moved closely toward those circles known as "evangelicals"... ultimately becoming a member of the National Association
of Evangelicals'. He went on:

> In recent times we have been made a target for misunderstanding on the
> part of many who have not understood our continuing connection with
> agencies of the National Council, both within and without our fellowship.
> We believe and feel that these criticisms have been unjust and unfounded;
> nevertheless, we have come to the place where active membership in an
> agency of the National Council of Churches would be discontinued. This
> is for the sake of harmony and effectiveness within our own ranks and is
> the reason behind the resignation...[118]

The letter is an especially poignant one, for it reveals the depth of
McGlasson's own commitment to the task of cooperation at a variety of
levels. His closing paragraph sums it up very well:

> The kindness, consideration, and Christian fellowship extended to us
> through the years makes the decision [to resign] more difficult. Present
> and past members of your staff, and members of the committees and
> boards of Church World Service, have contributed largely to the tie of

117. R.T. McGlasson to Bishop Fredrick B. Newell, 9 August, 1961.

118. R.T. McGlasson to Bishop Fredrick B. Newell (and Executive Committee
of C.W.S.), 9 August, 1961, p. 1.

fellowship which we have known. We do not consider this a severance of
such fellowship for the church of Jesus Christ is in fact a larger body of
which He Himself is the head. Our fellowship in spiritual matters and our
cooperation in other matters of mutual interest will continue.[119]

The Assemblies of God continued to hunker down under the assault
as the criticisms of still others attacked its original convictions. By June,
1962 the New York Office of the Foreign Missions Department was
closed. David du Plessis was invited to meet with the Executive
Presbytery at the time of the General Council, August 23-29, 1961.
Asked to respond to certain conditions placed before him in order to
maintain his ordination with the Assemblies of God, du Plessis struggled,
finding it futile to try to explain. Finally, in September, 1962 the decision
was made by the Executive Presbytery that his relationship as an
ordained minister of the Assemblies of God should be terminated. His
termination was said to be a result of problems surrounding his continued involvement with the National and World Councils of Churches.[120]

The National Council of Churches continued to make cordial advances
to the Assemblies of God but was rebuffed at every turn.[121] Carl
McIntire continued pressing his case against the National Council of
Churches and shaming and pummeling the Assemblies of God into
further submission to the fundamentalist agenda. McIntire published an
eight-page tract titled 'National Council of Churches 1963' in which he
accused the Assemblies of God, among others, of denying membership
in the National Council of Churches while entering into the Council
by the 'back door', citing a listing of 'Non-Member Communions—
Approved for Membership in Units of the National Council' released by
the Council on May 10, 1963.[122] R.T. McGlasson was asked to explain
this latest revelation to Thomas Zimmerman and suggested only that it

119. R.T. McGlasson to Bishop Fredrick B. Newell (and Executive Committee
of C.W.S.), 9 August, 1961, p. 2.
120. Bartlett Peterson to David J. du Plessis, 14 September, 1962, p. 1.
J. Roswell to Rev. David J. du Plessis states clearly the reason the issue would even
be raised is the embarrassment du Plessis posed to 'the officers of the General
Council'.
121. Cf. J. Quinter Miller to Mr Thomas F. Zimmerman, 7 May, 1963, and
General Superintendent to Mr J. Quinter Miller, 23 May, 1963.
122. C. McIntire, 'National Council of Churches 1963', (Collingwood, NJ:
Twentieth Century Reformation Hour, no date).

must be the result of an internal communication problem in the National Council.[123]

The fact that Carl McIntire published the list in which the Assemblies of God was to be found among the 'Non-Member Communions Approved for Membership' moved Bartlett Peterson to notify all departments at the headquarters building of the Assemblies of God that the National Council was using the presence of even one Assemblies of God person at any of its meetings for its own publicity purposes. The Executive Presbytery, therefore, had made a new request that 'no representative shall be sent to any meetings of the NCC or its units'.[124]

In spite of all these actions, questions continued to be addressed to Thomas F. Zimmerman regarding the actual relationship between the Assemblies of God and the National Council of Churches. The General Presbytery was asked to make a statement on 'the Ecumenical Movement', and that statement was essentially affirmed by the 1965 General Council.[125] Revised slightly, it was adopted in its present form at the 1969 General Council. It reads

The General Council of the Assemblies of God disapproves of ministers of churches participating in any of the modern ecumenical organizations on a local, national, or international level in such a manner as to promote the Ecumenical Movement, because

a. We believe the basis of doctrinal fellowship of said movement to be so broad that it includes people who reject the inspiration of Scripture, the deity of Christ, the universality of sin, the substitutionary atonement, and other cardinal teachings which we understand to be essential to Biblical Christianity.

b. We believe the emphases of the Ecumenical Movement to be at variance with what we hold to be biblical priorities, frequently displacing the urgency of individual salvation with social concerns.

c. We believe that the combination of many religious organizations into a World superchurch will culminate in the religious Babylon of Revelation 17 and 18.

123. Memo from R.T. McGlasson to T.F. Zimmerman, 6 June, 1963.

124. Memo from Bartlett Peterson to All Departments, 5 September, 1963.

125. The resolution as adopted, appeared under the Bylaws of the organization as Bylaws, Article XXIII, Section 16, titled 'the Ecumenical Movement', *Minutes* 1965, p. 138.

(This is not to be interpreted to mean that a limitation may be imposed upon any Assemblies of God minister regarding his Pentecostal witness or participation on a local level with inter-denominational activities.)[126]

4. *Conclusions*

This story suggests that the break between the Assemblies of God and the larger church world was complete by 1965. Future studies will have to tell us whether or not that is the case. In spite of this uncertainty, several things are clear from this survey.

From its childhood, the Assemblies of God had a yearning to participate within the Church which it understood to be larger than itself. As a small, struggling, often criticized child it had needs which had to be met. It is not unusual to see various denominational groups cooperate with one another when they have such needs. We need only to think of how cooperation between Christians was so important under the reign of communism in the former Soviet Union to realize that they were better off working together than if they had been in isolation.

Nor is it surprising to find that one of the first places ecumenical cooperation takes place in the life of the Church is in the Foreign Missions Department. It was the Edinburgh Missionary Convention of 1910, after all, which really started the ball rolling that culminated in the formation of the World Council of Churches. In many countries it was and is still more important to have a united Christian witness than it is to have a denominational witness. A strongly Muslim context demonstrates that fact very quickly.

Then there is the issue of stewardship. One of the reasons the Assemblies of God was formed in 1914 was to coordinate diverse missionary efforts for the sake of good stewardship. It should come as no surprise, then, that the Assemblies of God would look to find partners in mission who could help them to be more effective in their own efforts. And familiarity builds trust. Dialogue and mutual interaction bring to an end mistaken or misunderstood stereotypes.

It should come as no surprise that those who were closest to the ecumenical scene from 1920 until 1965 were also those who believed in

126.   Bylaws, Article IX.B, Section 11, The Ecumenical Movement. *Minutes of the 46th Session of the General Council of the Assemblies of God* Convened at St Louis, Missouri, August 8–13, 1995 with Revised Constitution and Bylaws (Springfield, MO: General Secretary's Office, 1995), p. 149.

the possibility that the relationship of the Assemblies of God to parts of the so-called Ecumenical Movement was a good thing, that they were not being compromised, that it should be continued. It should also come as no surprise that those who were least involved with the Ecumenical Movement, whether it be the fundamentalist Carl McIntire, or the Evangelical James DeForest Murch, or the Pentecostal Thomas F. Zimmerman, were also the least willing to trust its potential.

What is surprising is that the relationship between the Assemblies of God and the ecumenical impulse of the historic churches represented by the Foreign Missions Conference of North America, Church World Service, and the National and World Council of Churches could last so long without a greater level of commitment from the whole denomination. That comes, I suspect, from the fact that the Foreign Mission Department was encouraged to do what was best for Assemblies of God missions, but because it was not easily explained to the people of the Assemblies of God, they were not brought along. As a result, two strategies developed. For the Foreign Missions Department it was a strategy to aid its mission by cooperating with various ecumenical ventures, secretly. For the rest of the Assemblies of God it was a strategy to gain acceptance among those people with whom it found its greatest theological compatibility, Evangelicals, by entering publicly into their battles, battles in which Pentecostals had no real place.

It is a surprise, too, to realize that the Assemblies of God ultimately submitted itself to the agenda which Carl McIntire had set, a clear condemnation of the Ecumenical Movement and a commitment to separatism, even sectarianism; an agenda to which not even the National Association of Evangelicals had submitted. One can understand this, I suggest, only if one looks at the various players within the context in which they lived and recognizes that this submission was made in the belief that it was the right thing to do. It is always easier to be a 'Monday morning quarterback' and to try to discover the motivation behind the action than it is to participate in the event. But there are still clues in the text of history.

It is not only a surprise, but also a disappointment that those who were involved in the decisions to break with the long history of what had been repeatedly experienced as a positive relationship as portrayed by J.R. Flower, Donald Gee, David du Plessis, Robert T. McGlasson, Gustave Kinderman, Noel Perkin and others, could not or would not enter into the experience. Instead they led in decisions which cut off long-standing friendships in order to submit to an obvious enemy. And they called it good.

One can only wonder what might have happened had the Assemblies of God leadership openly acknowledged that major theological differences and emphases in ministry existed between it and other churches in the Foreign Missions Conference, but that its commitment to the unity of God's Church was so strong that it would cooperate with them where they could and where they could not they would openly work to show them a more excellent way. One can only wonder what might have happened had the Assemblies of God leadership openly challenged the sectarian attitude which sought to divide the Evangelical Movement and to condemn the Concilior Movement by doing so in love, thereby showing by its actions a more excellent way. One can only wonder how the modern Ecumenical Movement might now look had Assemblies of God leadership acted upon the pensive ponderings of J.R. Flower when he wondered whether Evangelicals should jump fully into the Movement and dominate it for Christ and the Gospel. One can only wonder how effective the missionary endeavor, not only of the Assemblies of God but of the whole Church, might look now had Assemblies of God leadership determined to cooperate, not only for its own social concern which saw vast sums of money expended on resettlement, food and clothing distribution, and government lobbying, but in the full work of evangelism and social concern to which the whole Church is called.

One can only wonder, because in the end, Assemblies of God leaders, for whatever reason, found it more expedient to break with old friendships, embrace the agenda of an old enemy, capitulate to questions of a new set of 'friends', and compromise what appears to be a basic Pentecostal distinctive with the enactment of a Bylaw which limits with whom Pentecostals can talk or work, than they did to act without guile. The earliest Pentecostals including the Assemblies of God believed that their way was the answer to Jesus' prayer in Jn 17.21.

But one can also hope that the foundation of ecumenical cooperation laid by General Superintendents from E.N. Bell to Ralph M. Riggs, by Missions executives from J. Roswell Flower to Noel Perkin, by staff members such as Kinderman, McGlasson, and Walegir, or ecumenists such as Gee and du Plessis will, in the end, prove to be substantial enough to bear the weight of a Fellowship now approaching a new millennium.

WHAT TO READ IN NEW TESTAMENT SPIRITUALITY
AND BEYOND: A BIBLIOGRAPHIC ESSAY

Russell P. Spittler

Amid the softly emerging color of Ozark foliage during the fall of 1958, my family and I arrived in Springfield, Missouri. We had come from the Boston area, where I completed seminary in the days before there was any such Pentecostal institution. Central Bible Institute—'CBI', as it was affectionately known—had expanded its faculty. To my delight, I became an office mate to William Menzies, known earlier by name to me through a Wheaton College classmate, Doris Dresselhaus, later to become Mrs. Menzies. As a boy growing up in Pittsburgh, Pennsylvania, everyday I drank milk brought by trucks from the Menzies Dairy—some relationship exists, I think. In those early days in Springfield, the Menzies boys were nextdoor neighbors and backyard playmates with the Spittler girls. My wife, Bobbie, and I salute our honored friends.

After four years of teaching at CBI (now Central Bible College), Bill Menzies and I (and Robert Cooley at the same time) went off in different directions for doctoral studies in the fall of 1962, but not before a firm and lasting friendship emerged. From the life and example of William Menzies I learned that intellect and character need not be alternatives. His life furnished a model of spirituality as it should and could be. For that reason, I am honored to contribute to this volume a bibliographic essay which links spirituality with New Testament studies.

1. *Introduction*

In this information age, bibliographies can be gotten wholesale—600 megabytes at a time on CD ROMs or through the mushrooming on-line library catalog services easily accessible through the Internet and the World Wide Web. This list tries to do some sorting for persons with dawning interests in the field of spirituality. So it has only a few of the thousands of published titles.

The aim in this article has been to identify useful reference works in the broad field of spirituality, to show where to start regarding selected New Testament themes, and to sample the breadth and depth of the whole field of spirituality. I try to delineate the more technical works that nuance the motifs of spirituality which characterize the New Testament.

But I omit standard reference works in the field of New Testament studies. In spirituality, something akin to what physical scientists call 'pure research' could occur through lexicographical mining in volumes like C. Brown's *New International Dictionary of New Testament Theology* (4 vols.; Grand Rapids: Zondervan, 1976–78) and C. Spicq's *Theological Lexicon of the New Testament* (3 vols.; Peabody, MA: Hendrickson, 1994). I include also practical titles easily accessible to interested non-specialists. The result confessedly presents a bibliographic coat of many colors.

The practice of spirituality is one thing, its study another. Books that deal with both approaches appear here. The term *spirituality* has lately become something of a marketing buzzword. I was asked once to write a chapter in a book presenting a variety of views on sanctification. Before the book was published, 'spirituality' was shoehorned into the title. That made some of the chapters look irrelevant to the title of the book.

Many works that could be cited as important feeders to current spirituality were called in past decades 'Christian classics', 'devotional classics', or something similar.

The question of how to define spirituality could be raised, too. In this article I assume a simple, common-sense definition of spirituality—whatever cultivates the spiritual life, in this case *reading*. More precise definitions can be found in the general entries under the term 'spirituality' in the encyclopedic works mentioned below (Wakefield 361-63; Downey 931-38, with cross-referenced articles). Teachers serving in higher education may specially like to consult B.C. Hanson's *Modern Christian Spirituality: Methodological and Historical Essays* (American Academy of Religion Studies in Religion, 62; Atlanta: Scholars Press, 1990) described in the section below on academic treatments.

1.1 *Approaches*
Certainly one fruitful avenue to classic spirituality takes the form of disciplined reading in the writings of Christian authors in the first five or six centuries. A clarion call to do just that comes from T.C. Oden in a

volume that I place in the top ten books any seminary student should read. There's enough autobiography in it to trace clearly Oden's pilgrimage from a rank liberalism to classical conservative Christianity. In *After Modernity, What? An Agenda for Modern Theology* (Grand Rapids: Zondervan, 1992), Oden, a professor of theology at Drew University in New Jersey, issues a rousing call to return to Christian sources, the texts penned by early Christian writers.

Such an enterprise becomes doable with the inexpensive availability of all 38 volumes of the Ante-Nicene Fathers (ANF) as well as the Nicene and Post-Nicene Fathers (NPNF) with two different series under this second title (ed. A. Roberts *et al.*; Grand Rapids: Eerdmans, 1980). Amazingly, the entire series can be had (at this writing) for less than eight dollars per volume. The latest republishers, Hendrickson in Peabody, MA, have added a useful topical index to boot, one that was not part of the original series published over a century ago. Users of the series will have to put up with sprawling and flowery Victorian English. But nowhere can so much of the heritage of heart and head of the Christian Church be gotten for so little.

Much more readable contemporary English appears in a series titled 'Ancient Christian Writers' (New York: Newman Press, 1946–92), which covers similar ground to the ANF/NPNF. Such contemporaneity accounts for the considerably higher costs of the volumes from Paulist Press (copyright for the ANF and NPNF series expired long ago).

The same publisher, Paulist Press, produces still another series of interest in the broad field of spirituality. The 'Sources of American Spirituality' series embraces, to date, nearly three dozen titles focusing either on persons like Charles Hodge, Phoebe Palmer and Elizabeth Seton, or on cultural subgroups like the Pennsylvania Dutch, or upon theological perspectives such as the volume edited by J.P. Chinnici, *Devotion to the Holy Spirit in American Catholicism* (Mahwah, NJ: Paulist Press, 1985).

Still another approach to spirituality could be to read the works of a particular contemporary author. The books below and their notes refer to many of these. Contemporary writers worth deep reading include Roberta Bondi, Richard Foster, Morton Kelsey, Richard Lovelace, Henri Nouwen, James I. Packer, Eugene Peterson, Agnes Sanford, Ron Sider, Philip Yancey, Adrian Van Kaam, Dallas Willard—many more could be named.

1.2 *The Fast Track*

Robert M. Meye, Dean Emeritus of Fuller Seminary's School of Theology, has been credited with inventing the field of New Testament spirituality. A good start can be made with use of his article 'Spirituality', in G.R. Hawthorne and R.P. Martin (eds.), *Dictionary of Paul and his Letters* (Downers Grove, IL: InterVarsity Press, 1993, pp. 906-916). For a single book to read on the subject, try, on the *practice* of spirituality, D. Willard, *The Spirit of the Disciplines* (San Francisco: HarperCollins, 1988).

On the *study* of spirituality—which can fruitfully lead into much reading—consult the work edited by C. Jones, G. Wainwright and E. Yarnold, *The Study of Spirituality* (New York: Oxford University Press, 1986). Chapters are written by experts, and coverage moves from the New Testament to the lives of the saints, movements (Celtic spirituality), subcultures (Black Worship), other religions (Hinduism), and an appealing section on 'Pastoral Spirituality' (Group Prayer, Retreat)— along with thoughtful analyses by the editors and others dealing with the varieties and theologies of spirituality. I consider this volume, available in paperback at less than twenty dollars, the single best book available for a comprehensive survey of the whole field. This is surely the one book to have on spirituality, whatever else is acquired. Its rich bibliographic suggestions at each chapter, often carefully classified, afford a wealth of guidance for deeper reading. It is hard to overrate this book of over 600 pages as a guide to the *study* of spirituality, something of course quite different from the *practice* of spirituality.

Two quite different books come from the same institution, Regent College in Vancouver. First, M. Green and R.P. Stevens, *New Testament Spirituality* (Guildford, Surrey: Eagle Imprint/Interpublishing Service, 1994). The range of topics is comprehensive, the style is devotional and homiletic, a book offering practical help and easily accessible to lay folk. A sturdier start in the field would be J.I. Packer and L. Wilkinson (eds.), *Alive to God: Studies in Spirituality Presented to James Houston* (Downers Grove, IL: InterVarsity Press, 1992). These thoughtful essays mildly reflect the Brethren heritage that lies behind the dedicatee and the institution he established, one that furnished many of the contributors. Apparent here are features long known to mark that noble group of Christians—unrelenting piety, faithful Bible study, and in the case of the Regent cluster, gallant engagement with intellectual culture.

2. *Study Aids*

2.1 *Reference Works*

Several major dictionaries exist in the field of spirituality. G.S. Wakefield (ed.), *The Westminster Dictionary of Spirituality* (Louisville, KY: Westminster/John Knox, 1983) provides one example, fairly recent and comprehensive; something of a standard. M. Downey (ed.), *The New Dictionary of Catholic Spirituality* (Collegeville, MN: Liturgical Press, 1990) takes stock of post-Vatican II developments.

The mother of all dictionaries speaks French and is over sixty years old: M. Viller, *Dictionnaire de spiritualité ascétique et mystique, doctrine et histoire* (17 vols.; Paris: G. Beauchesne et ses fils, 1932–). The age of the set confirms that among Roman Catholics the field of spirituality is no new invention. From this work has been translated and published separately J. Guillet *et al.*, *Discernment of Spirits* (Collegeville, MN: Liturgical Press, 1970). French Roman Catholics have a tradition of high interest in spirituality.

A brief history of the whole field of spirituality in less than 150 pages appears in B.P. Holt, *Thirsty for God: A Brief History of Christian Spirituality* (Minneapolis: Augsburg, 1993). This slender work includes as well some spiritual exercises that could be undertaken to imitate some of the forms spirituality has taken throughout the history of the Church. For example, the author suggests an intentional exercise of the practice of *lectio divina*, reading aloud slowly and reflectively.

2.2 *Comprehensive Studies*

R.J. Foster and J.B. Smith have produced a single volume containing a very useful selection of the *Devotional Classics: Selected Readings for Individuals and Groups* (San Francisco: HarperSanFrancisco, 1993). Not only does this convenient paperback offer a sample of such texts over the centuries. It reflects as well an instructive taxonomy of spiritualities that identifies five principal strands of spirituality within the Christian movement: the contemplative ('the prayer-filled life'); holiness ('the virtuous life'); charismatic ('the Spirit-filled life'); social justice ('the compassionate life'); and evangelical ('the word-centered life').

One useful volume that may seem a bit out of place is the first of a series titled 'A History of Private Life' (Philippe Aries and Georges Duby edit the series): P. Veyne (ed.), *From Pagan Rome to Byzantium* (Cambridge, MA: Harvard University Press, 1987). By tracing the intimate social lives of ordinary persons through (and beyond) the New Testament period, this book provides ample background to understand the private social world within which early Christian spirituality developed.

Two quite early works reflect particular points of view. P. Pourrat produced four volumes, divided historically, with the overall title *Christian Spirituality* (4 vols.; Westminster, MD: Newman Press, 1953–55). This work, which bears the official *nihil obstat* and *imprimatur,* represents a decidedly early twentieth-century Roman Catholic outlook. In conception, the work is not unlike that of Louis Bouyer mentioned below (this page).

A quite different perspective appears in D.W. Riddle, *Early Christian Life* (Chicago: Willett, Clark & Co., 1936). Reflecting the outlook of the sociologically oriented 'Chicago School' of the 1930s, the author abandons any canonical criterion and uses all early Christian literature to track early Christian life.

There is a classic series now out of print that may be found in some bookstores: L. Bouyer, J. Leclercq and F. Vandenbroucke, *A History of Christian Spirituality* (New York: Seabury, 1986). The three volumes bear separate titles: L. Bouyer, *The Spirituality of the New Testament and the Fathers* (I); J. Leclercq, F. Vandenbroucke and L. Bouyer, *The Spirituality of the Middle Ages* (II); and L Bouyer, *Orthodox Spirituality and Anglican Spirituality* (III). Bouyer believes that, on principle, one should not treat as history what is going on in the present time, so this series has little to say of the twentieth century. Louis Bouyer also produced an *Introduction to Spirituality* (Collegeville, MN: Liturgical Press, 1961). The work is suggestive, though it is decidedly pre-Vatican II Roman Catholic.

A 25 volume series bears the title 'World Spirituality: An Encyclopedic History of the Religious Quest'. Three volumes in the series deal with Christianity. The most relevant for biblical spirituality is the first (vol. 16 in the series), B. McGinn and J. Meyendorff (eds.), *Christian Spirituality: Origins to the Twelfth Century* (New York: Crossroad, 1989). The other two volumes are: J. Raitt and B. McGinn (eds.), *Christian Spirituality: High Middle Ages and Reformation* (New York, Crossroad, 1989), XVII; and L. Dupré and D.E. Saliers, *Christian Spirituality: Post-Reformation and Modern* (New York, Crossroad, 1989), XVIII.

Another attractive volume in the series is XV, A.H. Armstrong (ed.),

Classical Mediterranean Spirituality: Egyptian, Greek, Roman (New York: Crossroad, 1986)—useful for its depiction of spiritual quests among the neighbors of Jews and Christians.

Still another major contemporary series bears the title 'The Classics of Western Spirituality: A Library of the Great Spiritual Masters'. With more than 80 volumes in print by 1995, the writers represented vary widely from Julian of Norwich to Meister Eckhart to Jeremy Taylor. Some volumes are thematic: Quaker Spirituality, Safed Spirituality, Anchorite Spirituality, Apocalyptic Spirituality. Paulist Press puts out this series.

The most comprehensive systematic spirituality comes in the five-volume series by A. Van Kaam, *The Science of Formative Spirituality* (Pittsburgh: Epiphany Association, 1145 Beechwood Boulevard, Pittsburgh, PA 15206–4517). This highly technical work should be approached through less opaque writings of the same author, with my vote going to *Spirituality and Gentleness* (Pittsburgh: Epiphany Association, 1994).

Several volumes in a major series titled 'Studies in Early Christianity', edited by E. Ferguson, D.M. Scholer and P.C. Finney, treat topics in spirituality. These volumes conveniently reprint significant articles on the subject theme. For example, E. Ferguson (ed.), *Acts of Piety in the Early Church* (New York: Garland, 1993), XVII. Or in the same series, E. Ferguson (ed.), *Christian Life: Ethics, Morality, and Discipline in the Early Church* (New York: Garland, 1993), XVI.

We are now at the stage where comprehensive practical handbooks are emerging, with practicing clergy in mind. Two examples: R.W. Wicks (ed.), *Handbook of Spirituality for Ministers* (Mahwah, NJ: Paulist Press, 1995). M.A. Kimble *et al.* (eds.), *Aging, Spirituality and Religion: A Handbook* (Minneapolis: Fortress Press, 1995).

2.3 *Commentary Series*

Roman Catholics, it seems, never lost the category of spirituality. Among mainstream Protestants, until recently, the rise and hegemony of scientific biblical criticism often displaced any personal religious implications of scholarship as irrelevant at best, injurious at least. There are three (maybe two and a half) commentary series with express interests in extracting spiritual values—all from Roman Catholic sources.

Students anticipating a pastoral or teaching ministry, even a counseling career, may well like to consider acquisition of such works and series as these, alongside the more usually suggested technical exegetical commentaries listed in such works as D.A. Carson, *New Testament Commentary Survey* (Grand Rapids: Baker, 4th edn, 1993).

One recent series that covers the entire Bible in 15 volumes is titled the 'Message of Biblical Spirituality'. The series is edited by Carolyn Osiek. The volume on the second Gospel was written by K.A. Barta, *The Gospel of Mark* (Wilmington, DE: Michael Glazier, 1988), IX. (Michael Glazier titles are now distributed by the Liturgical Press, Collegeville, MN). This volume exemplifies the mix of informed exegesis and spiritual sensitivity which marks the series.

A series titled *Geistliche Schriftlesung*, edited by Wolfgang Trilling and others, came into English about a generation ago from German Roman Catholic sources. The series bears the title 'New Testament for Spiritual Reading' (NTSR) and is edited by John L. McKenzie, a Jesuit biblical scholar.

Here are a few samples of the 25 individual volumes of the NTSR: R. Schnackenburg, *The Gospel according to Mark* (2 vols.) (NTSR, 3; New York: Herder & Herder, 1971), I; and (NTSR, 4; London: Sheed & Ward, 1970), II. M. Zerwick, *The Epistle to the Ephesians* (NTSR, 16; New York: Herder & Herder, 1969), the same author who gave to grateful Greek students *A Grammatical Analysis of the Greek New Testament* (Rome: Biblical Institute Press, 1981)—a blended parsing guide, vocabulary list and light commentary. Zerwick on Ephesians has to be one of the best of the series. More: E. Walter, *The First Epistle to the Corinthians* (NTSR, 13; New York: Herder & Herder, 1971); and, combined in a single volume, F.J. Schierse, *The Epistle to the Hebrews* and O. Knoch, *The Epistle of St James* (NTSR, 21; London: Burns & Oates, 1969).

Another series of commentaries, perhaps half a series (limited to the Gospels and written by one person), is now handled by a publisher[1] other than the original one: L. Doohan, *Luke: The Perennial Spirituality* (Santa Fe: Bear & Co., 1985). Also, *idem, Matthew: Spirituality for the 80s and 90s* (Santa Fe: Bear & Co., 1985); *Mark: Visionary of Early Christianity* (Santa Fe: Bear & Co., 1986); *John: Gospel for a New Age* (Santa Fe: Bear & Co., 1988). Here, a reader suspects marketing use of the term spirituality.

---

1.   Resource Publications, 160 East Virginia Street #290, San Jose, CA 95112-5876.

2.4 *Journals*

Periodicals in the field of spirituality vary enormously, specially if the list were to include primarily devotional journals reflecting the interests of particular traditions. An example, one helpful beyond the borders of its origin, is *The Plough* (Spring Valley Bruderhof, Farmington, PA 15437–9506)—published by the Hutterian Brethren. A journal for spirituality of wide interest is *Weavings: A Journal of the Christian Spiritual Life* (PO Box 11672, Des Moines, IA 50347–1672).

More focused, specialized journals include *Studies in Spirituality,* published yearly in one volume, with an intent to 'promote spirituality as a science'. Articles may appear in English, German, French, Spanish. *Creation Spirituality Magazine* (815 44th Street, Oakland, CA 94608), edited by Matthew Fox, will delight or distress with its New Age inclinations. *Syzygy: Journal of Alternative Religion and Culture* offers a scholarly journal for those interested in new religious movements, such as New Age, new thought, neo-paganism, astrology, UFO groups and the like. Articles occur in English or French. *Spirituality Today* ceased publication in 1992, but past issues of this journal may be of interest. It is described as a 'thoughtful but not academic exploration of contemporary spirituality'.

Duquesne University in Pittsburgh operates an Institute for Formative Spirituality, mentioned again below. From here comes *Studies in Formative Spirituality* three times a year, reflecting more technical, discipline related studies. On a less formal level, from the same source, *Envoy* bears 'reflective reading bringing the word of God into everyday life', according to bibliographic reference descriptions.

The entire issue of *Concilium* 9 (1965) gathers round the theme 'Spirituality in Church and World'. This periodical also reflects Roman Catholic sponsorship.

2.5 *Newsletters*

In the evangelical Protestant tradition, perhaps the first newsletter to mention would be *Renovaré* (8 Inverness Drive East, Suite 102, Englewood, CO 80112–5609). Richard Foster, who edits the letter, ranks as a pioneer in revitalizing and popularizing spirituality with his books, *Celebration of Discipline*: *The Path to Spiritual Growth* (San Francisco: Harper & Row, 1978), and *Money, Sex, and Power* (San Francisco: Harper & Row, 1985).

The Pecos Benedictine, newsletter of the Benedictine Abbey (Pecos,

NM 87552), comes from a Roman Catholic monastery expressly established as a charismatic monastery. It operates a School for Charismatic
Spiritual Directors. Morton Kelsey is a frequent speaker at this place.
The former abbot of Pecos Monastery, David Geraets, relocated a few
years ago to San Luis Obispo on the central California coast—where
another charismatic monastery has been established and another
newsletter produced—*Resurrection Life* (Monastery of the Risen Christ,
Box 3931, San Luis Obispo, CA 93403–3931). Both monasteries
intentionally blend Benedictine and charismatic spirituality with depth
psychology. Schools for spiritual direction are held occasionally.

2.6 Academic Treatments of Spirituality
It is easily imaginable that, in today's climate, any consideration of
spirituality in the academy would be laughed out of court. Not so. For
four years, 1984–88, the prestigious American Academy of Religion
convened a Seminar on Modern Christian Spirituality at its annual meetings. One outcome appears in Hanson, *Modern Christian Spirituality*
(see above, p. 152). Perspectives broadly diversify here, but the material
struggling with how to define and how to study spirituality make it a
volume not to be missed by higher-level teachers of the subject.

Two doctoral theses will interest readers of the Menzies Festschrift.
Using anthropological ritual theory, D.E. Albrecht in 1993 collected a
PhD from the Graduate Theological Union, Berkeley, California, with a
dissertation entitled, 'Pentecostal/Charismatic Spirituality: Looking
through the Lens of Ritual'.

An Emory University PhD thesis lies behind S.J. Land, *Pentecostal
Spirituality: A Passion for the Kingdom* (JPTSup, 1; Sheffield, UK:
Sheffield Academic Press, 1993). This is the first major study of
Pentecostal spirituality, as well as the premier volume in the *Journal of
Pentecostal Theology* Supplement Series. Land's volume can be read
profitably along with a review of it by Harvey Cox, Harvard theologian,
followed by Land's response. Both appear in the *Journal of Pentecostal
Theology* 5 (1994), pp. 3-16.

The work of Albrecht and Land represent assessments of *Pentecostal*
spirituality, which has a certain appropriateness for this volume—just as
the James Houston Festschrift reflects the piety of the Brethren. The
spirituality of other traditions has been studied, of course. A list of them,
which lies beyond the boundaries of this article, suggests a sub-discipline
that might be termed *comparative spirituality*.

2.7 *Graduate Programs*

Speaking of doctoral studies, this may be the place to mention the handful of institutions where spirituality can be studied on a Master's or Doctoral level.

The Graduate Theological Union, Berkeley (GTU)—blends the resources of a cluster of Protestant, Catholic and Orthodox schools and institutes with the academic riches of the University of California at Berkeley. The PhD in Spirituality can be done there, as well as at several eastern Roman Catholic schools: Catholic University in Washington, DC; Fordham in New York; and Duquesne in Pittsburgh. At Saint Paul University in Ottawa, the PhD in Spirituality requires students to use both French and English. Seattle University and Creighton University in Omaha offer programs at the Master's level. It is always wise to check the current status of any such programs, academic tides do ebb and flow.

3. *Selected Topics*

3.1 *Biblical and Early Christian Spirituality*

A variety of books, many recent, explore themes of spirituality in sectors of the New Testament and the early Church. Here is a starter list that moves through sectors of the New Testament, into the early Church, and then to reflections of biblical scholars on spirituality.

G.A. Raymond, *Communion with God in the New Testament* (London: Epworth Press, 1953) might be styled as the closest thing to a systematic New Testament spirituality. This is a very substantial work that engages prior scholarship. It follows an arrangement much like that of standard biblical theologies, treating in order the Synoptics, the Johannine literature, the Paulines, and so on. A fairly technical work that will repay serious engagement.

S.C. Barton, *The Spirituality of the Gospels* (London: SPCK, 1992) makes positive use of redaction history to conclude distinctive emphases on spirituality by each of the evangelists.

M.H. Crosby, *Spirituality of the Beatitudes: Matthew's Challenge for First-World Christians* (Maryknoll: Orbis Books, 1981) evinces liberationist perspectives in matching Matthew's portrait of Jesus with issues of social justice in the first and the twentieth centuries. The same author penned *House of Disciples: Church, Economics, and Justice in Matthew* (Maryknoll: Orbis Books, 1988).

A ranking Pentecostal scholar of the New Testament, J.C. Thomas, published his Sheffield dissertation as *Footwashing in John 13 and the Johannine Community* (JSNTSup, 61; Sheffield: JSOT Press, 1991). Very few treatments of any sort exist on this significant aspect of spirituality.

B. Thurston, *Spiritual Life in the Early Church: The Witness of Acts and Ephesians* (Minneapolis: Augsburg–Fortress, 1993) asks first what spirituality is, answering that its emphasis on unseen realities contradicts the modern age. The author then takes specific motifs in Acts and Ephesians to unfold the spiritual life of the early Church. These motifs include prayer, breaking of bread, and an interesting study of 'the Name' in Acts 1–10.

J. Murphy-O'Connor, *Becoming Human Together: The Pastoral Anthropology of St Paul* (Wilmington, DE: Michael Glazier, 1982). This book blends critical biblical scholarship with spirituality. It maintains that the perfect humanity of Christ, which does not diminish his deity, makes thinkable the acquisition of authentic humanity within the sphere of Christian community.

R.C. Bondi, *To Love as God Loves: Conversations with the Early Church* (Philadelphia: Fortress Press, 1987); *idem, To Pray and To Love: Conversations on Prayer with the Early Church* (Minneapolis: Fortress Press, 1991). A specialist on early Church writers reflects on simple but profound spiritual themes found in their writings.

L.T. Johnson, *Faith's Freedom: A Classic Spirituality for Contemporary Christians* (Minneapolis: Fortress Press, 1990). Reflections of a prominent New Testament scholar concerned to integrate his professional biblical scholarship with personal faith. The result is a thoughtful testament of personal spirituality from the hands of a scholar and a New Testament professor. From a quite different quarter, similar things could be said of F.F. Bruce's autobiography, *In Retrospect: Remembrance of Things Past* (posthumous edition; Grand Rapids: Eerdmans, 1993). Teachers of the New Testament might consider a successive reading of these volumes as, as it were, professionally flavored personal devotions.

W. Pannenberg, *Christian Spirituality* (Philadelphia: Westminster Press, 1983). densely packed essays on guilt consciousness, eucharistic piety, sanctification and politics, authenticity. Another marketing use of the term 'spirituality'?

3.2 *Spiritual Gifts*

One place to begin is J. Koenig, *Charismata: God's Gifts for God's People* (Philadelphia: Westminster Press, 1978), a mainstream approach. A classic among Pentecostals is D. Gee, *Concerning Spiritual Gifts* (Springfield, MO: Gospel Publishing House, 1980).

Among the gifts listed in 1 Corinthians, glossolalia has surely been the most studied in this century. Despite its density, one book cannot be omitted in any technical approach to the subject: H. Newton Malony and A. Adams Lovekin, *Glossolalia: Behavioral Science Perspectives on Speaking in Tongues* (New York: Oxford University Press, 1985). It is a Baedecker's guide to a century of social science research. W.E. Mills indexes 1150 more titles in *Glossolalia: A Bibliography* (Lewiston, NY: Edwin Mellen, 1985).

As for the other gifts, prophecy and healing have received the most attention, both in technical and in popular works. Titles on healing appear below. Backgrounds to prophecy in the Mediterranean cultures are traced by D. Aune, *Prophecy in Early Christianity and the Ancient Mediterranean World* (Grand Rapids: Eerdmans, 1983), and foregrounds by C.M. Robeck, Jr, *Prophecy in Carthage: Perpetua, Tertullian, and Cyprian* (Cleveland: Pilgrim Press, 1992). More technical background appears in D. Hill's monograph, *New Testament Prophecy* (London: Marshall, Morgan & Scott). Two additional works concern themselves with relating biblical prophecy to contemporary prophecy in the charismatic movement: W.A. Grudem, *The Gift of Prophecy in the New Testament and Today* (Westchester, IL: Crossway Books, 1988) and C. Hill, *Prophecy Past and Present* (Crowborough, East Sussex: Highland Books, 1989).

3.3 *Sexuality*

A generation ago, P. Sorokin predicted *The Sexualization of American Culture* (Gloucester, MA: Peter, 1956). He could not have been more correct. The arrival of what P. Gardella called *Innocent Ecstasy: How Christianity Gave America The Ethic of Sexual Pleasure* (New York: Oxford University Press, 1985) certified Sorokin's prediction even before the scandals of the televangelists in 1987–89. Gardella's point, a debatable one, is that Christianity, from Catholic sensuality to evangelical ecstatic rebirth, paved the way for the modern sexual revolution in North America.

Given that the religious and the sexual impulses rank among the highest of human experiences, where is the sane volume that describes, in sensitive Christian terms, the spirituality of sexuality?

3.4 *Fasting, Gluttony*

Nearly all a serious student needs to know about fasting can be gotten from J.F. Wimmer's book, *Fasting in the New Testament* (New York: Paulist Press, 1982). This slender work of around 125 pages starts with hermeneutics, ends with 'Fasting Today', but in between it reviews the practice as mentioned in the Old Testament, in the Hellenistic world, and in intertestamental literature. Then it treats the major New Testament texts, with careful attention to the triple-layered character of the Gospels (redaction, tradition, history). The chief New Testament references to fasting, it turns out, are almost all found in the Gospels. The ascetically motivated textual additions of 'and fasting' here and there come in for consideration, too. And there is no fasting while the bridegroom is here (Mk 2.18-22). The useful bibliography (pp. 125-30) ranges from Rudolf Bultmann to Derek Prince and includes much in French and German (with one or two titles in Italian and Spanish). In many ways, this is a model monograph.

S.C. Juengst, *Breaking Bread: The Spiritual Significance of Food* (Louisville, KY: Westminster/John Knox, 1992), offers some thoughtful devotional reflections on aspects of eating like bonding, celebration and hospitality. They arise from participation in the culture of Zaire, where she and her husband served a decade as missionaries. Of quite different stock is the book by E.N. Rogers, *Fasting: The Phenomenon of Self-Denial* (Nashville: Thomas Nelson, 1976) before that press was acquired by a charismatic publisher. Rogers's work is a sort of secular survey of the range of reasons why people do not eat—religious, political and health-related.

A. Wallis, *God's Chosen Fast: A Spiritual and Practical Guide to Fasting* (repr.; Fort Washington, PA: Christian Literature Crusade, 1987 [1968]), constitutes a simple, practical guide to fasting and prayer.

One interesting sociological study showed that the contemporary practice of fasting occurs predominantly among Pentecostals *and* for the purpose of securing spiritual power. J.B. Tamney, 'Fasting and Dieting: A Research Note', *Review of Religious Research* 27 (March, 1986), pp. 255-62.

3.5 *Prayer, Exorcism, Spiritual Warfare*
The technical details in the New Testament text can be gotten through two works: J.H. Charlesworth, *The Lord's Prayer and Other Prayer Texts from the Greco-Roman Era* (Valley Forge, PA: Trinity, 1993), and J. Jeremias, *The Lord's Prayer* (Philadelphia: Fortress Press, 1964). Background on demonology can be found in E. Ferguson's book, *Demonology of the Early Christian World* (Symposium Series, 12; Lewiston, NY: Edwin Mellen, 1984). For a more modern, sociological assessment, see F.D. Goodman, *How about Demons? Possession and Exorcism in the Modern World* (Bloomington: Indiana University Press, 1988). The lofty role of religious magic centered in southwestern Asia Minor can be learned in C.E. Arnold, *Ephesians: Power and Magic, The Concept of Power in Ephesians in Light of its Historical Setting* (Grand Rapids: Baker, 1992).

While the Western world bifurcates reality into spheres of science and religion, third-world cultures take for granted an in-between realm of this-worldly but supernatural beings (ancestors, animal spirits, ghosts, and the like). This modern Western myopia P.G. Hiebert calls 'The Flaw of the Excluded Middle', *Missiology: An International Review* 10 (January, 1982), pp. 35-47. Fuller Seminary missiologist C.P. Wagner does seminars on the subject of spiritual warfare, using his books such as *Warfare Prayer: How to Seek God's Power and Protection in the Battle to Build his Kingdom* (Ventura, CA: Regal Books, 1992); *idem, Breaking Strongholds in your City: How to Use Spiritual Mapping to Make your Prayers More Strategic, Effective, and Targeted* (Ventura, CA: Regal Books, 1993); *idem, Prayer Shield: How to Intercede for Pastors, Christian Leaders, and Others on the Spiritual Front Lines* (Ventura, CA: Regal Books, 1992). Useful too are T.B. White, *The Believer's Guide to Spiritual Warfare: Wising Up to Satan's Influence in your World* (Ann Arbor: Servant Books, 1990) and *Breaking Strongholds: How Spiritual Warfare Can Reap a Harvest of Evangelism* (Ann Arbor: Servant Books, 1993).

Catherine Marshall founded Breakthrough—an intercession ministry. A 32-page publication, *The Breakthrough Intercessor* (The Catherine Center, PO Box 121, Lincoln, VA 22078), appears bi-monthly. The September–October 1993 issue has a spiritual warfare theme.

Those with psychological interests may find particularly interesting C.P Michael and M.C. Norrisey, *Prayer and Temperament: Different Prayer Forms for Different Personality Types* (The Open Door, PO

Box 855, Charlottesville, VA 22902, 1984). The book draws on the Myers–Briggs personality assessment instruments.

E. Peterson, *Answering God: The Psalms as Tools for Prayer* (New York: Harper & Row, 1989), is also worth a mention.

3.6 *Pastoral Care*

The larger context can be gotten in W. Clebsch and C. Jaekle, *Pastoral Care in Historical Perspective* (Englewood Cliffs, NJ: Prentice–Hall, 1964). Not merely a history, this work uses texts as illustrations of the ministry of pastors. N.S.T. Thayer's book *Spirituality and Pastoral Care* (Philadelphia: Fortress Press, 1985) comes as part of a series titled 'Theology and Pastoral Care'. By the author's own admission, the book is written primarily for those whose idea of persons has been formed by Freud, Erikson, Jung and Rogers—for the psychologically trained, in other words. That orientation may account for his taxonomy of prayer as centering, verbal and imagistic (pp. 81-22).

K. Leech has a book with the same title, *Spirituality and Pastoral Care* (Cowley Publications, 1989). A work with an Anglican flavor, the book offers timely counsel on topics like spirituality as struggle. The same author wrote *Soul Friend: The Practice of Christian Spirituality* (San Francisco: Harper & Row, 1977). This volume mostly concerns the practice of spiritual direction—use of a designated counselor, called a spiritual director, in intentional spiritual growth, a practice much more formally developed among Roman Catholics than within Protestantism.

3.7 *Poverty and Riches*

Two very readable, though technical, works by German theologians cover the topic, respectively, in Jesus and Paul. W. Stegemann's thin little work (72 pages) gives valuable information beyond its size: *The Gospel and the Poor: A Theology of Poverty* (Nashville: Abingdon Press, 1982). This author clarifies the economic situation in the Mediterranean world, showing that the early Christians were, as a whole, from the poor classes—but not from the destitute, with whom they were regularly challenged to form solidarity. The translator of the work added certain English titles, making the book of use to North Americans.

M. Hengel's book, *Property and Riches in the Early Church: Aspects of a Social History of Early Christianity* (London: SCM Press, 1974) extends, in less than a hundred pages, beyond the New Testament and focuses on property and attitudes toward it. D. Georgi, *Remembering the Poor: The History of Paul's Collection for Jerusalem* (Nashville: Abingdon Press, 1992) focuses on 2 Corinthians 8–9—which might be titled the most relevant chapters in scripture related to giving. Georgi's work represents decades of reflection on the subject, informed by his own experience in university administration at Frankfurt—nick named 'Bankfurt', the financial center of Germany, he observes. Both Stegemann and Georgi draw responsible conclusions for Christian spirituality today.

Any serious look at the New Testament's treatment of poverty and riches must sooner or later get to Luke–Acts. One can start (or end?) with D.P. Seccombe, *Possessions and the Poor in Luke–Acts* (SNTU, B.6; Linz [Austria]: A. Fuchs, 1982). This Cambridge doctoral dissertation includes a lengthy bibliography to the publication period.

A careful assessment of the economic views of early Christians, through Augustine, drew the attention of Justo Gonzales, a historian of Christian doctrine: *Faith and Wealth: A History of Early Christian Ideas on the Origin, Significance, and Use of Money* (San Francisco: Harper & Row, 1990).

3.8 *Money*

Baker Book House (1955) reprinted a massive A-to-Z tome (two volumes in one) by H. Landsell. *The Sacred Tenth: Or Studies in Tithe-Giving Among Ancient and Modern* (Grand Rapids: Baker, 1955) actually starts with the Egyptians and Babylonians and includes a chapter on 'Tithing in the Apocrypha'. Originally published in 1905, the work gives a massive history and conventional apologetic. The essential New Testament data are covered succinctly in three dozen pages in L. Vischer, *Tithing in the Early Church* (Facet Books, Historical Series, 3; Philadelphia: Fortress Press, 1966). In a small book of just over a hundred pages O. Piper sketches thoughtfully *The Christian Meaning of Money* (Englewood Cliffs, NJ: Prentice–Hall, 1965). Similarly useful is J.R. Crawford, *A Christian and His Money* (Nashville: Abingdon Press, 1967). Biblical backgrounds are traced by B.W. Frier, 'Interest and Usury in the Greco-Roman Period', in D.N. Freedman (ed.), *Anchor Bible Dictionary* (6 vols.; Garden City, NY: Doubleday, 1992), III, pp. 423-24.

But the first book to reach for today on the subject of money may well be J. Ellul, *Money and Power* (Downers Grove, IL: InterVarsity Press, 1984). Thoughtful, high caliber reflections derive from a French professor of the history and sociology of institutions. Necessary ground-work to any thoughtful reflection on money.

Risking titles that may seem out of place, I will report that I have found much practical help on money matters in two books repeatedly revised over the past three decades. These are *How To Avoid Financial Tangles*, no author listed in the January 1995 edition, and *How To Invest Wisely*, the February 1994 edition edited by L.S. Pratt. Both titles are put out by the American Institute for Economic Research, Great Barrington, Massachusetts 01230, a non-profit organization which offers other useful publications for management of personal finance.

3.9 *Lord's Day Observance*

The article on 'Sabbath', in J.B. Green *et al.* (eds.), *Dictionary of Jesus and the Gospels* (Downers Grove, IL: InterVarsity Press, 1992, pp. 716-19) makes a good starting point and contains a short list of the impor-tant work related to the topic in the Gospels. An article by Samuele Bacchiocchi, an Adventist scholar whose doctoral studies focused on early Christian sabbath practices, gives a good overview: 'How It Came About: From Saturday to Sunday', *BAR* 4 (1978), pp. 32-40.

In the early 1970s, a British biblical research group, Tyndale Fellow-ship, sponsored a thematic project dealing with *Sunday*. One outcome was a thorough collection of essays on the subject edited by D.A. Carson, *From Sabbath to Lord's Day: A Biblical, Historical, and Theological Investigation* (Grand Rapids: Zondervan, 1982). The introduction to this work (pp. 13-19) summarizes the important research in the last generation. Finally, P.K. Jewett admitted, in *The Lord's Day: A Theological Guide to the Christian Day of Worship* (Grand Rapids: Eerdmans, 1971), that the *exegetical* case for the shift from the seventh to the first day is not as strong as an argument drawn from early Christian *practice*.

There are at least two organizations devoted to strengthening the practice of the Lord's Day: the Lord's Day Observance Society (9 Kingsburgh Road, Edinburgh EH12 6DZ) in the United Kingdom and the Lord's Day Alliance of the US (The Baptist Center, 2930 Flowers Road, Suite 107, Atlanta, GA 30341).

In M. Dawn, *Keeping the Sabbath Wholly* (Grand Rapids: Eerdmans, 1989), the author takes no side in the Saturday/Sunday debate. Under the rubrics Ceasing, Resting, Embracing, Feasting, she goes for the essence of the Sabbath. A good place to start on the topic—or end.

3.10 *Friendship and Hospitality*

Volume XV of the Boston University Studies in Philosophy and Religion, edited by Leroy S. Rouner, gathers the results of a consultation on *The Changing Face of Friendship* (Notre Dame: University of Notre Dame Press, 1994). The published results provide a sort of philosophical infrastructure for the topic. K. Leech, S*oul Friend: The Practice of Christian Spirituality* (see p. 168), links friendship with its institutionalization. Tad Dunne offers some help as well, in *Spiritual Mentoring: Guiding People through Spiritual Exercises to Life's Decisions* (San Francisco: Harper-SanFrancisco, 1991).

J. Koenig, *New Testament Hospitality: Partnership with Strangers as Promise and Mission* (Philadelphia: Fortress Press, 1985), can be mentioned here as one of the few treatments of this neglected theme in spirituality.

3.11 *Martyrdom*

A useful way to begin is to read the *Letter of Ignatius to the Romans* and the *Martyrdom of Polycarp*—both found in the usual collections of the Apostolic Fathers. Historical studies include W. Horbury and B. McNeil (eds.), *Suffering and Martyrdom in the New Testament* (Cambridge: Cambridge University Press, 1981) as well as W.M.C. Frend, *Martyrdom and Persecution in the Early Church: A Study of a Conflict from the Maccabees to Donatus* (repr.; Grand Rapids: Baker, 1981 [1965]).

Martyrdom is no bygone phenomenon: recent annual total deaths have ranged from 150,000 to 250,000—according to church statistician D.B. Barrett. Since 1985, in the January issue of the *International Bulletin for Missionary Research*, he has provided statistical updates based on his magisterial *World Christian Encyclopedia* (New York: Oxford University Press, 1982; a new edition is in preparation).

3.12 *Healing*

A general historical review of the healing ministry in the Christian Church appears in M.T. Kelsey, *Psychology, Medicine, and Christian Healing: A Revised and Expanded Edition of Healing and Christianity* (San Francisco: Harper & Row, 1988). An Episcopalian priest, Kelsey represents—along with Agnes Sanford and her son John A. Sanford— what might be termed a Jungian charismatic school. The pristine work here was A. Sanford, *The Healing Light* (St Paul, MN: Macalester Park

Publishing Co., 1947). Besides the many writings of Morton Kelsey, one can see J.A. Sanford, *Healing and Wholeness* (New York: Paulist Press, 1977); *idem, Healing Body and Soul: The Meaning of Illness in the New Testament and in Psychotherapy* (Louisville, KY: Westminster/John Knox, 1992).

For a description of the ministry of healing that mingles theory and practice, the two books by Francis McNutt can be consulted: *Healing* (Notre Dame: Ave Maria Press, 1974) and *The Power to Heal* (Notre Dame: Ave Maria Press, 1977). Another practical presentation comes in C.P. Wagner, *How to Have a Healing Ministry without Making your Church Sick* (Ventura, CA: Regal Books, 1988).

Remarkable results of a study of the effect of prayer on heart patients, showing clearly measurable superior medical outcomes for those for whom prayer was offered, are summarized in an article in a medical journal: R.C. Byrd, 'Positive Therapeutic Effects of Intercessory Prayer in a Coronary Unit Population', *Southern Medical Journal* 81 (July, 1988), pp. 826-29.

Psychological healing falls outside the boundaries of this essay, as I see it. But it is useful here to name J.W. Ciarrocchi's book, *The Doubting Disease: Help for Scrupulosity and Religious Compulsions* (Mahwah, NJ: Paulist Press, 1995). Scrupulosity, the habit of finding sin where there is none, rates surely as one of the least noticed pathologies of spirituality. By their high and long interest in moral theology, however, the Romans have long known the problem. There is even an article on 'scrupulosity' in the *New Catholic Encyclopedia* (New York: McGraw–Hill, 1967), XII, pp. 1253-55.

3.13 *Jungian Spirituality*

Especially among Episcopalians and, to a lesser degree, Roman Catholics there exists what may be termed a Jungian school of spirituality. Jung argued the existence of a collective unconsciousness—a sort of universal residual human memory across all cultures. Agnes Sanford's writings may have been the initial popularization of this approach, while Morton Kelsey's books probe many of its implications.

R.J. Moore (ed.), *Carl Jung and Christian Spirituality* (Mahwah, NJ: Paulist Press, 1988), gathers a collection of articles on the approach over the years. This work seems to anchor a Paulist Press series titled, 'The Jung and Spirituality Series'. Among the titles: J.A. Hall, *The Unconscious Christian: Images of God in Dreams* (New York: Paulist

Press, 1993)—Jung's sustained interest in dreams gives his work a ready 'scientific' connection point with spirituality; S.A. Galipeau, *Transforming Body and Soul: Therapeutic Wisdom in the Gospel Healing Stories* (New York: Paulist Press, 1990); R.L. Moore and D.J. Meckel (eds.), *Jung and Christianity in Dialogue: Faith, Feminism, and Hermeneutics* (New York: Paulist Press, 1990); J.L. Hitchcock, *The Web of the Universe: Jung, the 'New Physics', and Human Spirituality* (New York: Paulist Press, 1991); and D.J. Meckel and R.L. Moore (eds.), *Self and Liberation: The Jung–Buddhism Dialogue* (New York: Paulist Press, 1992). Despite the title, here also belongs M.L. Santa-Maria, *Growth through Meditation and Journal Writing* (New York: Paulist Press, 1983).

4. *Miscellany*

The expanding popularity of spirituality has led to unbelievably broad applications of the theme. I list here examples of such a trend.

Paulist Press marks a segment of its catalog with the heading, 'environmental spirituality'. Among the titles: C. Cummings, *Eco-Spirituality: Toward a Reverent Life* (Mahwah: Paulist Press, 1991); S. Jung, *We Are Home: Spirituality of the Environment* (New York: Paulist Press, 1993).

Regional spirituality has arrived: V. Fabella, P.K.H. Lee and D. Kwang-sun Suh, *Asian Christian Spirituality* (Maryknoll: Orbis Books, 1992). This book lets Asians speak for themselves in describing and defining spirituality in the Asian context. It includes information on the Korean Minjung tradition.

The addiction recovery movement has its own literature and history, which have predated the voguish rise of 'spirituality' as a publisher's marketing tool. One place to start is with G.G. May's *Addiction and Grace: Love and Spirituality in the Healing of Addictions* (San Francisco: HarperSanFrancisco, 1991).

Women's and children's spirituality have received separate attention as well. Once such title is R.S. Keller, *Spirituality and Social Responsibility: Vocational Vision of Women in the United Methodist Tradition* (Nashville: Abingdon Press, 1993). P. Gillespie and M. Matthews, *Voices from within: Faith-life Stories of Women in the Church* (Hope Publishing House, Box 6008, Pasadena, CA 91116) presents the journeys of women initially gathered by the Collegeville (MN) Institute for

Ecumenical and Cultural Research. See also R. Coles, *The Spiritual Life of Children* (Boston: Houghton Mifflin, 1990).

D.S. Ferguson, *New Age Spirituality: An Assessment* (Louisville, KY: Westminster/John Knox, 1993) offers a critique by some very close to the movement. A. Faivre and J. Needleman, *Modern Esoteric Spirituality* (World Spirituality, 21; New York: Crossroad, 1992) treats subjects like anthroposophy, theosophy, freemasonry, rosicrucianism, C.J. Jung, Rudolf Steiner, distant planets in the galaxy of spirituality.

Finally, I include two curious titles, just to show where things have gone. R. O'Connor, *Blossom of Bone: Reclaiming the Connections between Homoeroticism and the Sacred* (San Francisco: HarperSanFrancisco, 1993), presents itself as a history of gay male spirituality. E. Stevens, *Spiritual Technologies: A User's Manual* (New York: Paulist Press, 1990), will strike many as bizarre. It gives specific instructions for touching and breathing, body awareness—a sort of physiology of meditation, with lots of Eastern echoes.

Why not, however, stay mainstream? Get a copy of C. Jones *et al.* (eds.), *The Study of Spirituality* (see above, p. 154), for your head— solid guidance over the breadth of the Christian Church in time and space. And for your heart, say, a copy of H. Nouwen, *The Wounded Healer: Ministry in Contemporary Society* (Garden City, NY: Doubleday, 1972). Read texts, not just textbooks. Value the rich contributions from the Roman Catholic tradition. And then, follow the Apostle's summary advice: 'Make love your aim' (1 Cor. 14.1, RSV).

THE HOLY SPIRIT: THE MISSING KEY IN THE IMPLEMENTATION OF THE DOCTRINE OF THE PRIESTHOOD OF BELIEVERS

Benjamin Sun

1. *Introduction*

AD 2000 is just a few years away. Will the Church be able to fulfill the Great Commission by the turn of the century? There is no simple answer to that question. However, I believe it is possible, if every Christian empowered by the Holy Spirit would commit to the task of winning the lost and discipling new believers. How could this happen?

It has been rightly observed that 'the Priesthood of all believers has never been entirely lost nor has it been fully received'.[1] Since the rediscovery of the doctrine of the priesthood of all believers during the Reformation, the Church has gained much understanding on the subject. Many books have been written and conferences held focusing on the laity. Yet, in reviewing the history of the Christian Church, we see only partial fulfillment of involving the laity in ministry as the New Testament describes it and the early Church practiced it. We have the knowledge and the means, but the dynamic power needed to move the teaching of the priesthood of all believers beyond slogan or paper document into practice seems to be missing.

A new Reformation was needed.[2] Then, in God's timing, the Pentecostal Revival began on April 9, 1906 in Azusa Street. Speaking of the revival in Azusa Street, Harvey Cox says, 'the power fell' and 'a spiritual fire roared forth around the world and touched millions of people with warmth and power'.[3] The emphasis the Pentecostals and the

---

1. O.E. Feucht, *Everyone A Minister: A Guide to Churchmanship for Laity and Clergy* (St Louis: Concordia, 1974), p. 54.

2. G. Ogden, *The New Reformation: Returning the Ministry to the People of God* (Grand Rapids: Zondervan, 1990), pp. 11-25.

3. H. Cox, *Fire from Heaven* (Reading, MA: Addison–Wesley, 1995), pp. 56, 46.

charismatics put on the person and work of the Holy Spirit added a new dimension to the mobilization of the laity for ministry. They identified the missing key, the Holy Spirit, as the foundation of the doctrine of the priesthood of all believers.

The purpose of this paper is to offer a brief study on the Biblical teachings and the impact of the Pentecostal and charismatic movements on the laity. Hopefully, insights will be gained in developing future strategies to mobilize dedicated men and women to put into practice their Christian calling in all sectors of life and society. 'We live in a moment of history', writes Greg Ogden, 'when ministry is potentially returned to the people of God'.[4]

2. *The Priesthood of Believers in the Bible*

The English word 'laity' has its original source in the Greek word λαός which means 'people'. The often-used New Testament phrase ὁ λαός τοῦ θεοῦ means 'the people of God'. This term applies to all who are 'in Christ' with no distinction in status, prestige and power, but distinction in gift, function and ministration. In the New Testament it is the whole people of God who are called to be the Church. All the members are joined to grow up into maturity, to the stature of the fulness of Christ (Eph. 4.15).[5]

In the Septuagint, λαός is used with amazing consistency to translate the Hebrew word עַם (people).[6] This image links the Church with Israel and all God's people throughout history. The following is a study of some of the key passages in the Bible concerning the λαός, the people of God.

2.1 *Exodus 19.5-6*
In this narrative, which describes God's making of the covenant with Israel at Sinai, the message is clear. First, Israel was chosen by God to enter into a special relationship with him, to be God's people. Secondly, Israel was to be a kingdom of priests and a holy nation, which means, they were to propagate the will of God by holy character and active

4. Ogden, *The New Reformation*, p. 29.
5. C. Van Engen, *God's Missionary People* (Grand Rapids: Baker, 1991), p. 151.
6. T.D. Lea, 'The Priesthood of All Christians According to the New Testament', *Southwestern Journal of Theology* 30 (Fall, 1987), p. 15.

witness.[7] Israel was chosen by God not just for her own good pleasure, but to be a channel of God's blessing to all people.

2.2 *1 Peter 2.4-10*

The term λαός which is used in the Old Testament to describe Israel as the people of God is applied here to the new Israel (Mt. 21.43), the Christian community. By God's calling and choice, all who are in Christ belong to the priesthood. As priests, the new Israel, like the original Israel, is called to fulfill God's mission in the world (v. 9). The λαός is the ministering people of God, the active, involved, serving body of Christ. They are 'to minister to God' (1 Pet. 2.5), 'to each other' (1 Pet. 4.10), and 'to the world' (1 Pet. 2.9).

2.3 *Acts 1.8*

How can the λαός enter into effective ministry? The answer is found in Lk. 24.49 and Acts 1.8, where Luke records Jesus' last instructions to His disciples: 'You shall receive power when the Holy Spirit has come upon you; and you shall be My witnesses' (Acts 1.8, NASB). Luke's intent in these passages is to show the primary and foremost purpose of the Spirit's coming in power is to equip believers for service. The entire book of Acts powerfully documents the work of the Holy Spirit in equipping believers to carry out the work of Christ in the world. F.J. May states,

> Our examination of the church in the Book of Acts has shown almost total involvement in ministry by all believers. The people were endued with the power of the Holy Spirit; they were praying people; there was anointed preaching; there were supernatural signs and wonders; there was cultural and cross-cultural evangelism, and they began new churches rapidly. This was, indeed, a well-mobilized church! The growth of the church was fantastic.[8]

2.4 *Ephesians 4.1-6*

In this classic passage, Paul repeatedly stresses that every believer has been given a ministry for which he or she has been called (v. 1) and gifted (v. 7). No one is a spectator, but each is a channel for the manifestation of the Spirit. Paul uses the imagery of the physical body with

7. Lea, 'The Priesthood of All Christians', p. 16.
8. F.J. May, *The Book of Acts and Church Growth: Growth through the Power of God's Holy Spirit* (Nashville: Bethany, 1990), p. 157-58.

its various parts to speak of the body of Christ (1 Cor. 12.15-26), stating that all rightly belong and that all are vital to the body. When each member of the body of Christ performs his or her God-given ministry, the body is able to function normally.

The gifts of the Holy Spirit are for ministry in the body of believers (1 Cor. 12.7; 1 Pet. 4.10). They are for the upbuilding of the Christian community (1 Cor. 14.26) so that God's people might be built into the stature of the fullness of Christ. Such fullness is not possible unless all members exercise their God-given gifts and calling. Out from among the λαός, God calls and gives gifts to some to be apostles, prophets, evangelists, pastors and teachers of his people. They have a 'specialized' ministry.[9] Their unique function is to equip the laity for the work of the ministry (vv. 11-12), and to develop maturity in them. To equip means to prepare, complete, put in order, and make ready the people of God for service.[10] It all fits together (1 Cor. 12.14-27). The relationship between clergy and laity is characterized by mutual submission and mutual service. They are partners in ministry.

2.5 *Summary*

Let us draw some conclusions from the above study:

1. All people are called to a special relationship with God. Only with a right relationship with God will one move into meaningful and dynamic Christian service. In the New Testament, character not intellect is essential for ministry. Those who desire to be of the Master's use must keep themselves 'clean' (2 Tim. 2.20-24; Eph. 4.1). Ministry is not just doing but also being.

2. The priesthood of all believers means not only that every Christian believer can approach God directly, but also that every Christian as a priest has a ministry to perform. The call to be the people of God is also a call to ministry.[11] Ministry is to be shared by all members (Rom. 12.4-8). Ministry in the assembly rests not on the shoulders of a few, or worse, just the paid staff, but each member is to assume a responsible role of service. Each member is a 'minister', and each one has a unique and vital part to contribute to the whole. The

9. J. Garlow, *Partners in Ministry: Lay and Pastors Working Together* (Kansas City: Beacon Hill, 1981), p. 42.

10. Ogden, *The New Reformation*, p. 115.

11. D.C. McCarty, *The Inner Heart of Ministry* (Nashville: Broadman, 1985), p. 14.

prevailing misguided attitude that the primary responsibility for doing God's work rests upon the clergy must be corrected by a strong biblical teaching on the call and giftedness of the people of God.

3. The people of God are gifted for ministry. Spiritual gifts are supernatural endowments of the Holy Spirit which enable a person to do the work of the ministry effectively. The Christian's responsibility is to discover what his or her gift is, and then use it for the building of the body as a whole. All the gifts have their proper and essential place in the full function of the body of Christ. Those gifted with the enabling ministries are to equip and develop others for ministry (Eph. 4). They are to help multiply and not monopolize ministries.[12]

4. The Holy Spirit is the source and power for dynamic ministry. William Menzies says, 'the emphasis of Acts 1.8 is power for service, not regeneration, not sanctification'.[13] When a believer is baptized in the Holy Spirit, that one is 'clothed with power from on high' (Lk. 24.49), becoming a potential channel of dynamic witness to the world. All believers are encouraged to receive this Pentecostal gift (Luke 11.13).[14] Like the early Church, the Church today needs the empowering dimension of life in the Spirit to evangelize the world and to build the Body of Christ.

3. *The Unfinished Reformation*

If the doctrine of the priesthood of all believers is such a clear teaching in the Bible, why has the Church taken so long in applying the truth? Many factors have contributed to this shortfalling. Kenneth Haugk has listed thirteen barriers. I will summarize them as follows: 1) The inertia of tradition. For centuries, the clergy have ministered, and lay people have received ministry. To change that pattern is not easy. No one deserves all the blame: clergy and laity both have resisted change. 2) The seductiveness of intellectualizing. Orthodoxy is easier than orthopraxis. Sometimes professional church workers and intellectually inclined laity enjoy educational, cognitive activities more then translating them into

12. J.R.W. Stott, *The Message of Ephesians* (Downers Grove, IL: InterVarsity Press, 1979), p. 167.

13. W.W. Menzies, *Bible Doctrines: A Pentecostal Perspective* (rev. and expanded S.M. Horton; Springfield, MO: Logion, 1993), p. 124.

14. R.P. Menzies, 'Coming to Terms with an Evangelical Heritage—Part I: Pentecostals and the Issue of Subsequence', *Paraclete* 28 (Summer, 1994), p. 26.

practice. This hinders the church from action. 3) Biblical interpretations—abridged versions. Conveniently omitting the Bible's emphasis on
the practice of the priesthood of all believers. 4) Institutional preservation
versus human needs. 5) Glory-seeking. 6) Fear of losing power and
control. 7) Failure to use appropriate power and authority. 8) Un-
equipped equippers. Students in Bible schools and seminaries learn a
great deal about doing ministry, but comparatively less about equipping
others for ministry. To become an equipper is not easy, it requires training, planning, hard work and risk taking. 9) The paid-minister syndrome.
10) The specialization trap. 11) Apathy. 12) Lack of faith. 13) Priorities.[15]

Haugk's comprehensive list, however, failed to list what I believe to
be a major reason why the Church has not been able to mobilize the
laity fully for ministry beyond the time of the early Church: the lack of
emphasis on the role of the Holy Spirit in the doctrine of the priesthood
of all believers. A study of Howard Grimes's summary of the historical
development of the lay ministry in the following paragraph will also
reveal the same fact.

Bill Leonard, in 'Southern Baptists and the Laity', summarizes
Howard Grimes's argument in *The Rebirth of the Laity*, saying:

> A general study of the role of the laity reflects the following develop-
> ments: 1) The sense of unified ministry for the whole people of God in
> the New Testament and post-apostolic period; 2) The growing distinction
> between clergy and laity in the patristic era; 3) The rise of clerical authority
> and status in the middle ages; 4) Monastic and sectarian reassertion of lay
> ministry in the church; 5) The Reformation emphasis on vocation and the
> priesthood of the believer; 6) The rise of the Free Church tradition, demo-
> cratic polity, and voluntary church membership; 7) The growing trend
> toward ministerial professionalism in the modern church; 8) The reasser-
> tion of the role of the laity through lay renewal; 9) The growth of the
> clerical authoritarianism among evangelical Protestants.[16]

In Grimes's summary, and other literature written on the same topic,
one seldom sees mention of the Holy Spirit's work or the proper attention given to the impact of the Pentecostal and charismatic movements
upon the development of the laity in ministry.[17] This is an issue that

15. K.C. Haugk, 'Lay Ministry: The Unfinished Reformation', *The Christian
Ministry* (November, 1985), pp. 5-8.
16. B.J. Leonard, 'Southern Baptists and the Laity', *Review and Expositor* 84
(Fall, 1987), p. 633.
17. More and more literature has been written with emphasis given to the work
of the Holy Spirit and the Pentecostal and charismatic influence on the laity. Some of

should not be overlooked or neglected. James Dunn says,

> Now is the time to reaffirm the root of all ministry as the charismatic Spirit given variously to members of the body, to recognize our starting point as the New Covenant of the Pentecostal Spirit, and not the old covenant of the priesthood.[18]

4. *Pentecostal and Charismatic Laity in Action*

4.1 *A Brief Historic Review of the Pentecostal and Charismatic Movements in the Twentieth Century and Their Contributions to the Body of Christ*

The turn of the twentieth century witnessed the beginning of what has been called the Pentecostal Movement, a movement with great world-wide implications. Historians usually associate the origin of modern Pentecostalism with a revival in Topeka, Kansas, that began on January 1, 1901.[19] This does not discount the significance of other occurrences which took place earlier or about the same time.[20] It was this revival, however, which made a decisive impact on the events which followed. Charles F. Parham, a holiness evangelist and founder of Bethel Bible College, assigned his students, during his absence, to do a study on the baptism in the Holy Spirit of Acts 2. He returned to discover that they had concluded that the biblical evidence of such baptism was always speaking in tongues. The students and teachers began to seek the Lord in prayer. Agnes Ozman became the first to receive the Holy Spirit with the expected evidence of glossolalia and others followed.[21] With this, a distinct Pentecostal movement had begun.

However, exerting a greater and more international influence on the

---

the examples are the books referred to in this paper: *Spiritual Power and Church Growth* (see n. 37); *Called and Empowered: Global Mission in Pentecostal Perspective* (n. 28); *The New Reformation: Returning the Ministry to the People of God* (n. 2); and *Azusa Street and Beyond* (n. 35).

18. Ogden, *The New Reformation*, p. 54.

19. W.W. Menzies, *Anointed to Serve: The Story of the Assemblies of God* (Springfield, MO: Gospel Publishing House, 1971), p. 34.

20. G.B. McGee, 'A Brief History of the Modern Pentecostal Outpouring', *Paraclete* (Spring, 1984), pp. 19-20. See also G.B. McGee's paper, 'Pentecostal Phenomena and Revival in India: Implications for Indigenous Church Leadership', given at the 24th meeting of the Society for Pentecostal Studies, November 10-14, 1994 at Wheaton College, Wheaton, IL.

21. Menzies, *Anointed to Serve*, p. 37.

formation of the Pentecostal movement was the Azusa Street Revival of 1906–1907, which took place in Los Angeles, California. It caught the attention of the secular world. The Wednesday edition of the Los Angeles Times reported, 'Breathing strange utterances and mouthing a creed which it would seem no sane mortal could understand, the newest religious sect has started in Los Angeles'.[22] Azusa Street became the center from which the Pentecostal message spread around the world.

Under the leadership of William J. Seymour, a black holiness preacher and others, unusual services took place day and night in a tumbled-down shack on 312 Azusa Street, California. Those meetings were marked with spontaneous worship and shouts of praise to the Lord, fervent prayers, dynamic preaching, cries for repentance, yearnings for sanctification, manifestations of the gifts of the Holy Spirit and testimonies. Crowds gathered with the simple desire to 'see what the Holy Spirit would do'.

Reports of the continuing revival at Azusa drew seekers from around the world and some of them returned to their homes as evangelists of the new movement. From Azusa Street Pentecostalism spread to Canada, Europe, India, China, Latin America, Africa and other parts of the world. Within the last few decades, the influence of the Pentecostal message has resulted in charismatic segments of older Protestant denominations, the Roman Catholic Church, and the evangelical churches.

The charismatic movement is usually dated from the Sunday morning in 1959 when Dennis Bennett announced to his Episcopalian congregation in Van Nuys, California, that he had been baptized in the Holy Spirit and spoken in tongues. In little more than a year, similar events were happening in a variety of Protestant congregations in the United States: Church of Christ, Methodist and Presbyterian.[23] The movement spread to every continent of the globe and into every major Christian denomination in less than two decades. In 1967 the charismatic movement reached the Roman Catholic Church in the United States. By the 1980s, Catholics in 120 countries were actively involved.[24]

Then in the last quarter of the twentieth century, the Spirit began to break out in the mainline evangelical churches. This movement is known

22. E.W. Blumhofer, *The Assemblies of God: A Popular History* (Springfield, MO: Radiant, 1985), p. 29.

23. L. Christenson, *Welcome, Holy Spirit: A Study of Charismatic Renewal in the Church* (Minneapolis: Augsburg, 1987), p. 18.

24. Christenson, *Welcome, Holy Spirit*, p. 19.

as the 'third wave'. David Barrett estimates that worldwide there are some 20 million 'third wave' believers.[25]

From inauspicious beginnings, Pentecostalism has mushroomed into the largest Christian movement in the twentieth century.[26] Today, Pentecostals and charismatics form the second largest Christian group in the world, outnumbered only by the Roman Catholic Church. A study by Vinson Synan estimated 372 million Pentecostals and charismatics worldwide. The study also counted 962 million Roman Catholics, 295 million evangelicals and 179 million Eastern Orthodox believers. The ranks of Pentecostals and charismatics are growing at a rate of 19 million per year.[27] David Barrett projects that there will be 562 million Pentecostals and charismatics by the year 2000.[28] And the projection by the World Council of Churches is that by the year 2000, over 50% of all Christians in the world will be of Pentecostal or charismatic variety.[29]

Church Growth expert, Peter Wagner, observes that there are several factors that have contributed to the phenomenal growth of the Pentecostal-charismatic churches: (1) Conservative evangelical theology is unquestioned. (2) Strong pastoral leadership is encouraged. (3) Prayer is a significant, explicit, and up front component of the churches' philosophy of ministry. (4) Openness to the person and work of the Holy Spirit is always maintained. (5) Abundant financial support is readily available. (6) Worship is a central feature of church life. (7) Participation in lay ministries is expected of all church members. (8) Extensive Bible-teaching ministry is focused on the felt needs of church members.[30]

The contributions of Pentecostals and charismatics go beyond the purely statistical. They have offered new and creative ways to energize

25. C.P. Wagner, 'Third Wave', in S.M. Burgess, G.B. McGee and P.H. Alexander, *Dictionary of Pentecostal and Charismatic Movements* (Grand Rapids: Regency Reference Library, 1988), p. 844.

26. G. Wacker, 'America's Pentecostals—Who They Are', *Christianity Today* 31 (October 16, 1987), p. 14.

27. V. Synan, 'Foreign Missions News: Recent Study Cites Worldwide Growth of Pentecostalism', in *Mountain Movers* [magazine] (Springfield, MO: Division of Foreign Missions of the Assemblies of God, January 1993), p. 13.

28. C.P. Wagner, 'A Church Growth Perspective on Pentecostal Missions', in M.A. Dempster, B.D. Klaus and D. Petersen (eds.), *Called and Empowered: Global Mission in Pentecostal Perspective* (Peabody, MA: Hendrickson, l991), p. 266.

29. Christenson, *Welcome, Holy Spirit*, p. 19.

30. C.P. Wagner, 'America's Pentecostals: See How They Grow', *Christianity Today* 31 (October 16, 1987), pp. 28-29.

the life of the Church in worship, Bible study, prayers, use of ministry gifts, mobilizing the laity, church growth and missions. 'Without the contributions of Pentecostalism', says the editor of *Christianity Today*, 'today's church would be far poorer'.[31]

4.2 *The Influence of the Wesleyan and Keswick Movements on Pentecostalism*

A large part of the heritage of modern Pentecostalism is found in the nineteenth-century Holiness and the Higher Life (Keswick) movements in England and America that emphasized 'second blessing' sanctification and the baptism in the Holy Spirit as an endowment of power for service.[32] The quest for holy living and power for service were distinct characteristics of the early Pentecostal movement.

Another important influence that the Wesleyan movement had on Pentecostalism was the enlisting of laity in various ministry and leadership functions. Wesley appointed large numbers of 'lay preachers' to lead the class meetings. The classes were held in house churches in the various neighborhoods where people lived, they served both an evangelistic and discipling function. The lay preachers were not the educated or the wealthy, but laboring men and women with spiritual gifts and an eagerness to serve. These lay preachers were directly under Wesley's supervision. Wesley saw his lay preachers as exercising a charismatic office. They were persons who demonstrated gifts for ministry, and Wesley put them to work, confirming their gifts. They would 'rise at four and preach at five o'clock, to scatter books and tracts, to live by rule, and to die without fear'.[33] Howard Snyder observes that 'the rapid growth of Methodism could never have happened without the traveling preachers'.[34]

Many of the laity who received the baptism in the Holy Spirit in the early Pentecostal revival were convinced that God was in their midst and had chosen them for a special work. They believed that the divine purpose in the Baptism was an enduement with power for witnessing and service. While the early Pentecostals lacked in education, they were

31. T. Muck, 'Spiritual Lifts', *Christianity Today* 31 (October 16, 1987), p. 14.

32. V. Synan, 'Classical Pentecostalism', in Burgess, McGee and Alexander (eds.), *Dictionary*, p. 220.

33. H.A. Snyder, *Signs of the Spirit: How God Reshapes the Church* (Grand Rapids: Zondervan, 1989), p. 230.

34. Snyder, *Signs of the Spirit*, p. 225.

filled with the power and gifts of the Holy Spirit as divine equipment for the work of evangelization. These Pentecostals had a fiery passion for souls like the early Methodists.[35] They believed that since every believer can experience the Spirit-filled life, each one should actively be serving Christ. Clearly, within the Pentecostal movement, the distinction between clergy and laity has often been minimized.[36]

4.3 *Some Selected Examples of the Pentecostal and Charismatic Laity in Action*

If the rapid growth of Methodism could never have happened without the traveling lay preachers that John Wesley had appointed, it would be equally true that the phenomenal growth of the Pentecostal and charismatic movements would not be possible without the participation of the laity. The following are some examples:

4.3.1 *Latin America*. The Christian Church in Latin America has experienced rapid growth in the twentieth century. It is evident from the following statistics:

> In 1900 there were about 50,000 Protestants in Latin America
> In the 1930s membership passed 1 million
> In the 1950s it passed 5 million
> In the 1960s it passed 10 million
> In the 1970s it passed 20 million
> By the end of the 1980s Protestant membership passed the 50 million mark, with 137 million projected by the year 2000.[37]

In 1986 it was estimated that three out of every four Protestants in Latin America were Pentecostals.[38] According to David Barrett, the total number of Pentecostal and charismatic church members in Latin America in 1988 was 78,404,910, which was 18.95% of the total church

35. D.J. Du Plessis, 'Golden Jubilees of Twentieth-Century Pentecostal Movements', in L.G. McClung, Jr (ed.), *Azusa Street and beyond: Pentecostal Missions and Church Growth in the Twentieth Century* (South Plainfield, NJ: Bridge Publishing, 1986), p. 40.

36. G.B. McGee, 'Pentecostals and Their Various Strategies for Global Mission: A Historical Assessment', in Dempster, Klaus and Petersen (eds.), *Called and Empowered*, p. 206.

37. C.P. Wagner, *Spiritual Power and Church Growth* (Altamonte Springs, Florida: Strang Communications, 1986), pp. 26-27.

38. Wagner, *Spiritual Power*, p. 27.

membership of the world.[39] Two of the three largest churches in the world are in Latin America, and they are Pentecostal.[40]

How is all of this happening? What are the secrets of the explosive, sustained growth of the Pentecostal churches in Latin America? Among other factors, two of the significant reasons behind the rapid growth of Pentecostal and charismatic churches in Latin America are the active participation of the laity in the church and the effective in-service training programs for believers.[41]

Paul Pierson has identified active lay participation and in-service training as crucial factors in the accelerated growth of the Pentecostal Church in Brazil. In a similar way, Peter Larson, who studied the Argentine Pentecostal group, *Iglesia Evangelica Pentecostal Misionera* (IEPM), linked the effectiveness of the IEPM in church planting with the apprentice-type in-service development of a broad cadre of leaders for such purposes.[42]

To most Pentecostals in Latin America, being a Christian means, among other things, serving God. The Pentecostal pastor provides the leadership and organizational functions of the church, but most of the ministries out on the street and in the home are done by the laity. A practical requirement for a sincere and true conversion experience is that a believer agrees to go out on the street to give his or her testimony immediately after making a decision for Christ. This experience not only strengthens the believer's faith in Christ, but also helps him or her feel like an active participant in the ministry of the church. Latin Pentecostals are effective in incorporating converts into a community of faith by giving them immediate responsibility and training.[43]

4.3.2 *China*. The growth of Christianity in China has been phenomenal. In 1949, after Mao's war of liberation ended 150 years of Western mis-

39. D.B. Barrett, 'Global Statistics', in Burgess, McGee and Alexander (eds.), *Dictionary*, p. 816.

40. Barrett, 'Global Statistics', p. 188.

41. For more information on the topic, please refer to the following resources: E.A. Wilson, 'Passion and Power: A Profile of Emergent Latin American Pentecostalism', in Dempster, Klaus and Petersen (eds.), *Called and Empowered*, pp. 87-88; B.D. Klaus and L.O Triplett, 'National Leadership in Pentecostal Missions', in Dempster, Klaus and Petersen (eds.), *Called and Empowered*, p. 229; Wagner, *Spiritual Power*, chs. 3 and 7.

42. Klaus and Triplett, 'National Leadership', p. 229.

43. Wagner, *Spiritual Power*, p. 44.

sionary work, China had less than one million Protestant believers. By the mid-1980s, the number was conservatively estimated at 50 million.[44] It is estimated that 85% of the Chinese believers are, phenomenologically, Pentecostal-charismatic.[45] Supernatural signs and wonders have played an important role in the spread of the gospel in China.[46]

Christianity is flourishing in China in the face of persecution. Jonathan Chao, Director of the Chinese Christian Research Center, says the suffering of the Church in China has led to revival.[47] The 'blood of the martyrs' has been the 'seed of the church'. Chao asserts that through suffering, the Chinese Christians have experienced the transforming power of Christ. Suffering tested and refined their faith, and enabled them to experience a deeper relation with Christ. Because of persecution, many church leaders were imprisoned. As a result, lay leaders were developed within the churches. House groups developed with laity taking the leadership. Many a pastor was released from prison to find that his church had grown under lay leadership.[48] It is estimated that for every one hundred churches in China, there is only one pastor.[49]

Itinerant evangelists have played a significant role in the growth of Christianity in China. Chao states,

> Most of the itinerant evangelists in the house church movement have never received any formal theological training. They learned to preach by preaching. They waxed strong by experiencing the power of the Holy Spirit. They developed a strong faith and bold courage through field ministry and frequent suffering. Younger men and women began to follow itinerant evangelists on their preaching tours as helpers and then as junior evangelists. As they shared the load of preaching and counseling, they soon became gifted and experienced itinerant evangelists themselves.[50]

In the mid-1980s, a Chinese Christian who could not even read proposed a training program for evangelists known as the 'Seminary of the Field'.

44. C.P. Wagner, 'Church Growth', in Burgess, McGee and Alexander (eds.), p. 182.

45. Wagner, 'Church Growth', p. 183.

46. Wagner, 'Church Growth', p. 190.

47. J. Chao, *The China Mission Handbook: A Portrait of China and Its Church* (Hong Kong: Chinese Church Research Center, 1989), p. 55.

48. D. Wang, 'The China Paradox', *Asian Report* 27 (September 12, 1994), 18.

49. C. Qian, 'Whither Chinese Theological Students?', *Bridge* 34 (March–April, 1989), p. 4.

50. Chao, *China*, p. 57.

In eight short years, the number of 'Seminaries of the Field' has grown beyond ten.[51]

4.3.3 *Korea*. The Korean Church has grown miraculously in the one hundred years of its mission history. From the time when the first Protestant missionary, Horace N. Allen, arrived in 1884 to the present, the society has been significantly impacted by the gospel. It is estimated that 25% of South Koreans are Christians.[52] Among the various factors pertaining to Korean church growth, the contribution of the laity is undeniable.[53] Laypeople in Korea are willing to pay a high price for mission. During the climax of 'Here's Life, Korea' in the 1980s, every night 2 million people rallied on Yoido Plaza for testimonies, songs and inspirational messages. Then a million and a half stayed there all night to pray. At the end of the campaign, over a million people pledged to spend a year—at their own expense—as lay missionaries either at home or abroad.[54]

Christianity has spread rapidly since the 1950s and Pentecostalism is a part of this success story in Korea. Pentecostals have a 742% decadal membership growth rate from 1969–82 (DGR), while the second-place Baptists are showing a 240% DGR.[55] In 1982, Pentecostals became the third largest denomination in Korea in terms of membership.[56] The largest church in the world is in Korea, the Yoido Full Gospel Church, a Pentecostal church pastored by David Yonggi Cho. The church had a membership of over 600,000 in 1989. After collapsing from overwork and stress in 1964, Cho put much emphasis in training and delegating responsibilities to others. Under his leadership there are 633 pastors, 400 elders, and 50,000 deacons or deaconesses shepherding this rapidly

51. Chao, *China*, p. 58.

52. Sang-Yong Kim, 'Lessons from The Pentecostal Movement in Korea in The Twentieth Century' (D.Miss. thesis; Fuller Theological Seminary, 1990), p. 9.

53. For more information on the subject of the laity and Church Growth in Korea, please see the following research theses: Kwan-Seog Chun, 'Church Growth and Laity Education, with Special Reference to Hwa-Do Methodist Church' (D.Min. thesis, Fuller Theological Seminary, 1987); Sang-Yong Kim, 'Lessons from the Pentecostal Movement in Korea in the Twentieth Century' (D.Miss. thesis; Fuller Theological Seminary, 1990); Soo-Sin Kim, 'A Study of the Layman Movement and its Influence on the Growth of the Korean Churches' (DMin thesis, 1987).

54. Cox, *Fire*, p. 233.

55. Wagner, 'Church Growth', p. 190.

56. Sang-Yong Kim, 'Lessons', p. 89.

growing congregation. The church operates a Sunday School program with an enrolment of more than 26,000, a ten-week training course for home-cell leaders, a sixteen-week training course for church officers and lay leaders, and a three-year Bible Institute for training pastors.[57]

Cho attributed the establishment of the home cell groups as one of the significant reasons for the phenomenal growth of his church.[58] The church membership is divided into 50,000 home cell groups in 406 sub-districts throughout Seoul.[59] These home cell groups are centered on prayer and Bible study and they provide every church member an opportunity to participate in the ministry of the church. The exercising of spiritual gifts is encouraged in the home cell groups. Church members find this kind of involvement very rewarding and evangelism has multiplied because of it.[60]

4.3.4 *North America: Pentecostal churches.* The Pentecostal churches in North America experienced good growth rates during the first half of the century. But it was after World War II that their growth became phenomenal. For example, the Assemblies of God, which was founded in Hot Springs, Arkansas, in 1914 with 300 members, had grown to 2.3 million by 1987 in the United States and 23 million worldwide. Energized by the Holy Spirit and filled with a passion for the lost, the laity of the Assemblies of God has been a key factor in the rapid growth of the movement.

Missionary zeal at home and on foreign fields has been a hallmark of the Assemblies of God from its beginning. Today there are 3,207 home missionaries and 1,725 foreign missionaries serving in 140 countries. The Assemblies of God Division of Foreign Missions is highly regarded as spearheading one of the most successful missionary enterprises of the twentieth century. The Assemblies of God laity—boys and girls, youth, men and women—have taken an active part in missions. The total giving for foreign missions in 1994 was over 109 million dollars. During 1993–1994, 556 construction teams worked overseas, and 368 people

---

57. M.R. Mullins, 'The Empire Strikes Back: Korean Pentecostal Missions to Japan', in K. Poewe (ed.), *Charismatic Christianity as a Global Culture* (Columbia: University of South Carolina Press, 1974), p. 89.

58. P. Yonggi Cho, *Successful Home Cell Groups* (Plainfield, NJ: Logos, 1981), p. 81.

59. Mullins, 'The Empire Strikes Back', p. 90.

60. Cho, *Cell Groups*, p. viii.

participated in summer ministry under the Missions Abroad Placement Service (MAPS) program. 5,817 teens participated in Ambassadors In Mission (AIM) trips during 1993–95, reporting more than 112,060 conversions.[61]

4.3.5 *North America: Mainline Protestant churches.* The charismatic movement began as a renewal movement among the mainline Protestant churches in North America in the 1960s. Among other influences, it has brought forth a significant change in the role of the laity in the mainline churches. Spirit-gifted laity are increasingly ministering with evident and acknowledged spirituality. They are taking a more active role in the ministries which traditionally were expected from the clergy: leading in worship, visiting the sick, counseling, and teaching basic doctrines.

Larry Christenson notes, 'The increased attention that the charismatic renewal has given to spiritual gifts is helping make the doctrine of the priesthood of all believers more than a theological phrase'.[62] And similarly, J.I. Packer notes, 'The current stress on the universality of the gifts and God's expectation of every-member ministry in the body of Christ was long overdue, for the New Testament on both points is explicit and clear'.[63] This is an important breakthrough that has brought renewal to the life of the Church.

4.3.6 *North America: Full Gospel Business Men's Fellowship International.* So far the focus has been on the lay movement within the Pentecostal and charismatic churches. The following is an example of the lay movement within a parachurch organization: The Full Gospel Business Men's Fellowship International (FGBMFI).

FGBMFI was founded by Demos Shakarian, a successful Californian dairyman and a layman raised in a Pentecostal home. When FGBMFI was organized in 1951, it was originally intended as a means for stimulating fellowship among Pentecostal laymen, cutting across Pentecostal denominational lines. By 1955, it began to shift focus. When non-Pentecostal people began to receive the baptism in the Holy Spirit,

61. '1993–1994 Biennial Report of the General Council of the Assemblies of God', *Advance* (Fall, 1995), pp. 1-35.

62. Christenson, *Welcome, Holy Spirit*, pp. 290-91.

63. J.I. Packer, *Keep in Step with the Spirit* (Grand Rapids: Fleming H. Revell, 1984), p. 28.

FGBMFI began to promote the charismatic renewal.[64] It played a major role in introducing the charismatic experience to many laymen and ministers from the historic Protestant and Catholic churches.

Focusing on business and professional men, the fellowship's non-denominational monthly meetings gave laymen opportunity for prayer, fellowship, encouragement and service. Often speakers were laymen who told of God's remarkable and miraculous intervention in their lives and business. They prayed for the sick, people were healed, saved and filled with the Holy Spirit in these services. These meetings were used as times of outreach as well, with members being encouraged to invite local businessmen and other friends to attend.

Many Pentecostals and charismatics shared the excitement and vision of the fellowship. But others raised their concerns. Some pastors and leaders disliked the time and money their members devoted to the FGBMFI. Over the last three decades FGBMFI has evolved into one of the Christian community's most active ministries to, of and for laity, claiming a membership of 65,000 in 87 countries with 3,000 chapters.[65]

Energized by the Holy Spirit, the laity from Pentecostal and charismatic churches around the world are actively engaging in ministry. They have played a vital role in making the Pentecostal and charismatic movements the largest Christian movements in the twentieth century.

5. *How Pentecostals and Charismatics Equip the Laity for Ministry*

5.1 *Baptism in the Holy Spirit*
Peter Wagner writes,

> Martin Luther's doctrine of the priesthood of all believers had an important soteriological function in the churches of the Reformation, but he did not clearly see the pneumatological implications. In fact, it was only with the advent of the Pentecostal movement that a practical application of Luther's doctrine began to be made for the ministry.[66]

The Holy Spirit empowers the λαός for ministry. By putting emphasis on the baptism in the Holy Spirit, Pentecostals and charismatics have added a new dimension to the mobilization of the laity for ministry.

Pentecostals put strong emphasis on the Holy Spirit in the training of believers. Practical teachings on the person and work of the Holy Spirit

---

64. W. Menzies, *Anointed to Serve*, p. 338.

65. B. Bird, 'Facing Frustration and the Future', *Charisma* 11 (January, 1986), p. 25.

66. Wagner, 'A Church Growth Perspective on Pentecostal Missions', p. 277.

are taught. Individual Christians are encouraged to seek and to experience the dynamics of the Holy Spirit in their lives. They have learned how to minister in the power of the Holy Spirit in leading worship, in personal evangelism, in praying for the sick, in casting out evil spirits, and in the exercising of spiritual gifts.

Pentecostals and charismatics stress the necessity of depending on the Holy Spirit in the practice of ministry. They believe that the baptism in the Holy Spirit enables one to receive power for effective service (Acts 1.8). They wait for the Holy Spirit to anoint and empower them so they might move dynamically beyond their natural abilities into the realm of the supernatural.

Pentecostals and charismatics are especially effective in power evangelism, which is the unleashing of God's supernatural power through signs and wonders, resulting in effective evangelism and a new depth and commitment among individual Christians.[67] Power evangelism accounts for the rapid growth of the Pentecostal churches in many parts of the world.

5.2 *Every Christian is Gifted for Ministry*
Throughout Church history specific groups of people had known and exercised spiritual gifts.[68] It was the Pentecostal and charismatic movements of the twentieth century that brought a revival of exercising spiritual gifts to the Christian Church in every denomination around the world. Spiritual gifts are essential to the practice of the doctrine of the priesthood of all believers.[69] Every Christian believer has a ministry to perform, and to be effective, it should be done with God-given gifts.

Donald Gee, an outstanding Pentecostal leader, believed the gifts of the Spirit were divine equipment for the work of world evangelization. To him world evangelization should involve a demonstration of spiritual gifts in action. He said, 'There is no need to choose between a passion for souls and a desire for spiritual gifts, they are mutually inclusive, not exclusive'.[70]

---

67. C.P. Wagner, *Church Growth: State of the Art* (Wheaton, IL: Tyndale, 1986), p. 223.

68. C.P. Wagner, *Your Spiritual Gifts Can Help Your Church Grow* (Glendale: Regal Books, 1974), pp. 26-27.

69. D. Lim, *Spiritual Gifts: A Fresh Look* (Springfield, MO: Gospel Publishing, 1991), p. 34.

70. D. Gee, 'Spiritual Gifts and World Evangelization', in McClung, (ed.),

Peter Wagner notes that, 'Worldwide, Pentecostal churches grow when the Holy Spirit is free to manifest His miracle power through believers'.[71] An example is the explosive church growth in China mentioned earlier. Wagner believes such rapid growth is a result of God's immediate supernatural work of healing, casting out of demons, and miracles.[72] The emphasis on spiritual gifts has also led to what J.I. Packer calls 'an unprecedented willingness to experiment with new structure and liturgical forms for church life, so as to make room for the full use of all gifts for the benefit of the whole congregation'.[73] This gives rise to a more spontaneous and dynamic form of worship and the use of small groups in building Christian community.

5.3 *Life Preparation is the Foundation of Ministry*
Rooted in the holiness movement, Pentecostals see life preparation as essential to ministry. Spiritual disciplines like fasting, praying and Bible study are vital parts of the training of Pentecostal leadership. Trainees are taught and encouraged to walk in the Spirit as well as to minister in the power of the Holy Spirit.

Pentecostals seek to choose their leaders from people with sound moral character and proven ministries (Acts 6.1; Timothy). A study of the Protestant clergy in Chile shows that Pentecostal pastors in comparison with non-Pentecostal pastors are for the most part older and more experienced.

5.4 *Using Creative Ways to Equip the Laity for Ministry*
Pentecostals are known much more as doers of the Word rather than writers of the Word.[74] Pentecostal training is functional and geared for effectiveness in ministry. Pentecostals put more emphasis on the practice of ministry than the learning of theology. They employ various methods of training which bring successful results.

5.4.1 *Bible School training.* Bible schools are an important aspect of Pentecostal national leadership development. The Assemblies of God

Azusa Street and Beyond, p. 63.

71. C.P. Wagner, 'Characteristics of Pentecostal Church Growth', in McClung (ed.), *Azusa Street and Beyond*, p. 129.

72. Wagner, 'Characteristics of Pentecostal Church Growth', p. 129.

73. Packer, *Keep in Step*, p. 29.

74. Wagner, *Spiritual Power*, p. 86.

leads all evangelical organizations in the number of overseas Bible schools with approximately 330 schools and over 32,000 students. Pentecostal Bible schools appear in a variety of forms, and programs may range from one to four years. Practical field ministry is an important part of their curriculum. Success and effectiveness in ministry is more important than the awarding of a diploma. Graduation is not just a matter of receiving a certificate but a confirmation through actual experience that God has called the students and has given them gifts for ministry.[75] One Pentecostal Bible institute in Central America has an unusual graduation requirement. After students have completed their first year of study, they are sent to a new field to plant a church. They can only be readmitted for further studies after they have successfully planted a church, which in turn is able to support them in their continuing education.[76]

5.4.2 *The apprentice-type training.* The strength of the Pentecostal leadership lies in the employment of this type of training, which has led to the emergence of large numbers of gifted and zealous leaders. There are several advantages to this type of training: 1) A larger number of people can participate. 2) Training requires a shorter period of time but with desirable results. 3) People who received training do not have to leave their place of ministry; they feel that the best place to learn how to minister is to be with people and not with scholars. 4) Training puts strong emphasis on the discovery and development of gifts. 5) People receiving training are equipped with skills for evangelism and church planting.[77]

5.4.3 *Training by correspondence: ICI University.* Pentecostals continue to be creative in developing programs for training national leadership. One of these is the ICI University, which is an Assemblies of God institution. It offers correspondence courses on evangelism, discipleship and ministerial training. A network of 129 national directors and extension offices make ICI University a global distance education school.

Since its beginning in 1967 more than nine and a half million students have enrolled. Over 600,000 people have sent in written testimonies of conversion. Thousands of students study discipleship and lay workers

75. McClung, *Azusa Street and beyond*, p. xiii.
76. Wagner, *Spiritual Power*, p. 89.
77. Wagner, *Spiritual Power*, p. 92.

training courses at any given time. Students from 160 nations are able to study Bible-based courses in up to 97 languages. ICI University also offers a four-year Bachelor of Arts and a Master of Arts degree.[78]

5.4.4 *Mobile leadership training.* Through mobile leadership training Pentecostals bring to their leaders already in ministry the continuing education enrichment so needed for their growth and for improving effectiveness in ministry. The Latin American Advanced School of Theology (LAAST) and the Caribbean School of Theology (CST) are two examples of this innovative form of leadership training.[79]

There is a close parallel between the teachings of the Bible and the dynamic ways Pentecostals and charismatics equip and mobilize their laity for ministry. They have taken the doctrine of the priesthood of all believers seriously, and have clearly identified the Holy Spirit as the key to successful implementation of the doctrine. Their creative and practical training programs have enabled them to prepare many effective leaders for their churches. However, the significance of the impact of the Pentecostal and charismatic movements on the laity calls for further research and theological reflection.

6. *Conclusion*

It has been said that Pentecostalism is a 'movement without a man'. Instead of having an outstanding founder such as a Luther, a Calvin, or a Wesley, like the other religious movements, the distinctive mark of the Pentecostal movement lies in the ordinary men and women of faith and courage who, having experienced the power of the baptism in the Holy Spirit, are willing to lay down their lives in fulfilling the Great Commission of Christ.[80] This brief study has shown that the laity is an important contributing factor to the dynamic growth of the Pentecostal and charismatic movements around world.

As the church approaches the year 2000, its attention is focused on winning the world with the Gospel of Jesus Christ. To reach the goal, we need to involve every Christian believer in the task. May we draw

---

78. 'Our Campus Is the World', ICI University pamphlet, Irving, Texas.

79. Klaus and Triplett, 'National Leaders', p. 230.

80. V. Synan, *The Twentieth-Century Pentecostal Explosion: The Exciting Growth of Pentecostal Churches and Charismatic Renewal Movements* (Altamonte Springs, Florida: Creation, 1987), p. 189.

insights from the Pentecostals and charismatics as we formulate our strategy for equipping and mobilizing the laity for ministry.

TRANSCENDENCE, IMMANENCE, AND THE EMERGING
PENTECOSTAL ACADEMY

Del Tarr

The original target audience for this paper was made up of the over 100
registrants at the National Educators Conference, including professors,
administrators and staff of the 18 post secondary schools of the
American Assemblies of God.[1] I believe it is cogent and relevant for
Pentecostals of other countries and denominations, especially as the
reader remembers the original context.

1. *The Terms and The Task*

A certain professor, an expert on zoology, was leading an expedition
into the wilds of the Upper Nile. One day, a student ran up to him in
great excitement. 'Professor', he cried, 'something dreadful has just
happened. Your wife has been eaten by an alligator.' A deep look of
concern came over the Professor's face. 'Surely, Jackson', he said, 'you
mean a crocodile.' Meaning is very important to all of us, but for some
it is *all* important. In using the words of the title, I hope we can agree on
a less exacting insistence than the professor! In preparing for this paper I
discovered very disparate definitions from my friends for these old
philosophical concepts. African perception would influence me to see
them in rather cyclical juxtapositions, but definitely not linearly, while
Asia could easily place them in a *Yin Yang* interrelationship.

---

1.   Originally presented at the National Educators Conference, General Council
of the Assemblies of God, St Louis, Missouri, 1995. The address will retain its
'conversational speech style' from an actual oral presentation. This is intentional for
two reasons. Most of the essays in this book will, of necessity, conform to a more
traditional academic mode because they were written for the purpose of print. Thus,
this essay will provide a variety in style. Secondly, my experience and training have
led me to observe the efficacy of an extemporaneous style for many audiences.

For some time theologians have been using the term 'transcendence' to mean other than the classical philosophical understanding. 'Theological transcendence'[2] speaks of the 'othernesss' of God in relation to the world where God is best expressed in categories of the holy and of mystery. Immanence is not used here as by the Greek naturalists before Socrates (absolute immanentism) which excluded transcendence, but rather with the Augustinian sense which recognizes the mutual complementarity of immanence and transcendence, though still retaining their basic distinctions.

For this paper, let me get from fancy sounding titles (needed for publication deadlines) to the practical. Even as God transcends all, he has formed in us some values we hold and defend because of their relative 'otherness'. We will make educational choices from that persuasion. We should not necessarily expect the world's secular social systems to understand our rationale. This transcendent God, however, wants to relate to us, and equip us for the task of Christ's ascension mandate with supernatural gifts (tools) that demonstrate his power in immanence. Pentecostals believe this enablement is still available, by faith, for any earnest born-again seeker. There are two topics I will address in the context of what Pentecostals believe, about God and us, and educational matters. First, the issue of Pentecostal Christian Education which must interface with a post-Christian secular culture. The dilemma is that we can neither ignore this culture, nor allow it to erode our theological postulates; Secondly, and more importantly, the problem of 'third generational declension' from our traditional beliefs as a Pentecostal movement. I submit we are facing big changes because we as a movement are at a watershed where traditional beliefs are being reinterpreted/re-evaluated in a fast changing materialistic and secular social climate. As it looks to the future, the scope of this paper will, of necessity, be limited to only these two (of the many) elements of change facing us.

1.1 *Intersection with Culture and Change*
One must not think that education as we know it in Pentecostalism will go on as it is, at least not in our movement. I believe we are facing change more rapid and encompassing in scope than most of us imagine. Decisions that will affect our destiny will be made on many fronts.

---

2.   'Theological Transcendence', in Karl Rahner *et al.* (eds.), *Sacramentum Mundi: An Encyclopedia of Theology* (6 vols.; New York: Burns & Oates, 1970), VI, pp. 276-77.

Readers are no doubt aware of the great electronic communications medium, which for some represents a 'threat' that is already revolutionizing the industry. Delivery systems not dreamed possible ten years ago will make some of us as obsolete as the Smith Corona typewriter company that went 'belly up' in July, 1995! Some of us will adapt without pain, others with much discomfort and resentment. As educators we are both resilient and intransigent at times. We are a diverse representation of one of the finest and most dedicated segments of the USA Assemblies of God ministerial ranks. There is no doubt that the educational personnel of other communions and countries are equally as commendable. I salute you!

I believe you are the audience that should hear my thoughts because you are indeed the salt of the earth (and vastly underpaid). Some of the members from your ranks, past and present, who taught at North Central Bible Institute in the 1950s challenged a young lad to make good on his announced call to Africa—way back when a whole semester's tuition was $112 (one-twentieth of today's cost). I remember few tests or test questions from that era. What I remember was biblical *spirituality and character modeled by instructors.* Those were elements possessed by many of those teachers back then, and if you have them today, teacher or administrator, they will still carry you into the twenty-first century, no matter in what electronic medium your lecture is presented.

I speak of men and women of God who smelled like integrity. They sacrificed to teach at the college. Some pumped gas all summer, or checked out groceries to supplement their meager salaries so they could pray with us and teach us and watch us grow spiritually. They were not satisfied until the touch of Pentecost was all over us! They were not satisfied until the cross of Christ was central to our thinking. They could see the future Church through us, as unlikely as that must have seemed at the time. Yes, I am talking about *discipleship and the impartation of faith.*

I thank God for those of you that still have those priorities and qualities. Those qualities have little to do with chronological age. I fear I may not have been as grateful to you, then, as I am today. Aside from my parents, you, the professors of North Central were the most important architects of my life: Frank Lindquist, Ivan O. Miller, Ray Levang, Ione Soltau, M.C. Nelson, John Phillips, Arvid Kingsriter, T.J. Jones, L.B. Larson, and I am surely missing some. Had I known then what I know now (while I was not an ungrateful student), I would have expressed my love and gratitude even more.

2. *Looking Back—Looking Ahead*

Not one of those professors had an earned doctorate while I was there. Some went on to get one; others, a masters in their field. Today North Central Bible College in Minneapolis, Minnesota has 16 doctorates and 26 teachers with masters degrees. I could go down the list of all of your colleges. We do not look today like we once did. Of the ten Assemblies of God schools in America with accredited four year programs there are 441 earned degrees on the faculty and administration. Of that number, 238 have masters degrees (54%) and 167 have their doctorates (38%). We've come a long way! Or have we? No one here doubts the wisdom of combining education and spiritual formation for the servants of God, whatever their calling. But though I have tried to get excited about being a 'futurist' in this paper and challenge you with the marvels of the potential of education for tomorrow through technology, I cannot. I cannot because I have been touched by this century's revival with all its awesome fury and wonder. I am concerned that it may have passed some of us by. (I will gladly let you prove me wrong.) I am even more concerned about your replacements coming on in the pipeline. *Are they going to be Pentecostal?*[3] When I say 'Pentecostal', I mean first of all someone who has been touched by the Spirit. I mean biblical, committed people who courageously believe that only God's presence in New Testament power will begin to meet the threatening forces of destruction let loose in our own culture. I mean holy living where character is more important than image or talent. Pentecostal means more than noise or just talk. I thank God for all of you Spirit-filled teachers who have a well-developed syllabus, but also have the spiritual depth to let the Spirit breathe into the classroom in his timing, because his truth and his touch are indispensable for a student's maturity.

There was a day when 'Pentecostal scholar' was some people's favorite oxymoron (along with 'Civil War'). We all rejoice that Pentecostal scholarship around the world is growing very fast. Thank God we can soon begin to abandon those Reformed textbooks and 'do theology' and speak of all of God's plan from a matrix of Full-Gospel orientation.

---

3. By 'Pentecostal' do not read noisy or excited or weird as a precondition, although a Pentecostal might be so described by some.

If you do not know what I am talking about, then you are probably described above in my fears. Will our own Assemblies of God academy, now forming, be a 'guild society' that is basically rejected by the church because it will have become estranged and alienated through insensitivity to the church's needs and its original *raison d'etre*? Or will it become the instrument of renewal that the Assemblies of God presently needs, like that which all church organizations have needed at similar times in their own journeys?

A global awakening to New Testament Christianity is occurring in all its dynamic glory and grace. By New Testament awakening I mean where the centrality of Christ's cross, the centerpiece of redemption, is proclaimed in the fullness of the Spirit's power with all the accompanying tools (gifts) of combat accounted for and shiny with use. (I am describing the overseas churches, not the majority of North American churches.)

With our General Superintendent, I believe the Assemblies of God in America needs revival or renewal. Not only has our growth largely stopped, we are embracing materialism and the 'fantasy of success' so that there is a decreasing distinction between a Christian and an unbeliever. *The good news is that I believe our educational institutions can once again be the major instruments in a new Great Awakening!*

Many voices in our movement have long given their rationale for fearing education in general as the source of the apostasy of past generations. But we must be gentle with them. Not everyone has the same definition for 'revival'. Some can only accept revival if it conforms to their model or method. If God graces our instrumentality with his move, we must expect critics of 'our' revival who claim they too want revival. Dave Roberts, a British journalist studying current revivals calls them:

> Ultra-subjective people, armed with a legalistic philosophy of ministry, will use their 'sense of peace' and their 'check in the spirit' as a blunt instrument of prejudice, accusation and superficial spiritual judgment. They will see demons under every stone, and they will leave none unturned. Beware those people whose entire identity is wrapped up in 'protecting the faithful'. They can sometimes destroy the faithful with division, accusation and false words of knowledge.[4]

You and I know that the colleges of America were the locus of great

---

4. D. Roberts, *The Toronto Blessing* (Eastbourne, Sussex: Kingsway Publications, 1994), p. 150.

revivals in our history. In the 1790s and the 1890s, the record is most clear. The Spirit of God visited Christian students on college campuses with an outpouring of revival spirit that gave them visions for renewing the churches and affecting USA culture. Who will lead the Great Awakening of the 1990s? Will one of your campuses repeat what happened in Williams College in 1806 where five students prayed together regularly until revival came to the campus and region. Similar facts can be recounted about the revivals of Finney in the 1830s and the revival of 1858 which began on college campuses. The list of spiritual leaders from campus revivals reads like a Who's Who of world missions: John R. Mott, E. Stanley Jones, Robert Wilder, Samuel Zwemer, Robert Speer, and many others.[5]

Many of our fearful critics have forgotten that the Pentecostal revival of this century did not first start at a mission on Azusa street in Los Angeles, but in a Bible School in the state of Kansas. Brothers and Sisters, let us lead the way again!

To focus more precisely on my topic of the day, I will start with an example from the Southern Baptists and then come to my concerns for our movement.

3. *Turbulence in Today's Post-Christian Era*

In a recent address to the Fellowship of Evangelical Seminary Presidents,[6] the new president of the Southern Baptist Seminary in Louisville, Kentucky, Dr. Albert Mohler spoke on the future of Theological Education. His presentation was not welcomed warmly by everyone in attendance. In fact, the house was quite divided. Mohler took the theme

---

5. D.M. Howard, *Student Power in World Evangelism* (Downers Grove, IL: InterVarsity Press, 1970). For good documentation of the history of this phenomenon see also: D.L. McKenna, *The Coming Great Awakening* (Downers Grove, IL: InterVarsity Press, 1990). For further research on early revivals in America and their 'charismatic' manifestations, see the following: P. Dixon, *Signs of Revival* (Eastbourne, Sussex: Kingsway Publications, 1994); J. Edwards, *On Revival* (Edinburgh: Banner of Truth, 1991); E. Evans, *The Welch Revival of 1904* (Cardiff, Wales: Evangelical Press of Wales, 1969); J.I. Packer, *God in our Midst* (Dallas: Word Books, 1987); J. Weir, *Heaven Came Down* (repr.; Belfast: Ambassador, 1987 [1860]).

6. A. Mohler, 'The Future of Theological Education in America', an address to the Fellowship of Evangelical Presidents, Phoenix, AZ, January 1995.

for his thesis from C.P. Snow's book, *The Two Cultures*.[7]

Mohler writes that when seminaries were worried about finances and worried about existence, they knew their mission. Today they are endowed and do not know what they are about. As you may all know, the Southern Baptist convention has been quite divided and stormy over the issue of the scriptures and confessional 'truth' for over a decade. The conservative element in the church has carried the day and scores of 'liberal' professors (who call themselves moderates or progressives) have been ousted from their main seminaries. The battle for the Bible still rages in that, the largest Protestant denomination in the USA. Listen to his perception of theological education that has gone awry in his arena:

> The autonomy of the academy.
> The faculty are self-appointing and they govern the schools.
> Specialization of disciplines runs counter to institutional 'wholeness'.
> Secularization of the academy.
> Academics too focused on programs and less on pragmatics.

All the above, for Mohler, represents *a move away from a confessional ethic*. Under the spell of his church's struggles and looking at many other Protestant churches now in drastic decline after facing many of the same choices (of course in the context of their own time frame and experience), this new and controversial president in his 30s sounds an alarm welcomed by the majority of his church in America. The 'moderates', however, feel they have been betrayed and misunderstood.

If you have been following this great church as it has turned on itself in the last decade, you have formed your own opinions about the reasons. I take no joy in watching the weakening of the Southern Baptist Convention. I pray they will see that coming to a healthy doctrinal agreement can include both factions. Mohler warned those of us who are seminary presidents that the pluralism of education, so espoused by the Association of Theological Schools (ATS) and the regional accrediting bodies (North Central Association etc.) may well eventuate in drastic measures. For those of us determined to stay in touch with the spiritual constraints of our sponsoring churches, we may have to leave ATS and go it alone. This same argument, of course, is now being waged in Assemblies of God circles by those who oppose leaving the

7. C.P. Snow, *The Two Cultures* (Cambridge: Cambridge University Press, 1959).

American Association of Bible Colleges (AABC) accreditation and going solely with a regional agency. Who can predict the social and political forces in our own hedonistic society and how they may impact on spiritual convictions of how best to educate our youth?

Our own academy is suddenly taking on life, really for the first time. Its very existence is a cause for concern by our Assemblies of God traditionalist faction. I believe heartily in the words of president Dodds of Princeton: *'Ideas should not be made safe for students, but students should be made safe for ideas'*. The ultra traditionalists in our company still believe that teachers should protect the modern student from competing ideas (education by inoculation or indoctrination) and thus preserve our Pentecostal youth. I reject that defensive view, based on fear and a sense of inferiority. I believe that a good portion of the 50% of the youth lost from our churches is lost because we have failed to instill in them the truth and power of Pentecost. This, I believe, will stand up in the marketplace of ideas, like the Bible stands. If you agree, I hope you are telling not just students (who are notorious for distorting information) but ministers and pastors. May I suggest that you go to your own District Councils (in the USA) and show your zeal for God and fire for witness. When they see 'degrees without temperature', many of our pastors are anxious. Two-thirds World educators do not generally face the same issue in this regard as their church leaders seldom fear education outright.

3.1 *Progressives versus Traditionalists*

When I look to the future in Assemblies of God education I see that we too must make decisions concerning the dividing line between progressives and traditionalists. This controversy has already surfaced on the issue of whether secular majors should be offered in a school where once only ministerial degrees (or diplomas) were available. Will our schools be held accountable to the regulative faith of the church? Or will the norms of the academy hold the day? As I travel the districts here at home and listen to the debate about the regional colleges, I hear an increasing criticism of a bent towards a Spirit-less rationalism and materialism. Some of these arguments are put forward by wise and informed heads. Others are not. It will be a tragedy if dialogue is not allowed. Dialogue facilitates analysis and reflection. Sadly, some of the loudest voices on these issues are the least informed. I believe implicitly that: *It is always better to debate a question without settling it, than to settle a question without debating it.*

Bertrand Russell, a British philosopher, typified the thinking of the world (and many times the Church too) when he said, 'The fundamental cause of trouble in the world today is that the stupid are cocksure while the intelligent are full of doubt.' Unlike the world's thinking, the believer knows that the Bible is right side up. To get the right-side-up thinker (about spiritual matters) to also keep his or her head about change is the key. The difference between winning and losing this battle in our church will be how the preachers in the Assemblies of God movement view change as it comes at them. If they see it as a threat, as an ill wind to be resisted by keeping our heads down and digging our feet in, we will be the losers. But if we, the educational community, can demonstrate that we are full of the Holy Ghost while we provide the educational tools, and are encouraged to use them, all will be well. When our ministers see change as synonymous with opportunity, the church will advance all around the world! I will have more to say on the topic of the academy and Pentecost below.

We will not best prepare young people for the rigors of the next century until we accept that our greatest challenge is not financial but theological. We are in the middle of third generational declension in the Western Church. Modern technology threatens the essence and content of theology. Let us recognize how our own discourse tends toward naturalistic and scientific jargon that betrays our departure from biblical belief. The spirit of the academy without the Spirit of Truth allows no place for truth claims. The traditional academy seldom allows transcendence! *Our Pentecostal schools must make clear our commitment to the truth of the doctrines of the Church, while we maintain the rigor of the educational process.*

I submit that Pentecostals must cease to be content to let Evangelicals, by default, determine the shape and content of the hermeneutical and theological agenda.

3.2 *Agenda by Default*
When Peter Wagner wrote the foreword for *The Kingdom and The Power*, he set out in clear terms the main subject of today's paper. Wagner gives a quick and somewhat controversial overview, nevertheless, outlining the topic well:

When the Pentecostal movement burst on the scene at the beginning of our century, the knee-jerk reaction of more traditional Christians was to write them off as a false cult along with Mormons and Jehovah's Witnesses. But that obviously carnal position could not be maintained, given the clear manifestations of the fruit of the Holy Spirit and the unprecedented numerical growth of the movement. After WW2, God raised up leaders such as Thomas Zimmerman of the Assemblies of God to mainstream Pentecostals into the National Association of Evangelicals and Evangelicalism. *The price for this, however, was a gradual de-emphasizing of the signs, wonders and other miraculous ministries so outwardly characteristic of the first and early second-generation Pentecostals.* Evangelicals could live with the Pentecostals as long as they were polite enough not to raise issues such as speaking in tongues or power ministries in mixed company such as the Lausanne Committee for World Evangelization. Just when things seemed to be settling down, the charismatic renewal came on the scene in the early 1960s. Many Pentecostals regretted this because for one thing they did not know how to relate to Lutherans and Episcopalians who spoke in tongues as well as drank beer; and for another, they could not understand how God could baptize Roman Catholics in the Holy Spirit. To complicate things more, the charismatics began giving signs and wonders and slaying in the Spirit the high profile that Pentecostals once did.[8]

Dr. Gary McGee, Professor of Church History at Assemblies of God Theological Seminary (AGTS), like most of his colleagues at the seminary, resonates with what we feel God wants to do with us in Springfield as an instrument of renewal in these end times. Traveling together on a recent trip in Europe, he visited with me on the topic of this paper. He wrote it out for me:

> Throughout the history of the Pentecostal movement, concern has always been expressed that Pentecostals might follow in the steps of the Methodists, meaning loss of their revival heritage, power, and zeal. In my opinion, the Assemblies of God, now in the later stages of a revival movement has already entered a 'post-Pentecostal' phase of its history.[9] This may come as a shock to many, but the facts become more obvious every year: decline in charismatic leadership, uncertainty about aspects of Pentecostal spirituality (a dilemma created in part by Evangelical scholar-ship and the slow development of Pentecostal scholarship), decline in

8.   P. Wagner in G.S. Greig and K.F.N. Springer (eds.), *The Kingdom and The Power* (Venture, CA: Regal Books, 1993), p. 15. Emphasis mine.

9.   See W.M. Menzies, *Anointed to Serve: The Story of the Assemblies of God* (Springfield, MO: Gospel Publishing House, 1971), pp. 379-83.

church growth, and the continuing propensity to exalt political power over holiness of character (fruit of the spirit).

It has been easy in recent years to boast about our remarkable church growth abroad and that the AG 'does it best', meaning that there is little to learn from others. We have viewed ourselves as superior to charismatics—they lean to excesses, lack sound biblical doctrine, are less committed and stable than we are. But beyond the hype of our self-generated triumphalism, is it possible that the Emperor 'has no clothes'? It is time to repent and open our hearts to the Spirit and seek for His leading.

The academic marketplace of the Assemblies of God plays a crucial role in the direction of our spirituality. The exegetical, historical, and theological examination of Pentecostal spirituality must be a top priority. However, the study of the Spirit's work in our lives must be a combination of scriptural truth and praxis. This confronts us with a major question: Can Pentecostal-charismatic spirituality and leadership be taught within the framework of standard Evangelical collegiate and seminary curricula? Will we be willing to break new ground by pulling theory and praxis together in creative avenues which provide more effective mentoring in Pentecostal students? The long-standing arrangement of presenting theory in the classroom and modeling in the chapel has been successful, but it has not been enough.

Many of the old 'spiritual masters' who taught in our schools have gone to be with the Lord. Retaining the Pentecostal heritage and preventing further entry into a post-Pentecostal future, requires the emergence of a new group of spiritual masters, well-trained academically and tutored by the Holy Spirit.[10]

I want to pick up on McGee's description of many of the more modern Pentecostals being 'uncertain about certain aspects of Pentecostal spirituality', and relate this to Evangelical theology. Bill Menzies, quoted above, writes of this in the foreword to Paul Pomerville's *The Third Force in Missions*.

From the age of Enlightenment, scholastic Protestantism has extended its influence on modern Evangelicalism. This influence is disclosed in an uneasiness with the supernatural manifestations of God's power, in an eagerness to ascribe as 'superstition' a serious belief in the demonic. Pentecostals, conscious of God's power to take authority over evil spirits and satanic power, at this point are not quite equal to their Evangelical 'cousins'.[11]

10. G.B. McGee, personal conversation, Bressanone, Italy, July 1995.
11. W.W. Menzies, 'Foreword', in P. Pomerville, *The Third Force in Missions* (Peabody, MA: Hendrickson, 1985), p. 14.

The early Enlightenment led scholastic Protestantism to the notion that grasping the whole counsel of God consisted mainly in arranging the 'facts' of scripture into their prearranged categories of systematic theology. To them Christianity was a religion of reason. Benjamin Warfield, a leader of the 'twentieth-century Princetonian Presbyterians' writes:

> It is the distinction of Christianity that it has come into the world clothed with the mission to reason its way to its dominion. It is solely by reasoning that it has come thus far on its way to its kingship. And it is solely by reasoning that it will put all its enemies under its feet.[12]

3.3 *Western Cultural Distortion*

What distortions have resulted due to the impact of Western culture on the gospel? The erosion of the sense of the supernatural has to be at the top of the list of distortions, as well as the eclipse of the experiential dimension of the Christian faith. The dynamic biblical theologizing represented by the notion of ethnic theologies is in stark contrast with a static, rationalistic, scholastically oriented systematic theology of Westerners.[13]

> Under the impact of the Enlightenment the post-Reformation period produced a scholastic theology. Theology was a theoretical discipline, an abstract technical science, a logical system of belief cast in an Aristotelian mold. It was static in nature, with an emphasis on a rational defense of a settled deposit of doctrine.[14]

Many sources speak of this 'theological deposit' which represented a systematizing of the theological writings of the Reformers. McClintock and Strong state concerning this fact:

> Whenever the Church begins to let the writings of any of its eminent ministers stand between it and a free and direct interpretation of the Scriptures in light of intuition and experience, that moment it enters its scholastic stage... The view of scholastic theologians was that they were working with a 'finished' theological deposit which allowed them to live in its systematic form and jump over a dynamic process where biblical revelation was constantly interacting with historical and cultural contexts.[15]

12. J.E. Meeter (ed.), *Selected Shorter Works of B.B. Warfield* (Nutley, NJ: Presbyterian & Reformed Press, 1973), p. 98.

13. Meeter, *Warfield*, 25.

14. P. Pomerville, 'A Case Study in the Contextualization of the Gospel: A Critique of the Reformed View of Scripture in the Post-Reformation Period' (MA thesis; Seattle Pacific University, 1980), p. 94.

15. J. McClintock and J. Strong, *Encyclopedia of Biblical, Theological, and*

Rationality and system were characteristic of the methodology of scholastic theologians then, and one wonders to what extent the same forces are not at work today? Pomerville adds,

> The primary role of reason in the eighteenth century theological work was the result of a philosophical shift. Augustine's 'I believe that I may understand', which emphasized reason's subordination to faith, shifted under the impact of the Enlightenment to Protestant Scholasticism's 'I know that I may believe'. Such a confidence in reason led to a naive realism, which in turn led theologians to believe that there was a direct correspondence between their western perception and reality. Human reason was elevated to such a point in Reformed Scholasticism, under the influence of Scottish Common Sense philosophy, that theologians assumed that they were thinking the thoughts of God after him.[16]

3.4 *The Loss of Spiritual Power*

This rational focus often has been accompanied by an indifferent attitude toward spiritual experience and power. David Boot states that pneumatology began to be neglected as early as the second century.[17] Rolland Allen reminds us of early missions, before this century: 'Missionary work as an expression of the Holy Spirit has received such slight and casual attention that it might almost escape the notice of the hasty reader'.[18] Melvin Hodges describes this neglect as an indispensable qualification for the relative success of Pentecostal evangelistic efforts. The 'place' that Pentecostals give to the Holy Spirit is similar to that which the New Testament believers gave to him.[19]

The reluctance of some Evangelicals to pursue the experiential dimension of the Christian faith, however, goes deeper than avoiding existential theology.

> It involves the excessive impact of the western worldview and scholastic theology on Evangelicalism. Some Evangelicals may be content with the unhappy combination of a warm conversion experience and a cold

Ecclesiastical Literature (Grand Rapids: Baker Book House, 1970), IX, p. 422.

16. P. Pomerville, *The Third Force in Missions* (Peabody, MA: Hendrickson, 1985), p. 67.

17. D. Boot, *Witness to the World: The Christian Mission in Theological Perspective* (London, England: Marshall, Morgan & Scott, 1980).

18. R. Allen, *The Ministry of the Spirit* (Grand Rapids: Eerdmans, 1960), p. 21.

19. M. Hodges, *Theology of the Church and its Mission* (Springfield, MO: Gospel Publishing House, 1977), p. 149. See also H. Boer, *Pentecost and Missions* (Grand Rapids: Eerdmans, 1961).

intellectual doctrine and apologetic, but the Pentecostal cannot afford that
tension. The very center of his distinctive is jeopardized, the dynamic,
charismatic experience of the Spirit in the Christian life.[20]

John Ruthven both chides and encourages Pentecostals to abandon
the 'wrong road taken' by Calvinists (among others) in America who do
not do justice to Calvin's insights concerning revelation. Pentecostals,
like other American Fundamentalists, ignored Calvin's teaching of the
testimonium of the Spirit in interpreting scripture, but rather followed, to
one degree or another, the rationalistic premises of the Princetonians.
The scholars from Princeton failed to include that part of Calvin's thesis
where the *acts* of God are also instructive for revelation.

In this context, American Pentecostalism's appeal to 'experience'
almost never sought to displace the authority of Scripture so much as it
attempted to prove it, or at least some interpretation of it (like some
rationalistic apologetic). When tongues first reappeared at the turn of the
century, they were perceived as explaining a theological truth, rather
than *applying* theology. He refers to the Topeka outbreak of tongues
as only a means of finding a rationale, or as providing 'evidence' for
theological truths already categorized (finished—approved—catalogued).
Pentecostals accepted the paradigm concerning 'experience' that implies
a religious authority based on subjective mysticism, thus unverifiable and
untrustworthy. This evangelical paradigm insisted that tongues were a
new word and thus unacceptable as an addition to the Canon. Ruthven
cleverly shows how Pentecostal theology can respond to this miscon-
ception with an appeal to Calvin's doctrine of the *testimonium* of the
Spirit, but more so to the biblical concept of 'word' as referring, not
primarily to scripture, but more essentially to divine revelation in its
variety of forms, for example, as in a prophecy, revelation or miracle,
with scripture emerging as a result of these processes.[21] Ruthven says:

> The word of God, then, is appropriated from scripture on a continuum of
> experience with its original appearance. The revelatory action of the Spirit
> is required for scripture to fulfill its work (1 Cor. 2.12,14; 2 Cor. 3.14-
> 17). The Sadducees' position in Mk 12.24 parallels the contemporary
> bifurcation of 'word' and 'experience': *Jesus' answer is that failure to
> 'know' (in the biblical sense of 'experience', rather than 'intellectually*

20. Pomerville, *Third Force*, p. 14.
21. See the explanation of B. Klappert, 'Word', in Colin Brown (ed.), *New
International Dictionary of New Testament Theology* (Grand Rapids: Zondervan,
1978).

grasp') the power of God is also a failure to 'know' scripture itself. Hence any attempt to understand scripture from a lack of miraculous experience is to fail, though this is the essence of some recent Evangelical hermeneutics.[22]

4. *The Curse of Reformed Theology and The Supernatural*

Since the days of the reformation, many Protestant theologians have argued that the gifts of the Spirit were temporary in nature. The reformers had two reasons for formulating and systematizing theological arguments against contemporary miracles. First, their enemies, the Catholics, appealed to Catholic miracles in support of Catholic doctrine. In effect they said, 'We have miracles that show God approves of our doctrine. Furthermore, we have a long history of miracles stretching back to New Testament times. What miracles can you point to that show that God approves of your doctrine?' This attack led the reformers both to deny the validity of Catholic miracles, past and present, and to formulate theological arguments against contemporary miracles.[23]

Secondly, the reformers' lack of experience of the miraculous was the major reason for their distinctive stance. Had they witnessed noteworthy miracles, they would never have attempted to argue that miracles were meant to be temporary. Thus the reformers were confronted with a choice—was their lack of experience of the miraculous due to a defect in their experience or to a divinely planned obsolescence of miracles? They chose to believe the latter. They now had the monumental task before them of explaining why God was so liberal in giving miracles to the first-century Church and so stingy with miracles in the centuries that followed. The trick was to prove that miracles were meant only to serve temporary purposes in the first century.

They could not produce one specific text of Scripture that taught that miracles or the supernatural gifts were confined to the New Testament period. Nor has anyone else since then been able to do that.[24] Thus it

22. J. Ruthven, 'Pentecostal Spiritual Formation: Its Ground and Expression' (Society of Pentecostal Studies Conference Papers, 1992), p. 6 (italics Ruthven's); now largely incorporated in his book, *On the Cessation of the Charismata: The Protestant Polemic on Postbiblical Miracles* (JPTSup, 3; Sheffield: Sheffield Academic Press, 1993).

23. J. Deere, *Surprised by the Power of the Spirit* (Grand Rapids: Zondervan, 1993), p. 100.

24. J. Ruthven, '*Cessation of the Charismata*', pp. 41-111.

followed, in natural progression of this fabrication, that the reformers argued that miracles were needed to authenticate the apostles as trust-worthy authors of the Holy Scripture. Once this was achieved, miracles would no longer be needed.

This remains the primary argument of the cessationists. Many of you have come under the intense environment of these fine, scholarly teachers of the Word. While they may be intellectual giants, so many are experientially weak in spiritual power! Their rationality appeals to our basic conservative nature as academicians. Miracles are sometimes messy for us. The mysterious activity of God is too unpredictable for us. So why not buy into this neat clean evangelical power vacuum that has a certain prestige but very little risk? Dare we ask ourselves, where is the fruit of Pentecost in our life? Let us not hide behind our 'personality type' or a cognitive predisposition of a certain cerebral hemisphere! One need not be an 'evangelist type' to be a witness.

I have a colleague who recounts with some sadness the marked contrast he encountered in the spiritual orientation of his colleagues in one of our 18 post secondary institutions. Returning to the campus after a long absence, he discovered that younger faculty, having been educated in a rationalistic evangelical background had little experience or conviction of the Pentecostal model for ministry. There is a danger here, not so much that these individuals would speak openly against the reality of Pentecost, but it is demonstrable that attitudes prevail which are cool and sometimes scornful of certain legitimate expressions of Pentecostal-charismatic ministry and values. We must not be guilty of eroding the faith of students. I know the dangers of over-generalization, and this is not a blanket indictment. Of course I run the risk of being misunder-stood. I take that risk because we must, Brothers and Sisters, confront this issue in the open. Good academicians welcome open dialogue.

Do you exercise a spiritual gift in public ministry? Do you have an up-to-date prayer language? Do your students and associates hear you worship with it? (I am not talking of exhibitionism). *Brothers and Sisters, we can not come up to our full potential in God without the gifts and fruit in operation.* Do we regularly bind up the wounded? Are we disciplers in the mode of Benny Aker or Bill Menzies? (to name only two with whom I have worked). There are many more in our ranks and in the broader Full-Gospel Church worldwide. Who is going to replace Stanley Horton some day? Who is going to become another Gordon Fee? These persons have great academic minds *and* a fire in their souls.

They have demonstrated the supernatural in witness.

Is it reasonable to think we can standardize or systematize the Holy Spirit? By his Spirit, God moves in the affairs of humanity. In this mode, he is mysterious. If we have been influenced by reformed Protestant theological paradigms, can we even perceive the non-linear nature of God? How can we fit him into our boxes of neat predictability?

4.1 *The Domestication of the Holy Spirit*

In how many of our churches and classrooms is the Holy Spirit seen as a disturbing influence? Listen to Green's caricature:

> Let the Holy Spirit therefore be paid lip service, but for all practical purposes be shut up in the Bible where he can do no harm. Let his presence attend the confessional statement of our particular brand of Protestantism. Let the bizarre and miraculous elements which the NT documents narrate about his activity be relegated to those far-off apostolic days: It would be very embarrassing and doctrinally untidy if the Holy Spirit were to speak to men today, or to enable miracles to be performed and men to speak in tongues not their own. The Bible, accordingly is the safest place for the Spirit. That's where he belongs; not in the hurly burly of real life.[25]

Do you both teach and demonstrate for your students how God can deliver a drug addict? How about a transvestite? When is the last time some of us tarried with a seeker until he or she received the baptism in the Holy Spirit? Do we demonstrate *any* of the manifestation gifts in the chapel? Do we model only the intellectual side of our profession?

Probably by now some are saying 'enough already! Tarr why are you on this Signs and Wonders kick?' Because I am alarmed! Alarmed because of what I see dying in the Assemblies of God movement in the USA. We have successfully passed the torch of Pentecost and its message of 'deliverance to the poor' (Lk. 4.18-19) to 149 countries of the world. The difference in our 'foreign children' is the presence of New Testament power to witness, and power to confront the forces of darkness.

In hundreds of our USA churches (I am being conservative) there is no growth because there is no witness. I am alarmed at the few people coming to the altar for salvation and fewer being baptized in the Holy Ghost. We are raising a generation of Christians most of whom have never seen 'revival'. They have never experienced the overshadowing

---

25. M. Green, *I Believe in the Holy Spirit* (Grand Rapids: Eerdmans, 1975), p. 12.

presence of God around the altar, nor do they know anyone who has been healed. The majority have never spoken in tongues, and a good portion of them do not particularly want to.

Have you dared ask your beginning classes for a show of hands on how many have a daily prayer language? For us to survive as a viable Pentecostal movement in the future, our future ministers must get the biblical fundamentals of New Testament Christianity in your classrooms, *plus* the experiential (*praxis*) from your personal life. I care little if you are teaching Bible, Theology, the Social Sciences, Communications, Secondary Education, or Counseling. For me these are all ministry related and should be taught (by us) and 'caught' (by our students) from an environment of a Pentecostal world view.

I find a higher incidence of similar thinking about the immanence of God's mysterious power than even ten years ago. This is especially visible in the ranks of the academy in the West. Brothers and Sisters, the future of our movement will depend, in a large measure, on our determination to reverse this trend. You are the ones that make up the academic affairs committees of our institutions that determine the final curriculum. As teachers and administrators we must have Pentecost in our souls until it oozes out of our pores and 'contaminates' those wonderful lives that brush up against us in the academic scene. The New Testament specifically commands its readers to 'seek', 'desire earnestly', 'rekindle' and 'employ' certain 'miraculous' charismata (1 Cor. 12.31; 14.1, 4, 5, 39; 2 Tim. 1.6; 1 Pet. 4.10). You that are expert exegetes know that this command implies that simple neglect is all one needs to retard or suppress the appearance of the charismata. The current condition of the American Assemblies of God, in general, is testimony that this grace does not operate automatically.[26]

4.2 A Modern Example of Evangelical Exclusion

In a very recent article Gary McGee has just finished for *The International Bulletin of Missionary Research* on the legacy of Melvin Hodges, he points out a very revealing incident when Moody Press gained permission to print Hodges's seminal work, *The Indigenous Church*. Moody wanted to print the book as part of its Colportage Library, albeit with an important abridgment. In the chapter 'Pentecost and Indigenous Methods', the editors removed the following statement, among others,

26. D. Willard, *The Spirit of the Disciplines* (San Francisco, CA: Harper & Row, 1988), p. ix.

in order to de-emphasize the charismata which Hodges knew to be indispensable for powerful and effective evangelism. In fact *this distinctive* is the genius of Assemblies of God foreign missions along with a truly indigenous missiology. The paragraph left out reads:

> On the mission field, the emphasis which Pentecostal people place on the necessity of each individual believer receiving a personal infilling of the Holy Spirit has produced believers and workers of unusual zeal and power. Again, the emphasis on the present-day working of miracles and the healing of the sick has been the means in the hand of God of awakening whole communities and convincing unbelievers of the power of God. These have seen a Power at work superior to that of their own witch doctors and priests. The faith which Pentecostal people have in the ability of the Holy Spirit to give spiritual gifts and supernatural abilities to the common people, even to those who might be termed 'ignorant and unlearned', has raised up a host of lay preachers and leaders of unusual spiritual ability—not unlike the rugged fishermen who first followed the Lord.[27]

Protestant scholasticism represents the theological roots of the silencing of the Spirit in Western missions. Western missionaries' lack of supernatural belief was the biggest cause of the great Independent Church Movement in Africa. The West lays this phenomenon onto 'African' doings, as if the continent had distorted the 'true gospel' out of some innate depravity. Sengue sees the reason as a clash of Western thinking and African, not the clash of the gospel and African culture![28] Pomerville agrees as he quotes Peel:

> Christianity has been both cause and catalyst of social change in Africa; and one of the most prominent features of modern Africa has been the emergence of independent churches, founded by Africans in protest at some feature of the Christianity of the missionary societies. This clearly shows that the loss of the belief in and perception of the supernatural in Western culture is an all-important antecedent factor in the study of the independency movements.[29]

27. M.L. Hodges, *The Indigenous Church* (Springfield, MO: Gospel Publishing House, 1953). The Moody edition was entitled *On The Mission Field: The Indigenous Church* (Chicago, IL: Moody, 1953).

28. N. Sengue, 'Identity Crises in African Church', *EMQ* 17.2 (1981), pp. 9-99.

29. J.D.Y. Peel, *Aladura: A Religious Movement among the Yoruba* (Oxford: Oxford University Press, 1968), p. 1.

Pomerville continues:

> The fact that Pentecostalism has such a dynamic role in contemporary
> missions is directly related to its experiential dimension of the Christian
> faith. As such, it is not only a 'corrective' of post-Reformation Protestant
> Scholasticism, but the vehicle by which two-thirds world peoples satisfy
> their predisposition to transcendence and the supernatural to which the
> Western mind pretends to be superior.[30]

4.3 *On Revelation*

Pentecostals in the future must develop a more holistic understanding of
revelation that goes beyond the traditional static conciliar and Evangelical
understanding. No one here is implying a denial of the canon of
Scripture, but neither should we be bound by the *noetic* view (knowing
as information, reflection, propositional) which obscures the *ontic* (immediacy, presence, reality).[31]

Charles Kraft states:

> Personal truth and revelation are not static. A true person will speak truly.
> But our understanding of truth (especially in the biblical sense) should not
> be reduced to a concept of 'true information'. Jesus *did* the truth—not
> simply gave *information* about the Father. We need to learn to distinguish
> between such dynamic revelation and truth and the information that is
> inevitably a part but never the whole of either.[32]

A Pentecostal concept of revelation must include the activity of God
in the contemporary moment. If you will prepare students to be ministers to the inner cities of this nation, or the countries of the world, you
will of necessity impart to them this dynamic of Scripture and theology.
It represents a Divine contextualization, a true power encounter through
active faith against the demonic lifestyle growing so fast in this culture.
Pomerville again puts it so well:

> The concepts of Scripture and theology are distorted when the dynamic
> dimension of the Spirit is missing in revelation... The idea that revelation,
> Scripture, and theology have a dynamic dimension validates contempo-
> rary contextualization efforts. Divine activity can be expected in those

---

30. Pomerville, *Third Force*, p. 63. For a full review of this vital issue for
Pentecostals, see chapter 3, 'A Correction of a Western Distortion', pp. 63-78.

31. C. Kraft, *Christianity in Culture: A Study in Cross-Cultural Perspective*
(Maryknoll: Orbis Books, 1979), p. 178. See also B. Ramm, *Special Revelation and
The Word of God* (Grand Rapids: Eerdmans, 1961), p. 158.

32. Kraft, *Culture*, p. 178.

efforts. The supernatural witness of the Holy Spirit in the heart, the demonstration of the Word of God in transforming behavior, and the Word confirmed with 'signs following' could only be adequate authority in those circumstances. The Christian faith concerns the present activity and rule of God, not merely an intellectual faith. *This is the corrective message of Pentecostalism for an Enlightenment-impacted Protestant faith.*[33]

I am conscious that this paper may be sounding harsh, and for some, even uninformed or presumptuous. There are always some who do not think anyone but a highly trained theologian should ever speak about the science of God. Again, I do not pretend to be on a level of theological training like some of you who have made theology their specialty. I am rather a communicologist–anthropologist by training, and a pastor, missionary and teacher by experience. But from that matrix my privilege has been to train pastors and missionaries and a few evangelists for 35 years. I am starting to get a pretty good idea of the faith characteristics and consequent demonstration of a person's belief structure that make a significant difference in the kingdom. Please do not be angry with me. I am not aiming at individuals or any institution. I do not have a private agenda. Please do not interpret my intensity as something other than a heart full of sadness on one side, and hope on the other. I covet renewal in our midst and I dare to speak so pointedly because you are the people who can best turn us back to our roots (not back to the 1920's in time or repeated experience). But who better can articulate to the future generation the need to remint, like a worn coin, the ultimate intention of the Spirit than you who are dedicated to the task and have the intellect and verbal skills to accomplish it? Let the Holy Spirit of God again form us as individuals, and turn this move ment, into a shiny, clear, negotiable instrument for his commendation.

4.4 *Current Events*

In March of this year the Lord led the seminary to call a Signs and Wonders Conference in Springfield. This conference touched a need in the hearts of pastors across this nation. Over one thousand pastors came. The level of hunger and seeking demonstrated by altar times was both astonishing and gratifying. The reports of post-conference impact on local congregations in accounts of healings and deliverance and conversions

---

33. Pomerville, *Third Force*, p. 127. Emphasis mine.

reads like the book of Acts. There are hundreds of churches in our movement that have not seen revival, even in it's most conservative definition, for a generation or more. With some wonderful exceptions, many of our churches are sending young people to our schools who have not seen Pentecost, do not know how to pray for the salvation of a comrade, let alone pray with him or her for the baptism of the Holy Spirit. What a wonderful opportunity we have to model the New Testament concept of Pentecost and equip them to confront our present world. The supernatural power of God in the church and in your classroom is vitally needed. Let pastors of our districts no more stand in District Councils and decry the lack of spirituality in our schools! Of course we cannot ignore the case that can be made for a local Assembly's primary responsibility in this regard.

4.5 *A Sociological Reason for the Suppression of the Holy Spirit*

> The Assemblies of God shares with other movements the ever present danger of an erosion of charisma. The experience of God can readily give way to dogma, ritual, and organization, with a religious group becoming more intent on perpetuation of the institution than the religious experiences which birthed it.[34]

Thus does sociologist Margaret Poloma describe another, much more sociological reason for the loss of Pentecost as we once knew it. She continues: 'Perhaps no single issue within the Assemblies of God can better reflect this process than an analysis of the role of women.' The story of women in Assemblies of God ministry (in America) elaborates a passing observation made by Max Weber in his classic work on the sociology of religion.[35] Weber says that those involved in any social movement of the 'common folk' are characterized by the tendency to allot equality to women, but that this state rarely extends beyond the formation stage. No doubt the rise and success of a professional clergy in our own movement, like any other, is not only a sign of moving from the 'sect' status to that of a denomination, but no matter how important this may be for the establishment of a denomination, it also paradoxically undermines charisma.[36] Let me be clear in quick summary. The decrease

34. M.M. Poloma, *The Assemblies of God at the Crossroads* (Knoxville, TN: University of Tennessee Press, 1989), p. 101.

35. M. Weber, *The Sociology of Religion* (Boston, MA: Beacon, 1963), p. 104.

36. E. Hoffer, 'The True Believer on the Role of "Prophet" and "Priest" in Social Movements', *The True Believer* (Perennial Library Edition; New York:

in the (ministerial) role of women in our church does not *cause* the cooling off of Pentecostal fervor, but the same internal organizational forces that find the influence of women less desirable also find the role of the prophet, and especially the prophetess, less desirable. That is regrettable and certainly less than the Holy Spirit intends for the influence of women in ministry in a New Testament church. The very success of the denomination is luring it away from a healthy fear of institutionalism and toward accommodation into the larger culture, which favors efficiency and pragmatism over charisma and prophets who tend to be critical of the establishment. Here, then, is why I am so solicitous for the classrooms of our 18 schools in the USA (and the 400 plus overseas) to hold high the value of God's 'in-breaking' immanent power, and transcendence above rationalistic thinking concerning that supernatural power to equip all of us. We, the teachers and professors must first show the fruits of the Spirit-filled life and in turn *impact our students with the blending of heat and light, of academic rigor and spiritual fervor*. I call it 'knowledge on fire'. Unless I am wrong, if we march into the twenty-first century without first repenting of our carnal love of power, our materialism and compromise with secularism so rampant in our society, we may very well be 'marching' in 2010 with our Pentecostal banner hanging in shreds on the altar of expedience to social influence and the heady wine of respectability and acceptance.

Let us in academia lead the way back to the New Testament. Let us show students and their pastors alike that God's power through the cross of Christ makes possible miraculous healing as much as it does sanctification, endurance, and suffering for the gospel, by the power of God (2 Tim. 1.8). We may not know all things about how these elements are interrelated (e.g., is healing in the atonement at the same level as salvation of the soul?), but that must not keep us from also teaching of the sovereignty of God. Let's be encouraged! We know that the same discipline that it takes to achieve an educational goal, will give us the perseverance to bear fruit in our lives and those we must touch.

Harper & Row, 1966). For further explanation of this concept see C. Barfoot and G. Sheppard, 'Prophetic vs. Priestly Religion: The Changing Role of Women Clergy in Classical Pentecostal Churches', *Review of Religious Research* 22 (1980), pp. 2-17.

5. *Future Sight*

I see a day when some of our present instruction will not limit students to the controlling sphere of Bible-restricting, mind-choking, 'narrow' dogma. I speak of boundaries built of fear, and weakness of experience, that hedge in the largest diameter an issue could span; the smallest degree of arc of diversity to be considered relevant; the absolute length of the radius of truth. I see a day when we as a greater Pentecostal movement will shed our inferiority complex and finally lift our heads in humility, not pride or triumphalism, to affirm that 'this is that spoken by the prophets'. This is the biblically based truth that delivers human-kind's captives by attacking the roots of satanic power. Why? Because it is the genuine article Jesus promised.

I see a day when we do not hang our heads in embarrassment in an ecumenical meeting. Nor will we carnally project a powerful air of 'in your face' when our inner city churches thrive and attract the wounded world to their front steps, or when soon we are acclaimed the largest Protestant church in the world.

I see a time when our electronic delivery systems will have more substance than just the shine of technological hardware. Then the message of Christ's cross can march out to the marketplace with power to transform. We will then surely attract the full scorn of Satan's social empire, for that is a *sine qua non* of Christ's Church militant. I see a day when the violence put upon our church in Iran will be a common theme in our expectations and you will train your students for the grace of martyrdom.

I see a day when defensiveness and suspicion about dialogue in our community will give way to the examination of a subject to be held at arm's length and scrutinized in the clear light of current scholarship. 'By what process was this conclusion reached?', one will ask. Was the information forced through a certain epistemological grid to arrive at a forced conclusion? What data was ignored in the process? I believe the pristine truth of Pentecost will not only stand up under such scrutiny, but gain strength and glimmer by the rigor of the exercise! But the participants will neither seek nor tolerate the plaudits of people or Church in so doing.

I see a day when we Pentecostals no longer can be classified as Evangelicals-plus on the issues of social justice. When sociologists chart us on issues of racism and intolerance, today, they can chart us along with the worst of them. I believe the Holy Ghost is moving us back to the path we left in the 1920's when this movement chose preservation over the prophetic.[37] We must go back to the constraints of Pentecost which cannot be separated from a prophetic voice that cries out against the injustices of a sinful society. We seem to have lost our way on this issue. We cannot be both Pentecostal and *non-prophetic*.

I see a day when God again calls us (the rich) to a *conversion* to the poor. Our job in the spirit of Jesus is not done when we simply build 'them' a chapel or give food and clothing. This we must also do. When I read my Bible, it suggests that I get more involved than just some impersonal charity fund of non-involvement. Yes, Jesus also reached out to the rich, but look at the context of his words (Mt. 19.16-30). He always insisted that the best expression of faith in him would be best demonstrated by releasing the poor from their bondage by a change of *our own attitude* (Lk. 4). It gets even worse! God loves it when I get so close to the object of his love that I smell like them! I call it the *smell of sheep*. When I get close enough and really relate to God's sheep (think of Peter after the resurrection, 'feed my sheep'), I will even be in the position to receive ministry from them. There is a blessing by the poor of this world: the charismata of the poor.

I see a day when a spirit of repentance settles on us like a cloud. There never has been a revival in history without deep repentance. We could start by asking forgiveness about our glib conclusion that God has 'cut a covenant' with the Assemblies of God movement (in particular) like he did with Abraham. We could continue by seeking forgiveness about accusing God of poor aim when the Holy Spirit is poured out on any group over which we have no control, as if the first decade of this century was the only model God has. No one can hide behind 'corporate repentance'. I, as an individual, must seek his forgiveness in all areas where I have offended him.

5.1 *The Heart of the Matter*

The United States and many Western European nations have just commemorated the fiftieth anniversary of the end of World War II in May of this year. Depending on your age, you may or may not remember those dramatic moments when first Hitler and then Hirohito and their war machines were beaten by the Allied powers. Between the

---

37. H. Kenyon, 'An Analysis of Ethical Issues in the History of the Assemblies of God' (PhD Diss.; Baylor University, 1988), pp. 401-403.

victory in Europe and the final victory of Japan, Norman Corwin, called 'America's unofficial poet laureate' and a masterful radio broadcaster, was asked to write a program for broadcast on the day of victory in Europe. Everyone knew in advance that the occasion could not be celebrated as a victory in any final sense, because the war was still continuing in Asia. It was in this context of limited triumph that he approached the task and wrote and directed what is no doubt one of the great classics of radio. It is still being broadcast 50 years later![38] Corwin writes about the task:

> It was in this context of limited triumph that I approached the task. Instead of delivering merely a paean to military victory I thought to consider what had been wrought, and why—what the victory had cost—what, if anything we had learned—and what lay ahead.

The parallels between his radio program 'On a Note of Triumph' and the American Assemblies of God movement are striking, in my opinion. In the program the voice of a young soldier who looks at the staggering cost of conflict and the lessons from history humankind fails to learn, asks *'Is it going to happen again?'* I have no doubt that the Assemblies of God worldwide and other Pentecostal movements will, if they do not already, face this challenge.

When one studies Church history and counts the number of times the Church has repeatedly 'ruled out' the New Testament role of the Holy Spirit, and when at age 61 I see the perceived drift from Pentecostal experience and witness to a more evangelical intellectualizing of his role in theology and praxis, I can hear that young voice, *'Is it going to happen again?'*, in the middle of the greatest Christian advance in the history of the Church and in hundreds of foreign cultures and languages, and our own foreign missions enterprise leading the way. Paradoxically, when even many of the most traditionally resistant groups to the reality of Pentecost are beginning to accept the energizing of his power, are we moving in the opposite direction in America because of the stigma of being called an emotional 'experientially motivated' Christian? *Is it going to happen again?*

Listen to these words from Corwin's broadcast:

> Soldier, when the sweet morning comes and you're mustered out—when you get paid off—and there's a ticket in your wallet that guarantees delivery to street and number—and the faces you've dreamed about in

38. Norman Corwin, 'On a Note of Triumph', ABC, May 8, 1945.

foxholes—you mustn't forget to take along your homework in the barracks bag. For there's no discharge in the war. You are on probation only!
You and the faces you've dreamed about—and all the rest of us. Hence-
forth we must do a little civil thinking—every day. Vigilance pays interest
and compounds into peace. Whereas bland unconcern and the appeasing
cheek draws blitzkrieg as a lightning rod attracts a thunderbolt. A little
civil thinking every day—that's the homework. Yes, shooting your mouth
off against the bad appointment and the shoddy referendum. Storming the
redoubts of the local schilkegrouper. Voting in season and demanding of
your representative that he be representative.

Is it going to happen again? Listen—peace is never granted outright. It
is *lent and leased.* You can win a war today and lose the peace tomorrow.
Win in the field and lose in the forum. Peace has a mind of its own. It
doesn't follow victory around. You can make war quickly, but you make
peace slowly. It takes a second to break a peace, but a long time to put it
together again. It took only eight minutes to declare war on Germany and
in the same session it took only five minutes to declare war on Japan.

I paraphrase: Listen Spirit-filled believer of the 90's, you who are living
in an age when more people are asking to be baptized in the Holy Ghost
in one year than the total number of critics of us Pentecostals from 1907
to 1970! Is it going to be on your watch that the Mother Church in
America loses her power to witness and stops growing? When you've
been recognized by all the respectable national organizations and are
courted by the local ministerial associations to be their leader; when the
'wrong side of the tracks' syndrome is all forgotten and your movement
is known for its multimillion dollar edifices with stainless steel kitchens,
you mustn't forget to take along your homework in your barracks bag
college professor. For there's no discharge from the war the devil wages
on the Church's practice of New Testament Pentecostalism. You are on
probation only. And the pioneers who faithfully went before us—who
knew the dangers of the excesses; who knew the need for a balance of
the Fruit of the Spirit and the Gifts—they watch from the balcony
above. Your probation reminds you that you can't pass up deep and
costly primitive Church theology and its inevitable price of ridicule. It
must not be exchanged for a more glamorous and less ego-punishing
Evangelicalism that risks very little public ridicule and scorn, with its
weakened grasp on God's supernatural (transcendent) power to encounter the god of this world and his hold on modern humankind.
Vigilance pays interest and compounds into power for witnessing and
holy living. Whereas bland unconcern and the appeasing compromise of
convictions of clear Biblical distinctives attracts the cessationist's poison

like a lightning rod attracts a thunderbolt. Worshipping God everyday in your prayer language as you agonize over lost men and women in your neighborhood (and college classroom)—that's the homework. Opposing social ills and decadent materialism in a culture drugged by the success fantasy. Living a lifestyle that mentors your students by example. Demonstrating servant leadership that baffles and contradicts the world's and the church's political systems.

5.2 *Is it Going to Happen Again?*

New Testament Christianity in its fullness is never granted outright. It is *lent* to us by faith and *leased* to those who will maintain it. You can be a Pentecostal Church in 1950 and lose your power to witness by 1980. You can have Pentecost at the altar and lose it in the classroom as well as the district office. You can have a 'Pentecostal revival' quickly—but you build a life of fruitbearing and powerful witness slowly! We have learned painfully that like peace among nations, spiritual vitality doesn't have a life of its own. It must constantly be maintained through conscious choice. Church history shouts at us with clarity: Beware Pentecostal! *Holiness and piety will not maintain this elusive tool for witness*, yet a lack of holiness will surely snuff it out. Pentecostal power will only be gained and maintained by repentance and faith. Faith—what a simple word; what an indispensable essence in God's plan for the Spirit-filled life.

WHEN GOSPEL AND CULTURE INTERSECT:
NOTES ON THE NATURE OF CHRISTIAN DIFFERENCE[*]

Miroslav Volf

1. *Introduction: In Praise of Marginality*

At the threshold of the twenty-first century, there is a profound sense of crisis in many churches in the West. Once they were dominant social forces; today they find themselves on the margins, with a past they like to boast about and future they seem to dread. Occasionally they still try to insert themselves as major players in the big social game. Invariably, however, they find out that none of the old tricks they knew so well work anymore; they trip over the ball, they don't know how to pass, let alone how to score. So the coaches put them on the bench where they either yell angry and fruitless shouts at the enemy or try to comfort the members of their own team when they come bruised from the field, all this while secretly hoping that they themselves will some day be allowed to step onto the field and present themselves to the world in all their glory. Increasingly, however, there is less and less space for them even on the bench; other, more able, players are already occupying the space. And so the churches find themselves pushed up into the crowd of spectators, rooting for their favorite teams, scheming up ever new and useless ways to return to the field or reminiscing about the good old days when they were still young.

For anyone who remembers the days when the Church *was* young and vigorous, there is something profoundly odd about the present sense of crisis. The early Church was not simply on the sidelines, it was not even among the cheering spectators. A slandered, discriminated against, even persecuted minority, a thorn in society's flesh. Yet, notwithstanding the temptation to backslide or accommodate, the early Church

---

[*] This paper was prepared for 'The Gospel in Our Pluralistic Culture: A Theological Consultation on Missiology and Western Culture' in Bad Urach, Germany, July 4-8, 1994.

celebrated hope in God and proclaimed fearlessly the resurrected Lord as it walked in the footsteps of the crucified Messiah. It was he who taught them:

> Blessed are those who are persecuted for righteousness' sake, for theirs is the kingdom of heaven. Blessed are you when people revile you and persecute you and utter all kinds of evil against you falsely on my account. Rejoice and be glad, for your reward is great in heaven, for in the same way they persecuted the prophets who were before you (Mt. 5.10-11).

For the early Church, to be on the margin was not a cause of alarm, but grounds for rejoicing. To be tucked in the dark corner of the public arena was not a sign of failure, but of keeping good company. Much like many persecuted churches in the world today, the early Church had resources to deal with its marginality. We in the West do not. And so we despair as we find ourselves unwanted players in the large-scale social game.

The reasons the early Church could rejoice in situations in which the contemporary Western Church moans are many and complex. To claim that there is a simple road that leads from where we are today to where they were then is not to engender hope but to sow seeds of more despair. There is, however, no doubt that one major reason for the difference between the early and contemporary churches lies in expectations: we have come to expect to be major players in the first league in our social world; the early Church expected nothing more than to be left alone to play their own game, inviting their neighbors and friends to join in and learn the rules. The difference in expectations reflects the difference in attitudes toward culture at large, which in turn reflects social position in that culture. We have come to consider it our home and are frustrated to find ourselves losing control over it; for them it was a land occupied by a foreign force.

There is no need here to trace historically the road which brought us to where we are today. Instead, I wish to look toward the future, to re-imagine the relation between the gospel and multiple cultures in contemporary societies, to explore the nature of Christian presence in these societies. My desire is to defuse the sense of crisis and generate new hope for the Church facing the twenty-first century—both a more modest and a more robust hope than the churches in the West have had in recent history. To state my goal more pointedly, *I want to make us more comfortable with our marginality so that from there we can influence the multiple centers of our societies, more at home with our irrelevance so that from there we can gain new confidence about our relevance.*

My outline is simple. First I will point out four major features of contemporary societies and the kinds of relations between Church and culture these societies do or do not allow. Secondly, I will name three inadequate ways to live as Christians in these societies. Thirdly, I will tell you a better way. Finally, I will draw some implications for mission and theology.

2. *Social Context*

Before I reflect about the nature of Christian presence in modern societies, let me indicate briefly four features of these societies. They describe the framework in which we need to place our discussion about Christian identity and difference.

1. *Voluntarism*. Churches can come into existence and continue to live only through the decisions—choices—of their members. Certainly, it takes more to have a church than the will of its members to belong to a church. Furthermore, much in ecclesiology depends on how we understand theologically the decisions of its members to be a church. Still, without the conscious will of the people to belong to a church, churches cannot exist as social realities. No amount of talk about rediscovery of community and tradition can negate this fact; the community that is being rediscovered today is a (post-modern?) *intentional* community, not a pre-modern 'natural' community.

2. *Difference*. Churches will be able to survive in modern societies only if they attend to their 'difference' from the surrounding cultures. Without difference, churches will dissolve. This is something one can complain about or celebrate, depending upon one's theological scruples. Irrespective of our scruples, the following principle stands: whoever wants the Church must want its difference from the surrounding culture. The dispute among those who want the Church can intelligently take place only regarding what ecclesial difference should look like, not whether one should actively pursue it or not.

3. *Plurality*. According to Ernst Troeltsch 'church' affirms the world whereas 'sect' denies it. Today, however, the one world which 'church' could affirm or 'sect' deny, has splintered into a plurality of worlds that exist in an overarching social framework. These worlds are partly compatible and partly incompatible, partly mutually dependent

and partly independent; they form partly overlapping social spaces and create ever-changing hybrid cultures. Simple denial or affirmation of 'the world' will not do. Similarly, the simple claim that the Christian message is (or can be made) intelligible to 'the world' will not do. More complex ways of relating to multiple cultures will have to be developed to take into account the complexity of the social worlds that make up modern societies.

4. *Self-sufficiency.* What sociologists call functional differentiation of society—the fact that various subsystems specialize in performing particular functions, such as economic, educational, or communication activity—implies (relative) self-sufficiency and self-perpetuation of social sub-systems. And self-perpetuation means that the subsystems resist influence through outside values. Unlike in traditional societies, there is no symbolic or actual center holding societies together, through which influence on the whole can be exerted. To be adequate to the nature of contemporary societies, reflection on the social influence of the Church will have to take into account this (relative) self-sufficiency and self-perpetuation of social systems. Otherwise our rhetoric will give us a fleeting sense that we are doing something significant, but in the long run only engender frustration. The result will be increased marginalization of the churches in modern societies.

3. *The Liberal Program: Accommodation*

How should we think of the presence of the Christian Church in the world given these four features of contemporary societies? Let me first look at what I have come to think are misplaced proposals; in critiquing them, I will be paving the road for getting at what I think is a better way to think about the relation between gospel and culture, Church and society in contemporary Western societies.

The liberal answer to this question about the nature of Christian presence runs something like this: translate the message into the conceptualities of the culture in which one lives, accommodate to the social practices of the surrounding modern culture. If you do not, you will be run by it. It is not hard to see why Christians would be tempted to reduce distance from their social environments by acculturating. The place of Christian communities in modern societies has become problematic. They appear socially superfluous. Things go their own way, with churches or without them. Being close to a particular culture and its centers of power would let us 'push' things in God's direction—or so it would seem.

Notice, however, what one needs to do in order to maintain closeness to a given culture in contemporary societies—one must be involved in constant reconstruction of the patterns of belief and practice to make them fit the changing plausibilities of that culture. What one gains is that the message appears plausible in a given context. This important gain does not come, however, without a significant loss. In modern societies churches are no longer capable of shaping plausibility structures of the cultures in which they live; other, more powerful forces are at work. So you have to acculturate to what you have not helped shape. As a consequence, all reconstructions which are guided by existing plausibility structures carry in themselves seeds of Christian self-destruction.[1] As Hauerwas and Willimon put it: 'Alas, in leaning over to speak to the modern world, we had fallen in. We had lost the theological resources to resist, lost the resources even to see that there was something worth resisting.'[2] In the best case, what remains for churches to do is to appear after a non-Christian show and repeat the performance in their own way for a few remaining visitors with Christian scruples. The voice of the Church is an echo of a voice that is not their own.

4. *The Post-Liberal Program: Reversing the Direction of Conformation*

The post-liberal answer to the question about how we should think of the presence of the Christian churches in modern societies comes out of profound dissatisfaction with the liberal answer. In the words of Nicholas Wolterstoff it consists in 'reversing the direction of conformation'.[3] Instead of translating the biblical message into the conceptuality of the social world that one inhabits, as modern theology has done, Christians should describe anew the social world they inhabit with the help of the biblical story.

But when one has nested oneself into the biblical story, what happens to conversation with the culture at large? Has one not closed oneself

---

1.   P. Berger, *A Far Glory: The Quest for Faith in an Age of Credulity* (New York: Free Press, 1992), pp. 3-24.

2.   S. Hauerwas and W.H. Willimon, *Resident Aliens: A Provocative Christian Assessment of Culture and Ministry for People Who Know That Something Is Wrong* (Nashville: Abingdon Press, 1989), p. 27.

3.   N. Wolterstorff, *What New Haven and Grand Rapids Have to Say to Each Other* (Grand Rapids: Calvin College, 1993), p. 2.

from it? The post-liberal answer to this question would be, of course, 'no'. But for the 'no' to stick, two conditions need to be satisfied—two conditions to which post-liberals such as George Lindbeck or Hans Frei have not given sufficient attention.

First, there must be at least some significant symbolic compatibility between the Christian communities and the non-Christian cultural worlds. Even when the churches need to say something that does not quiet make sense to the cultural worlds they inhabit, they must still say it in the language of their culture. Churches are distinct communities of discourse, yet they do not speak their own language. Rather, *they use the existing language in a different way*. Religious language of Christians does not come in place of the language of the wider culture, neither does it exist side by side with it. Religious language is rather *a way of using the language of one's culture* (hopefully not an obsolete dialect of that language!).

Secondly, conversation with non-Christians presupposes readiness to listen and learn on the part of Christians. It would be not only arrogant but also foolish of churches to interpret their social environments from their own perspective, not paying attention to how these social environments interpret themselves or how they interpret the churches. Here we come up against the limits of the metaphor of 'reversing the direction of conformation'. Wolterstorff asks rightly:

> But is the relation of the Church theologians to the non-theological discipline exclusively that of melting down gold taken from the Egyptians? Isn't some of the statuary of the Egyptians quite OK as it is? Does it all reek of idolatry? Isn't there something for the Church theologian to learn from the non-theological disciplines?[4]

A more selective approach to the question of conformation seems required than what the metaphor of 'reversal of conformation' suggests. Christians ought to be able to decide case by case in which direction the conformation should go. From some neutral standpoint? Such a standpoint is not available. From the standpoint we have taken: God's revelation in Christ as mediated to us through the community of faith. God's word in Jesus Christ is 'final and decisive for us'. Yet we occasionally need to revise our understanding of God's revelation in the light of what transpires, say, in the sciences (while at the same time being

---

4.   Wolterstorff, *New Haven and Grand Rapids*, p. 45.

alert to the functioning of sciences as an instrument of domination rather than simply as a neutral tool for finding the 'truth').

It would seem that the two conditions for Christian conversation with non-Christian cultural worlds call into question the difference of Christian communities, their distance. Both the partial symbolic compatibility and the readiness to learn require a good deal of closeness. If we take these conditions seriously, what happens to distance? Do not the dangers of accommodation lurk around the corner? Yet it would be rather bizarre for Christians to run the risk of parroting as soon as they opened their mouths to speak and ears to hear. So we come up against the important issue of how we should think about the *presence* of the Christian difference in modern societies.

5. The Separatist Program: Retreat from the World

One way to think about the *presence* of Christian difference 'in the world' is to imagine churches as Christian islands in the sea of worldliness. They would then have their own territory that is as clearly set apart from the social environment as are the rocks that protrude from the waters.

In *The Cost of Discipleship*, Dietrich Bonhoeffer describes churches as being 'in the midst of the world' but as those who are 'taken out of the world'.[5] Their environment is 'a foreign land' to them. Or, using a more dynamic image, he thought of Christians as strangers 'only passing through the country' (p. 303), like a 'sealed train', as he put it. Bonhoeffer continues,

> At any moment they may receive the signal to move on. Then they will strike tents, leaving behind them all their worldly friends and connections, and following only the voice of their Lord who calls. They leave the land of their exile, and start their homeward trek to heaven.

In writing these words, Bonhoeffer was, of course, giving pastoral advice to a church facing a godless Nazi regime. If one extracts them from the situation and elevates them to a program for Christian presence in the world, serious problems arise. One could ask: Where would Christians go when they strike tents and leave the land of exile? Literally to heaven, like Enoch? Did Enoch not walk with God for 300 years

---

5.   D. Bonhoeffer, *The Cost of Discipleship* (trans. R.H. Fuller; New York: Macmillan, 1963), p. 311.

before 'he was no more, because God took him' (Gen. 5.24)? Do not
Christians rather move at the bidding of their Lord to a different place
in the land of exile? And how is it that the homeward trek starts *after*
leaving the land and not while still in it? This is because the Bonhoeffer
of *The Cost of Discipleship* thinks of Christian presence as *passage* —as
the 'wandering on earth' of those who 'live in heaven' (p. 304).

If Christian communities only wander on earth, but live in heaven, if
they are like islands surrounded by a sea of worldliness, then they will
have their own truth and their own values that are determined alone by
the 'story' of Jesus Christ and that have nothing to do with truth and
value outside of their boundaries. Christian difference would then be in a
given social world, but would remain completely external to it, one
would be 'in God' but could not be at the same time 'in Thessaloniki'
(1 Thess. 1.1; see 1 Cor. 1.2)—in Lima, Los Angeles, Delhi or Nairobi—
at least not as its genuine citizen.

The trouble with such an external view of Christian presence in the
world is a wrong notion of 'Thessaloniki'. It presupposes that the social
environment in which churches live is a foreign country pure and simple.
Yet this certainly is not the case. The God who gave Christians the new
birth is not only the 'Father of our Lord Jesus Christ' (1 Pet. 1.3) but
also the creator and sustainer of the universe. From that perspective, *the
environment in which Christians live is not a foreign country, but rather
their own proper homeland, property of their God. If they are alien in
it, it is because and insofar as their own land has been occupied by a
foreign power*; if they are estranged from the world, it is because and
insofar as the world is estranged from God.

Every social world is God's territory. Hence Christians should not
seek to leave it and establish a settlement outside. Rather they should
remain in it and change it—subvert the power of the foreign force and
bring their environment back from the estrangement into communion
with God. Put more abstractly, Christian difference must be always
internal to a given cultural world.

6. *Metaphorizing the Dominant Order*

How should we imagine Christian presence as *internal* difference? Here
I find some aspects of Michel de Certeau's thought helpful. Reflecting
on the uses people make of cultural goods that are produced for them
he writes:

users make innumerable and infinitesimal transformations of and within the dominant cultural economy in order to adapt it to their own interests and their own rules.[6]

He explains this creativity of users by looking at that painful process which started on October 12, 1492 when the Spaniard ships sailed up to the shores of Latin America—at the colonization of the indigenous Indian population. We sometimes fail to see that in spite of their oppression and powerlessness, the indigenous population were not simply passive recipients of an imposed culture. He writes,

> the Indians often used the laws, practices, and representations that were imposed on them by force or by fascination to ends other than those of their conquerors; they made something else out of them; they subverted them from within—not by rejecting them or by transforming them (though that occurred as well), but by many different ways of using them in the service of rules, customs or convictions foreign to the colonization which they could not escape. They metaphorized the dominant order: they made it function in another register. They remained other within the system which they assimilated and which assimilated them externally. They diverted without leaving. Procedures of consumption maintained their difference in the very space that the occupier was organizing.[7]

The image of conquest and colonization is certainly not adequate to describe the relation between cultures and churches. For one, it inverts the direction of the process: cultures do not colonize churches, but churches spring up within the existing cultures. They can be more or less distant from the culture, but they certainly do not first exist outside of culture so as to be able then to be colonized by it. Secondly, the culture is not simply a negative power against which one has to fight, but a space in which one lives, the air one breathes. Apart from such inadequacies, however, the image of metaphorizing the culture, subverting it from within is helpful. It rightly suggests that churches should neither abandon nor dominate their cultural environments, but rather live differently *in* them, that their difference should be internal not simply to the cultural space, but cultural forms.

What does this mean concretely? What are some paradigmatic options open to churches? First, it will be possible for Christians simply to adopt some elements of the cultures in which they live, possibly putting them

6. M. de Certeau, *The Practice of Everyday Life* (trans. S.F. Rendall; Berkeley: University of California Press, 1984), p. xiv.

7. De Certeau, *Everyday Life*, p. 32.

to different use guided by the values that stem from their being 'in God'. They may live in the same kind of houses, drive the same kinds of cars; they might listen to the same music and enjoy some of the same visual or culinary arts. What Christians might do differently is put their houses, cars or musical arts to partly different uses than their non-Christian neighbors do. A house can be a vehicle of service; a meal, an occasion of worship.

Sometimes putting things to different uses will require changes in the things themselves. To be a good vehicle of service, a house might need a guest room and larger community room. Some type of technology might foster more humane kinds of work if it is constructed in a certain way. Which brings me to the second possible way of living Christian difference within a given culture: the majority of the elements of a culture will be taken up but transformed from inside. For instance, one would be using the same words as the general culture does, but their semantic fields would be occupied by new contents that partly change and partly replace the old ones. Take a basic term in Christian vocabulary such as 'God'. It is a term that Christians did not invent; they inherited it form the Hebrew people of God, and these in turn from their environment. Yet just like for Jews the term 'God' came to mean the God of Abraham and Sarah, the God of Moses and Miriam, so also for Christians the semantic field of the term 'God' was partly changed to mean 'the God of Jesus Christ'. A host of other Christian terms would show similar inner transformation. The same is true of Christian practices. Christians take part in particular culturally defined practices, but shape them on the basis of their dominant values. Take marriage, for instance. Many of its elements are the same for Christians as they are for anybody else—or so I take it. Yet for Christians the love between partners in marriage is informed by the sacrificial love of Christ for the Church.

Thirdly, there might be some elements of a given culture that Christians will have to discard and possibly replace by other elements. Take slavery: it simply had to be discarded. Since in Christ there is 'no longer slave or free', but 'we all are children of God through faith' (Gal. 3.26-28), the runaway slave Onesimus should be received by Philemon as 'a beloved brother', and that not only 'in the Lord', but also 'in flesh' (Phlm 16). The gospel required an inner transformation of this cultural institution of such magnitude that it eventually amounted to discarding the institution itself.

Taking these three complementary ways of relating to culture together we can say that *Christian difference is always a complex and flexible network of small and large refusals, divergences, subversions, and more or less radical alternative proposals, surrounded by the acceptance of many cultural givens. There is no single correct way to relate to a given culture as a whole, or even to its dominant thrust; there are only numerous ways of accepting, transforming, or replacing various aspects of a given culture from within.* This is what it means for Christian difference to be *internal* to a given culture.

7. Some Implications

The notion of Christian presence as an internal difference has radical implications for mission and theology. I will name here only four.

1. Strictly speaking, Christians never have their own proper and exclusive cultural territory—their own proper language, their own proper values, their own proper rationality. To be more precise, their own proper territory is always already inhabited by somebody else: they speak the language they have learned from their neighbors, though they metaphorize its meaning from within; they have inherited the value structure of the culture at large, yet they change more or less radically some of its elements and refuse to accept others; they take up the rules of what makes sense in a given culture, and yet they subvert them and occasionally refuse to follow where they lead. They belong, and yet do not belong; they are present, and yet distant. To become Christian means to divert without leaving; to live as a Christian means to keep inserting a difference into a given culture without ever stepping outside to do so.

2. For Christian difference to be internal to a given culture means that Christians have no place from which to transform the *whole culture they inhabit*—*no* place from which to undertake that eminently modern project of restructuring the whole social and intellectual life, no virgin soil on which to start building a new, radically different city. No revolutions are possible; all transformations are piece-meal—transformation of some elements, at some points, for some time, with some gain and possibly some loss. These transformations are reconstructions of the structures that must be inhabited as the reconstruction is going on. As a result, what Christians end up helping to build resembles much less a suburban development project, all planned out in advance in architectural bureaus, than an ancient city with its 'maze of little streets and

squares, of old and new houses, and of houses with additions from various periods; and this surrounded by a multitude of new boroughs with straight regular streets and uniform houses'. This, it will be remembered, is how Ludwig Wittgenstein described our language; and this is how we should think of the results of the insertion of Christian difference into a given culture.

3.   Accommodation should not be part of the Christian project. We are used to hearing that kind of a message from old-style fundamentalists. And in this one thing they were right (though they often failed to live up to their own rhetoric of difference and accommodated in surprisingly banal ways). The children of fundamentalists no less than their older siblings, liberals, do not like to hear diatribes against accommodation. They like to be at the center, to be mainstream—theologically and culturally. They want influence—for the good of the Church, of the society, of the world, of course. And so they accommodate. But the accommodation strategy has been a bad investment, and, given the nature of contemporary societies, its yield will diminish even more.

We need to retrieve the stress on difference. *It is the difference that matters*. Erase the difference and literally nothing will remain that *could* matter. Without boundaries, groups dissolve. Our task should not be accommodation, but distance from a given culture—a critical distance, to be sure, not a naive distance unaware of its own captivity to what it thinks it has escaped; a productive distance, not a sterile self-insulating distance of those who let the world go to hell. Accommodation is a given. It takes place whether you want it or not. Difference is not a given. Rather it is an arduous task that needs to be accomplished anew all the time. *Difference*, not accommodation, is the reason why theology needs to be fresh.

4.   If accommodation is out, must not inculturation also be unacceptable? In answering this question let me step back briefly to take a look at what happens at conversion. When we become Christians the gospel disrupts the equilibrium of our cultural identity; when we receive it, we become estranged from our culture because every culture is estranged from God. If one feels uncomfortable with that disruption, one might as well feel uncomfortable about becoming a Christian. *Without disruption there can be no Christian faith.*

It is essential, however, that this disruption remain *internal* to a given culture. This is the main thrust of my study. The question therefore is not whether but how inculturation should take place. Theologians are good for many important things (at least the good ones are), but they have not proven so good for formulating the gospel in terms of culture at large (except, maybe, in terms of the limited intellectual culture of which they are a part). Inculturation is best done by the faithful people of God themselves. *(Western* theologians—or theologians trained in the West—are good for many things, but not for giving advice to non-Western believers on how they should go about inculturating the gospel.[8]) Inculturation takes place when people in their own contexts receive the one gospel of the crucified and resurrected Jesus Christ and run with it, living out and expressing the Christian difference in their own terms and symbols, and through their own practices. Theologians do have a role to play in the process of inculturation, but it is a critical one rather than a creative one. Here their task is to lay bare the captivities of the Church to the spirit of the age, of every church and in every culture. Which is to say that instead of *in*-culturating the gospel they should rather think about whether they may need to *de*-culturate it, free it from contamination by those elements of culture which have been pervaded by the spirit of the age.

When the gospel comes into a culture, it always disrupts.[9] But if it comes in an authentic way, in a way that honors both the creative and redemptive work of God, the disruption will remain *internal to a given culture.* Why? Because the people to whom the gospel comes will remain part of their culture; they will divert without leaving. And if they do this, inculturation will take care of itself. The real question is not how to inculturate the gospel. They key issue is how to maintain Christian difference from the culture of which we are a part and how to make that difference a leaven in the culture.

8. *In Place of a Conclusion: Difference and What to Do with it*

Let me conclude. I have sung the praises of difference and some of you may have been disturbed. You fear that the ghosts of obscurantism and fundamentalism will be attracted or that the demons will rush in that

8.   See S. Billington Harper, 'Ironies of Indigenization: Some Cultural Repercussions of Mission in South India', *International Bulletin of Missionary Research* 19 (January 1996), pp. 13-16, 18-20.

9.   On the dialectic between disruption and affirmation see Miroslav Volf, *Exclusion and Embrace: A Theological Exploration of Identity, Otherness and Reconciliation* (Nashville: Abingdon Press, 1996), chapter 1.

make things fall apart and the center unable to hold. But consider once again, no more generally, the importance of difference. Level the difference and what you have left will be *nothing*—you yourself along with everything else will be drowned in the sea of undifferentiated 'stuff' that is indistinguishable from anything. To erase the difference is to undo the creation, that intricate pattern of separations that God established during those unique six days when the universe was formed out of *no*-thing. Literally *every*-thing depends on difference.

Now apply this claim about creation to the relation between gospel and culture. Here too, everything depends on difference. If you have difference, you can have the gospel; if you do not, you cannot: you will either have just plain old culture or the reign of God, but you will not have the gospel. Gospel is always about difference; after all it means the good *news*. The trick is to know *what* the Christian difference is and where precisely it needs to surface and where not; the trick is how to keep ourselves open to God and God's reign and at the same time remain internal to a given culture. As I see it, *this* is what the problem of the relation between gospel and culture is all about.

Part III

THE MISSIOLOGICAL CONTEXT

THE DECLINE OF CONFUCIANISM
AND THE PROCLAMATION OF THE GOSPEL IN CHINA[*]

Li Yue Hong

It is estimated that there are currently over 63 million Protestant Christians in China,[1] the vast majority of which may be characterized as Pentecostal or Charismatic. This represents a dramatic increase from the less than one million Protestant believers in China just prior to the Communist revolution of 1949. Much of this growth has occurred since the end of the Cultural Revolution in 1976. The following article seeks to discuss reasons for the phenomenal growth of Christianity in China in the last two decades. In view of the legacy of Pentecostal missions and the large number of Pentecostal believers in this great country, the following article clearly has tremendous relevance for the Pentecostal movement today. It is written by a capable young Chinese scholar who in the summer of 1992 had the opportunity to meet and converse with William W. Menzies. The author has expressed his desire to honor William Menzies with this 'humble' contribution — the editors.

The history of Christianity in China spans a period of approximately 1350 years, from the days of the Tang dynasty when the first Nestorian missionaries set foot on Chinese soil until today. Throughout this period, Christianity has encountered countless hardships and frustrations. Indeed, it is widely acknowledged that through the centuries China has been one of the most difficult regions for Christianity to penetrate. The sixteenth-century Roman Catholic missionary, Alexander Valignani (1538–1606), peering across the sea toward the China mainland from his home in Macao, shouted, 'Rock, Oh, Rock, when will you crack?'

---

[*]   Translated by Xu Qin Sun and Robert Menzies.

1.   Statistics concerning the Christian population in China come from the Chinese Church Research Center in Hong Kong (*China Prayer Letter*, 123 [Oct–Dec, 1992], p. 1). This CCRC report cites an unpublished Chinese government source which concluded that in China '75 million believe in some form of Christianity', including 63 million Protestant and 12 million Catholic believers.

Of all the obstacles to the growth of the Christian Church in China, none has been more significant than Confucianism, for centuries the dominant force shaping Chinese culture. The China mainland was the cradle of Confucianism, nurturing over the centuries a variety of schools of Confucian thought. Confucianism is most deeply rooted in the culture of mainland China, exerting a dominant influence for a period more lengthy than in other Confucian-based countries or regions.

Sinologists frequently highlight many factors detrimental to the growth of Christianity in present-day China, but the role of Confucianism is often ignored or minimized. However, the past 20 years have witnessed unprecedented growth for the Church in China and they are particularly revealing. During this period the Church in mainland China has grown much faster than its counterparts in neighboring regions (e.g. Hong Kong, Macao, Taiwan), in spite of the fact that all of these regions have experienced political conditions more favorable to the advance of the gospel. Significantly, these neighboring regions have also been deeply impacted by Confucian thought.

There are many reasons for the recent surge of Christianity in China and the lack of any such a surge in surrounding regions. Yet, one of the most significant reasons is that in modern mainland China (unlike in Hong Kong, Taiwan, etc.), Confucianism has been dealt a series of violent blows, resulting in a sharp decline in its status and influence. Scholars discussing the problems encountered by Christianity as it has sought to take root in China tend to relate them to external forces, accidental occurrences, or even individual personalities. Yet they often consciously or unconsciously minimize the role Confucianism has played as an impediment to the advance of the gospel. These scholars are reluctant to speak of any contradiction between Christianity and Chinese culture. They fear that in so doing, they might dampen the confidence and impede the evangelistic efforts of Christians in China. Their concern is understandable. I also do not believe that the Confucian-based Chinese culture is totally incompatible with Christianity, as water with fire; on the contrary, as an ancient culture which inevitably bears the mark of the creator, Confucian-based Chinese culture has many points of contact with biblical Christianity. These truths, when sifted from less desirable elements, can be readily integrated into a Christian worldview. However, when Confucianism exists as a comprehensive explanation of reality and occupies a dominant position of influence, it is incompatible with the Christian faith. In China, the decline of Confucianism and the corresponding rise of Christianity offer ample support for this thesis. The following essay will examine the relationship between Confucian thought and the rejection of Christianity in China. I shall also analyze the unique circumstances in mainland China which have contributed to Confucianism's decline. It is my hope that this essay will contribute to a more accurate understanding of the rapid growth of Christianity in China.

1. *Confucianism and the Rejection of Christianity*

Tang dynasty Nestorianism and Yuan dynasty *Arkaun* (the Mongol name for both Nestorianism and Roman Catholicism) both disappeared from the interior of China. The reasons for the repulsion and demise of these Christian groups, in addition to economic and political factors, include the impact of Confucianism as the representative of traditional Chinese culture.

In this essay, owing to limitations of space, I shall focus on the formative events during the Ming and Qing dynasties. Christianity entered China for the third time during this Ming–Qing era. It was in many respects a splendid era in the history of Christianity in China. Nevertheless, during this period Christianity suffered severe attacks and hardships, none of which were related to external forces. This conflict culminated in the repression of Christianity during the high point of the Qing dynasty. This cycle of Christianity's ascent and decline is especially representative of the antagonism between Chinese traditional culture and Christianity. During this period, the famous Jesuit missionary, Matteo Ricci (1552–1610), observed various aspects of the Chinese political system and traditional culture. On the basis of this experience, he determined that he must study the Confucian classics, not simply the Chinese language. So, he began to propagate the Christian faith as a form of Confucianism, focusing on the upper class of Chinese society. Ricci utilized Western scientific knowledge and gadgets, his knowledge of the Confucian classics, and a disciplined moral life in order to gain friends and influence among the literati, officials and even the emperor. Emperor Kang Xi (1662–1722) called this approach 'the Ricci method',[2] and initially it was very effective. Emperor Wan Li (1573–1620) not only received Ricci's gadgets; he also granted Ricci a personal audience

---

2.   Zheng Tian Ting (ed.), *Ming Qing Shi Zi Liao* [*Ming and Qing Dynasty Historical Documents*] (Tianjin: Tianjin Ren Min Publishing House, 1981), II, p. 363.

and queried him concerning the Christian faith. As a result, the emperor gave Ricci an administrative office and commanded the Ministry of Rites to treat Ricci with respect, to provide him with housing in Beijing, and to grant him a stipend covering his living expenses. Many high officials also held Ricci in high esteem.

Ricci's influence soon bore fruit. Several leading Chinese intellectuals embraced the faith, becoming 'the three pillars of Chinese Roman Catholicism'. Xu Guang Qi (1562–1633) was a *Jin Shi*, the title given to those who successfully completed the highest level of imperial examinations, a scholar in the prestigious Wen Yuan Academy and a high official, governing the Ministry of Rites. He was the first government official and Confucian scholar to become a Christian. Li Zhi Zao (1565–1630) was also a *Jin Shi* and a high official in the Ministry of Works in Nanjing. The third member of this holy triumvirate, Yang Ting Jun (1557–1627), also a *Jin Shi*, became the first ardent Buddhist to convert to Christianity.

In spite of this initial success, Ricci's method produced a foundation that was flawed. Many of the intellectuals and officials who received Ricci with favor, and even those who made professions of faith, failed to grasp the essence of the Christian faith. For example, after Matteo Ricci's death, Emperor Wan Li decreed that Ricci should be revered because 'he came from afar seeking righteousness, ardently studied, came to know the truth, and wrote noble books'.[3] The emperor's decree implies that Ricci found 'the truth' in China, probably a veiled reference to Confucianism, and makes no reference to the Christian message. It indicates that the emperor did not understand Ricci's real motives nor the essential matters of the Christian faith. Moreover, it suggests that the emperor thought of Ricci as, above all, an admirer of Confucian values.

The emperor was not unique is his failure to grasp the essence of the Christian faith. The desire to interpret and shape the Christian message purely in the light of the prevailing culture was immense. Many other examples could be cited, but an examination of 'the three pillars' alluded to above is especially instructive. Xu Guang Qi, for example, found the Christian faith entirely compatible with the Confucian-based Chinese culture of his day. He stated that 'in all the books and writings which expound the Roman Catholic faith, one cannot find one word which contradicts the essence of [the key Confucian virtues of] loyalty and

---

3.   Wang You San (ed.), *Zhong Guo Zong Jiao Shi* [*The History of Religion in China*] (Ji Nan, Shandong: Qi Lu Publishing House, 1991), p. 877.

filial piety, nor can one find one word which contradicts the morals and social standards of the day'. He also asserted that Christianity could 'help sustain the rule of the emperor by supporting Confucian values and correcting Buddhist errors'.[4]

Li Zhi Zao held similar beliefs. He affirmed that Ricci, in his teaching, 'did not deviate from the six Confucian classics'.[5] Furthermore, Li stated that 'Roman Catholicism and Confucianism could be unified into a single, coherent whole'.[6] Li felt that, in essence, there was no contradiction. Roman Catholicism could complement and support Confucianism.

Yang Ting Jun was also convinced that Roman Catholicism and Confucianism were compatible, stating that they shared 'the same perspective'. Yang urged his Chinese compatriots not to view 'Roman Catholicism as heretical'. According to Yang,

> God has endowed human beings with noble qualities love, justice, propriety, and wisdom. The Christian Scriptures declare, in conformity with Confucianism, that this God-given nature contains the highest virtues. Evil deeds are the result of human error, not a corrupt nature.[7]

Here one sees clearly that Yang has used Confucius' and Mencius' emphasis on the inherent goodness of human nature in order to interpret and explain Roman Catholic thought.

These examples reveal that the 'three pillars' employed Confucian principles in order to understand, evaluate and confirm Roman Catholic doctrine. This is entirely understandable when it is remembered that the three pillars' knowledge of Roman Catholic thought came, not through their own study of the Bible, but rather, through their study of Ricci's writings, especially *The Essentials of Roman Catholicism* (*Tian Zhu Shi Yi*), which attempted to contextualize Christianity through the use of Confucian principles. Although Ricci's knowledge of Roman Catholicism and Confucianism as a whole was unsurpassed, it appears that he did not

4.   Xu Guang Qi, *Bian Xue Zhang Shu* [*Analytical Studies*] (ancient book, no publication data).

5.   The six Confucian classics include: The Book of Songs; The Book of History; The Book of Rites; The Book of Changes; The Spring and Autumn Annals; The Book of Music (this last book is not extant).

6.   Li Zhi Zao, *Tian Zhu Shi Yi Xu* [Preface to *The Essentials of Roman Catholicism*] (ancient book, no publication data).

7.   Fang Hao, *Fang Hao Liu Shi Zi Ding Gao* [*A Collection of the Writings of Fang Hao: Compiled by the Author in his 60th Year*] (Taiwan: Taiwan Xue Sheng Publishing House, 1969), I, p. 217.

fully understand the fundamental nature of Confucianism. However, it is also possible that Ricci was more fully aware of the contradictions between Christianity and Confucianism than his writings suggest, and that he simply chose to tolerate these contradictions temporarily in order to enable Christianity to take root in Chinese culture. For Ricci, Confucianism clearly served a strategic purpose. For example, when Ricci first arrived in China, he took on the name and appearance of a Buddhist monk. However, when he found that Buddhist monks were not respected by the upper class, he donned the robes of a Confucian scholar, discarded his Buddhist name, and attacked Buddhism with Confucian principles.

Shortly after Ricci's death, two controversies erupted. The first debate centered on Ricci's use of Confucian principles and terminology as a vehicle for propagating Christianity. Some Roman Catholic missionaries felt that Ricci's method was valid and useful, while others felt a clear distinction between Christianity and Confucianism must be maintained. This debate included the critical question concerning how the name of God should be rendered in Chinese: should terminology from traditional Chinese culture be used (e.g. *Shang Di*), as Ricci advocated, or should new and different terms be employed (e.g. *Tian Fu*, *Tian Zhu*)? The second debate dealt with the question of whether it was permissible for Christians to participate in traditional memorial ceremonies honoring their ancestors, Confucius and Heaven.

Both debates are often referred to as 'the rites controversy'. Although the questions of appropriate terminology and rites did not deal with the essential nature of Confucian thought, these questions did represent a challenge to a Confucian-based form of contextualization. Thus, when 'the rites controversy' erupted, Confucian scholars began to criticize aggressively the doctrines of Roman Catholicism. A number of Buddhist monks, eager to repudiate Christianity, also joined in the fray. In spite of the fact that Ricci had sought to marshall Confucian ideology against Buddhism, a coalition of Confucianism and Buddhism emerged, and side by side these forces entered into battle.

This religious conflict produced a number of important works, including the massive eight volume critique of Christianity entitled, *Fight the Heresy (Po Xie Ji)*. Although space does not permit a full discussion of this significant resource, I shall discuss the criticisms of church affairs in Nanjing in 1615 which it contains. Although many historians describe the Nanjing incident as the result of one individual's (Shen Que)

polemical writings, in reality the conflict reflected larger issues. While it
is true that the Nanjing incident was initiated by government officials, it
should be noted that it was preceded by 54 separate incidents instigated
by peasants. Shen Que, the ostensible instigator of the tensions, was an
intellectual lightweight with very limited understanding. He only saw a
small portion, bits and pieces, of the conflict between Christianity and
Confucianism. The accusations he leveled at Christianity and its
representatives where far-fetched and based on ignorance. In spite of this
fact, his criticisms clearly illustrate the contradictions between
Christianity and Confucianism.

Shen Que's first work, 'Report on the Expulsion of Foreigners', was
subtitled 'The Unauthorized Entry of Foreigners into the Capital and
their Secret Plan to Subvert Imperial Authority'. Here the phrase,
'Imperial Authority' (*wang hua*), refers to Confucian values and the
authoritarian culture they helped support. In this work, Shen's perspective is given clear expression:

> I have heard that the emperor rules the nation in accordance with
> Confucian values and social law and, on this basis, he administers judg-
> ment and confers rewards. In this way, he turns his subjects from evil to
> good and protects them from the insidious influences of foreigners. The
> moral fabric of the nation is thereby elevated.[8]

Shen affirms Confucianism and rejects the foreign influences of Roman
Catholicism in order to protect traditional Chinese culture and maintain
order in society. His criticisms were especially directed at those missionaries who opposed ancestor worship:

> I have also heard that missionaries incite and confuse the peasants,
> declaring that they need not venerate their ancestors; rather, they should
> only honor God, and thereby ascend to heaven and escape hell. Buddhism
> and Daoism both speak of heaven and hell, but they also encourage the
> practice of filial piety and fraternal duty. This indicates that those who do
> not fulfill their filial duties shall be judged for their sins. In this regard,
> Buddhism and Daoism both support Confucian values. Currently, how-
> ever, the Roman Catholic missionaries deliberately attempt to convince
> the people not to participate in ancestor worship and teach them not to
> show filial respect. The result is that the distinction between the emperor
> and his servants is blurred and the difference between father and son

---

8.   Shen Que, 'Nan Gong Shu Du Can Yuan Yi Shu' [Official Documents
Concerning the Expulsion of Foreigners], in *Po Xie Ji* [*Fight the Heresy*] (ancient
book, no publication data), I.

becomes unclear. From whence does this evil doctrine come? How could one deliberately teach such falsehood? These are the enemies of Confucianism. Now is the time to act! We must destroy this doctrine. How can we encourage the people to listen to these insidious concepts.[9]

Shen Que also slandered the missionaries for attempting to correct the Chinese calendar: 'They carelessly transgress the ways of Heaven.'[10]

Shen's criticisms reveal the great gulf between Christianity and Confucianism. Shen's memorials to the emperor and the subsequent Ming government official notice all emphasize that the missionaries came 'to establish Roman Catholicism and mislead the people, their evil schemes are unfathomable'.[11] This charge of political subversion appears to be a pretext for establishing laws which prohibited missionaries from entering into China. The Ming government did not fear foreign aggression. The real motive for such strident rhetoric is rather the conflict between Christianity and Confucianism.

This was a crucial period, for the relationship between the imperial court and the missionaries had been very amicable. The Yuan dynasty Emperor Shun and the Ming dynasty Emperor Chong Zhen, as well as later emperors of the Southern Ming period, all had very good relations with the missionaries. For example, during Chong Zhen's reign Roman Catholicism not only spread to 13 provinces, but could also boast of over 100 believers within the walls of the imperial palace. Nevertheless, with the 100 year ban on Roman Catholicism, the differences and contradictions between Christianity and Confucianism became much clearer.

At the outset of the Qing dynasty, as during the time of Ricci, the relationship between the emperor and the missionaries was very good. Initially Shun Zhi ruled the land, and he was followed by his son, Emperor Kang Xi. J.A. Schall von Bell (1591–1660) and Ferdinand Verbiest (1623–1688) are two well known missionaries from this period. The relationship between these rulers and missionaries was especially warm and cordial. However, it was not built on the similarities between and synthesis of Christianity and Confucianism; rather, it was based on the traditional Chinese concept of 'the wise emperor and loyal officials'. In order to elucidate the nature of this relationship, rather than assessing the missionaries' personal motives, I shall focus on their actions, at least as they were perceived by the emperor.

9.   Shen Que, 'Nan Gong Shu', in *Po Xie Ji*, I.
10. Shen Que, 'Nan Gong Shu', in *Po Xie Ji*, I.
11. Shen Que, 'Nan Gong Shu', in *Po Xie Ji*, I.

The missionaries' high moral character, special skills (e.g. they revised the calendar system and helped manufacture powerful cannons), loyalty, devotion and discipline, quickly won the favor of the emperor. In his stele inscription entitled, 'Declaration Concerning Roman Catholicism', Emperor Shun Zhi states:

> Western scholars are capable of calculating the times and seasons [including solar eclipses] with great skill and precision. Were not men such as these, with knowledge of the seasons, sent by Heaven to serve the emperor? J.A. Schall von Bell has lived in China for over twenty years and, with a sincere heart, he has steadfastly and diligently maintained and advocated his religious practices and belief in God. If all of the emperor's subjects served the emperor as Schall von Bell serves his God, no one could criticize their service as lacking in any way. I greatly admire him.

After Ferdinand Verbiest's death, Emperor Kang Xi sent court officials to honor him. The emperor had the following inscription etched in stone:

> Ferdinand Verbiest, with his simple and unadorned nature, was a multi-talented man. He traveled a great distance and braved stormy seas in order to come here and serve with a sincere heart. He served the court for many years and demonstrated his ability. He viewed the heavens with clarity and enabled us to measure time and the seasons with precision. He served as a capable astronomer and also helped provide munitions for our armory, using his intelligence to help us create great weapons capable of destroying the fortifications of our enemies. His diligent labor greatly helped us.

Emperor Qian Long, as famous and capable as Kang Xi, was, of all the succeeding emperors, the most courteous to the missionaries after their religious activities in China had been officially restricted. However, his motive was to utilize the technical skills of the missionaries. Qian Long had no interest in their religious beliefs and he did not fundamentally alter the restrictive policies of the past. Emperor Kang Xi also viewed the evangelistic activity of the missionaries with disdain. In the middle of 'the rites controversy' Kang Xi addressed the missionaries, dismissing their significance: 'Your religious activity has no influence in China. Whether you come or go is irrelevant and of no concern.'[12] While it is probably inaccurate to say that Kang Xi and the other emperors had absolutely no interest in the Christian faith, it does appear that their interest was rather superficial, flowing more out of common curiosity

---

12. Zheng Tian Ting (ed.), *Ming Qing Shi Zi Liao*, II, p. 362.

than any genuine thirst for knowledge. Furthermore, their interest in Christianity emanated from their desire to defend Confucianism.

After recognizing the spurious nature of the charges brought against the missionaries (for tampering with the Chinese calendar) by Yang Guan Xian, Emperor Kang Xi issued a public proclamation lifting the ban on their religious activities. He declared: 'Roman Catholic doctrine and Chinese traditional beliefs are harmonious.'[13] The high point in Kang Xi's relationships with the missionaries came in 1700. Kang Xi was suffering with malaria and his fever raged. One of the missionaries gave the emperor medicine and he recovered. Out of gratitude, Kang Xi gave the missionaries a plot of land on which to build a church, and with his own hand presented them with inscriptions: 'Without beginning and without end, with form and sound as fate has decreed'; 'Displaying benevolence (*ren*) and righteousness (*yi*), the benefactor and judge of men'. Although these enigmatic inscriptions mark a watershed in Kang Xi's relationship with the missionaries, it should be noted that they emphasize Confucian concepts (note especially the key terms, *ren* and *yi*) and do not move beyond the boundaries of orthodox Confucian thought.

This brief survey reveals that the warm relationship between the early Qing emperors and the missionaries resulted from the practical value Qing leaders attached to the missionaries' skills in calendar reckoning and building cannons. The relationship was further rooted in the Qing emperors' perception that the evangelistic activity of the missionaries did not constitute a threat or hindrance to Confucianism. However, as soon as the emperors discovered that Roman Catholic doctrine did not fully conform to Confucian thought, they ruthlessly suppressed the evangelistic activity of the missionaries.

Confucianism was also central to 'the rites controversy', which finally led to 'the 100 year ban' on missionary activity in China. While this controversy resulted in conflict between two different perspectives within the Roman Catholic Church (represented by the Franciscans and the Dominicans), at its deepest level, the controversy stemmed from the contradictions between Christianity and Confucianism. The questions discussed during the rites controversy are relatively clear: Should the veneration of Confucius and one's ancestors be considered idolatrous? Should the traditional Chinese terms *Tian* and *Shang Di* be used as names for God? The final verdict was to reject the Chinese rites as

13. Wang You San (ed.), *Zhong Guo Zong Jiao Shi*, p. 914.

idolatrous and to refrain from using traditional Chinese terms as names for God. This verdict led to missionary practices which differed widely from the methods advocated by Matteo Ricci and, more specifically, to the rejection of the veneration of Confucius and the ancestors. This in turn led to conflict between the Vatican and the imperial court and ultimately, to 'the 100 year ban' on missionary activity. 'The rites controversy', it might seem, centered on superficial questions pertaining to form, not with fundamental divisions between Christianity and Confucianism. However, in actuality, the controversy revealed a deeper truth: the sacred and inviolable standing of Confucianism within Chinese society and the fact that a social system so completely and deeply influenced by Confucian thought could not tolerate a dissenting voice, whether it be that of Christianity or any other. Regardless of its relative strengths or weaknesses, the prohibition of the veneration of Confucius in practice challenged the sacred place of Confucianism within Chinese society. The prohibition of the veneration of ancestors also undermined the core Confucian concept of filial piety.

If the emperor's attitude toward Roman Catholicism was utilitarian at best, then the attitude of court officials and local magistrates toward the Catholic faith was even less hospitable. Even in the best of times during the reign of Kang Xi, the emperor was often concerned about the strength of the imperial court's opposition to Roman Catholicism. Generally speaking, if in the interest of the nation the emperor gave the missionaries preferential treatment, the attitude of the court officials, apart from the notable exception of 'the three pillars' cited above, remained rather hostile. This hostility was reflected in subsequent events, including the repression of religious activity and the Boxer rebellion of 1900.

'The 100 year ban' on missionary activity came to an end in 1840 with concessions obtained in the wake of the Opium War and a display of foreign military power. Thus, it was against this backdrop of very special circumstances that evangelistic activity resumed in China. However, Chinese antagonism toward Christianity still continued and intensified, culminating in the Boxer rebellion of 1900. Chinese hostility now emphasized repulsing foreign military, political and economic imperialism, not simply conflicts with Christian doctrine and practice. Nevertheless, at this time it is easy to see points of contradiction between Christianity and various aspects of Confucian thought representative of Chinese traditional culture. For example, Shan Dong Province, the region which gave rise to the Boxer rebellion, was also home to Confucius and the birthplace of Confucianism. As a result of this strong Confucian heritage, government officials and the literati of Shan Dong Province, even after the repeal of 'the ban', continued to oppose the entrance of missionaries into the province. Additionally, the origins of the Boxer uprising are instructive. The Boxer uprising flowed from earlier anti-missionary movements in the Shan Dong/Chao Zhou region which were suppressed by Qing government forces. Later, however, the cry of the Boxer's became 'support the Qing, repulse the foreigners'. Thus, this movement marshalled intense nationalism and cultural pride in an effort to reject foreign power and the influence of Christianity.

With the overthrow of the Qing dynasty, the concrete expression of Confucianism in the form of a feudal state came to an end. During this period, Christianity in Beijing experienced rapid growth. However, in spite of the demise of feudalism, Chinese traditional culture was still a potent force and able to hinder and obstruct evangelistic efforts, as well as undermine the faith of some Chinese believers. In the intense atmosphere of cultural and nationalistic pride which marked the times, many Chinese became deeply committed to traditional Chinese culture, and especially Confucian values. There was a struggle in the Chinese soul between new thoughts and allegiances, and the influence of cultural traditions. As one scholar has described, 'there developed in the minds of people a form of double allegiance in which it was difficult to distinguish between master and servant'.[14] In other words, it was often difficult to determine to what extent individual Chinese embraced new thought patterns, including those advocated by Christian missionaries, or retained the traditional patterns of thought passed down through the centuries.

The result was that many Christians interpreted Christianity through the lenses of Confucianism and forcibly reconciled various conflicts between the two perspectives, even at times using Christianity to safeguard Confucian values. In this way, many Christians submitted to Chinese traditional culture, and various forms of 'Confucianized Christianity' or 'Buddhistic Christianity' emerged. This inevitably resulted in a distortion of Christianity and a weakening of its independence and authority. Moreover in the 1920s, a powerful and dynamic 'anti-

14. Lin Rong Hong, *Feng Chao Zhong Fen Qi De Zhong Guo Jiao Hui* [*The Church in China: Growth in the Midst of Adversity*] (Hong Kong: Tian Dao Publishing House, 1990), p. 102.

Christian movement' developed. Originally, this movement stemmed from the prevailing scientific outlook and the opposition to religion it engendered, the connection in the minds of many between Christianity and Western imperialism, and the influences of Marxism. However, the intellectual outlook and method of the movement was largely shaped by the pragmatism of traditional Chinese culture. Christianity was measured essentially by utilitarian standards: could it serve to save the country from foreign oppression? Could it serve to encourage economic development and raise the people's standard of living? In reality, the radical forms of contextualization noted above (e.g. Confucianized Christianity) were also expressions of this traditional pragmatism.

The distortion of Christianity through syncretism with Chinese traditional culture reached its fullest expression in the Taiping revolutionary movement. Hong Xiu Quan, the leader of the Taiping movement, came to understand (and subsequently use) Christian doctrine through the realities of revolutionary life and various essential features of Confucianism. This was the case despite the fact that he consciously attacked Confucius and Confucianism. For example, Hong used Confucian concepts of society (e.g. the patriarchal clan system) to explain Heavenly realities: if there is a father, there must be a son; and if Jesus is the eldest son, there must be a younger son. Hong went so far as to declare that he was this younger brother of Jesus. Moreover, since Jesus did not have a son, Hong gave his own son to Jesus as an adopted son. In this way, Hong's son was to carry on the family line of both Jesus and Hong. These ideas come straight from Confucius's dictum: 'There are three forms of unfilial or disrespectful behavior; the greatest of these is not having a son.' The motives for these views are found in Hong's desire to perpetuate the feudal practice of dynastic succession.

Another Taiping leader, Yang Xiu Qing, asserted that he was an oracle of God the Father and that Xiao Chao Gui, yet another Taiping, was the oracle of Jesus Christ. In their words, the will of God could be found. These views were undoubtedly influenced by Chinese folk witchcraft and related traditions which supplement orthodox Confucian doctrine. All of these views, of course, are widely divergent from the central tenets of the Christian faith.

2. *The Decline of Confucianism*

The historical evidence clearly reveals the central role that Confucianism, as the representative of traditional Chinese culture, has played in China's earlier and widespread rejection of Christianity.[15] This brief survey also suggests that, while Confucianism is not totally incompatible with Christianity, there are a number of fundamental contradictions which cannot be ignored. I have noted that Confucianism contains an authoritarian or powerful controlling element, and thus was a key force in Chinese resistance to early attempts at evangelization. This indicates that a precondition for effective evangelism in China is a weakening of the dominant role of Confucianism within Chinese society and culture. In terms of the Christian mission, the influence of Confucianism must be undermined. A study of history also suggests that Christians, whether missionaries or Chinese believers, have not been particularly well-placed to complete this task. However, other forces which historically have been viewed as opponents of Christianity, such as the modern scientific outlook and especially Maoist-Marxism, have the capacity to fulfill this task. An analysis of the rise and impact of the radical Cultural Revolution offers ample evidence in support of this thesis.

2.1. *The May Fourth Movement of 1919*

The New Culture Movement, which was given impetus and strength by the May Fourth Movement of 1919, represents the first vigorous attack on Confucianism in the history of the Chinese people. It was an unprecedented event: emotions ran deep and the anti-Confucian rhetoric was fierce. The May Fourth Movement, which was called 'the Anti-Imperialism, Anti-Feudalism Movement', and the more recent 'National Salvation and Enlightenment Movement', were shaped by essentially the same concerns: the former emphasized what was to be discarded or attacked; the latter, what was to be preserved and safe-guarded. The motive and impetus for both movements sprang from a deep desire to combat imperialism and to save the nation, and resulted in attacks upon feudalism and the encouragement of a more progressive, enlightened perspective. The motives cannot be separated from the results.

The May Fourth attacks on feudalism stimulated much soul-searching on the part of the Chinese people and resulted in ideological conflict and debates concerning the nature of Chinese culture. From 1840 onwards,

15. Owing to limitations of space, I have focused on Confucianism. The adversarial roles of Buddhism, Daoism and Chinese folk religion in relation to Christianity are self-evident. I shall discuss various specific aspects of the relationship between Christianity and Confucianism, especially those areas of confrontation or difference, in subsequent articles.

China had been greatly humiliated and her people became painfully aware of the decayed state of the imperial court. The Revolution of 1911, led by Sun Zhong Shan (Sun Yat-sen), finally overthrew the Qing dynasty. However, the revolution was not able to eradicate the political and economic legacy of feudalism. Confucianism, the heart of feudalistic culture, remained untouched. Moreover, Yuan Shi Kai and Zhang Xun utilized Confucianism in their attempts to revive the monarchy and dynastic rule. Yet the failures of the Revolution of 1911 made the Chinese people painfully aware of a crucial fact: if China was to develop into a prosperous nation, then feudalistic culture would have to be swept aside. The link between feudalism and Confucianism was inseparable, and so the latter as well as the former would have to go. Chen Du Xiu, the intellectual leader of the May Fourth Movement, criticized those who saw reform and the affirmation of Confucian values as compatible: 'The three cardinal virtues of Confucianism are the source of Chinese ethical and political theory. If we seek to establish a Republic and continue to maintain the three cardinal virtues as the basis of our ethical theory, we will not succeed.'[16] Thus, a central aim of the May Fourth Movement was to repudiate Confucian values and reform Chinese society. From the use of colloquial language (*bai hua wen*) to contemporary literary works, from political theory to cultural and religious attitudes, the revolutionary faction sought to utilize every tool in its fight against feudalism.

Extensive and unprecedented debates between the revolutionaries and the conservatives raged until 1927. The debates focused on the relative strengths and weaknesses of traditional Chinese and Western culture, with discussion of Confucianism being especially prominent. The views of these opposing groups were clearly expressed: the revolutionaries were eager to embrace Western culture and mercilessly attacked Confucianism; the conservatives, by way of contrast, sought to use every means possible to defend Confucianism and deprecate Western culture.

The revolutionary perspective was based upon Western democracy, scientific methods and Marxism. Chen Du Xiu declared,

> Modern civilization has been developed by Europeans; it is Western civilization...the three characteristics of modern civilization, endowing it with the ability to reform ancient methods and to create new attitudes in

16. Chen Du Xiu, 'Wu Ren Zui Hou Zhi Jue Wu' ['Our Final Awakening'], *Qing Nian Za Zhi* [*Young People's Journal*] (February, 1916).

the hearts of people, are an emphasis on human rights, biological evolution, and socialism.[17]

These three elements were not always given equal emphasis. At the outset democracy and science were heavily stressed. Chen insisted that

> in order to support Mr. Democracy, we must oppose Confucianism, Confucian rites and morality, and outdated ethical and political theories. In order to support Mr. Science, we must oppose old forms of artistic expression and old religious views. In order to support Mr. Democracy and Mr. Science, we must oppose the essence of Chinese culture. We now maintain that only Mr. Democracy and Mr. Science can dispel the dark clouds which envelop and inhibit Chinese political, moral, academic, and intellectual achievement. Without Mr. Democracy and Mr. Science, inevitably every government oppresses and every society descends into bitter conflict, shedding much blood and lopping off many heads.[18]

Later, Marxism began to gain more attention and was given greater emphasis. Marxism was also allied with the anti-imperial and anti-feudal cause, and viewed as a means by which the nation might be saved. The conservatives of this period, apart from those who did not understand Western culture, stressed the negative aspects of Western culture. This contributed to the emergence of Marxism, above democracy and science, as the defining feature of the revolutionary perspective. In addition to an emphasis on Confucianism, the conservative arsenal relied heavily on criticisms of various maladies which plagued Western civilization.

World War I was decisive in this regard. When the war in Europe broke out, it gave conservatives ammunition with which to attack Western civilization. The war also disillusioned those who had favored the capitalist system and left them in doubt about Western civilization, some of them even turning to the side of advocates for Confucianism. Thus, after the victory of the October Revolution and the foundation of the Chinese Communist Party, Western ideas that were associated with capitalist theories were replaced by Marxism, which eventually became a major source employed in criticizing Confucianism. In other words, the critical stance characteristic of Marxism was not only recognized as a powerful weapon against imperialism and feudalism, but it was also

17. Chen Du Xiu, 'Fa Lan Xi Ren Yu Jin Shi Wen Ming' ['The French and Modern Civilization'], *Qing Nian Za Zhi [Young People's Journal]* (September, 1915).

18. Chen Du Xiu, 'Ben Zhi Zui An Zhi Da Bian Shu' ['A Response to Critics of Our Journal], *Xin Qing Nian [New Youth]* (January, 1919).

treasured as an efficient means for national salvation. In this way, Marxism began to dominate the ideological arena in China. Consequently, revolutionists felt better equipped to attack conservatives who, from the very beginning, fought back in a defensive and anxious manner. This was the case even though the conservatives constantly changed their defensive strategies by, for example, making comparisons between the moral doctrines of Confucianism and the materialism of Western culture; by contrasting what was believed to be lacking in Western culture with what was held valuable by Confucianism; by distinguishing the authentic doctrines of Confucianism from those of the meta-Confucianism developed in the Song and Ming dynasty, and by relegating all sins and evils to the later adaptations so as to make Confucianism innocent.

The revolutionists kept fighting mercilessly and uncompromisingly, and eventually they were able to remove Confucianism from the national pedestal. Academically, however, this cultural campaign did not achieve what had been expected by its initiators. This was in part due to the painstaking classification of Confucian principles which regulated virtually every aspect of life. Confucianism, though no longer so dominant as it had been before, still had a great impact in academic circles and was always popular in the countryside.

In this cultural campaign, although many aspects of the cultural and social life of the country were rigorously debated—such as the relationship between materialism (matter) and consciousness (mind), between desire and morality, between the virtues of science and humanity—the point of religion was seldom discussed in an adequate way. It was mentioned rather casually as one of the human activities. The attitude of the revolutionists towards traditional Chinese religions was entirely negative, and the attitude of the conservatives was not very positive either. But, with respect to Christianity, their opinions were divided and, at times, fickle. This is witnessed by the fact that in one essay Christianity might be appreciated; while in another by the same author, it might be deprecated. This vacillating attitude characterized such key revolutionary figures as Chen Du Xiu and Li Da Zhao.

A good example is found in the comparisons made between Orientalism and Occidentalism by Li Da Zhao in his 'Fundamental Differences between Eastern and Western Civilization' and 'Material Change and Moral Development'. According to Li, Oriental religions sought after a way to escape the dread of death, whereas Occidental religions 'are rooted in culture and society, inspiring their believers to discover the origin and values of life. The gospel and prayer ringing in churches are powerful enough to lead to the pursuit of the truth of life'.[19] One year later, however, his attitude toward religion changed fundamentally as he wrote:

> Since morality is such a thing that no earthly standards could verify its substance, some people seek to flee their earthly life and take refuge in religion. They believe that the only place for them to go to find the root of morality is the religious world where they can live a seclusive, super-natural life. It is not until the second half of the nineteenth century that the motive to pursue the virtue of morality was justified by two scholars, Charles Robert Darwin and Karl Marx.[20]

Such changes of attitude were also popular among conservatives who, for instance, did not even have a proper name for Christianity. They either called it 'Hebraism' or 'Occidentalism' or 'Western religion', rather than Christianity. This shows, at the very least, that by that time Christianity had not yet been rooted in the Chinese ideological system. As Hu Shi put it: 'It cannot be denied that Christianity and its religious ceremonies are held among Chinese intellectuals either in contempt or in neglect.'[21]

Nevertheless, since Western ideas were borrowed as weapons in the campaign against Confucianism, Christianity was given a vigorous push forward in China. In April 1920, for example, the Chinese Christian Association arranged for a conference in Beijing at which a number of eminent scholars expressed their opinions on Christianity. Both Christians and non-Christians were invited to discuss 'the renaissance of Christianity'. The 11th Conference of the World Students' Christian Union was held at Qinghua University in April 1922 and Christianity appeared to be enjoying rapid development in China.

However, in 1922 an anti-Christian campaign was also launched. The campaign was stimulated by several factors: first, the conflict between science and religion peaked internationally at this time; secondly, the

19. Li Da Zhao, 'Dong Xi Wen Ming Zhi Gen Ben Yi Dian' [Fundamental Differences between Eastern and Western Civilization], *Yan Zhi* [*Political Discourse*] (July, 1918).

20. Li Da Zhao, 'Wu Zhi Bian Dong Yu Dao De Bian Dong' ['Material Change and Moral Development'], *Xin Chao* [*New Wave*] (December, 1919).

21. Li Zhi Gang, *Ji Du Jiao Yu Jin Dai Zhong Guo Wen Hua Lun Wen Ji* [*Essays on Christianity and Modern Chinese Culture*] (Hong Kong: Yu Zhou Guang Publishing House, 1993), II, p. 201.

history of Christianity in China, particularly the last 50 years, had been inextricably linked with foreign imperialism; and thirdly, both proponents and opponents of Confucianism found common ground in their anger against imperialism. During this anti-Christian campaign, speeches and articles against Christianity were delivered one after another by many national celebrities, including such notable figures as Chen Du Xiu, Li Da Zhao, Cai Yuan Pei, Li Shi Zeng and Wang Jin Wei.

There was, however, a positive side to this outburst of criticism. The critical speeches and articles, along with the different opinions expressed at the conference of 1920, all seemed to support the observation that Christianity in China had emerged from its former state of being neglected and despised by the Chinese literati. It had begun to find its place in the ideological system and academic circles of China. More importantly, when the anti-Christian campaign came to an end, a more indigenous and authentically Chinese form of Christianity emerged. This Christian renaissance found its full expression in the Three Self Movement (self-governing, self-supporting and self-propagating). Li Zhi Gang offers a description of this dynamic period: 'During that period of time, educators were so abundant, ideas so dynamic, and industries so progressive, that nothing like it had ever been seen before.'[22] In short, the historical record suggests that the anti-Confucian campaign significantly helped to promote the growth of Christianity in China.

2.2 *China as a Feudal Society*
The polemical discussions concerning the social character of China gradually faded away in the mid-1920s. During the five years from 1929 to 1934, however, the same issues once again made their way back into the political and academic arena. Many people participated in the debate, most of whom were intellectually minded young people. The influence of this latter debate was even more far-reaching than the former. More than 140 essays and 30 books were published. Because some of the opinions reflected in these publications were relevant and similar to, though sometimes different from, those held by the Chinese Communist Party, Li Ze Hou affirmed that the discussion has 'political insight, serves certain political purposes and manifests the spirit of the Chinese Communist Party'.[23] The subject at issue was the classification of the

22. Li Zhi Gang, *Ji Du Jiao Yu Jin Dai Zhong Guo*, II, p. 217.
23. Li Ze Hou, *Zhong Guo Xian Dai Si Xiang Shi Lun* [*Modern Chinese Thought: Historical Essays*] (Dong Fang Publishing House, 1987), 70.

social system of China: was it a capitalist society, a socialist society, or a feudal society? Three views were presented. Two held that Chinese society was capitalist; while the third, echoing the Chinese Communist Party, believed that China was still a feudal society. Since the classification of Chinese society as feudal reflected more accurately the realities of the day, this view gradually became dominant. Once the classification of Chinese society as a semi-feudal, semi-colonial society was academically established, the task set for the Chinese Communist Party became even clearer: to fight against imperialism and feudalism.

2.3 *The Anti-Feudalism Campaign*

The slogan 'Down with Confucianism' emerged from the May Fourth Movement and continued to be heard throughout literary circles as late as 1949. But the Chinese Communist Party was not content with what had already been achieved. It was determined to put its political propositions into practice. It worked quickly to extend the anti-feudalism campaign from the intellectuals to the countryside, where feudalism had built its stronghold. In one of his most famous essays about the anti-feudalism campaign carried out in the countryside, Mao Tse-tung wrote:

> These four authorities—political, clan, religious and masculine—are the embodiment of the whole feudal-patriarchal system and ideology, and are the four thick ropes binding the Chinese people, particularly the peasants. The fact is that the great peasant masses have risen to fulfill their historic mission and that the forces of rural democracy have risen to overthrow the forces of rural feudalism. To overthrow these feudal forces is the real objective of the national revolution. In a few months the peasants have accomplished what Dr. Sun Yat-sen wanted, but failed to accomplish in the forty years he devoted to the national revolution. This is a marvelous feat never before achieved, not just in forty, but in thousands of years.[24]

In spite of the fact that this anti-feudalism campaign was aborted soon afterwards due to a sudden change in the political landscape (the split between the Chinese Communist Party and the Kuomintang), this sort of radical mass movement, first advocated by Mao, proved to be so powerful in the anti-feudalism campaign that it was eventually adopted by the Chinese Communist Party and its army in order to fulfill their mission.

As the land-reform movement launched by the Chinese Communist

---

24. Mao Tse-tung, *Mao Ze Dong Xuan Ji* [*Selected Writings of Mao Tse-tung*] (One volume edition, 1969), p. 31 (first citation), pp. 15-16 (second citation).

Party was progressing steadily throughout the countryside, the feudal system, theoretically at least, collapsed. To wipe out feudalism completely, forms of mass media such as literature and drama were successfully employed by the Chinese Communist. For one and a half decades, starting from the early 1940s, the most frequently used phrase in China was 'feudal mind', referring to any stick-in-the-mud attitude. In spite of all the efforts and achievements made in the anti-feudalism campaign, this was not the end of feudalism. Culturally, Confucianism was still highly appreciated and was therefore frequently attacked in each political movement after 1949.

2.4. *The Story of Wu Xun*

The year 1951 saw another ideological campaign against feudalism. This campaign was sparkled by a film entitled 'The Story of Wu Xun'. In an authoritative document, Mao Tse-tung commented,

> The end of the Qing dynasty was an age when Chinese people were fighting against invaders on the national level and feudalism on the domestic level. Wu Xun, unlike his contemporaries who were engaged in the campaign against feudalism and its economic base and superstructure, turned to the other side and prostrated himself at the feet of feudal lords, allowing himself to be used for the propaganda of feudalism. Should such repulsive acts be crowned with glory? The staging of 'The Story of Wu Xun' along with so much blind sympathy and admiration for both the story and the protagonist simply suggests what confusion has emerged in our ideological life![25]

Mao's antipathy for feudalism was clear and he allowed no tolerance of it. Although this campaign originally was not aimed at feudalism, feudal culture represented by Confucianism was given one more heavy blow.

2.5 *The Great Cultural Revolution*

The next great political campaign, the Great Cultural Revolution, sent shock waves around the world. The Cultural Revolution was initiated by the issuance of the programmatic '5.16 Document' which stated,

> Our country is faced with the climax of the Great Proletarian Cultural Revolution. This climax is charging with great force on the ideological and cultural stronghold where remnants of capitalism and feudalism are protected.

25. Mao Tse-tung, *Ying Dang Zhong Shi Dian Ying, 'Wu Xun Zhuan', De Tao Lun* [*Discussion Concerning the Importance of the Movie, 'The Life of Wu Xun'*].

Although the task of the Cultural Revolution was 'to purge those capitalist heads in authority', feudal culture represented by Confucianism once again received severe criticism. The criticism came in three distinct stages. The first stage started early in the Cultural Revolution with the 'Against Four Olds and for Four News' Movement (the 'four olds' are old ideas, old culture, old customs and old habits; while the 'four news' are their opposites). Consequently, not only were ideas associated with Confucianism criticized, but sacrifices to ancestors were banned, religious temples were destroyed, and superstitious customs repressed. Christians were also severely persecuted: most churches were closed; and some nuns and friars were forced to return to secular life.

The second stage was marked by another national campaign. This one, launched by Mao Tse-tung and lasting from the fall of 1973 through the end of 1974, was directed against Confucianism and Lin Biao. It was rumored that this campaign was originally aimed at Lin Biao and his gang because Lin Biao was once a secret believer of Confucianism and Mencianism. But the real purpose of this campaign was to justify the Cultural Revolution so that Mao Tse-tung could maintain his absolute authority. The Great Cultural Revolution, as its name suggests, was great in the sense that no other cultural campaign so far could be compared with it both in scale and in the vigor of its attacks against Confucianism. It seemed for a time as if Confucianism and Mao Tse-tung thought were fire and water: one's existence would mean the other's extinction.

The campaign soon swept over the nation, from the Politburo to Party committees at the basic level, from such scholars as Guo Mo Ruo and Feng You Lan to illiterate peasants, from large cities to rural villages; no one was spared. Intellectuals were either forced to commit self-criticism or to make verbal attacks on Confucianism; ordinary people were forced to read poems, novels, picture-books and limericks designed to criticize or ridicule Confucianism. Take the Chinese word *Zi*, as used in male names in ancient times. Originally, prior to the Qin dynasty, *Zi* was an honorific title given to scholars. The character was used after their family name, thus Kong Zi (Confucius), Meng Zi (Mencius), Mo Zi (Mohcius), Lao Zi (Laocius) and Zhuang Zi (Zhuangcius). Later, however, this practice lost its original meaning and no longer suggested honorific connotations. During the campaign against Confucianism and Lin Biao, however, Kong Zi was deliberately avoided when speaking of Confucius. Instead, Confucius was known as Kong Qiu or Kong Lao Er (Lao Er means the second child of a family), both in written documents and in speech. But, while this campaign reached its climax in China, an anti-climax was seen in Taiwan where the Kuomintang and its citizens continued to sacrifice to Confucius.

The third and final stage came in 1975 when a minor cultural movement was triggered by a Chinese classic literary work entitled, *Outlaws of the Marsh*. Hu Sheng accurately describes the defining moment:

> When Mao Tse-tung, at the request of a young teacher at Beijing University, gave his personal reflection on *Outlaws of the Marsh*, the Gang of Four immediately seized the opportunity and heralded it to the press. For Jiang Qing, one of the crucial points with the book was the attempt to make Zhao Gai a mere figurehead. Thus, she framed a case against Zhou Enlai and Deng Xiao Ping, accusing them of making Chairman Mao a mere figurehead.[26]

In many respects, this was another influential, nationwide campaign against Confucianism. Song Jiang, one of the protagonists in *Outlaws of the Marsh*, was severely criticized for being a 'faithful believer of Confucianism and Mencianism'. He was portrayed in the book as a person of blind faith, one who would not waver in his faith or devotion. Even when wronged and then forced to become an outlaw, Song Jiang tried by every means to prove his faith and devotion to the imperial court. He eventually accepted an amnesty offered by the emperor and began to work for him, repressing other rebels. Thus, Song Jiang was identified in the campaign as a capitulationist rather than as the heroic figure of the book. Accordingly, this literary work was labeled as a book that advocated capitulationism, and was derisively associated with Confucianism.[27]

In retrospect, it may be said that in all of the major cultural campaigns after the May Fourth Movement of 1919, especially in those after 1949, Confucianism was fundamentally debased. As a rule, once a principle or an idea has received severe criticism in mass movements, it is almost impossible for the idea or principle to reestablish its previous reputation.

26. Hu Sheng (ed.), *Zhong Guo Gong Chan Dang De 70 Nian* [*The Chinese Communist Party: 70 Years of History*] (Ren Min Publishing House, 1991), p. 456.
27. *Pi Pan 'Shui Hu' Zi Liao Ji* [*Essays Critiquing 'All Men Are Brothers'*] (Shan Xi Teachers College Chinese Department, 1975), p. 14.

3. *Conclusion*

The impact of these cultural and political movements, culminating in the Cultural Revolution, was that Confucianism was marginalized and stigmatized in the ideological realm as a source of feudal ideas. Take for example one of the most important documents issued by the Central Committee, 'The Central Committee of the Chinese Communist Party: Resolution of Several Post-1949 Historical Questions', which describes factors that gave rise to the Cultural Revolution:

> China is a country with a long history of feudalism. The feudal regime and its impacts on politics and ideology are impossible to clean up in a short time. This naturally affords grounds for the growth of an excessive centralization of power, leading to personal dictatorship and idolization. Therefore, it was almost impossible for the Party and the country to kill the Great Cultural Revolution in the cradle.[28]

This view is also held among scholars:

> It was at the end of the Opium War that China entered its semi-feudal, semi-colonial stage. Judging from all domestic factors, the feudal regime then was much stronger than the newly-born national bourgeoisie which, due to the lack of a material base and an independent ideology, was not strong enough to fight against feudalism. As a result, the task unfinished by the national bourgeoisie was passed down to the proletarian class and its party for fulfillment.[29]

The Great Cultural Revolution and tragedies of this kind were believed to be the outcomes of the impact of feudalism. In conjunction with the introduction of new approaches to social science and the subject of psychology, researchers provided further explanations for the observation that the deep-rooted social psychology of Confucianism was fertile soil for personal idolization and dictatorship, even among those who claimed to be revolutionaries. Accordingly, the attitude towards traditional culture became rather negative. Particularly noticeable was the rejection of ideas and practices associated with Confucianism, especially

---

28. *Zhong Guo Gong Chan Dang Zhong Yang Wei Yuan Hui Guan Yu Jian Guo Yi Lai De Ruo Gan Li Shi Wen Ti De Jue Yi* [*The Central Committee of the Chinese Communist Party: Resolution of Several Post-1949 Historical Questions*].

29. Cao Wei Jing and Wei Cheng En (eds.), *Zhong Guo 80 Nian Dai Ren Wen Si Chao* [*Intellectual Trends in China: The Humanities in the 1980s*] (Shanghai: Xue Lin Publishing House, 1992), p. 558.

'the three cardinal guides' (the ruler guides the subject; the father, his son; and the husband, his wife) and 'the five constant virtues' (benevolence, righteousness, propriety, wisdom and fidelity).

While classical Confucianism was undergoing such harsh treatment in mainland China, among the overseas Chinese a new current known as Modern Neo-Confucianism had begun to emerge. The genesis of this new movement can be traced back to the early 1920s. Neo-Confucianism was founded and developed by scholars of Confucian philosophy during the Song and Ming dynasties. It differed from classical Confucianism in that it sought to blend traditional Confucian philosophy with contemporary Western ideas in the quest for a better future for Chinese culture and society. The development of Modern Neo-Confucianism roughly underwent three stages. During the first period (1920s–1940s), advocates of Modern Neo-Confucianism attempted to give Chinese culture an ideological base for the study of Western philosophy.

The second period (1950s–1960s) saw the newly-established academic base move from the mainland of China to Hong Kong and Taiwan. Many outstanding scholars also went abroad to resume their research. There they began to reshape the value system of Chinese culture in the light of Western philosophies: while Confucianism was still regarded as the core of Chinese culture (and the virtues of Chinese culture were still held against the ills of Western culture), more positive Western ideas were adopted by Modern New-Confucianists.

The third period has emerged quite recently. Again, the major impetus has come from outside the China mainland, although its influence began to be felt on the mainland once again when China opened up to the outside world in late 70s and early 80s. Although mainland scholars are interested in the new approaches and accomplishments of Modern Neo-Confucianism, their attitude towards it is generally quite cautious and reserved, with some rejecting it outright. In response, an academic wave of national study is pushing its way throughout China. But many scholars are concerned this new wave will be highly politicized.

More than five decades of constant waves of cultural and political movements had eventually washed away the ideological foundation of Confucianism, leaving China an intellectual and religious wasteland. When the critical floods came, they not only swept aside Confucianism, but other ideas and schools of thought as well, including some appropriated from the West to combat feudalism and even aspects of Maoist-Marxism. Before 1949, for instance, the task set for the Chinese revolution was to move the 'three mountains': imperialism, feudalism and bureaucratic capitalism. After 1949, however, the three mountains changed. Only the mountain of feudalism remained (even here a change from 'uprooting' to 'criticizing' feudalism can be observed). The three mountains which now needed to be moved were feudalism, bourgeoisie tendencies (instead of bureaucratic capitalism), and revisionism (instead of imperialism). Changes were also noticed with respect to other concepts and ideas, including those previously advocated in the campaign against feudalism. Revisionism became a widely used term and referred to any attempt, theory or practice employed to explain Marxism by Mao's political rivals (e.g. leaders of the former Soviet Union, Liu Shao Qi and Deng Xiao Ping). According to the Central Committee of the Chinese Communist Party:

> Many ideas and theories which were mistakenly criticized as principles of revisionism and capitalism during the Cultural Revolution are in fact those of Marxism and socialism. Quite a few of them were even set forth and advocated by Mao Tse-tung himself.[30]

Not surprisingly, the constant upheaval of critical movements did not allow sufficient space for new perspectives or theoretical systems to develop. If Confucianism, so deeply rooted in the Chinese psyche, had been wiped out, how could anything else survive?

The critical movements and political campaigns outlined above have created an important new reality: today, the position and influence of Confucianism is much less significant in mainland China than in Hong Kong, Taiwan, and other regions inhabited by overseas Chinese. The fact that Christianity is growing at a relatively slow rate in Hong Kong and Taiwan in particular, suggests that the loss of faith in traditional religion, especially the collapse of Confucianism, is a major factor in the current rapid growth of Christianity in China. So far, the spread of Christianity has met little apparent resistance in intellectual and cultural circles in China. Will obstacles arise? If so, what will be their nature and how great their impact? Of course, it is too early to predict any likely outcome. But one point is certain: whatever obstacles do arise, they will not impose the same sort of difficulties which Matteo Ricci and his colleagues had to face. Certainly, contemporary Christians no longer

---

30. *Zhong Guo Gong Chan Dang Zhong Yang Wei Yuan Hui Guan Yu Jian Guo Yi Lai De Ruo Gan Li Shi Wen Ti De Jue Yi.*

need to utilize and blend together Confucian values and terms in order to address the Chinese of the mainland.

I have suggested, then, that the cultural and political campaigns of the past 70 years represent an important stimulus to the present rapid progress of Christianity in mainland China. This observation should not be taken as a sign that these campaigns meet with my approval or that I applaud them. Obviously, these revolutions were not initiated to encourage others to embrace Christianity or any other religion. I do, however, believe that several factors help explain why Christianity, unlike Confucianism, has met with little resistance as of late from cultural and intellectual leaders: first, unlike Confucianism, Christianity in China has never enjoyed nationwide popularity and, due to its distinctive nature, it did not and will not impede the positive work of revolutionary forces. Secondly, the policies of the Chinese Communist Party concerning religion (e.g. 'the united front') have insured that Christianity has never been directly attacked, though it has been restricted by Maoist-Marxist perspectives and policies. Thirdly, in spite of the fact that many in China do not know much about Christianity, the public attitude towards Christianity is generally quite sympathetic. There is no hostility. All this seems to suggest that the miraculous arrangement of events which marks the past 70 years could never have come about simply through the effort of mortal hands. It was not possible for Christianity by itself to vie with systems as dominant in China as Confucianism, Marxism and Mao Tse-tung Thought. However, critical means are used for criticism, not for construction. When the most radical forces had eventually cleared the way, their mission was over, leaving the thirsty land ready for the timely rain of truth.

A COMPARISON OF TWO WORLDVIEWS:
KANKANA-EY AND PENTECOSTAL

Julie Ma

This study probes worldviews which shape two distinct belief systems: that of the tribal, animistic Kankana-ey in the Philippines on the one hand, and that of twentieth-century Pentecostals on the other. This inquiry further examines present-day Kankana-ey Pentecostal beliefs. Once these beliefs are delineated and juxtaposed according to various categories, several implications emerge. First, comparison of Kankana-ey and Pentecostal worldviews suggests several contact points which may serve as a means to facilitate evangelism. Secondly, such comparison helps to identify what elements of the Kankana-ey and Pentecostal belief systems have made their way into currents of Kankana-ey Pentecostal belief and practice.

The Kankana-eys inhabit the mountainous northern Philippines and engage in native gold mining and slash-and-burn farming. Like other animistic groups, they are keepers of their own distinct cultural and sub-cultural heritage. The Kankana-eys as animists are also ancestral worshipers.

This study of the Kankana-ey worldview was prompted by the success of Pentecostal missions in their midst. Bill Menzies and his wife have lived among these people for the past seven years. The present small study is a humble offering of my personal appreciation to them for constantly challenging people to be faithful to the truth, not only in the classroom, but also 'out there', always with the aim of reaching the unreached.

In this comparative study, several key religious concepts of each group will be examined: the understanding of God or gods, the Holy Spirit, revelation and the spirit world. For this study, various methods have been employed. For the worldview of Kankana-ey Pentecostal Christians, an extensive survey interview was conducted in the early summer of 1995 among at least fifteen Kankana-ey Assemblies of God

churches in Benguet Province.[1] For data on the native Kankana-ey
worldview, library research has been complemented by personal observations through my own missionary involvement among the Kankana-
eys. The survey of Pentecostal belief is not a presentation of a standard
theology. Only fundamental basics are culled from the biblical references.
Our primary concern is rather with 'grass-roots' Pentecostal theology. It
is deduced from their theological orientation expressed in prayers,
preaching and testimonies.

1. *Blessings*

In most religions, fortune as well as misfortune are ascribed to the will of
the deities. Pentecostals view God as a loving father, faithful and good.
The loving father blesses his children as they present their desires to him.
God is faithful to meet their needs. Kankana-ey Christians likewise
experience God's blessing and believe in God's provision. They believe
that God cares for his people.

1.1 *Traditional Kankana-eys*
The traditional Kankana-eys not only believe in spirit beings, but also in
these beings' intimate involvement in the daily activities of Kankana-ey
life. The deities thus function in roles which are significant for people.
The most relevant and tangible expression of divine power is felt in the
forms of blessings and curses endowed or inflicted by the deities. The
people believe that their gods bless every aspect of their lives. The gods
are believed to be the ultimate source of blessing. Thus, the Kankana-eys
frequently perform rituals to receive blessings. The gods are sought so
that the people may obtain power to meet their needs and resolve
conflicts.

The Kankana-eys believe that the deities have arbitrary power to
bring fortune or misfortune to human beings. All aspects of life are in
their domain, including bountiful harvests, prosperous family life, the
increase of herds, and successful business ventures. The tribal Kankana-
eys operate on the assumption that the ancestors grow the crops, raise
the animals, and rule over daily societal activities.[2] Such notions are

1.   I would like to take this opportunity to express my appreciation to the
churches, pastors and our ministry team members. A more extensive analysis is
found in my forthcoming dissertation.
2.   S. Russell, 'Ritual Persistence and the Ancestral Cult among the Ibaloi of the

deeply internalized. Accordingly, the more they want to be blessed, the more animals they feel compelled to offer.

In every phase of their agricultural calendar, from the preparation of the seedbeds, through the sowing of the seeds, the transplanting of seedlings, and the actual storing of crops in the granary, the Kankana-eys accompany their work with rituals to secure flourishing growth and abundant blessing from the spirits.[3] When the harvest is not bountiful, they examine the rituals they have performed to determine whether or not they have been satisfactorily conducted.

The following discussion describes several occasions in which the pagan Kankana-eys attempt to receive blessing from the gods. A newly married couple, for example, is encouraged to perform a ritual for two or more days following the wedding festival. The ritual prescribed by the priest involves several stages of performance, for the new couple wants to secure a pleasant and prosperous married life. As the ritual is performed, they anticipate that their gods will bless them and bring them good luck.

Ritual performance is also required before a baby is born. The young couple desires safe delivery for the baby. This wish is fulfilled only through performing a ritual. The villagers are invited for the occasion. The priest carefully observes the liver of the sacrificial animal to determine if the shape is auspicious or ominous. For example, the presence of two biles in the liver, many pockets or many parts means good luck will be with the baby. The priest orders the young couple to butcher a large pig as an expression of their thanksgiving to the gods.

A traditional Kankana-ey family, upon the completion of a new house, is expected to perform a ritual to express their gratitude to and to secure more blessings from the deities. The priest (*manbunong*) offers a prayer of blessing. His typical prayer is that the family would offer even greater rituals to honor the gods, especially if the occupants of the new house become rich.

The Kankana-eys also believe that the gods have power to control the success or failure of crops, their primary source of sustenance. Rituals during the planting and harvesting seasons are thus the most celebrated.

Luzon Highlands', in S. Russell and C.E. Cunningham (eds.), *Changing Lives Changing Rites: Ritual and Social Dynamics in Philippine and Indonesian Uplands* (Ann Arbor: University of Michigan Press, 1989), p. 24.

3. W.H. Scott, *On the Cordillera* (Manila, Philippines: MCS Enterprises, 1969), p. 145.

Various smaller rituals likewise are offered for occasions such as mending irrigation channels, hunting, gold mining, cockfighting, and so on. The Kankana-eys perceive the gods as having control over natural resources. For community projects such as irrigation work, village people or groups of individuals agree on an appropriate performance of ritual.

The Kankana-eys trust that their wishes and blessings will be realized through the community priest's proper appeal to the gods along with the proper performance of ritual. They recognize the gods' power to bless and bring good luck to their lives. Every activity of the Kankana-eys is complete only insofar as the deities are invoked to intervene. This invocation is achieved solely through the appropriate means of ritual performance. The ritual provides a meaningful avenue by which the people have their felt needs met.

1.2 Pentecostals

The Pentecostal theology of blessing is not much different from that of traditional Christian theology. However, Pentecostals believe that God intervenes tangibly when they ask and specific blessings are therefore expected. Pentecostal belief is characterized by a sense of expectancy and an experiential focus.

What characteristics of God assure the Pentecostal of God's blessing? First of all, God is faithful. The Hebrew word *amen* (אמן, 'truly') is derived from one of the most outstanding Hebrew descriptions of God's character, reflecting his certainty and dependability. The Pentecostals use *amen* to express their assurance of God's ability to answer prayer.[4] God reveals his faithfulness by keeping his promises: 'Know therefore that the Lord your God is God; he is the faithful God, keeping his covenant of love to a thousand generations of those who love him and keep his commands' (Deut. 7.9).[5] The psalmist confesses, 'You established your faithfulness in heaven itself' (Ps. 89.2). Pentecostals frequently confess God's faithfulness declaring, 'His mercies are new every morning; great is thy faithfulness' (Lam. 3.22). This verbal pronouncement is more than a mental exercise. They anticipate that they will experience his faithfulness. Paul contrasts the human and the divine natures as follows: 'If we are faithless, he will remain faithful, for he cannot disown himself' (2 Tim. 2.13). God's dependability is absolute,

---

4. R.E. Joyner, 'The One True God', in S. Horton (ed.), *Systematic Theology; A Pentecostal Perspective* (Springfield, MO: Logion, 1994), p. 125.

5. Scripture quotations are taken from the NIV.

because God is faithful (Deut. 32.4; Ps. 89.8; 1 Thess. 5.23-24; Heb. 10.23; 1 Jn 1.9). The dependable and faithful God keeps the promise of his blessing as his people ask and seek for it.

Secondly, God by his nature is good. During the days of creation, God periodically examined his work and declared that it was good, in the sense of being pleasing and well-suited for his purpose. The psalmist expresses the same thought: 'The Lord is good and his love endures forever' (Ps. 100.5). He also expresses praises: 'The Lord is gracious and compassionate, slow to anger and rich in love. The Lord is good to all; he has compassion on all he has made' (Ps. 145.8-9). Pentecostals often celebrate his goodness in praise and worship. They believe that God who is good will meet his people's needs. In fact, he is willing to bless and provide for his people (Acts 14.17).

Thirdly, God is love. He is the God who loved the world so much that he gave his only begotten son. This reveals God's particular kind of love—unconditional, sacrificial love. God displays his love by providing for his people rest and protection (Deut. 33.12). The highest form and greatest demonstration of his love is found in the cross of Christ (Rom. 5.8). Because of his love and grace, the world is redeemed and sinners are saved. His lavish love is also revealed through his blessing and careful provision for his people.

The expectation of God's blessing has as its basis God's own character which is exhibited in his relationship with his people. The character of God discussed above is formed of integral dimensions and dynamics, and these features never change. God's promise of blessing to his people is based on this divine integrity. His blessing is intended for his people to experience in daily life. It is not meant only to be transcendent but also to be immanent, tangible and empirical as well. For this reason, Pentecostals do not hesitate to seek such blessing from God. Experience enhances their relationship with God as they are drawn closer to him, and this leads them into deep faith.

1.3 *Kankana-ey Pentecostals*

The Kankana-ey Christians want to experience God's blessing in the whole spectrum of their daily life. When any unexpected disaster strikes them, they earnestly seek God's help and blessing. During the monsoon season, for a period of six to eight months, a series of typhoons pummels the region, and the people often suffer great losses and destruction. Their farm products, their major source of sustenance, are most significantly affected. In such critical situations, the Kankana-ey Pentecostals intensely look for God's help and blessing.

Through the interviews of this study, conducted among the Kankana-ey Pentecostal Christians, questions were asked so as to register their views concerning God's blessing. These interviews revealed a simple yet profound understanding of God's blessing. Their theological perspective has been established primarily through empirical, daily life experiences, where they exist as Christians in a pagan community.

First of all, they view God as the Provider of their needs. They have learned to request of God what they need. After conversion, they come to know that their provider is no longer the whole array of pagan gods but rather the one God who created the universe and humankind. The Kankana-ey Pentecostals hold to what the Bible says: he never forsakes nor neglects his children, but he always cares for them. Thus, when they encounter disasters in their business, they above all seek the Provider for help and blessing. They confess, 'We want to exercise our faith in such difficult circumstances'. Practicing faith typically leads them to endurance and further experience of his blessing.

Secondly, they have an immanent orientation to God. They believe he is able to supply the basic needs of his people. When the Kankana-ey believers face financial crisis, they earnestly beseech God for help. They frequently expect that God can and will improve farming and mining production. They actively believe and anticipate that God will intervene in their circumstances and assist in their affairs. They express their trust in various ways. In times of crisis, they seldom wrestle with problems by themselves. They often share their concerns broadly. It is thus not uncommon to have an hour-long time of testimonies during any given service. They freely share their thanksgiving as well as their prayer needs. Considering their traditional timidity, this is a rather unusual scene. They often call together fellow Christians for corporate prayer. This practice clearly expresses their oneness as they are surrounded by 'persecuting' relatives and neighbors. They simply believe that blessing will truly come when they ask for it.

Thirdly, they believe that God is the source of all blessing. Prior to receiving their Christian faith, they say, they believed that the pagan gods were the ultimate source of their blessing. Facing calamity, they used to seek the village priest to prescribe an appropriate ritual for blessing and thus secure their future. After becoming Christians, they came to believe that God is the only one who can bless. God is trusted as the one who is in charge of their lives. One Kankana-ey Pentecostal Christian stated, 'He cares for us and brings blessing to us when we look for it'. Thus God is viewed as the abundant Blesser.

Fourthly, God blesses because he is faithful. The Kankana-ey Pentecostals' experience of God in his faithfulness may be dramatically contrasted with their former relations to gods who were unpredictable and who constantly changed their demands. The capricious and demanding nature of these gods is reflected in the rituals in which the number of sacrificial animals increases, beginning with one, then three, five, seven, and so on. They also understand God's faithfulness as supplying the needs of his children. As they believe in his faithfulness, they wait on his blessing. This perseverance results in their growth in faith and trust in God. Some of them articulated their view of God as follows: 'We frequently recall the experience of God's faithfulness in his blessing', or 'It helps us to wait on what is anticipated to come'.

To summarize, the Kankana-ey Pentecostals view God in terms of his blessing. He is viewed primarily as the Provider who is faithful and as the source of all blessing—the one who has power to bless. It seems reasonable to assume that their firsthand experience of God's blessing has contributed to the formation of such a view of God's blessing. They particularly believe that God's power is manifested through blessings. Their focus on concrete realities seems to generate simple belief and trust. God is higher than any other god, and his power is greater than any other god's power.

2. *Curses*

Whenever non-Christian Kankana-eys experience disaster or difficulties, they attribute them to the gods and spirits. The acts of the gods are considered either as curses or judgments. Calamity occurs, according to their understanding, when they offend any of the gods or spirits. The Pentecostal similarly believes that in God's judgment, they may suffer when he is offended. God is the Lord of love and judgment. Judgment is to be expected when one commits sin. The Kankana-ey Pentecostals experience curses as they are embodied by non-believing members of the community, especially when the Christians no longer participate in traditional religious practices.

2.1 *Traditional Kankana-eys*

The traditional Kankana-eys hold to a notion that the gods bring curses when a ritual is not properly offered or omitted. The offended and an-gered spirit-beings bring affliction as a form of curse, causing poor harvests, illness, hearing problems, sleepiness, drowsiness, headaches, inability to procreate, or the like. Sometimes the spirits, the Kankana-eys believe, cause acute depression for an extended period of time. This affliction naturally keeps one from normal activity and renders the victim unproductive in daily life. The only way to counter such affliction is to appease the offended deity. The requisite appeasement involves careful execution of an animal sacrifice, or the appropriate material offerings. This activity is not voluntary worship, but rather an attempt to appease the anger of capricious gods.

Here are several examples which illustrate the worldview underlying these activities. A village complains of sleeping problems. During a ritual the *manbunong* carefully observes the bile of the sacrificial animal's liver, the organ most commonly inspected for signs or omens. If the bile is partly covered by the liver, this is interpreted as a sign that a spirit, called *Tomongao*, does not wish to release the afflicted person. The *manbunong* orders the family to offer more chickens or pigs until the desired bile is finally obtained.[6]

When a newly married couple cannot bear a child, the *manbunong* consults with the couple and identifies *Kabunyan* (one of the gods) as responsible for this problem. In fact, the deity is asking for gifts from the couple.[7] The couple meet the requirements so that they may have children.

A person has performed a ritual in the past and offered a single animal, without knowing that the ritual requires a pair of animals. Certain rituals require animals in pairs, male and female, according to the belief that a pair of animals multiplies once it is taken to the skyworld. As a result of the person's oversight, he becomes ill. For such a ritual mistake, another ritual is deemed mandatory before any healing can occur. Similarly, a sick woman is bathed by a family member. Every one in the family anticipates imminent death. Then, the sick woman is brought to a female *mansip-ok* (priest). The *mansip-ok,* after hearing

---

6.   W.D. Sacla, *Treasury of Beliefs and Home Rituals of Benguet* (Baguio City, Philippines: BCF Printing, 1987), p. 71.

7.   Sacla, *Beliefs*, 72.

from her, says, 'Your third generation ancestor in the third ascendant generation performed this ritual. In this ritual, a female and male carabao (Philippine water buffalo) were to be offered. Since a female carabao was the only available sacrificial offering at that time, the ritual was not performed according to the conditions requiring a pair of sacrificial offerings to be butchered.'[8] Another ritual must then be performed with strict adherence to the wishes of the gods.

A pair of animals is butchered according to the wish of certain gods. Since the purpose of performing this ritual is to comfort and soothe the angry gods in order to expedite the healing of the afflicted, detailed observation of the animals' entrails is required in order to detect any omen. The Kankana-eys believe that the performer's ancestors come down for the completion of this offering. G. van Rheenen states that the only way dead ancestors can tell their wishes and communicate with the living is by causing illness and misfortune, or by similar evil means.[9] Malevolent deities afflict or attack when persons offend them. The degree of offense against the gods determines the degree of punishment to be meted out.[10]

The curse normally comes upon the offended party from *Adikaila*, the highest god and god of justice and fairness. If an individual is suspected of stealing someone's animal, the owner brings the suspect to the members of the village council. The priest presides over the council and proceeds with the case. The priest first offers a prayer to the deity. Then, one of the council members interrogates the accuser as well as the one accused. The first question is addressed to the accused: 'Do you believe that the guilty party will be cursed by the highest spirit?' The suspect answers, 'Yes'. It is implied that he asserts his innocence. Then, the council asks the accuser, 'If there is no truth in your charge, are you willing to suffer the curse of *Adikaila*?' The farmer indicates his willingness. The council then asks the final question of the suspect, 'You claim your innocence, while the accuser is positive in his accusation. In this case, we cannot give judgment but leave the case to *Adikaila*'. Then the council presents to the suspect a selection of several curses that he or she should suffer. In this particular case, the selections are: 1) that he

8.   Sacla, *Beliefs*, pp. 77-78.
9.   G. van Rheenen, *Communicating Christ in Animistic Contexts* (Grand Rapids: Baker, 1991), p. 185.
10.   Sacla, *Beliefs*, p. 4.

shall live a very poor life; 2) that lightning will strike him; 3) that a snake will bite him; or 4) that he may not live long.[11]

In sum, the pagan Kankana-eys perceive the gods as having power to bring curses. It is, therefore, of crucial importance for them to avoid offending the gods in any degree. Appropriate avoidance and appease-ment will protect them from unfavorable occurrences and will secure favor. Offering sacrifices restores normal states of life. The gods are also capable of discerning if a person is guilty or not, and they will curse society's offenders.

2.2 *Pentecostals*

The Pentecostals understand God as a God of justice. The justice of God includes judgment (Deut. 7.9-10). His character is dependable in the ethical or moral realm. 'Rightness' is a quality of his character and action.[12] He judges his people in righteousness and justice (Ps. 72.2).

According to a biblically informed Pentecostal worldview, there are several types of guilt (Gen. 26.10; Jas. 2.10). Individual or personal guilt may be distinguished from the communal guilt of societies. Objective guilt ascribes to the actual sin, whether realized by the guilty or not. Subjective guilt refers to the experience of guilt as it is perceived by a person. Subjective guilt may be honest, leading to repentance (Ps. 51; Acts 2.40-47).[13] God's justice does not compromise with sin (Ps. 11.5; Rom. 1.18). Penalty or castigation inflicted by an authority on sinners is the just result of sin, a chastisement predicted on guilt.

Scriptures further teach that the impact of sin is apparent in non-human creation. The curse pronounced in Genesis 3.17-18 marks the beginning of this evil. Romans 8.19-22 elaborates on the continuous state of frustration in nature. The creation groans expecting the consum-mation of Jesus Christ. The Greek ματαιότης, 'frustration', 'emptiness' (Rom. 8.20), describes the incessancy of corruption that is set in motion when something is separated from its original intent, epitomizing in one term the overall futility of the present state of the universe itself. The condition may range from plants and animals to quarks and galaxies.[14]

11. Sacla, *Beliefs*, p. 16.
12. R.E. Joyner, 'The One True God', p. 130.
13. B.R. Marino, 'The Origin, Nature, and Consequences of Sin', in Horton (ed.), *Systematic Theology*, p. 286.
14. Marino, 'Sin', p. 285.

Judgment, however, renders the guilty motivated to replace what was taken or destroyed. This can be a witness of God's work in a life (Exod. 22.1; Lk. 19.8). Deterrence, for example, involves using castigation of the guilty to discourage others from behaving similarly and such deterrence may often be seen in divine warnings (Ps. 95.8-11; 1 Cor. 10.11). Remediation enables the guilty not to sin in the future. It is an expression of God's love (Ps. 94.12; Heb. 12.5-17).

Issues of justice are to be dealt with in the Church, over against the reality and problems of sin, as part of the truth of love. God's justice and love are central to a Christian worldview. Pentecostals accordingly transmit the good news of Christ as containing both justice and love. Pentecostals believe that the world should hear this balanced, two-edged message of Christ.

2.3 *Kankana-ey Pentecostals*
The Kankana-ey believers frequently are cursed by non-believing relatives and neighbors, when the former do not follow Kankana-ey traditional religious practices. Sharing the gospel also elicits curses from non-believers. According to the interviews, Kankana-ey Christians typically counteract cursing with prayer. They say, 'We trust God to prevent and protect us from the curses of the non-believing people'; 'We believe in the power of prayer, that the curses from the pagans will not occur'.

Although they are cursed, these believers still return the love of Christ. This response is possible only through the help of the Holy Spirit. The Kankana-ey Christians know that love is an essential element of Christianity and that they have to show it to pagan people. They continue to demonstrate the loving kindness of Christ to those who curse. Cursing is not something Christians are taught to do. The Kankana-ey believers are taught instead to bless the non-believers who curse them. To bless those who curse is a sign of spiritual maturity. They believe that they demonstrate a biblical pattern when as Christians they do not return cursing for cursing.

They do rebuke the curses of pagan people, invoking the power of God. However, rebuking does not mean that they confront unbelievers. Rather, they exercise spiritual power granted to them so that they will be protected from the curse. This typical behavior shows that they indeed take cursing seriously. It also implies that they rely upon God's authority. In this sense, the Kankana-ey Pentecostal believers are verbally bold in declaring the power of God. One stated, 'Whenever we need to proclaim God's power, we do so'.

The Kankana-ey Christians also counter curses with the word of God. They understand that God's words are a great spiritual weapon. They constantly read the Bible to gain strength in God. They stress that 'God is with us when we go through suffering and difficulty'. They believe that God's word literally provides a 'refuge'.

They believe that God with his power is able to protect them from curses. They trust that he would never allow his children to be cursed, because God's power is greater than that of any other god. He is viewed as capable of keeping his children from any harm. Accordingly, they regularly pray as they travel that the blood of Jesus will cover their ways.

3. *Healing*

Healing is one prominent area of concern for all three groups involved in this study. The pagan Kankana-eys, like other animists, are spirit-conscious people. They believe that the spirits are responsible for diseases. And they also believe that their ancestors' spirits have obtained power to heal. Human beings can induce the healing power of the spirits via ritual performance. Pentecostals acknowledge healing as the work of the Holy Spirit. They frequently invite the presence of the Holy Spirit when his healing touch is needed. The Kankana-ey Pentecostal Christians frequently experience manifestations of the power of the Holy Spirit. For them, the Holy Spirit is the one who readily helps, encourages and heals.

3.1 *Traditional Kankana-eys*
When a family member becomes sick, pagan Kankana-eys seek the counsel of the priest, (*mansip-ok*), who is gifted in discernment. The priest analyzes the information supplied by the sick person. Often dreams and/or omens around the time of the onset of sickness bear significance to the cause. The *mansip-ok* determines the cause of illness from them.[15] Often the spirit of a deceased brother or sister communicates to family members through these means. The *mansip-ok* determines which specific spirit is responsible for the sickness. One example of interpretation is this: a certain ancestral spirit needs blankets,

---

15. Tito Inio, personal interview, Baguio City, Philippines, 1991.

clothes, garments, food or animals. The family of the sick person has to meet these demands. The *mansip-ok* also prescribes a specific ritual for healing.

In some instances, a normal person may suddenly lose his or her sense of hearing without any noticeable cause. The advice is immediately to conduct a ritual called, *bosal-lan*. In this ritual, first of all, the *manbunong* constructs a replica of a small hut, about one foot wide and a foot high, within the vicinity of the house of the victim's parents. Then the *manbunong,* who has shared power with the spirits,[16] performs a ritual beside this little hut. He offers a chicken to appease the deafness-causing spirit. The *manbunong* persuades the spirit to leave the ear and to be transferred to the newly constructed hut, for the hut is a better dwelling place. As the *manbunong* prays, the sick person simultaneously plucks wing feathers out of the chicken and puts them inside the small hut for the spirit to follow. After this procedure, the chicken is singed, sliced, cooked and eaten.[17]

The spirits of the deceased are not totally separated from the visible world, their families, or their descendants. Rather, they intimately inter-act with them. Since the spirits have no direct means of communication with living kin, they employ dreams, omens, signs or sickness to tell their descendants what they want. It is believed that although the spirits are out of body, the spirits still need for their use items such as, blankets, clothes, garments, food and animals. To obtain power to heal from the spirits, the living comply with their demands. The spirits possess power—power which the Kankana-eys believe is released when living people approach the presence of the deities through mediums in the worship of ritual.

3.2 *Pentecostals*

It appears that healing is one of the Pentecostals' distinguishing mes-sages. According to the Pentecostal worldview, when the Holy Spirit moves, healing takes place. Instances of healing are frequently recounted by Pentecostal believers. Such testimonies often serve to bring people to Christ.

16. M. Wiber, 'The Canao Imperative: Changes in Resource Control, Stratifi-cation and the Economy of Ritual among the Ibaloi of Northern Luzon', in Russell and Cunningham (eds.), *Changing Lives Changing Rites*, p. 58.

17. L.T. Igualdo, 'The Social World of the Kankana-eys' (D.Ed. thesis, Baguio Central University, Baguio City, Philippines, 1989), p. 231.

Pentecostals believe that healing was an essential part of Jesus' ministry during his earthly life. His authority to heal was a sign that the kingdom of God had arrived in and through his presence and ministry. Matthew quotes Isa. 53.4, saying, 'He took our infirmities and bore our diseases'. This reference reminds listeners that Jesus used his power for the purpose of serving people (Mt. 20.28; 26.28).[18] Pentecostals rightly argue that the gospels attest to the abundant healing ministry of Christ (Mk 1.29-34, 40-42; 2.1-12; 3.1-6; Jn 4.46-54; 9.17; Mt. 8.1-4; 12.9-13).

Pentecostals also argue that the healing ministry of Christ is intended to bring people into the kingdom of God. When people see and experience the power of healing, their attention is arrested and they are more likely to believe that Christ is who he claims to be (Lk. 10.1-9). This evangelistic significance is well attested in Jesus' commissioning of the seventy (or seventy-two; Lk. 10.1-2). They are equipped with power and commanded to 'heal' (Lk. 10.9).

Pentecostals further note that baptism in the Spirit was a necessary prerequisite for the disciples' mission. Only after this experience were the disciples to leave Jerusalem and begin fulfilling the great commission. They needed power to witness (Acts 1.8). The concepts of the Holy Spirit in the New Testament and that of the Spirit of God in the Old Testament are intimately connected with power. Consider the pattern of Jesus' ministry after the appearance of the Holy Spirit at his baptism. It is not difficult to assume that the 'power' he received included more than dynamic verbal capability. It included power to heal. The healing account recorded in Acts 3 is taken by Pentecostals to be a typical case. This event immediately drew a large crowd, and Peter was given an opportunity to present the message of Jesus and his salvation.

The history of the mountain Pentecostal churches in the northern Philippines is that of healing and miracles. These occurrences were particularly frequent during the early stage of the Pentecostal ministry, around 1945. The power of the Holy Spirit was revealed through the healing of various sick people. One woman missionary working on her own, Elva Vanderbout, had a significant impact. Her burning desire to bring people to Christ impelled her boldly to share the gospel among the pagans. Her first revival meeting was held in Tuding, Itogon, Benguet Province. In this meeting, the Holy Spirit moved mightily among the people. Many were saved, and more than 150 were baptized in water. Countless number of people, young and old, including small children,

18.   R.H. Smith, *Matthew* (Minneapolis: Augsburg, 1988), p. 133.

shared wonderful testimonies of the power of God. They usually refer to God's power with reference to his miraculous ability to save souls and to heal sicknesses.[19]

At subsequent Sunday night services, many people were also baptized with the Holy Ghost and fire (Acts 2.4). It was like old time Pentecost. With a tremendous sense of anticipation people came to the services to hear the message of Christ. God's power was revealed vividly through the message and through prayer. The power the people experienced was something different from the power of ancestral spirits mediated by pagan priests.

Vanderbout held a revival meeting for salvation and healing in Baguio City. Located at 6,000 feet above the sea level, Baguio is a central crossroads city for various mountain tribal people. Baguio City thus provides access to several provinces. During the revival meeting, one girl, eighteen years of age, who had been a deaf-mute for twelve years, was instantly healed. During each morning and evening service, the sick lined up for healing.[20] The Holy Spirit moved so mightily among the people that the sick were healed by the scores. The blind were enabled to see. Paralytics were healed. People suffering with tuberculosis and many other diseases were healed. One woman was healed of a very large goiter. It was partly reduced when she was prayed for on Saturday night, and when she came back to the services on Sunday morning, it had completely disappeared. A man, twenty-eight years of age, who had been a deaf-mute all his life, was also instantly cured one morning.[21] Healing and salvation characterized Vanderbout's eight-day crusade. In fact, healing and miracles not only drew large crowds, but also convinced them that God through the Holy Spirit works miracles. Through manifestations of healing, many pagans turned to Christ and abandoned their traditional beliefs. The healings continued to take place by the power of the Holy Spirit throughout the mountain ministry. It is likely that the people's religious expectations contributed greatly to the frequent manifestations of the Holy Spirit's healing power. As a result, the Assemblies of God opened many works and erected numerous churches throughout Benguet Province and beyond. The successful penetration of

19. J.B. Soriano, 'Pentecost in the Philippines', *Pentecostal Evangel* (August 7, 1948), p. 1.

20. E. Vanderbout, 'Salvation-Healing Revival in Baguio City, Philippines', *Pentecostal Evangel* (June, 1955), p. 4.

21. Vanderbout, 'Revival', p. 2.

the Assemblies of God into this animistic mountain region is thus largely attributable to the active manifestation of the power of the Holy Spirit in healing.

3.3 *Kankana-ey Pentecostals*

Kankana-ey Pentecostal Christians expect the Holy Spirit to work in their lives on a regular basis. They believe that the Holy Spirit readily works when the people of God urgently beseech him. When a family member gets sick, Kankana-ey Pentecostals pray intensely for the intervention of the Holy Spirit. They believe that when the Holy Spirit is present, healing will take place. Peace and consolation will come as well.

Kankana-ey Christians say, 'God never fails us when we approach him in faith'. This phrase reflects their strong faith in the abiding God. The Kankana-ey believers frequently convene for corporate prayer. They customarily make their prayer requests known to fellow Christians. When prayer is answered, they publicly share their testimonies in a church service. Testimony time is the part of a church service allotted for anyone to stand up and share such testimonies.

Experience of healing power leads them increasingly to rely on the power of the Holy Spirit. The Kankana-ey Christians, particularly older believers, confess that they not only have seen many healings, but also have personally experienced God's healing touch in the past. In interviews, they testified, 'When a family member gets sick, we pray for healing, and God answers our prayer'. This experience of healing also makes the Pentecostal Christians an encouragement to non-Christian members of the tribe; especially when they are sick, they often want to seek the help of the God who heals.

An average Kankana-ey community lacks many basic provisions. There is no electrical power source, and in some places, there is not even an adequate water system. There is no medical service whatsoever, except in large villages where a health worker may be found, but without a supply of suitable medicine. Therefore, if anyone is ill, people either wait for a natural recovery or carry the patient many miles across the mountains to reach a hospital or a clinic. This adds to their financial hardship, for their farming barely sustains their living. In remote villages, cash income is almost non-existent. Thus, bringing the sick to the hospital and buying medication is very difficult. It is not unusual to find a sick baby cry all by him or herself, while all the other family members work in the fields. The last resort is performing a ritual. However, this costs dearly. Against this background, it is no wonder that healing from the Holy Spirit is so routinely sought among Kankana-ey Pentecostals. The experience of God's power leads them to the truth of and allegiance to God. The concrete mindset of the tribal people readily acknowledges the power and goodness of God who works healing wonders 'without cost'.

4. *Revelation*

By 'revelation' I mean communication by a spiritual being to humans. As in every religion, there are two kinds of divine communication to humans: voluntary and involuntary. By 'voluntary communication', I mean a message from a divinity readily revealed to humans. By 'involuntary communication', I mean a message the humans attempt to obtain from the spiritual beings by inducing them, often through ritual.

4.1 *Traditional Kankana-eys*

The traditional Kankana-eys' worldview regards omens and signs as real and powerful. These include dreams, strange animals, red birds, snakes, dogs and pigs. A disturbing or unusual dream signifies an impending accident or misfortune. When strange animals or birds enter a house, the traditional Kankana-eys believe that they may foretell future occurrences for the family. Birds with red colors signify either bad or good luck, depending on their entering movements. A snake crawling inside a house may foretell good or bad luck as well. These incidents must be referred to the priest (*mankotom*) or the elders for a prescription of the necessary ritual. If the movement of the animal signifies bad luck, the ritual *pukkay* is required. It is intended to counteract bad luck or misfortune caused by offended spirits. The sacrificial animal preferably is a dog, the barking of which is believed to drive the evil spirits away.

The traditional Kankana-eys also believe that a pig wallowing in the mud in the morning is a sign of bad luck for the family. The pig should be butchered immediately. A dog barking and wailing at night indicates the presence of evil spirits or an imminent death in the community. The owner of the dog must offer a *madmad* (prayer) ritual to drive away the malevolent spirits. The same owner must invoke the protection of the *Kabunyan*, to keep the community from evil or misfortune.[22] If a

22. Igualdo, *Social World*, p. 333.

person's clothes are immersed in river water, it is believed that a family member will be drowned. To dissuade spirits of such intent, a ritual is performed.

The traditional Kankana-eys are particularly sensitive to dreams. Frequently, deceased ancestors reveal the future through dreams. If a family member has a bad or unusual dream, he or she should refer it to the priest (*mankotom*) for proper interpretation and prescription of rituals. If a person who plans to travel dreams of a trip on the night prior to his or her departure, the individual should cancel the trip. If this warning is ignored, he or she will meet with accident or the planned business will not be successful. If a traveler meets a black bird flying across or opposite the way of travel, the person must return home lest death be his or her fate.

The traditional Kankana-eys, like many other animistic groups, believe that there are built-in messages in certain phenomena. The omens hold profound significance for they contain vital messages for the people's future welfare. Some omens and signs are universally understood, but there are others which require professional interpretation as well as proper measures to counter impending misfortune; hence the vital role of the priest.

4.2 *Pentecostals*

The Pentecostals share basic theological convictions with traditional Christianity. The primacy of the written word as God's revelation is never questioned. However, they also believe in God's direct communication through various other modes. Reports of visions, audible messages, and dreams are common. Prophecy in public settings and speaking in tongues with accompanying interpretation are also considered modes through which God reveals his will.

The Bible provides an ample amount of evidence that the above phenomena are manifestations of the Holy Spirit. The book of Acts records that people saw visions and prophesied after the Pentecost experience. After being baptized in the Holy Spirit, people frequently spoke in tongues and prophesied (e.g. Acts 8). Acts 8.12 indicates that signs and miracles were manifested after the Pentecostal experience. In Acts 5.1-10 we read that Peter, through the inspiration of the Spirit, foretold the deaths of Ananias and Sapphira. Peter's foreknowledge is understood by Pentecostals as God's special revelation for a specific context. It can be identified with the gifts of discernment and prophecy.

The Holy Spirit was with him so that he was able to exercise the gifts of God for ministry. Acts 10.9-16 describes a vision experienced by Peter. The account of the vision is detailed. The experience directly dealt with Peter's bias against the Gentiles. It further substantiated revealed truth (v. 15).

Paul experienced similar works of God. Acts 27.23-24 describes how an angel of God spoke to Paul and revealed God's plan for him. Visions, prophecies and dreams were frequently used by God to communicate his specific will and plan to Paul. On another occasion, the Holy Spirit directed Paul's path through a dream. When Paul received the Mace-donian call, he immediately understood it as God's revelation.

All these accounts share several commonalties which are observed by Pentecostals. First, direct revelation is never intended to replace the written word of God. The early Church cherished as God's inspired revelation what we today call the Old Testament. Frequently, direct revelation serves to affirm the principles revealed in the written word. Secondly, the occasions of direct revelation recorded in the Bible are very specific. As in the case of the Macedonian call, often it is an occasion of choice between equally acceptable options, rather than between good and evil.

Modern Pentecostals have distinguished themselves not merely by *remembering* but especially by *believing* what is written about the work of the Spirit or spirits in the Bible. 'Prophetic words' accordingly are often 'waited upon' in Pentecostal public services. Pentecostals believe that God's specific communication for specific contexts is accessible, and this is in addition to the written revelation.

4.3 *Kankana-ey Pentecostals*

If a Kankana-ey Christian has a horrible dream, for example, in which a dead ancestor appears, the family expects something will happen accord-ing to their long standing belief. Understandably, upon waking the individual often remains shaken by what he or she has seen in the dream. In such circumstances Kankana-ey Christians often seek the help of pastors to pray for 'deliverance' from fear. Incidents like these occur particularly among new Christians. Their immediate need is to be strong enough to resist old influences. It takes time to instruct the believer that the 'father' is not one's own father, but rather is a disguised evil spirit trying to intimidate the family. Taking the authority of the name of Jesus and claiming God's protection is a prayer theme often heard among these believers. Mature Christians see such cases as a means of testing their faith. They perceive evil dreams as an attempt of the enemy to destroy their faith. The spiritual dynamic is recognized as spiritual warfare, in which they must fight against the devil with the power of God. So upon waking from nightmares, they immediately 'check their spiritual state'.

In fact, many Kankana-ey believers have come to the Lord through deliverance from evil dreams. Some dreams have such a powerful effect that the individual cannot take any food or sleep for several nights. When one experiences the power of God delivering him or her from the effect and fear of the omen, that person in fact becomes free once-for-all.

On the other hand, the Kankana-ey worldview and previous religious orientation provides fertile soil for new spiritual experiences. Reports from the field frequently indicate that numerous people see visions as they pray. This phenomenon seems especially to occur among persons who have experienced the baptism of the Spirit. Some speak in tongues, and others are 'slain in the Spirit'. During these moments, they recall, they were filled with extraordinary peace. Such experiences are often accompanied by visions, fragrance and/or the audible voice of the Lord. During the prayer time in a church worship service, it is not unusual for several members to raise their voices and either prophesy or speak in tongues with other members interpreting.

Kankana-ey Pentecostals appear to have more experiences of this kind than average Christians, perhaps on account of the dual influences of native animism and Pentecostalism. They view God in a way which is immanent.

5. *Spirit World*

Belief in the spirit world clearly is evident in Kankana-eys' practices concerning life after death. The spirit world is not just a theological subject, but a reality one has to reckon with constantly. This worldview shapes the contours of this study.

5.1 *Traditional Kankana-eys*
The traditional Kankana-eys believe that there is a hierarchy of deities, and that they all have different effects on the human world. A deceased person is believed to join the other spirits in the skyworld. When the

Adikaila, the supreme being, summons the soul, the body becomes lifeless.[23]

The pagan Kankana-eys distinguish between the spirits of people who have long been dead and those who have recently died. The spirits of those who are long dead are called *Ap-apo.* These spirits are believed to live with *Kabunyan,* the second highest god in the Kankana-ey spiritual world. These spirits travel from the skyworld to the earth, to the underworld and back. The spirits of recently deceased humans are called *Kak-kading.* They remain on the earth. During rituals a host family offers and pours several drops of wine to acknowledge these spirits' presence in the ritual.[24]

The pagan Kankana-eys believe that spirits also dwell in the underworld. They are called *Anito.* They are of particular interest, since they are responsible for misfortune. *Anito* denotes groups of spirits. The particular dwelling places of some of these groups of spirits are as follows.[25]

Pinad-eng stay in the forest and, as owners of wild pigs and chickens, are spirits to whom hunters offer sacrifices to ensure successful hunting. *Tinmongao* dwell in the mountains and are called mountain spirits. They cruelly inflict sickness and injury on people who walk on the spirits' dwelling place. Victims are required to offer sacrifice to calm the spirits' anger. *Penten* dwell in water, and are called water spirits. They are believed to be spirits of those people who have died violently, by accident or by drowning. They cause rivers to rise when people cross during rainy days. *Butat-tew* live in caves, and are the spirits who group themselves at night and misguide humans from their path. They appear and disappear unexpectedly. *Ampasit* also live in caves. They generally are malevolent spirits and have power to steal the souls of people. They mislead people traveling at night.

The rest of the spirits dwell in big rocks, cliffs, ravines, caves, abandoned tunnels, abandoned buildings, bushy trees, bushes, waterfalls, creeks, springs, lakes, rivers, oceans, in the ground and various other places.[26] These spirits are easily offended when people trespass, forget to open wine for them, neglect sacrificial offerings, and commit other acts

23. Sacla, *Beliefs*, p. 60.

24. Sacla, *Beliefs*, pp. 17-18.

25. A. Bagamaspad and Z. Hamada-Pawid, *A People's History of Benguet* (Baguio City, Philippines: Baguio Printing, 1985), p. 103.

26. Sacla, *Beliefs*, p. 19.

of negligence. Offended spirits may cause illness, death and misfortune.

Since the pagan Kankana-eys believe in life beyond death, on the fifth day of a funeral, relatives and friends give *opo* (contributions), which can be money, any kind of fruit, or jars of wine, for the dead person to take along on the journey to the skyworld.[27] The priest (*manbunong*) announces to the dead spirit and spirits of the ancestors, who are waiting for this occasion in the skyworld, the names of the those people who made contributions. The Kankana-eys believe that if the spirits do not receive *opo*, anyone among the attendants may die or become sick. In such fear, they attempt to give ample *opo*. Because of their capability to bless or harm, the dead spirits are treated as living, conscious beings.

5.2 Pentecostals

The Pentecostals believe in life after death. However, they do not believe that the deceased become spirits who affect human life; nor do they treat the deceased as objects of worship.

The Bible reveals that the spirit world is a reality. There are angels as well as evil spiritual beings often called demons, evil spirits, or simply enemies. The angels serve God and execute his will. They are primarily 'messengers' as the Hebrew word מלאך indicates. However, they are also involved in human, especially believers', lives in various ways. The Bible appears to say that each one of God's children has guardian angels (Mt. 18.10). The angels are God's army (2 Kgs 6.17).

The scriptures are clear that evil spirits and demons cause physical and mental illness, although there are also other causes of maladies. On many occasions, demons recognized the Lord. They even pleaded with him not to cast them out (Mk 5.9-11). This behavior clearly illustrates that some diseases are caused by evil spirits or demons. They also create disturbances in the believer's life, especially in one's spiritual life (e.g. Dan. 10.13).

Today's Pentecostals, unlike many other evangelical Christians, take seriously the reality of the spiritual world. They regularly 'rebuke' the activity of the adversaries. They literally take authority in the name of Jesus and verbally pronounce their commands against them. In this sense, the Pentecostals often engage in spiritual warfare. In their thinking, 'power' is closely linked with the experience of Spirit baptism. A favorite passage of Pentecostals is Luke 10, in which Jesus commissions

27. N. Anima, *The Mountain Province Tribes* (Quezon City, Philippines: OMAR Publications, 1977), p. 88.

the seventy. The Lord simply commands them to 'cure the sick' (v. 9). When the seventy return, they report, 'Lord, even the demons submit to us in your name' (v. 17). The link between the healing ministry and the submission of the demons is clear. Yet the casting out of demons is not limited to healing. Any disturbance in daily or spiritual affairs is considered a hindrance or harassment of the enemy. In a public or private setting, whenever a prayer request is shared, people naturally rebuke the activities of the enemy. Their awareness of the spiritual world, and its influence distinguishes Pentecostals. Accordingly, they expect the Holy Spirit—but not necessarily angels—to 'protect' them from all evil.

5.3 *Kankana-ey Pentecostals*

The consciousness of the spiritual world and its effect upon human affairs is more evident among Kankana-ey Pentecostals than among other Pentecostals. This feature probably stands out because of their animistic background. They are particularly conscious of potential retaliation wrought by evil spirits, especially for the offense of abandoning the old allegiance and servitude to the spirits. These believers thus feel that they need added protection from the Lord. This orientation is also well attested in their responses to curses as discussed above.

A common testimony is that they have been deceived by evil spirits. When they thought they were offering sacrifices to their ancestral spirits, it was in fact evil spirits who pretended to be their ancestors. This realization sets it with the new biblical orientation, and it drives new Christians to 'hate and curse' the old spirits. Christians in general grow to pay much less attention to the deceased. So, they do not necessarily bury the dead within the premises of the house, the practice expected of non-Christian family members. The dead are regarded as having departed the living once-for-all. Furthermore, the believing family members do not go through the complex funeral process. The traditional funeral requires at least a week-long sacrifice, and this entails an enormous economic burden.

However, they remain aware that they are surrounded by hostile powers, and they frequently claim power in the blood of Jesus. Sometimes several frequently enunciated terms such as the 'blood of Jesus', the 'cross', and the 'power of the Holy Spirit' are pronounced with a sort of magical expectation. Perhaps this behavior reflects the influence of the word 'spirit' as it used to represent a lower deity who makes contact with human beings. Due to this orientation, they often pray *to the Spirit*.

Their assurance of life after death is significant. The animists always live in fear of the unknown future, especially that which occurs after death. The possibility of becoming an *Anito* haunts them. It is felt that large amounts of sacrifices might ensure a secure future for the non-Christian Kankana-eys. In contrast, Christians enjoy the security of a guaranteed future. Because of their poor living conditions, they put great emphasis on eternal life in heaven. This is their supreme hope.

6. *Summary*

This study has compared and contrasted the worldviews of the native Kankana-eys and the Pentecostals across five primary religious categories: blessings, curses, healing, revelation and the spiritual world. Kankana-ey Pentecostals have been examined as a third religious group which has been profoundly influenced by both belief systems.

The first two groups share many worldview features. First, both are clearly conscious of the spiritual world. Their religions, therefore, reflect the immanence of spiritual beings. God or gods and the Spirit or spirits are intimately involved in human affairs. They are not only worshipped but also expected to intervene in daily human situation. Both groups expect the spirit beings to bless, curse, heal and solve problems, and often their expectations are met through their religious devotion, although the Pentecostals would term this 'faith'.

In spite of these commonalties, however, there are several fundamental differences. The most obvious is the basis of their religions. The native Kankana-ey religion is structured according to the rudiments of animism. It is a religion of 'carrot and stick'. The promise of blessing and the fear of retaliation enslave the Kankana-eys. Their extravagant funerals epitomize the typical level of bondage. Occasionally, the family is not only expected but also explicitly commanded by the deceased ones through the priest to butcher every single animal in the house and even to buy more. This demand is met in exchange for blessings endowed from the spirit to the family. The other side of the story is that the spirit will retaliate severely if the demands are not met. In contrast, Pentecostal worship is characterized by celebration in song, testimony and words. The striking contrast between these two belief systems was stated by one Christian interviewed for this study: 'The new God never asks for anything. He instead gives and gives until he gives his own son.' The other distinguishing feature of Pentecostal worship is triumphalism. Often they use the expression 'claim'. They claim the victory in Jesus. They literally command the enemies to stop their activities and leave.

Another striking contrast lies in observing the roles of the religious specialists. In the native Kankana-ey religion, the authority and role of the priest is unchallenged. His prayers are uttered with murmurs, and some suspect that he may invite wrong spirits to bring adverse effects on the family. Interpretation, prayer, prescription of ritual, and actual performance of ritual require the expertise of the priest. When people do not receive expected blessings or healing, some look to blame improprieties of the priestly service. In contrast, Pentecostals are known for their 'ministry by gifts'. In actual ministry, the difference between clergy and lay people often is indistinguishable. Anyone who stands nearby a fellow sufferer or 'who feels led by the Spirit' is free to lay on hands and pray.

The Kankana-ey Pentecostals are distinct among other Christian groups in a number of ways. Their active and sometimes proactive attitude toward evangelism and 'spiritual warfare' stands in a sharp contrast to that of more reserved, 'spiritualized' Christians. Whereas other Christian groups appear to put old things behind completely, the Kankana-ey Pentecostal Christians seem to bring in some of the old religious orientations and enhance them in the new religious setting. Their active participation in prayer for healing is one noteworthy example.

The similarity of basic religious worldviews between the native Kankana-eys and the Pentecostals may explain the active and aggressive success of the Pentecostal churches in the region. Stories of God's miracles and healings spread rapidly, and this witness attracts many who are in need.

However, these similarities pose some unique challenges along with their possibilities. As stated above, the need to replace the animistic orientation with belief in a personal God is a constant issue. In the past, there were some pastors who adopted a system of teaching which used only Christian terms, but the beliefs reflected more of the traditional animistic orientation. That may be classified as 'Folk Pentecostalism' or Pentecostal syncretism. In fact, the true success of the Pentecostal message is not due to the occurrences of supernatural phenomena alone. Fortunately, in the Kankana-ey region constant ministerial care has been present in the work of missionaries and national church leaders. As Kraft has noted, this 'power-encounter' frequently opens the heart.[28] But it should be followed by 'truth-encounter', an encounter with God who is. This often takes the form of teaching. Then, the Kankana-ey Pentecostals cans flourish in a full 'allegiance-encounter', abandoning their former allegiance to the traditional spirits and deities, but pledging their new allegiance to the new found God, the Savior.

28. C.H. Kraft, 'Allegiance, Truth and Power Encounters in Christian Witness' (unpublished manuscript, Pasadena, CA: Fuller Theological Seminary, School of World Mission, 1991), p. 7.

THE SPIRIT OF GOD UPON LEADERS OF ISRAELITE SOCIETY AND IGOROT TRIBAL CHURCHES

Wonsuk Ma

In ancient Israel, leadership possessed a charismatic[1] character. Leaders were chosen or accepted primarily because they exhibited spiritual power. This was particularly the case before the monarchy, when formalized procedures for the succession or selection of leaders had not yet been developed. During this period, leaders emerged by virtue of the sovereign election of Yahweh and his empowerment. In order for the leader to be recognized by the people, he or she needed to present evidence of God's call. One of the most common ways this 'call' was established was through a demonstration of the presence of God's spirit.[2]

Frequently, the practices and perceptions of the ancient world are not so distant from those of our modern tribal world. The charismatic nature of Israelite leadership is a case in point. The process of election, call and commissioning of Israelite leaders and their acceptance by the people show marked similarities with those of contemporary tribal Christian leaders. The Igorot mountain tribes in the northern Philippines offer an excellent example of this phenomenon. Among the Igorots, a church leader is usually recognized as a community leader. It is also commonly observed that when the presence of the Holy Spirit is known to be upon the leader, the process of acceptance is significantly enhanced.

In the following study, I shall investigate the role of the spirit of God among the ancient Israelite leaders and that of the Holy Spirit among

---

1. M. Weber, *Ancient Judaism* (trans. and ed. H.H. Gerth and D. Hartindale; New York: Free Press, 1952), p. 465, uses this expression for the first time to denote a leader who is believed to possess almost magical superhuman ability, and his or her leadership is based on this common belief.

2. In the Old Testament, the Hebrew word רוח was not yet understood in the Trinitarian context. Hence, even though it is 'of God/Yahweh', its English rendering will be 'spirit' instead of 'Spirit'.

contemporary tribal Christian leaders. The former will be assessed through an examination of relevant Old Testament texts; the latter will be examined in the context of prevailing tribal leadership patterns. Then, these two will be compared to see if the spirit's role in ancient Israel has any correspondence with the role of the Holy Spirit in a contemporary tribal setting.

It will be important to note that in this study I shall compare *political* leaders, rather than *religious* leaders (e.g. prophets) of ancient Israel with modern tribal Christian leaders. Certainly, the early political leaders of Israel performed religious duties as well. Before the monarchy, this is a common feature of leadership, as well attested with Eli (1 Sam. 4.19) and Samuel (1 Sam. 7.15). A dichotomy between the secular and religious represents a later development in Israelite religion.

1. *The Spirit of God and Charismatic Leaders in Ancient Israel*

In this study of charismatic leaders, I shall include the judges and the first two kings of the united monarchy, Saul and David. Thus I will examine four charismatic groups or individuals: Samson, the judges, Saul and David. Most of the passages investigated are found in the Deuteronomic History. Although it is uncertain when the historical books received their final form, the antiquity of this material is evident, and most apparent in the books of Judges and Samuel.

1.1 *Samson (Judges 13–16)*
Samson, of all the judges, is the least idealized. He never leads an army to deliver Israel,[3] and the material pertaining to him is less developed theologically.[4] The near mockery of the tribe of Judah in 15.9-17 constitutes a striking contrast to the careful consideration given to the tribe through the inclusion of the Othniel story. The unvarnished nature of the narrative reflects a period of early theological reflection.

Chapter 13 begins the Samson cycle with the miraculous birth of the judge. The spirit of Yahweh is described as stirring Samson (v. 25). However, the narrative is silent of its immediate effect.

3. 'He judged for twenty years' (15.20) instead of the stereotyped 'forty years' (e.g. 3.11; 5.31).
4. There are several 'theological passages' which transform folkloric episodes into theological narratives, e.g. 14.4. See J.C. Exum, 'The Theological Dimension of the Samson Saga', *VT* 33 (1983), pp. 30-45; J.A. Wharton, 'The Secret of Yahweh: Story and Affirmation in Judges 13–16', *Int* 27 (1973), p. 142.

Once the story moves to ch. 14, however, the result of the spirit's inspiration is clearly recorded. As Samson goes down to Timnah, a lion confronts him. 'Then the spirit of Yahweh came mightily upon him and he tore the lion in pieces as one tears a kid, with his bare hand' (v. 6). When Samson encounters personal danger, the spirit rushes upon him. Empowering through the inspiration of (or even seizure by) the spirit is clearly implied here. The verb (צלח) employed here indicates what kind of action will follow. The extraordinary physical strength caused by the 'rushing' of the spirit of Yahweh does not have any political or social function. It is purely for personal exploits.

Verses 10-18 also picture Samson in imminent need. His enemies have answered his riddle and he is obliged to give them their reward. This story implies that Samson is in physical danger. Then 'the spirit of Yahweh rushed upon him' (v. 19). The sudden empowerment of the spirit enables him to kill 30 of 'their men' and secure the necessary payment.

In ch. 15 Samson again is in danger. He is tied and handed over by the men of Judah to the Philistines. At the appearance of the Philistines, 'the spirit of Yahweh rushed upon him, and the ropes which bound his arms became weak as though they were burnt flax; and his bonds melted from his arms' (v. 14). When the spirit of Yahweh 'rushes upon him (ותצלח עליו)',[5] he demonstrates extraordinary physical power by breaking the rope binding him.

In short, the spirit repeatedly empowers Samson as he faces personal danger, thereby saving his neck.

1.2 *Judges*

There are only three major judges, apart from Samson, who are said to receive the spirit of Yahweh. The first is Othniel (3.7-11). In this first and shortest account of the judges, the 'younger brother of Caleb' is called a 'deliverer'. The spirit of Yahweh was upon him, and he judged Israel. The 'judging' is more closely related to military activities than 'ruling' the nation.[6] As a result, he was successful in military matters. The identity of the foe is not certain because of its textual problem. Nor is the military success described in detail. Even the coming of the spirit

---

5. The identical words for the spirit upon Samson, except 13.25.

6. J.A. Soggin, *Judges: A Commentary* (trans. J. Bowden; OTL; London: SCM Press, 2nd edn, 1987), p. 1, contends that the 'judging' is mustering or organizing for war.

(ותהי עליו) does not indicate any mode of action. There is no suddenness or violence.[7] However, the military role of the spirit of Yahweh is firmly established. Here, undoubtedly, the presence of the spirit is an accepted sign of God's favor and choice, marking the 'person of the hour'.

The second judge associated with the spirit of God is Gideon (6.33-35). The expression of the spirit's coming is unusual. This is commonly rendered: 'The spirit of Yahweh clothed (itself) with Gideon.' Although the exact meaning is not certain, the overwhelming effect is evident. The expression seems to imply that the spirit of Yahweh executes the military activities, and Gideon becomes the spirit's human tool. In Gideon, the coming of the spirit signals God's commission, after the conclusion of negotiations between God and Gideon. The military action follows immediately. The long list of clans and tribes mustered by Gideon implies a strong emphasis on the mobilization process. The successful summoning of a tribal army with an enthusiastic and voluntary response is a 'sign of the acknowledgment of God's call upon the judge'.[8]

The third judge is Jephthah (11.29-33). Along with some unusual features in his story, the coming of the spirit is described in a casual and static notion (היה על).[9] This form is identical with that used in 3.10 for Othniel. The verb does not indicate exactly in which way, or with what demonstrable manifestation, the coming of the spirit is recognized.[10] Also lacking is any reference to the summoning of the tribal army.[11] Probably an army has already been summoned by the elders before Jephthah is elected to lead the people to war.

Here, the spirit has little to do with the ratification of Jephthah's judgeship. He was previously accepted as a judge (v. 11). So, Jephthah is

7. G.F. Moore, *A Critical and Exegetical Commentary on Judges* (ICC; Edinburgh: T. & T. Clark, 1976), p. 87, does not substantiate his reading of the 'sudden and violent seizure'.

8. R.G. Boling, *Judges* (AB, 6A; Garden City, NY: Doubleday, 1975), p. 83. R. Albertz, *A History of Israelite Religion in the Old Testament Period.* I. *From the Beginnings to the End of the Monarchy* (trans. J. Bowden; OTL; Louisville, KY: Westminster/John Knox, 1994), p. 80, argues that this is due to the lack of any 'institutional possibility of a central mobilization'.

9. Boling calls it a 'sober declarative statement' (*Judges*, p. 207).

10. Soggin, *Judges*, p. 219, fails to recognize the silence in other passages.

11. J.E. Hamlin, *At Risk in the Promised Land: A Commentary on the Book of Judges* (International Theological Commentary; Grand Rapids: Eerdmans, 1990), p. 117, is not clear if this refers to Yahweh's first direct intervention by causing his spirit to come upon a military leader.

a civil leader who later assumes a military role. The spirit of Yahweh comes upon him immediately before the military confrontation. Consequently, the spirit is closely linked to the subsequent military activities. It is the spirit which prompts him to launch the military campaign. Yet no heroic act of Jephthah is recorded. The victory is ascribed to God: 'Yahweh gave them into his (Jephthah's) hand' (v. 32). Yahweh's saving act on behalf of his people is the focus here. Boling rightly identifies the movement of the spirit with 'Yahweh's gracious ratification of the proceeding that had, in effect, been taking Yahweh for granted'.[12] God affirms the human selection.

1.3. *Saul*

Chapters 8–12 of 1 Samuel introduce Saul and the new institution. The coming of the spirit follows his anointing: 'And the spirit of Yahweh will rush upon you and you will prophesy with them, and you will turn into another man. And this came to pass' (10.9-10). The anointing in a private setting symbolizes God's consecration for specific tasks. As Saul is anointed, three signs are given to affirm the act of God's election (10.5-7), and the third is the only sign with a detailed account. It is the 'recapitulation of Saul's journey to Samuel' which culminates in his 'becoming another man'.[13] As Samuel promised, this is achieved by the coming of the spirit of Yahweh. The spirit 'comes mightily' upon (על) Saul. The verb (צלח) in this literary context denotes forcefulness and suddenness.[14] It is a powerful invasion evidenced by Saul's prophetic experience. In this case, the imagery is undoubtedly that of a rushing powerful wind. The foremost function of the spirit's presence is to serve as a 'sign'. The incident affirms the miraculous selection of a leader (נגיד),[15]

---

12. Boling, *Judges*, p. 207.

13. L. Eslinger, *Kingship of God in Crisis: A Close Reading of 1 Samuel 1–12* (Bible and Literature Series, 10; Sheffield: Almond Press, 1985), p. 322.

14. BDB, p. 857.

15. S.B. Parker, 'Possession Trance and Prophecy in Pre-Exilic Israel', *VT* 28 (1978), p. 275. However, it is not precise enough to view the rushing of the spirit as a 'legitimating element', C.E. Hauer, Jr, 'Does 1 Sam. 9.1–11.15 Reflect the Extension of Saul's Dominions?', *JBL* 86 (1967), p. 308; H.W. Hertzberg, *I & II Samuel: A Commentary* (trans. J. Bowden; OTL; London: SCM Press; Philadelphia: Westminster Press, 1964), p. 87. The narrator's intention is clear in this passage: his kingship or נגיד-ship has not been revealed yet. It is, so to speak, for private consumption only.

the creation of a 'new position within the theocratic regime'.[16] The
second role of the spirit's coming is rather implicit: the equipping of Saul.

What then are the consequences of the spirit's inspiration? There seem
to be three effects, and the most obvious one is the prophetic manifestation. From its outset, the passage makes it clear that the prophetic
experience is not intended to make Saul a prophet. Gunn states that he
is 'momentarily given the status of prophet, making him out as
Yahweh's servant'.[17] One should be reminded that this possession is
given as a sign: to affirm God's choice made through the prophet.
Therefore, this prophetic experience is temporary in nature: 'When he
finished prophesying, he went home' (10.13). A remarkably similar use
of the prophetic phenomenon as a means to demonstrate Yahweh's
approval is found in Numbers 11.

The second incident is recorded in 1 Sam. 11.5-11. Upon hearing the
brutal demand of the Ammonites (11.1-4),[18] 'the spirit of God rushed
upon Saul' and 'he became exceedingly furious' (v. 6). In this passage
Saul acts as a judge-deliverer. He is equipped through the spirit of God
for victory. Unlike the private and secretive nature of the first account
of Saul's election, this passage indicates that people are involved. This
also follows the established pattern of judgeship.[19] Halpern argues for a
three-part pattern of designation, battle and confirmation; while Knierim,
following von Rad,[20] argues for a pattern of anointing and military
'proof'.[21] Either way, spirit-inspiration is an element of the testing

16. Eslinger, *Kingship*, p. 322.

17. D.M. Gunn, *The Fate of King Saul: An Interpretation of a Biblical Story*
(JSOTSup, 14; Sheffield: JSOT Press, 1980), p. 61. Also R.R. Wilson, 'Prophecy
and Ecstasy: A Reexamination', *JBL* 98 (1979), p. 333. Contrary to this,
V. Eppstein, 'Was Saul Also among the Prophets?', *ZAW* 81 (1969), p. 289; and
also J. Mauchline, *1 and 2 Samuel* (NCB; London: Marshall, Morgan & Scott,
1971), p. 99, God 'not only gives him the gift of prophecy but the manifold gifts of
the spirit which a national leader requires'.

18. A.J. Soggin, 'Charisma und Institution im Königtum Sauls', *ZAW* 75
(1963), p. 63, contends that kingship especially in its formative stage is practically
identical with the charismatic office of the judges.

19. B. Halpern, *The Constitution of the Monarchy in Israel* (HSM, 25; Chico,
CA: Scholars Press, 1981), pp. 51-148; D.V. Edelman, 'Saul's Rescue of Jabesh-
Gilead (I Sam 11.1-11): Sorting Story from History', *ZAW* 96 (1984), p. 198.

20. G. von Rad, *Old Testament Theology* (2 vols.; trans. M.G. Stalker; New
York: Harper & Row, 1962), I, p. 329.

21. R.P. Knierim, 'The Messianic Concept in the First Book of Samuel', in
F.T. Trotter (ed.), *Jesus and the Historian: Written in Honor of Ernest Cadman*

process. The true proof of God's election and favor is obtained through God's favor in military expedition.

Therefore, the spirit of God plays a dual role: symbolic and functional. First, it is symbolic as the presence of the spirit affirms God's choice. Halpern contends that in the testing stage, regalia and weapons are bestowed as an act of investment and this can be 'associated with the bestowal of holiness and perhaps the spirit'.[22] Second, it is functional in the sense that all that follows, including the military success, is attributed to the spirit of God. The verb used here is a familiar one (צלח), whose literal meaning is 'to leap' or 'to rush'. Here the inspiration of the spirit, as in ch. 10, is temporary in nature.[23]

The third appearance of the spirit occurs in 1 Sam. 16.13–23. As David was anointed, 'the spirit of God came upon him' (v. 13), and 'the spirit of Yahweh departed from Saul and an evil spirit from Yahweh afflicted him' (v. 14). Verses 13 and 14 mark a dividing line between two eras. Many 'comings' and 'goings' characterize the passage. For Samuel, v. 13 marks the end of his involvement in the kingdom as the state prophet.[24] Also the spirit rushes on David, while the spirit departs from Saul (v. 14). And an evil spirit falls upon Saul. Thus, the status of Saul changes drastically. Even though he remains king hereafter, he has lost divine endorsement and favor.[25]

As the spirit of Yahweh comes upon David, the spirit 'departs' from Saul (v. 14). One does not need to ask if they are the same spirit, since this is 'the' spirit of Yahweh. Because the spirit has been the 'sign' of God's election and even God's 'obligation to him',[26] Saul rules the

---

Colwell (Philadelphia: Westminster Press, 1968), p. 26.

22. Halpern, *Constitution*, pp. 132, 137-38. Similarly Edelman, 'Saul's Rescue', p. 198. For Hertzberg, it is the 'description of the Lord's nomination' (*I & II Samuel*, p. 93).

23. On the contrary Edelman, 'Saul's Rescue', p. 207 views the spirit-possession in ch. 10 as temporary in nature, while in Gilgal, it is a 'permanent gift' at his coronation in 11.14-15. Apparently there is no reference to the spirit in these verses, and the endowment in v. 6 should be regarded as temporary due to the specificity of the task. Her argument appears to betray the text.

24. His subsequent appearances (e.g. 1 Sam. 19.20; 28.15) are not directly related to the affairs of the kingdom.

25. Edelman's dichotomy between an era under Yahweh's good spirit and under his evil spirit appears too simplistic, *King Saul in the Historiography of Judah* (JSOTSup, 121; Sheffield: JSOT Press, 1991), p. 33.

26. R.W. Klein, *1 Samuel* (WBC, 10; Waco, TX: Word Books, 1983), p. 162.

nation without this divine favor for many years. However, it is doubtful if the legitimation is also withdrawn.[27] The anointing is the act of election or 'king-making', while the endowment of the spirit serves as an affirming sign with an equipping role. This is how David understands Saul (24.6; 26.9). In 18.12 Saul considers it as the departure of Yahweh from him.

Then 'an evil spirit from Yahweh' (רוח רעה מאת יהוה) falls upon Saul. The grammatical construction does not contain any quality for the definite article. This expression resembles the 'lying spirit' from the divine council in 1 Kgs 22.22-23. This evil spirit severely 'torments' Saul, so that only the skillful playing of the lyre by David is able to soothe him. This is more than mental disturbance; it comes from an 'active, external power'.[28] In fact, the subsequent downfall of Saul is attributed to the evil spirit. Howard counts eight occurrences of רוח רעה or its variant, emanating from or belonging to Yahweh: once from Abimelech (Judg. 9.23) and the rest from Saul. In all these cases, the evil spirit is sent to counter sin;[29] that is, to effect evil to the subject.

The last appearance of the spirit of God is found in 1 Sam. 19.18-24. Not only Saul's messengers, but also Saul himself, experience the spirit of God, and they prophesy (v. 23). He even 'tore his garment and fell naked all that day and all that night' (v. 24). This prompts a reaction from the people: 'Is Saul also among the prophets?' (v. 24). Here, Wilson concludes that it is the evil spirit which drives him mad (18.10-11).[30] However, it is difficult to assume that the messengers are also under the working of the evil spirit, since the evil spirit has only fallen upon Saul. Rather, it is natural to assume that Saul is under the influence of the same spirit (i.e. the spirit of God) which animates the band of prophets. Nowhere does the text imply that the prophets have an 'evil spirit'. This experience is not a 'bout of his maniacal, homicidal frenzy', but rather an experience of Yahweh's presence and power.[31] There is no reason to question the genuineness of the experience.[32] However, the real purpose

27. Hertzberg believes that Saul is no longer a legitimate king (*I & II Samuel*, p. 140).

28. D.M. Howard, Jr, 'The Transfer of Power from Saul to David in 1 Sam 16.13–14', *JETS* 32 (1989), p. 482.

29. Howard, 'Transfer', p. 482.

30. Wilson, 'Prophecy and Ecstasy', pp. 334-35.

31. Mauchline, *1 and 2 Samuel*, p. 144.

32. In contrast, Edelman, *King Saul*, p. 152: Saul's nakedness implies the loss of royal dignity and power; or P.D. Miscall, *1 Samuel: A Literary Reading*

of the spirit's presence is to provide for David a way of escape from danger.[33] The spirit does not work on the recipient's behalf, but to achieve the will of Yahweh. After all, it is his spirit.

1.4 *David*

David's case can be examined by way of comparison with Saul's experience. David's secret anointing (1 Sam. 16.13) is often contrasted with that of Saul (1 Sam. 10.1), in spite of many similarities. Saul's anointing results in the immediate receiving of a new heart[34] and only later in the granting of the spirit of God, while David receives the spirit immediately. Also the effect of the spirit displays further differences.

First, the spirit comes mightily to David 'from that day forward'; that is, continually. Although 16.14 states that the spirit of Yahweh departed from Saul, this does not presume that the spirit has been constantly with him in the past. The two separate occasions of spirit-inspiration confirm their temporary nature. On the contrary, nowhere is it recorded that David received the spirit of God a second time; rather, the more permanent spirit of Yahweh replaces the charismatic spirit.

Secondly, in David, there is no reference to any demonstrable proof of the spirit's inspiration. This stands in sharp contrast to Saul's prophetic expression (ch. 10) and the charismatic manifestation (ch. 11) of the spirit's presence. Even though the designation-testing pattern is still part of the emergence of leadership, the heroic defeat of Goliath (1 Sam. 17) is never attributed to the equipment of the spirit of Yahweh.[35] Assuming

(Bloomington: Indiana University Press, 1986), p. 62, 'this prophesying can be a sign that Saul has lost his kingly status, that he is no longer another man with another heart'. Both readings seem to be arbitrary. First, the nakedness, especially in the cultic setting, is viewed not necessarily in a completely negative way. See David's case in 2 Sam. 6.16-20. For the same reason, the loss of the 'another heart' is not substantiated from the text.

33. Or to create a kind of 'force field' in Edelman, *King Saul*, p. 152.

34. It is when one does not follow Hertzberg's emendation.

35. The prophetic claim in 2 Sam. 23.2 is a later theologization of royal ideology. For the late incorporation of prophetic, royal and wisdom elements, G.T. Sheppard, *Wisdom as a Hermeneutical Construct* (BZAW, 151; Berlin: de Gruyter, 1980), pp. 151-52. For an early dating of the poem, but not necessarily for the introductory portion (v. 2), F.M. Cross, Jr, 'The Ideologies of Kingship in the Era of the Empire: Conditional Covenant and Eternal Decree', in *idem* (ed.), *Canaanite Myth and Hebrew Epic: Essays in the History of the Religion of Israel* (Cambridge, MA: Harvard University Press, 1973), p. 234.

that both serve as signs of legitimation, this may imply that the need for
any demonstrable sign no longer exists at this time. This could mean that
the new institution has attained its stability, the 'routinization of charisma' in Malamat's words.[36]

Thirdly, there is the lack of a charismatic element in David's experience. For both Saul (10.6, 10) and David, the same familiar verb (צלח) is
used with the only difference being in the prepositions that follow:
'upon' (על) for Saul and 'to' (אל) for David. It is not clear if this signals
different behavior.[37] The verb implies forcefulness but not necessarily
the subsequent activities of the recipient or their nature. The absence of
charismatic phenomena is clearly related to the close of the era of the
judges, which Samuel's disappearance may have signaled. Thus, from
this perspective, Saul belongs more to the period of the judges than that
of the monarchy. With the opening of the new era, spirit-endowment
loses its functional role and remains purely symbolic of divine election.

2. The Spirit's Role in Relation to Israel's Leaders

Of various spirit traditions, the above discussed passages deal with the
spirit of God in relation to the leaders of Israel. It is true that Saul
received the prophetic spirit of God. However, this did not make Saul a
prophet. Rather, the prophetic experience, as in numerous other texts,
signified the presence of God's spirit. Both here and in Numbers 11, the
emphasis is not on the prophetic message, but on the character's behavior and appearance. Based on the preceding discussion, we can identify
two major roles that the spirit of God played in the election of the
leaders.

2.1 Authentication
First, the spirit's inspiration affirmed God's election and commissioning
as a leader. This affirmation was primarily directed to the society or the
entire nation who were to be under the rule of the new leader. This was
true in the case of all of the major judges. Their recognition as divinely

---

36. A. Malamat, 'Charismatic Leadership in the Book of Judges', in F.M. Cross,
W. Lemke and P. Miller (eds.), *Magnalia Dei: The Mighty Acts of God: Essays on
the Bible and Archaeology in Memory of G. Ernest Wright* (Garden City, NY:
Doubleday, 1976), p. 164.

37. For instance, in 18.10, the same verb with אל is used, but there it produces
violent behavior.

appointed leaders was reflected in the successful and voluntary mustering of tribal armies. In this light, the presence of the prophetic spirit was not intended to raise a prophet, but to convince the people around the new leader of God's choice through a well received cultural phenomenon—prophetic, and probably ecstatic, experience. Conversely, one may conclude that the prophetic phenomenon was perceived in ancient Israel as the most common display of the presence of God's spirit.

Sometimes, God affirmed the prior human election of a leader. This was the experience of the seventy elders, Saul and David. However, in each of these stories, the initial election came from God. Yahweh secretly elected Saul and David in private settings before they were publicly elected by the people. However, God also validated the human selection process by giving his spirit to the newly elected leaders (1 Sam. 11.6 for Saul, and Num. 11.25 for the seventy elders). Charismatic leaders were ultimately elected by God himself. Thus his sovereign election was authenticated by the presence of his spirit.

This authentication was also intended for the leader himself. It was particularly evident at Samuel's anointing of Saul as the first king over Israel (1 Sam. 10.1). However, to this young lad who understandably doubted the truthfulness and implication of God's election, Samuel promised three signs (1 Sam. 10.2-27). The coming of God's spirit was the climax of the three signs. In view of the fact that neither Saul nor Samuel could publicize the election of a king, the signs were given for the sake of Saul, and so also was the presence of God's spirit.

2.2 *Empowerment*

The most explicit relationship between the divine spirit and stories of human empowerment are found in the book of Judges. Among them, the Samson cycle exhibits the most vivid description. As the spirit of God came upon Samson, he gained superhuman strength, and at times wisdom, to destroy his enemies. In these early stories, the spirit did not carry any moral implications. Samson did not muster a tribal army. The empowerment centered around physical strength in time of personal need.

However, when we move to the major judges, the spirit's coming had a direct bearing on the judges' deliverance of the nation from the foreign yoke. The empowerment appeared often in the form of military activities. The connection between the spirit and successful military activities is often explicit. Thus, among the major judges, the presence of the spirit affected a tribe or tribes. Also, the main manifestation was no longer physical might, but military strength and wisdom. However, the demonstration of power took place within a specific context. Ultimately the empowerment comes to meet an immediate need of the nation (or a person in the case of Samson). In a sense, a hero was born in time of need. When the people were convinced that their acute and immediate 'felt needs' were solved through divine empowerment, the human vehicle was accepted as a divinely appointed leader.

The two elements listed above are not mutually exclusive. In fact, the extraordinary solution of an immediate problem is a critical part of the authentication process. King Saul, for instance, became king only after he 'proves' his divine appointment by demonstrating Yahweh's supernatural empowerment with prophetic speech. The demonstration of the spirit's empowerment is an essential element in the emergence of a charismatic leader.

If this is the case, why is the empowering element missing in the story of David? It is possible to argue that the subsequent achievements of David were implicitly attributed to the spirit of God which was upon him 'from that day and onward' (16.13). Neve argues that from David on, in Judah, charismatic appointment was replaced by dynastic succession.[38] This is an adequate explanation as to why Solomon and the succeeding kings are not known to have God's spirit. A lengthy and complex process bringing David to the throne may put him outside the 'charismatic' category. David probably marks a significant transition in Israelite history, the movement from charismatic leadership to dynastic succession.

3. *Igorot Christian Leaders and the Holy Spirit*

The mountainous region of the northern Philippines is called the Cordillera. Its inhabitants are generally called *Igorot*s and they consist of eight major subtribal groups according to linguistic and cultural traits.[39] The Igorots successfully resisted four centuries of Spanish attempts to conquer and influence the mountain people religiously, politically and

38. L. Neve, *The Spirit of God in the Old Testament* (Tokyo: Seibunsha, 1972), pp. 26-27.
39. A.J. and A.M. de los Reyes (eds.), *Igorot: A People Who Daily Touch the Earth and the Sky*. I. *Ethnographies of Major Tribes* (Baguio: Cordillera Schools Group, 1987), Introduction, p. xi.

culturally. Hence, they retain their culture almost intact. It was only in the beginning of this century under the American colonial rule that the Igorots began to be exposed to the outside world. It was just in the first half of this century that their notorious headhunting practice gradually disappeared. However, the lack of social services, including educational opportunities and medical services, as well as poor infrastructure (e.g. inadequate road systems, communication facilities and power plants) hinder the improvement of their lives. Yet, communities which have been reached with the gospel show signs of change.

I shall begin my examination of Igorot leadership patterns by discussing the traditional role and qualifications of Igorot leaders. This will place the role of the Christian leaders and their work into a proper perspective.

3.1 *Emergence of the Igorot Leader*

As in many other tribal systems, an Igorot leader is not elected, but emerges. The influence of this kind of traditional leadership is immeasurable. It is the only leadership existent in a tiny community, generally called a *sitio*, where there is no administrative structure. Even in bigger communities where elected government officials exist, the influence of unofficial leaders, whose power stems solely from their place in society as defined by ancient traditions, is enormous. In fact, the authority of these unofficial leaders often surpasses that of the elected officials. The elected officials know that the traditional leaders are 'the most important and most influential people' in the community.[40] In small communities, the traditional leaders settle disputes, judge cases, determine punishment and compensation, officiate marriages, handle divorces, and bury the dead. They have the final authority in matters which affect the entire community. Their role is not limited to social matters; they also perform religious functions.[41] They preside over various religious rites and rituals, interpret dreams, diagnose sicknesses and determine the cause of misfortune through divination, and prescribe appropriate rituals to correct the situation. This traditional tribal leadership requires several common qualifications.

40. V. Encarnacion, 'Leadership in a Benguet Village', *Philippine Studies* 9 (1961), p. 571.

41. The elite members of a community are often children or relatives of a pagan priest. Of five traditional leaders whom Encarnacion studies, four are priests ('Leadership', p. 574).

3.1.1 *Old age*. Tribal leadership titles in various dialects are commonly translated as 'elder' in English. This literally means that they are aged people.[42] Even though descendants of past leaders are viewed as potential leaders, they must wait until they reach an appropriate age to receive serious consideration. This is true even if one has already acquired all of the other necessary qualifications for leadership.

Among the Bontoc Igorot, three or four male elders form an elder's council, called *intugtukon*. In this council, the elders decide social and religious community affairs and may, on behalf of the community, enter into a peace pact with a neighboring community.[43] As a typical tribal society, decisions made in the *ato*[44] impact everything from the planting of rice to the performance of rituals pertaining to marriage or the latest headhunting expedition. The council decides almost everything. Therefore, the council of elders is rightly called the supreme governing body, making rules and executing them. The members are considered wise and experienced elders. In a dispute with a neighboring village, each council of elders independently makes decisions, and there is no superior body to whom they must report. However, in some exceptional cases an individual performs a rite on behalf of the community. Normally the eldest member of the council offers a prayer to their god, *Lumawig*. Therefore, it is not uncommon for a priest (*manbunong*) to be included in the council. A respectably mature age is an essential qualification for an Igorot leader.

3.1.2 *'Rich men'*. For the Igorots, the term 'rich' does not refer principally to the accumulation of possessions, but rather to an elite social

42. Encarnacion, 'Leadership', p. 573, discovered that the average age of seven elected government officials was forty-one, while that of five traditional leaders was seventy-five.

43. Called *budong* by the Kalinga tribe: to ensure the safety and security of a community, villages enter into a bilateral covenant not to harm any member of the covenanted community. This practice is particularly common among headhunting tribes such as the Bontoc. See C. Cawed, *The Culture of the Bontoc Igorot* (Manila, Philippines: MCS Enterprises, 1972), pp. 23-28. The Bontocs call it *pechen*. See N. Anima, *And Now Comes* [*sic*] *the Mountain Province Tribes* (Quezon City, Philippines: OMAR Publications, 1977), pp. 37-38, for Bontoc *pechen*, and pp. 76-79 for Kalinga *budong*.

44. A male club house where unmarried male members sleep. It is also here that the council meets to discuss various issues. At the entrance of the *ato*, the jaw bones of headhunting victims are proudly displayed, Cawed, *Bontoc*, pp. 30-31.

class. The Ibaloi tribe has three classes: rich, average and poor. The leader called *bakang* comes from the 'rich' class. The Kankanaey tribe also uses the same term. A *bakang* is a 'rich man with power'. He has the most number of families under him—either through blood relations (consanguinal), by marriage (affinal), or by arrangement (fictive), such as servants.[45] Naturally the *bakang* has a responsibility to look after the families under him, including his servants' families. Most members are treated as if they are the *bakang*'s children. The servants call him father (*ama*).[46] Among the Ibalois, the *bakang* system is hereditary.

The Ifugaos dwell in the eastern mountain ranges of the Cordillera. The region is well known for its ingenious rice terraces. There are only two classes in Ifugao society: poor (*nawotwot*) and rich (*kadangyan*).[47] The rich are further divided into three categories according to their possessions, and leaders naturally come from the richest group (*himmagabi*). Their richness is judged by the number of rice paddies they possess. Among the Ifugaos, one can belong to the poor group even if his or her ancestors were once rich. Theoretically, the term 'rich' signifies not that one has accumulated many possessions, but rather that one's social status is high. The highest leader in an Ifugao village may not be the richest man in the community. However, in practice, families in the 'rich' class are generally materially rich.

The Igorots believe that classes and order in society are a reflection of the order in the spiritual world. *Anitos*, malevolent ancestral spirits, are under benevolent ancestral spirits often called *ap-apo*, which are in turn under superior deities called *Kabunyan*, *Wigan* or *Lumawig*. In a similar way, social hierarchy or status is believed to be an unbreakable order predestined in the spiritual world.

3.1.3 *Ritual requirements*. Among the Igorot tribes, the *cañao* is the highlight of their religious celebrations. It is offered for various purposes: to celebrate as a religious sacrifice, as part of a funeral rite, and to secure healing.[48] The *bakang* of the Ibaloi tribe, for example, regularly offer sacrifices to deal with various misfortunes or simply to celebrate. This

45. E.L. Pungayan, 'Kinship Structure among Benguet Ibalois', *Saint Louis University Research Journal* 11 (1980), pp. 1-54 (7).

46. Pungayan, 'Kinship', p. 14.

47. M.A. Dumia, *The Ifugao World* (Manila, Philippines: New Day, 1979), p. 10.

48. Pungayan, 'Kinship', p. 14.

gives him an opportunity to demonstrate his wealth and his care for the community members. The scale of the sacrifice commonly reflects one's wealth. There are numerous steps one must take before offering the *pedit*, the highest form of the *cañao*. This grants him the status of *bakang*. The *cañao* is offered either to *Kabunyan*, the supreme deity,[49] or to his ancestral spirits.[50]

In Ifugao, a *kadangyan* (a man of the rich class) attains the status of *himmagabi* by fulfilling prescribed ritual requirements. For a married *kadangyan*, an *uya-ry* (or *uya-oy)* sacrifice is required. This extravagant sacrifice normally lasts between a week and a month and is thought to bring honor and pride.[51] The *uy-uy* involves the butchering of many and various animals, preparing the traditional wine made of red rice, and the priestly prayer. This ritual is the final passage before a man and his wife obtain the highest status and respect. A *hagabi* sacrifice is offered with very rigid ritual specifications. During this period, a rich man's bed is made out of a tree, and this is called *hagabi*.[52]

According to Encarnacion, the *cañao* fulfills two social functions. It brings prestige to the family. It also affirms and strengthens the existing social structure and the (extended) family ties. The *cañao* plays a critical role in maintaining the existing social order.[53] In his survey, all five traditional leaders fulfilled the ritual requirements by offering thirteen native pigs. This prestige celebration begins with three pigs. Then the second ritual requires five, then seven and so on. In other words, the leader has performed at least seven *cañao*s before he offers the final one with thirteen pigs. He also butchers a Carabao, a Philippine water buffalo. The *cañao* involving thirteen pigs, therefore, is a sign of his wealth and prestige.[54]

49. Some argue that *Adika-ila* is the supreme Igorot deity above *Kabunyan*, for example, W.D. Sacla, *Treasury of Beliefs and Home Rituals of Benguet* (La Trinidad: Province of Benguet, 1987), p. 4. Even though *Adika-ila*'s existence is substantiated, presently *Kabunyan* is understood by the Igorots as the most powerful deity. If *Adika-ila* is, as Sacla argues, the creator, he is considered semi-retired. The rise and fall of a deity is commonly known in ancient religions. For example, in the Ugaritic world view, El, presently retired, is the Ugaritic creation god and 'the father of the gods'. Later, however, Baal is viewed as the most powerful god.

50. Especially *ap-apo*s, the spirits of recently deceased ancestors.

51. Anima, *And Now Comes*, pp. 5-6.

52. Dumia, *Ifugao*, p. 11.

53. Encarnacion, 'Leadership', p. 575.

54. Encarnacion, 'Leadership', p. 575, reports a similar case in the *pumapatay*, a

Wiber studied the Ibaloi economy in the second half of the sixteenth century. According to her research, the Ibalois engaged in extensive trade with the lowlanders. They traded their gold for cattle and other supplies. The cattle were not for breeding or growing, but for immediate consumption. Normally they killed the animals to offer them to the spirits, and later the meat was distributed to the entire community. This 'economic distribution' brought prestige and political power to a small number of families.[55] The *kadangyan* (rich) class not only enjoyed status, wealth and prestige, but also effectively prohibited other families from joining them. One method of achieving this was marriage within the class.[56] Any family which showed potential for upward mobility by the accumulation of possessions would be pressured into offering an expensive *cañao* by the *kadangyan* families.[57] By forcing the family to exhaust its possessions, the exclusiveness of the rich class was maintained.

This social system continues to function today much as it did three hundred years ago. The 'return of the meat' is an idiomatic expression for the pressure exerted by the rich families. The *kadangyan*s are easily noted by their share of meat in a ritual. They receive extra amounts of meat or choice portions. They also enjoy special parts of the animal, such as the liver, which are generally regarded as sacred.[58] When one loses a rice paddy, the community knows that the man who suffers such

Bontoc leader. He leads the community ritual called *tengao* and butchers the sacrificial animal. He must be an old man from the *katsangyan* (rich) class, and have offered many thanksgiving sacrifices. J.P. Romack, 'Toward a Contextualized Practice of the *Tengao* Custom of the Bontoc of Mountain Province, Philippines' (MA thesis; Pasadena, CA: Fuller Theological Seminary, 1991), p. 86.

55. M. Wiber, 'The "*Cañao* Imperative": Changes in Resource Control, Stratification and the Economy of Ritual among the Ibaloi of Northern Luzon', in S.D. Russell and C.B. Cunningham (eds.), *Changing Lives Changing Rites: Ritual and Social Dynamics in Philippines and Indonesian Uplands* (Michigan Studies of South and Southeast Asia, 1; Ann Arbor: Center for South and Southeast Asian Studies, University of Michigan, 1989), pp. 45-46.

56. Wiber, 'Imperative', p. 47.

57. Wiber, 'Imperative', p. 48, divides Ibaloi *cañao* into two categories: voluntary and involuntary. The former is offered in conjunction with marriage, harvest and income from gold mines, and the latter is occasioned by funeral, healing and 'demand from the ancestors'. This division can be applied to any Igorot subtribe. Often the voluntary ritual is offered either through a family's decision, or by the advice of village elders.

58. Sacla, *Benguet*, p. 38.

a loss must prepare a *cañao*. This ritual is not only sacred, but also expensive to the Igorots.

Hence, the *cañao* plays a vital role in reaffirming the existing order and status which has been determined in the spiritual world. It is also regarded as a means of influencing the gods and spirits to maintain the existing order.[59] In addition, the Igorots believe that fame, material blessing and good health are granted by the *Kabunyan* and the ancestral spirits. Therefore, it is natural for them to view present wealth as a reward for their religious piety expressed through many *cañao* sacrifices.[60] Today's *cañao* ensures tomorrow's blessing.

3.1.4 *Man of knowledge*. Until recently, there has been no formal education system available in many mountain communities. In such a setting, the elderly leaders, like the wise men of ancient Israel, offer advice for various matters, and make decisions for the community. Their wisdom is often demonstrated by their amazing ability to recite the names of any family's ancestors. In a community of extended families where everybody is related to the rest of the village, such knowledge has significance. The priest, who is often a leader as well, determines which spirits are to be invited to a ritual. He not only calls their names, but also describes their appearances. Considering their belief that the omission of any spirit to a ritual will result in serious retaliation from the spirit, the priest's knowledge of the gods and the spirits is crucial.

The leader's knowledge also includes extensive cataloging of various taboos, their interpretations, and preventative measures when one violates a taboo. Accurate interpretation of omens is another way to demonstrate the leader's deep knowledge. It is also thought that the accurate recital of myths can influence the spirits to act benevolently toward human beings. The leader's knowledge enables them to deal with these spiritual realities and everyday 'felt needs'.

59. T.C. Casiño, 'The Relevance of the Christian Concept of God to the Cordilleran's Search for Identity as a People' (STD thesis; Baguio, Philippines: Asia Baptist Graduate School of Theology, 1992), pp. 119-26.

60. Among the Ibalois, an irrigated rice paddy is considered the most valuable. Selling it for reasons other than offering a sacrifice to the ancestors is considered taboo. This would offend the ancestor who built the rice paddy. Also such property is to be sold only within the community. There are many cases in which the rich class takes advantage of this custom. Cf. Wiber, 'Imperative', p. 51.

3.1.5 *The leader's heritage.* Qualification for leadership is something that one can inherit from his ancestors. It includes not only possessions, but also social status. A man may inherit servants and subjects who have shown their loyalty and respect to the family. He may inherit a network of farmers who have lost their land to the family due to their debts and now work in the same land for the family. He may also inherit servants and their families. It is important for the new leader to affirm his status before the inherited extended family members and to the community by offering a *cañao*.

As the new leader has more opportunities to receive modern education, he has a greater chance to occupy elected positions. It is customary for government positions to be offered first to the traditional leaders who have great influence in the community. For this reason, it is almost impossible for members of non-rich families to move into leadership. Their only chance for 'success' is to become an elected official or professional through higher education.

3.1.6 *Leadership effectiveness.* A community normally tests a leader's ability, and the leader must 'earn the respect of the people'. In most communities, leadership is not vested in an individual, but in a group of elders, from which a chairperson often emerges. The chairperson represents the council of elders during community events. By offering a sacrificial animal in a community ritual such as *tengao* of the Bontoc tribe, the leader demonstrates control over the community. His ability is also realized by successfully summoning the community ritual. However, status does not automatically bring respect. Leadership is often examined and proved in two areas: resolving conflicts and performing rituals.

In a culture where a third party is favored in resolving conflicts, an elder is expected to play an important role in this area. However, this does not mean that he is the supreme leader. A family may choose to invite one particular elder to resolve a dispute. This involves more than negotiation skills, and the leader should also demonstrate some knowledge of the spiritual world. He becomes successful in resolving a dispute, either by offering a mutually satisfactory resolution, or by resorting to a divinatory scheme to discern who is the offender. As his reputation spreads, more people may invite this particular leader to resolve disputes.

The effectiveness of a leader is also measured by his ability to perform religious rituals. These rituals are offered for various reasons: to obtain healing, to ensure a good harvest, to guarantee a safe journey, to bless a headhunting expedition, and many others. The effectiveness of a ritual is contingent upon the labor of the leader, who must accurately and correctly interpret dreams and omens. Proper divination is often achieved by examining the internal organs of a sacrificial animal. The leader must choose the right day and time for the sacrificial ritual, with the right kind of animal. His prayer must be effective, for a family is free to invite another leader for their next ritual. If they exhaust all the leaders in the community, they 'import' a specialist from outside.[61]

The preceding discussion of six commonly observable qualifications reveals that, according to Igorot perception, leaders emerge either through the favor of spiritual beings or election by the gods. Their pious dedication to the gods and the spirits and their fearful reverence to them presupposes the belief of divine election. Wealth itself is a sign of divine favor. Their vast knowledge spans from matters of everyday life (ways of not offending the spiritual beings, including taboos) to knowledge of the deceased ancestors who are now spirits. However, the simple accumulation of cognitive information does not make one an effective leader. Nevertheless, the focus on this form of knowledge does indicate the strong religious role and root of Igorot leadership.

Of course, we have noted there are several other qualifications for Igorot leadership. Old age as a leadership requirement is a cultural norm. Wealth is also a significant requirement, but this wealth is associated with inherited social class and serves a practical purpose. Possessions alone are not definitive. In any event, experience of ritual performance, wealth of (spiritual) knowledge, and leadership effectiveness are required to ensure that a leader will have the divine equipment needed to meet the immediate 'felt needs' of the people. In the Igorot multiple leadership settings, the formal recognition of leadership status comes automatically. At stake is the perception of the leader's effectiveness, which hinges on the demonstration of spiritual empowerment. The leader's religious piety is believed to have secured the favor of the gods and spirits. The leader must know how to manipulate the gods and spirits for the benefit of human beings. One who can bring healing is most popularly recognized and accepted by the people. A leader who cannot prove his leadership effectiveness by meeting immediate needs through supernatural power will exercise limited authority. In a way, he is a leader in name only.

61. Kalango-ya priests are known for their effectiveness. When Kankana-ey or Ibaloi families cannot find effective priests among their own tribes, they normally invite a Kalango-ya priest.

3.2 *Igorot leaders and the Christian faith*

The following presentation is based on personal experiences and observations as a missionary to the Igorots. Material has been collected from over twenty Assemblies of God churches in the Kankana-ey region. In the past six years, I have been able to associate closely with many national leaders. Among them, I chose four typical church leaders who are also readily received as civic leaders in their respective communities. In terms of age, three are in their fifties and one is in his sixties. They are all male and have families. One has college-level education, another is a high school graduate, two received no education although they can read the Bible. One was a lay leader who was once elected as Barrio Captain, the highest elected official in the community. This public leadership experience complements his relatively limited (five years) ministerial experience. The other three are more typical tribal ministers, with more than twenty years of ministerial experience. Each of these three men pastor two to seven churches in different communities. Their ministry is characterized by frequent healings and the casting out of demons by the power of the Holy Spirit.[62] Their leadership is readily received not only among Christians, but also throughout their communities.

3.2.1 *Leader of a social institution.*

In a typical Igorot community, especially those in remote mountains, there is no visible social institution. The only recognizable social institution is a branch school which offers two or three year courses. However, the teachers often come from outside and most of them are young women. Being an outsider means being a foreigner to the host culture. This precludes any leadership potential. Furthermore, they receive benefits from the community through the favor of the elders. This comes in the form of food and lodging. As a beneficiary, the teacher is further removed from leadership potential.

In larger communities, there is barrio captain and councilmen. Their leadership authority as elected officials is perceived as subordinate and, therefore, relatively inferior to that of the traditional leader. The leadership of the elected officials needs to be endorsed by the traditional leaders. As seen in Encarnacion's study, most of the elected leaders are in fact related to the traditional leaders. Government posts can be regarded as an internship for true leadership in the future.

In such a setting, the church in most cases represents the only social

---

62. A good example is found in the ministry of Elva Vanderbout found in I. Sturgeon, *Give Me This Mountain* (Oakland, CA: Hunter Advertising, 1960).

institution. The pastor, by virtue of his leadership in the church, is easily recognized as a civic leader. The pastor has established his leadership among the Christians in the community and so he is viewed with respect in the community. Because of the visible nature of his ministry and the stature of the church in the community, the pastor's help is often sought out by community health workers, law enforcement agencies, and teachers. His ability to mobilize Christians is viewed as a significant part of his leadership effectiveness.

Among the *Igorot* people, visits from outsiders are very infrequent. About the only people to visit such communities are family members who have moved away. Consequently, visits from outsiders, with no familial ties to the community, are seen as very significant. In a family ritual, whether in a *cañao* or funeral, the family's prestige is drastically enhanced by the presence of outside visitors. In a small community, a visitor or group of visitors attracts the instant attention of the entire community. Thus, when the church receives visitors from the outside, whether they are from other provinces or other countries, the church receives an immediate image boost within the community. These visitors are not just seen as visitors of the church, but as visitors of the whole community.

The pastor is also viewed as someone who is not only willing but also able to assist people. Often the pastor is the only one who has some form of medicine in a remote village. The church also receives ministry teams from outside, including medical and humanitarian missions. As government assistance is inadequate, this service becomes extremely valuable, and accordingly the role of the pastor is enhanced in the community.

3.2.2 *Performer of religious rites.* Animists have high respect for religious specialists. This is due to their status as intermediaries as well as their ability to affect lives. Their special place in the community is visibly demonstrated through the officiating of, or active participation in, religious rituals. This role simply presupposes a divine call and commissioning. The role of Christian ministers corresponds to that of the native leaders as their role encompasses practically every aspect of the daily life of the Christians. That is, they not only offer and lead worship as a religious activity, but also offer counseling and help in domestic life, including marriages, funerals, birthday celebrations, and other social events.

The animistic mind would normally expect a response from the deity to whom a ritual is offered, which indicates that the supernatural realm touches everyday life. The Christian leader is viewed as having authority to bless the people. This perception involves much more than simply the ability to perform divinatory rites. There is an assumption that God has granted the ability to commune with him and his favor rest on the Christian leader. Just as native leaders affect lives by declaring the will of the gods; so also, through proclamation and prayer, does the Christian leader attain this priestly status.

3.2.3 *Man of knowledge*. As observed above, the most important knowledge a community leader can possess is that of the unseen spiritual world. Knowing the things of God and the Spirit is not something that one can learn through formal education, for they perceive that this knowledge is granted ultimately by God himself. Consequently, it is a rather rare scene in a traditional community for an elder or a minister to stand before a group of people with a big black Bible in his hand and teach the things of God. Their proclamation is not normally disputed because of their inherent authority.

The pastor's 'knowledge' is often displayed in a 'let's-talk' session among the elders of the community. Any new thoughts are tested publicly in front of the community. The pastor, often a man who grew up in the community with little education, generally displays an impressive knowledge of God. In spite of limited formal training, he has obtained considerable 'knowledge' through the 'big black book', the Bible. The Bible is a powerful symbol in a society where memorization is the only means of preserving valuable knowledge.

3.2.4. *Effectiveness in spiritual matters*. The foregoing qualifications are shared by all religious leaders, Christian and non-Christian alike. So, is every religious leader respected with due recognition of their leadership? Probably, yes. Their leadership, in religious as well as secular realms, is awarded popular recognition. At the same time, their leadership effectiveness is something that will be tested. This is where Pentecostal leaders have distinguished themselves. Through their unique manifestations of the power of the Holy Spirit, they are not only well received and respected, but even feared in a positive sense.

One may argue that other Christian leaders operate in the same spiritual realm. From the Christian viewpoint, it may be so. The Holy

Spirit is intimately involved in every facet of Christian life, from conversion to resurrection. However, from the perspective of the native animists, the presence of any divine element should be demonstrable. This religious orientation contributes to the frequent occurrences of healings and miracles. The preaching of God's miraculous power and ability to heal, therefore, is extremely relevant to them. Thus, the supernatural orientation of Pentecostal pastors facilitates the acceptance of their leadership role, even among non-Christian members of the tribal society.

The introduction of Christianity to an animistic community has an immediate spiritual effect. One does not have to believe in the idea of territorial spirits to recognize a fierce spiritual conflict. The enemy territory is invaded by the force of the light. The conflict is understood not only by the gospel preachers, but also by the tribal people. They traditionally call upon a spirit to remove the effect of another spirit. A native sacrifice is offered to a stronger and more benevolent spirit to undo the sickness which the inferior spirit has inflicted. The occurrence of a miracle, such as healing, is, therefore, viewed within this context of a spiritual conflict. The manifestation of God's power through the Holy Spirit is perceived as God's initial triumph. The Pentecostal minister is viewed as the representative of this powerful God. Miracles in turn prove the minister's call by God and his empowerment by the Holy Spirit.

On the part of tribal leaders, there is formidable resistance to or even enmity against the Christian leaders for 'despoiling' their traditional religion. It is not uncommon that they employ various measures including physical harassment to stop Christian preaching. People are extremely reluctant to abandon the old religion for fear of retaliation from the spirits they have served. At this point, Pentecostal and non-Pentecostal (Protestant as well as Roman Catholic) leaders show a marked difference. The Pentecostal preachers exhibit an added dimension when compared with other Christian leaders. They openly claim that God is able and willing to perform miracles as an expression of his power and grace. The presence and power of the Spirit is externally demonstrated by means of speaking in tongues, healing, miracles, and the casting out of demons. These manifestations of spiritual power provide tangible proof that the spirits, in their attempts to retaliate, will have no power over the God of the universe. As Charles Kraft states, the power encounter leads to an allegiance encounter.[63]

63. C.H. Kraft, 'Allegiance, Truth and Power Encounters in Christian Witness',

Through the ministry of supernatural power, the Pentecostal minister and church meet the felt needs of the people. In a community where medical service is largely non-existent, many traditional sacrifices are offered to receive healing from the spirits. This entails an enormous financial burden on the family. The Christian message and practice address these immediate and critical felt needs.

So, when ministry is accompanied by the manifestation of spiritual power, the Pentecostal Christian leaders receive instant recognition that they are called, commissioned and empowered by God. Their spiritual authority is significantly strengthened. This corresponds closely to the role of the spirit of God among the Israelite leaders. This commands spiritual fear even among non-believing community members. A typical reaction is found in a statement made by a pagan priest in Abatan. In a funeral setting, he experienced an instant healing through the prayer of a Pentecostal worker. He said, 'Be careful of the Pentecostals. God is with them.'

4. *Concluding Remarks*

The work of the Spirit in relation to the leaders in God's economy has a twofold function: authentication and empowerment. This applies to the leaders in the past as well as in the present. The empowering function is more crucial in that it strengthens the other function of authentication. This may explain why Pentecostal churches among the animistic Igorot people in the northern Philippines have experienced more success than non-Pentecostal groups. The Pentecostal church leaders are not only received as civic and community leaders, just as other Christian pastors, but are also respected as ministers who have divine appointment and favor. This is significant for the Igorots, who are 'a people who daily touch the earth and the sky'.[64]

Of course, this does not mean that every Pentecostal church is successful. Reasons for the success of a Christian ministry are rather complex. In other provinces in Cordillera, the Pentecostal churches are not as successful as in Benguet. This definitely indicates that there are important contributing factors to growth other than the manifestation of

---

in J.A.B. Jongeneel *et al.* (eds.), *Pentecost, Mission and Ecumenism: Essays on Intercultural Theology* (Studies in the Intercultural History of Christianity, 75; Frankfurt am Main: Peter Lang, 1992), pp. 215-30.

64. The subtitle of A.J. and A.M. de los Reyes (eds.), *Igorot*.

supernatural power. Having said that, it is unquestionable that the manifestation of the Spirit plays a decisive role in the success of ministry to the Igorots.

The observations chronicled above, pertaining to the pagan as well as Christian Igorots, are based on a decade of experience. Consequently, these conclusions will require further data in order to be substantiated. The comparison presented in this study should be taken as tentative. I am aware of the possibility of overgeneralization.

By offering these small insights, I wish to honor the life and ministry of William W. Menzies among the Igorot tribes. I also wish to encourage fellow Asian Pentecostals to pay close attention to the dynamic work of the Holy Spirit in often oppressive and challenging life settings.

'POWER FROM ON HIGH':
A HISTORICAL PERSPECTIVE ON THE RADICAL
STRATEGY IN MISSIONS

Gary B. McGee

During a prayer meeting at an obscure mission school in South India in the early 1860s, a young student arose and queried, 'God, by Joel, promised to pour out his Spirit in the latter days; these are the latter days. Has not the Spirit come?'[1] Regrettably, the record of the account fails to mention the missionary's answer. Today, the same question burns in the hearts of millions of Christians who long for manifestations of divine power in the life and ministry of the churches: are the 'signs and wonders' performed by Jesus and the apostles (Acts 2.22; 5.12) and promised to all (Jn 14.12) available for the life and mission of the churches?

In the last two centuries, Christianity has undergone several dramatic shifts, including the extraordinary attention currently placed on the ministry of the Holy Spirit. The nineteenth-century missions movement and the rush to evangelize the non-Christian world contributed to the development of modern Pentecostalism in its various forms. In fact, the Pentecostal movement cannot be properly understood apart from its eschatological and mission ethos. This study examines the link that Christians have made between paranormal phenomena and evangelism and missions, particularly in the last two hundred years; the emergence and significance of the 'radical strategy' in missions; and the impact of this new paradigm in shaping the Pentecostal movement, its mission enterprise, and later charismatic mission endeavors.

1. Miracles after the Apostles

Expectation of supernatural phenomena, notably miracles as well as the *charismata* (gifts of the Holy Spirit [1 Cor. 12.8-10]), continued in

1. H.E. Scudder, *Life and Letters of David Coit Scudder* (New York: Hurd & Houghton, 1864), p. 225.

sectors of Christianity long after the time of the apostles. The fourth-century 'desert father' Antony of Egypt became legendary for his orthodox (Nicene) Christology which enabled him to engage in 'spiritual warfare' with demons.[2] At about the same time, Nino, a slave girl taken captive to the Caucasus region of Georgia, prayed for the healing of a member of the royal family. The miracle then led to the conversion of the nation.[3] While much can be said for the story's reliability, later writers clouded her legacy with fantastic tales. Mediaeval accounts reflect the same problem. In Britain, the Venerable Bede recorded miracles that occurred during the evangelization of England in the sixth and seventh centuries. In one instance, a heavenly light appeared over the site where the Christian King Oswald had been martyred and buried; afterward, pilgrims visiting the shrine reported healings and exorcisms.[4] And ironically, reputed signs in the heavens and miracles inspired the first Crusaders in their quest to conquer the Holy Land and slaughter its Muslim inhabitants.[5]

With the coming of the Protestant Reformation (1500–1650), Protestant and Catholic theologians rattled their sabers over such issues as the nature of sin, justification by faith, the sacraments, and the authority of Scripture. By teaching the priesthood of all believers, Martin Luther, Huldrych Zwingli and John Calvin disavowed the Catholic doctrine of the communion of Mary and the saints, thereby dismissing the value set on the saints, holy relics, shrines, pilgrimages and the miracle stories that developed around them. Luther faced a more immediate challenge from charismatic prophets who insisted that God had given them new revelations which they viewed as superior to Scripture and contributed to social disorder.[6]

Later in the sixteenth and seventeenth centuries, Lutheran and

2. See Athanasius, *The Life of St Antony* (trans. R.T. Meyer; New York: Newman, 1978), pp. 78-79.

3. D.M. Lang (ed.), *Lives and Legends of the Georgian Saints* (Crestwood, NY: St. Vladimir's Seminary Press, 2nd edn, 1976), pp. 13-19.

4. Bede, *A History of the English Church and People* (trans. L. Sherley-Price; New York: Penguin, 1968), pp. 156-60.

5. Fulcher of Chartres, *A History of the Expedition to Jerusalem, 1095–1127* (ed. H.S. Fink; New York: W.W. Norton, 1973), pp. 76-77, 102, 219-21.

6. M. Luther, 'Against the Heavenly Prophets in the Matter of Images and Sacraments', in T.G. Tappert (ed.), *Selected Writings of Martin Luther* (Philadelphia: Fortress Press, 1967), III, pp. 157-301; also, G.H. Williams, *The Radical Reformation* (Philadelphia: Westminster Press, 1962), pp. 38-58.

Reformed theologians returned to the late mediaeval procedure of using philosophical reasoning, chiefly the form of logic cultivated by Aristotle, to assist in the building of doctrine. The fruits of their labors can be seen in conservative Protestant theology today and in large tomes of dogmatic theology whose chapters probe every conceivable crevice of doctrine. Nonetheless, the arid discussions of 'Protestant orthodoxy' took place at the very time when piety had declined in the churches.[7] Defending doctrine in part led theologians to fear that subjective religious experience would scuttle the Bible's authority; hence, they nurtured the religion of the head more than the religion of the heart.

2. *Doubts versus Heartfelt Salvation*

The great bombardment of reason against Scripture and doctrine commenced in the eighteenth century, the same period in which Evangelical awakenings flourished in Germany, England and America. The 'Enlightenment' or 'Age of Reason', aimed its fusillades of skepticism on anything considered miraculous. Humankind had only now come of age thanks to the liberation of rational thinking from superstition. Although much Enlightenment philosophy negatively impacted traditional Christian beliefs, the value set on scientific experimentation influenced the theology of evangelical revivalists: Experimentation, better described in this context as 'experience', when related to 'heartfelt' conversion brushed aside the nagging question of whether one had been predestined to salvation.[8] John and Charles Wesley in England and the later American revivalist Charles G. Finney, along with others, highlighted the personal certainty of redemption. Moreover, this provided a simple and comforting assurance of the truthfulness of Christian faith in an atmosphere of skepticism.

Experiential piety, however, unintentionally encouraged what many viewed as bizarre physical manifestations in revival services and camp meetings: believers falling down, laughing, weeping, shouting, barking and dancing. The popular piety of most American Christians included

7.   Concern over the decline of piety in the Lutheran churches in the seventeenth century found expression in two seminal works from the period: J. Arndt, *True Christianity* (trans. P. Erb; New York: Paulist Press, 1979); and P.J. Spener, *Pia Desideria* (ed. T.G. Tappert; Philadelphia: Fortress Press, 1964).

8.   D.W. Bebbington, 'Evangelical Christianity and the Enlightenment', in M. Eden and D.F. Wells (eds.), *The Gospel in the Modern World* (Downers Grove, IL: InterVarsity Press, 1991), pp. 66-78.

the possibility of miracles, although theologians contended they had ended with the apostolic period in practice if not in theory.[9] Evangelists who daringly prayed for the sick felt the sting of ridicule, despite reports of healings in their services. Because seekers often fell prostrate in her meetings, critics dubbed the itinerant preacher Maria B. Woodworth-Etter the 'Trance Evangelist'.[10]

It presently appears that as a rule, missionaries, both Protestants and Roman Catholics, doubted the availability of miracles as well.[11] Alexander Duff, the noted missionary educator to India, defended the sending of missionaries by writing in 1839:

> Missionaries of the Church of Scotland have been sent forth with a special commission to prosecute the only means within their reach, *in the absence of miracles*, towards rearing a superior race of 'native' teachers and preachers of the everlasting Gospel; they have been sent forth with an equally special commission to preach as they have opportunity.[12]

This qualification also surfaced at the 1860 international missions conference in Liverpool, England. When comparing modern missionaries to the apostles, the Reverend Frederick Trestrail, secretary of the Baptist Missionary Society, fluttering above the constraints of logic, triumphantly sounded this note: 'Divest the Apostles of miraculous power...and you have the *modern missionary*, a true successor of the Apostles.'[13] In place of supernatural demonstrations of power, Western missionaries confidently shared the blessings of their 'higher' civilization to further the gospel.[14] For most Christians, the post-millennial calendar with its optimism of Christianizing society nurtured the hope that after a lengthy period of progress, Christ would return. Therefore, mission schools 'civilized' and educated 'heathen' students so they would see

---

9. N.O. Hatch, *The Democratization of American Christianity* (New Haven: Yale University Press, 1989), pp. 30-46.

10. See W.E. Warner, *The Woman Evangelist: The Life and Times of Charismatic Evangelist Maria B. Woodworth-Etter* (Metuchen, NJ: Scarecrow, 1986), pp. 21-22.

11. A Catholic perspective on miracles and missions may be found in J. Schmidlin, *Catholic Mission Theology* (Techny, IL: Mission Press, S.V.D., 1931), pp. 341-53.

12. A. Duff, *India, and India Missions* (Edinburgh: John Johnstone, Hunter Square, 1839), p. xiii. Emphasis mine.

13. F. Trestrail, 'On Native Churches', *Conference on Missions Held in 1860 at Liverpool* (London: James Nisbet, 1860), p. 279. Emphasis is Trestrail's.

14. E.g. Duff, *India*, pp. 25-26.

the superiority of Christianity and embrace the faith. Nevertheless, the number of converts seemed meager indeed (only 3.6 million communicants and adherents by 1906) when compared to the enormous investment in personnel and monies by Western mission agencies.[15]

3. *The Radical Strategy*

The nineteenth century introduced an age of awakenings. One of the most significant, the great 'Prayer Revival', started just before the American Civil War in 1858.[16] It soon spread to Canada, Northern Ireland (Ulster), Wales, England, South Africa, and South India. Startled Presbyterians in Northern Ireland noted unusual happenings, especially hundreds of people falling to the ground—'stricken' or 'prostrated' by God's power under intense conviction of sin.[17] Even more surprising, followers of the South Indian Christian, John Christian Aroolappen, spoke in tongues, prophesied, recounted visions, fell prostrate, prayed for the sick, helped the poor, and evangelized non-Christians. The revival there also gave prominence to women, a notable feature in Pentecostal renewals (Joel 2.28-29; Acts 21.9).[18] Anglican missionary Ashton Dibb (Church Missionary Society) declared the impact to be unprecedented in the history of Indian missions: 'It certainly does seem to have at least the merit of being the *first entirely indigenous effort of the native church at self-extension*'.[19] Another missionary reported,

> There is little doubt but that the Spirit of the Lord is in an extraordinary manner at work in portions of our South India Missions. Church-of-England [*sic*] clergy are backward in accepting such movements as these; but the testimony is now pretty decided and unanimous. It is indeed a new

15. H.P. Beach, *A Geography and Atlas of Protestant Missions*. II. *Statistics and Atlas* (2 vols.; New York: Student Volunteer Movement for Foreign Missions, 1906), p. 19; cf. W.R. Hutchison, *Errand to the World: American Protestant Thought and Foreign Missions* (Chicago: University of Chicago Press, 1987), pp. 99-100.

16. For a survey of the revival, see J.E. Orr, *The Fervent Prayer: The Worldwide Impact of the Great Awakening of 1858* (Chicago: Moody, 1974).

17. Many such accounts appear in W. Reid, *Authentic Records of Revival, Now in Progress in the United Kingdom* (London: James Nisbet, 1860).

18. See G.H. Lang (ed.), *The History and Diaries of an Indian Christian* (London: Thynne, 1939), pp. 138-39.

19. A. Dibb, 'The Revival in North Tinnevelly', *Church Missionary Record*, 5 (NS; August, 1860), p. 178 (emphasis Dibb's).

era in Indian Missions—that of lay converts going forth without purse or
scrip to preach the Gospel of Christ to their fellow-country-men [*sic*], and
that with a zeal and life we had hardly thought them capable of.[20]

Years later, in another part of the world and unrelated to the Prayer
Revival, missionary Johannes Warneck recorded that the Indonesian
Christian community had increased after the appearance of similar
'Pentecostal' phenomena: dreams, visions, signs in the heavens, and
several instances where missionaries unwittingly drank poison given by
their enemies and remained unharmed (Joel 2.28-31; Mk 16.18).[21]
Convinced that they had 'fulfilled their purpose of pointing the stupefied
heathen to the gift of the Gospel', Warneck saw 'the power of working
signs and wonders' as temporary, just as they had been in early
Christianity.[22]

Believers who contended that supernatural 'signs' should normally
follow the preaching of the gospel (Mk 16.17-18) helped set the stage
for the *radical strategy*—an apocalyptic scenario of divine intervention
in signs and wonders to ensure that every tribe and nation would hear
the gospel before the close of human history (Mt. 24.14; Acts 1.8).
Those who reflected on the availability of miracles included Anthony
Norris Groves (Brethren missionary to India); Thomas Erskine (Scottish
lay theologian); Edward Irving (leader of a Pentecostal movement in
England); and Horace Bushnell (an American theologian).[23] This list,
however, would be incomplete without the name of George Müller, a
well-known philanthropist whose expectant faith for God's provision at
his orphan homes in Bristol, England, modeled the idealized 'faith life'
for many Christians.[24] Although not remembered for advocacy of signs
and wonders, his perspective on faith helped lay the theoretical basis.

Why did Christians become interested in miraculous power? To begin
with, a wide spectrum of Protestants, both at home and on the mission

20. Dibb, 'Revival', p. 185.

21. J. Warneck, *The Living Christ and Dying Heathenism* (New York: Fleming
H. Revell, 3rd edn, n.d.), pp. 175-82.

22. Warneck, *Living Christ*, pp. 182, 165.

23. G.H. Lang, *Anthony Norris Groves* (London: Thynne, 1939); C.G. Strachan,
The Pentecostal Theology of Edward Irving (London: Darton, Longman & Todd,
1973); T. Erskine, *The Supernatural Gifts of the Spirit* (ed. R.K. Carter; Philadelphia:
Office of 'Words of Faith', 1883); H. Bushnell, *Nature and The Supernatural* (New
York: Charles Scribner, 1858), pp. 446-528.

24. See A.T. Pierson, *George Müller of Bristol* (New York: Baker & Taylor,
1899).

fields, prayed throughout the century for the outpouring of the Spirit as predicted by the prophet Joel (2.28-32). After all, Jesus told his disciples that he would send 'the promise of the Father', but in the meantime they needed to 'tarry' in prayer in Jerusalem 'until ye be endued with power from on high' (Lk. 24.49 [AV]).[25] Effective evangelism and reforming society of its evils (e.g. slavery, drunkenness, political corruption) required divine empowerment.[26] However, ministers, missionaries and church leaders supposed that an outpouring would enliven but not change conventional (Western) forms of preaching, worship and church structure.

The slow advance of medical science and the cries of the terminally ill also prompted Christians (usually those with ties to the holiness movement) to examine scriptural promises of healing (e.g. Isa. 53.4-5; Jas 5.13-16).[27] Testimonies of healing from the ministries of Dorothea Trudel (Switzerland) and Johann Christoph Blumhardt (Germany) influenced the American healing movement whose leading lights included Charles C. Cullis (Boston), A.B. Simpson (New York City), A.J. Gordon (Boston), John Alexander Dowie (Zion City, IL), and Maria B. Woodworth-Etter.[28] Emphasis on healing opened the door wider to miracles since all of the charismatic gifts might too be restored (e.g. 'the working of miracles' [1 Cor. 12.10]).

Finally, after the Civil War a small but growing cadre of pre-millennialists began to assess human progress negatively. On their scorecard, the world would go from bad to worse before Christ's return.[29] With the end of the century nearing, an arms race heating up between the major powers, increasing political and military tensions ('wars and rumors of wars'), and Zionists calling for a Jewish homeland in Palestine, numerous believers speculated that Christ would return by 1900 or thereabouts.[30]

25. All scripture quotations are taken from the AV.

26. T.L. Smith, *Revivalism and Social Concern: American Protestantism on the Eve of the Civil War* (New York: Harper & Row, 1957), pp. 114-62.

27. L.I. Sweet, *Health and Medicine in the Evangelical Tradition* (Valley Forge, PA: Trinity, 1994), pp. 135-61.

28. For a survey of the healing movement, see P.G. Chappell, 'The Divine Healing Movement in America' (PhD thesis; Drew University, 1983).

29. For an analysis of millennial perspectives held by evangelical Christians, see M.J. Erickson, *Contemporary Options in Eschatology: A Study of the Millennium* (Grand Rapids: Baker, 1977).

30. See T.P. Weber, *Living in the Shadow of the Second Coming, 1875–1982* (Chicago: University of Chicago Press, 1987), pp. 13-42.

With deepening concern, keen observers of the missions scene wondered how the Great Commission could be accomplished in such a short time.

3.1 *From Theory to Praxis*

More than anyone else after mid-century, A.B. Simpson, the former Presbyterian minister who founded the Christian and Missionary Alliance (CMA), put theory into action by encouraging the faithful to trust God for miracles. Along with others, he believed that God would heal the sick and even considered it possible that the Spirit might confer known languages (i.e. speaking in tongues) to expedite preaching to every tribe and nation (Mt. 24.14).[31] Opponents scorned such notions as absurd and irresponsible. Fanny Guinness, editor of a missionary monthly, *The Regions Beyond*, sniffed that for the heathen, 'miracles cannot enlighten their dark minds, or soften their hard hearts. Our aim is to enlighten, not to astonish.'[32] She did not foresee the impact that healings and 'power encounters' (exorcisms, etc.) would have in capturing the attention of non-Christians in Third World countries. To Simpson, 'the plan of the Lord [is] to pour out His Spirit not only in the ordinary, but also in the extraordinary gifts and operations of His power as His people press forward to claim the evangelization of the entire world'.[33]

The praxis of the radical strategy, however, brought mixed results. John Condit, one of the first Alliance missionaries to the Belgian Congo (present-day Zaire), died from a fever in 1885, just months after his arrival.[34] Five years later, missionaries from Topeka, Kansas, allegedly influenced by Simpson arrived in Sierra Leone confident of biblical promises of healing and Pentecostal tongues.[35] After discovering their

31. A.B. Simpson, 'The Gift of Tongues', *Christian Alliance and Missionary Weekly* (February 12, 1892), pp. 98-99.
32. H. Grattan [Fanny] Guinness, 'Missionaries According to Matt. X: A Critique', *The Regions beyond* (April, 1889), p. 110.
33. A.B. Simpson, 'Connection between Supernatural Gifts and the World's Evangelization', *Christian Alliance and Missionary Weekly* (October 7 and 14, 1892), p. 226.
34. G.P. Pardington, *Twenty-Five Wonderful Years, 1889–1914* (New York: Christian Alliance Publishing, 1914), pp. 129, 193-94.
35. The Kansas missionaries' expectation of Pentecostal tongues caught the attention of the noted Anglican linguist, Robert Needham Cust; see his *Evangelization of the Non-Christian World* (London: Luzac, 1894), pp. 106-107.

need to learn the native dialect, they persevered, but three died from malaria, having refused to take quinine.[36]

3.2 *Enlarging the Strategy*

Clearly this revolutionary concept emerged from those few like Simpson, the Kansas missionaries, and others who believed that God would provide supernatural assistance. One radical, Frank W. Sandford, founded a community and the Holy Ghost and Us Bible School at Shiloh, Maine, to prepare an elite band of end-times missionaries. Affirming the importance of signs and wonders, he called his organization, 'The World's Evangelization Crusade on Apostolic Principles'.[37] Although he apparently did not speak in tongues himself, others did. In accentuating the cosmic dimension of spiritual warfare in confronting the powers of darkness on mission fields, Sandford later purchased a schooner and barkentine and led his followers on a cruise in which they sailed off the coasts of Africa and South America, praying that God would release his power in each country for its conversion.[38] Nearly a century later, charismatic mission enthusiasts proposed a slightly similar approach to bringing the nations under the dominion of God.[39]

With connections to Sandford's enterprise, Walter S. Black and Frances Black and Jennie Glassey testified to Spirit baptism and receiving new languages during an 1895 revival in St. Louis, Missouri.[40] In view of their new-found abilities, Walter Black, a Canadian Baptist minister, looked at contemporary mission endeavors and crowed that neither '20,000 nor 100,000 missionaries of the common sanctified type will [ever] evangelize this globe'. Instead, God's Church needed to operate 'with purely Holy Ghost machinery'. After a vision in which she was called to Africa and promised an African language (March 23, 1894),

36. H. Grattan Guinness, 'Faith-Healing and Missions', *The Regions beyond* (January, 1891), p. 31.

37. F.W. Sandford, *Seven Years with God* (Mount Vernon, NH: Kingdom Press, 1957), pp. 111-32.

38. F.S. Murray, *The Sublimity of Faith: The Life and Work of Frank W. Sandford* (Amherst, NH: Kingdom Press, 1981), pp. 360-74.

39. C.P. Wagner, 'Territorial Spirits and World Missions', *Evangelical Missions Quarterly* 25 (July, 1989): pp. 278-88; D. Shibley, *A Force in the Earth: The Charismatic Renewal and World Evangelism* (Altamonte Springs, Florida: Creation House, 1989), pp. 67-86.

40. This may be the same revival that Maria B. Woodworth-Etter refers to in her *Marvels and Miracles* (Indianapolis, By the author, 1922), pp. 68-70.

Glassey received a 'wonderful language lesson' on July 8-9, 1895. Black reported that

> the Spirit came in a vision and unrolled before her eyes a long scroll covered with strange characters. These were in the Croo language. The Spirit read them most rapidly, and she read them after Him. First the Psalms, for she was reared a Psalm-singer, a Scotch Presbyterian; and then the Bible. So rapid was the reading that she feared that she would not remember all, but has done so; and speaks the Croo language *with great fluency*. She was also taught several native tunes, which have been recognized by travellers from Sierra Leone with whom she has conversed.

She allegedly spoke in several African dialects: 'Housa' (Hausa), 'Croo' and 'Khoominar', and later the 'Chinese language'.[41] The Blacks too received languages, but through the 'laying on of hands' by members of their church in St. Louis and claiming the promise of Mk 16.17: 'And these signs shall follow them that believe; In my name shall they cast out devils; they shall speak with new tongues.'

Before long, they too headed for Sierra Leone led by 'signs, wonders, miracles, healings, tongues and prophecy'.[42] On their way in 1897, they stayed in Liverpool where Glassey spoke to an old sailor acquainted with the Khoominar language. Upon hearing her speak in the dialect, 'the power of God settled upon him, and then and there he broke down, confessed his sins, and became a Christian'.[43] In view of this, Black remarked,

> The same power that drove the arrow of conviction into the hardened heart of an old sailor as he listened to a young girl speaking a language she had never heard in the power of the Holy Ghost, that same power will convict unconverted people, even as it did on the day of Pentecost.

In looking to the future, he predicted that 'God Almighty is raising up such a movement, and the last mighty billow that is to sweep over this globe and prepare the way for the coming of the Son of Man, is the

---

41. 'Tongues of Fire'; 'Other Tongues', *Tongues of Fire* (April 15, 1896), pp. 58-59. Emphasis in extended quotation is Black's.

42. 'Commit Thy Way', *Tongues of Fire* (June 15, 1898), p. 93. After leaving Liverpool, the Blacks and Glassey accompanied Frank W. Sandford to Jerusalem; their immediate whereabouts after that are presently unknown. In 1904, Walter Black began pastoring Baptist churches once again. See Murray, *Sublimity of Faith*, pp. 180-91.

43. 'Tarry Until', *Tongues of Fire* (March 1, 1897), p. 38.

movement that will "Tarry Until"'.[44] Little did he know that four years later such a movement would appear and shortly after become international in scope. While it remains uncertain how he later viewed the Pentecostal movement, one can easily see that the contours of Pentecostals' adaptation of the radical strategy had already begun to take shape by 1890.

A Midwestern holiness preacher, Charles F. Parham, took special interest in Sandford's teachings and the missionary implications of Glassey's testimony, printing her account in his own *Apostolic Faith* (Topeka, Kansas) periodical in 1899.[45] In April 1900, he announced that a 'Bro. and Sister Hamaker' resided at his faith home in Topeka, Kansas, 'to labor for Jesus until He gives them an heathen tongue, and then they will proceed to the missionary field'.[46] During the summer, Parham visited Shiloh where he heard speaking in tongues for the first time. Convinced that the 'gift of languages' offered the key for unlocking a Spirit-empowered ministry in signs and wonders, Parham and his students at Bethel Bible School prayed in January 1901 for the fulfillment of Joel's prophecy. Participants testified, as others did at the later Azusa Street Revival (1906–1909) in Los Angeles, California, and elsewhere, that God had given them the languages of the world.[47] Indeed, one report from Los Angeles announced, 'God is solving the missionary problem, sending out new-tongued missionaries on the apostolic faith line, without purse or scrip, and the Lord is going before them preparing the way'.[48] In regard to Jesus' statement in Mk 16.15 ('Go ye into all the world, and preach the gospel to every creature'), an Ohio Pentecostal added: 'Without this gift one cannot fulfill the great commission to preach the Gospel to every creature he comes in contact with' (Mk 16.15).[49] Hence, missionaries could now bypass the nuisance of language school and leave immediately for the mission fields.[50]

44. 'Tarry Until', p. 38.

45. 'The Gift of Tongues', *Apostolic Faith* (Topeka, Kansas; May 3, 1899), p. 5.

46. Untitled news note, *Apostolic Faith* (April 1, 1900), p. 7, col. 2.

47. 'A Queer Faith', *Topeka Daily Capital* (January 6, 1901), p. 2; also, J.R. Goff, Jr, *Fields White unto Harvest: Charles F. Parham and the Missionary Origins of Pentecostalism* (Fayetteville: University of Arkansas Press, 1988), pp. 62-86.

48. *Apostolic Faith* (Los Angeles; November, 1906), p. 2, col. 4.

49. 'Utility of Tongues', *The New Acts* (July and August ,1907), p. 9.

50. 'Parham's New Religion Practiced at "Stone's Folly"', *Kansas City Times* (January 27, 1901), p. 55.

The origins of Pentecostalism (also known as the 'Apostolic Faith' or 'Latter Rain' movement) naturally include more factors than the quest to fulfill the Great Commission.[51] For example, speaking in tongues ostensibly resolved for Pentecostals the longstanding theological question in holiness circles about the evidence of Spirit baptism. Social and cultural factors also played major roles in shaping the various strands of Pentecostalism whether in North America, Europe or on the mission fields.[52]

4. *Radical beyond Reason?*

The language proposal severely tested the credulity of other radical Evangelicals, but retained an empirical tinge—languages could be verified. Yet, evidence that Pentecostals did indeed preach in new languages proved difficult to establish. By late 1906 and 1907, though still believing that tongues signified human languages or those of angels (1 Cor. 13.1), Pentecostals began to view tongues speech as 'glossolalia' (i.e. unknown tongues to speaker and hearer). Hence, 'praying in tongues', an exercise that Parham dismissed, brought empowerment through worship and intercession in the Spirit (Rom. 8.26-27).[53]

Critics branded glossolalia as nonsense. Moreover, Pentecostals had crossed the 'Rubicon' into irrational behavior and perhaps into the

51. For further examinations of the origins of Pentecostalism, see R.M. Anderson, *Vision of the Disinherited: The Making of American Pentecostalism* (New York: Oxford University Press, 1979); D.W. Dayton, *Theological Roots of Pentecostalism* (Metuchen, NJ: Scarecrow, 1987; repr., Peabody, MA: Hendrickson, 1994); E.L. Blumhofer, *Restoring the Faith: The Assemblies of God, Pentecostalism, and American Culture* (Urbana: University of Illinois Press, 1993); cf. W.J. Hollenweger, *The Pentecostals* (London: SCM Press, 1972; repr., Peabody, MA: Hendrickson, 1988); I. MacRobert, *The Black Roots and White Racism of Early Pentecostalism in the USA* (New York: St Martin's, 1988).

52. For a study of the reception of Pentecostal teachings in Central America, see E.A. Wilson, 'Passion and Power: A Profile of Emergent Latin American Pentecostalism', in M.W. Dempster, B.D. Klaus and D. Petersen (eds.), *Called and Empowered: Global Mission in Pentecostal Perspective* (Peabody, MA: Hendrickson, 1991), pp. 67-97; for India, see my 'Pentecostal Phenomena and Revivals in India: Implications for Indigenous Church Leadership', *International Bulletin of Missionary Research* 20 (July 1996), pp. 112-17.

53. E.g. A.G. Garr, 'Tongues, the Bible Evidence', *A Cloud of Witnesses to Pentecost in India* (September, 1907), pp. 42-44; A.A. Boddy, 'Speaking in Tongues: What is It?', *Confidence* (May, 1910), p. 100.

satanic realm. Evangelical Christians were already becoming aware of the encroachment of Theosophy, Christian Science and Spiritualism. Kenneth Mackenzie, a leader in the Christian and Missionary Alliance, warned the faithful in his *Anti-Christian Supernaturalism* (1901) that 'God's work of grace is ever paralleled by another force energising [sic] a contrary spirit'.[54] To make matters worse, not only did speaking in tongues appear among spiritualists, but Mormons as well.[55] If these threats failed to rattle the serenity of the faithful, Presbyterian missionary John L. Nevius did that by telling of exorcisms in China where demons had spoken in tongues.[56]

Scrutinizing the expansion of Pentecostalism, the fiery holiness bishop Alma White fumed that the 'old Red Dragon' had caused it to spread so quickly around the world.[57] Speaking in tongues might sound to some like a real language, but those who engaged in it had already been 'caught in the devil's delusive net', despite their liking to 'talk about the blood of the atonement, claim to heal diseases, and especially take up the theme of the second coming of Christ'.[58]

4.1 *Expecting Miracles*
Most Pentecostals taught that every Christian should seek for Spirit baptism with tongues and then for the gifts of the Spirit. In evangelizing, they prioritized seeking for spectacular displays of celestial power— signs and wonders, healing, and deliverance from sinful habits and satanic bondage. For example, on the home front, differences between Evangelical and Pentecostal tactics in evangelism become quickly apparent when one compares the early twentieth-century ministries of Billy Sunday and Aimee Semple McPherson. In 1912, Billy Sunday held an evangelistic campaign in Canton, Ohio, preceded by months of planning, construction of a wooden tabernacle, training of a 600 voice choir, and the support of the ministerial alliance. Thousands attended and in Sunday's words, 'hit the sawdust trail' (variously meaning to commit

54. K. Mackenzie, Jr, *Anti-Christian Supernaturalism* (New York: Christian Alliance Publishing, 1901), p. 11.

55. See J.L. Brooke, *The Refiner's Fire: The Making of Mormon Cosmology, 1644–1844* (New York: Cambridge University Press, 1994), pp. 220, 228, 291.

56. J.L. Nevius, *Demon Possession and Allied Themes* (New York: Fleming H. Revell, 1896), pp. 46-47, 58-59.

57. A. White, *Demons and Tongues* (Zarephath, NJ: Pillar of Fire, 1936), p. 99.

58. White, *Demons*, p. 16.

one's life to Christ, to commit to being a good American, and/or taking the 'pledge' not to consume alcohol).[59]

Nine years later, Aimee Semple McPherson arrived almost without any preparation. Permitted to use the civic auditorium, she began preaching and praying for the sick. Newspaper headlines immediately screamed: 'Cripples Are Cured When Woman Evangelist Prays', 'Sick of Soul and Body Are Relieved', 'Two Hundred Men Answer Call for Prayer', and 'Thousands Unable to Gain Entrance at Healing Meet'.[60] Seekers jammed the meetings nightly and several thousand professed salvation. McPherson attributed the results to 'preaching the great "I Am" instead of the great "I Was"'—that Jesus would do today what he had done for the sick and needy during his earthly ministry.[61] Her evangelistic campaigns, combined with those of other Pentecostal evangelists (e.g. Maria B. Woodworth-Etter, Raymond T. Richey, and Charles S. Price), led to the founding of thousands of congregations. The same expectancy of miracles characterized Pentecostal evangelism overseas. Pentecostals quickly became adept at planning, but maintained that 'well-oiled' campaign techniques could never substitute for demonstrations of supernatural power.

Reformulating the strategy to include tongues and spiritual gifts, however, occasionally led to unusual assertions. Alfred G. Garr, an early missionary from the Azusa Street Revival, brought discredit on the Pentecostal movement in India by endorsing an Indian Christian's prophecy that Colombo, Ceylon (present-day Sri Lanka) would be destroyed by an earthquake on September 23, 1907.[62] Levi R. Lupton,

59. E.T. Heald, *History of Stark County. III. Industry Comes of Age, 1901–1917* (Canton, OH: Stark County Historical Society, 1952), III, pp. 596-607; W.G. McLoughlin, Jr, *Billy Sunday Was his Real Name* (Chicago: University of Chicago Press, 1955), p. 97.

60. 'Cripples Are Cured When Woman Evangelist Prays', *Canton Daily News* (October 6, 1921), pp. 1, 4; J.V. McCann, 'Sick of Soul and Body Are Relieved', *Canton Daily News* (October 7, 1921); *idem*, '200 Men Answer Call of Woman Evangelist and Ask for Prayer', *Canton Daily News* (October 8, 1921), p. 1; 'Thousands Unable to Gain Entrance at Healing Meet', *The Evening Repository* (October 16, 1921), pp. 1-2.

61. A.S. McPherson, *This Is That* (Los Angeles: Echo Park Evangelistic Association, 1923), p. 378.

62. K. Wood Kumarakulasinghe, 'The Tongues Earthquake Scare in Ceylon', *Free Methodist* (December 17, 1907); also, F.B. Price, 'Manifestations Genuine and Counterfeit', *Indian Witness* (April 18, 1907), p. 251.

a holiness Quaker-turned-Pentecostal who founded the Pentecostal Missionary Union (U.S.A.), announced in 1907 that God had conferred the title 'apostle' on him.[63] Pentecostals and Lupton's wife soon became wary of such claims.

It should also be noted that expectancy of supernatural interventions continued in the ranks of less radical Evangelicals, despite the penchant of many Pentecostals to limit such happenings to those who had been Spirit baptized and spoken in tongues.[64] Notwithstanding, healings, exorcisms and other extraordinary events occurred in the ministries of pastors, evangelists and missionaries in the Christian and Missionary Alliance, National Holiness Missionary Society (later World Gospel Mission), Church of the Nazarene, and the Missionary Church Association, among others.[65] Although less well known, this has been true across a still broader spectrum of evangelical Christians from fundamentalists to members of the historic churches (e.g., Elijah Bingham, Dick Hillis, Corrie ten Boom, James M. Hickson, and members of the Order of St Luke [interdenominational]).[66] Yet, polemical controversy over the 'tongues movement' and healing evangelists produced hesitations that kept most fundamentalists and Evangelicals from seeking signs and wonders.

63. 'Apostle Levi, Says Vision', *The Alliance Daily Review* (June 26, 1907), p. 1. See my 'Levi Lupton: A Forgotten Pioneer of Early Pentecostalism', in P. Elbert (ed.), *Faces of Renewal: Studies in Honor of Stanley M. Horton* (Peabody, MA: Hendrickson, 1988), pp. 192-208.

64. E.g. R.M. Riggs, *The Spirit Himself* (Springfield, MO: Gospel Publishing, 1949), pp. 118-19.

65. E.g. C.W. Nienkirchen, *A.B. Simpson and the Pentecostal Movement* (Peabody, MA: Hendrickson, 1992), pp. 122-28; W.W. Cary, *Story of the National Holiness Missionary Society* (Chicago: National Holiness Missionary Society, 2nd edn, 1941), pp. 48, 189; R.V. DeLong and M. Taylor, *Fifty Years of Nazarene Missions*. II. *History of the Fields* (Kansas City, MO: Beacon Hill, 1955), pp. 291-92, 294; J.A. Ringenberg, *Jesus the Healer* (Fort Wayne, IN: Missionary Church Association, 1947), p. 76. Interestingly, Pentecostals have sometimes used books written by conservative Evangelicals and fundamentalists for biblical insights on demonology; examples include J.L. Nevius, *Demon Possession*; M.F. Unger, *Biblical Demonology* (Wheaton: Van Kampen, 1952); and C.F. Dickason, *Angels, Elect and Evil* (Chicago: Moody, 1975).

66. E.g. *Demon Experiences in Many Lands* (Chicago: Moody, 1960), pp. 11-14, 37-40; also J.M. Hickson, *Heal the Sick* (New York: E.P. Dutton & Co., n.d.); C. ten Boom, *Defeated Enemies* (Fort Washington, Penn.: Christian Literature Crusade, 1963).

4.2 *Crisis and Controversy*

By the 1940s, Pentecostals began coming out of sectarian isolation to identify with conservative Evangelicals. But in the estimation of some, the power of early Pentecostalism had waned. Fears that denominational structures, theological education, and new-found respectability quenched the freedom of the Spirit prompted another revival, the '*New Order* of the Latter Rain'.[67] This produced a division between those who said the Pentecostal movement had 'matured' in theology and practice, and others who championed a more open-ended view of the Spirit's gifts and workings, one not chained to denominational and sometimes even hermeneutical restraints.[68]

Controversy soon brewed over actions that denominational Pentecostal leaders, especially those in the Assemblies of God, considered unacceptable such as the impartation of the spiritual gifts through the laying on of hands, restoration of the offices of apostle and prophet, personal prophecies of guidance given to individuals, and insistence that the Spirit would dispense languages to missionaries. Opinions on the genuineness of the revival varied considerably, revealing a growing gap between 'establishment Pentecostals' and 'grass roots' or 'folk' Pentecostals. Not wishing to repeat what they perceived to be mistakes from their own past, church leaders who saw their institutions threatened by a new movement with questionable teachings distanced themselves and in certain cases officially condemned it.[69] To Pentecostal leaders, Latter Rain teachers had dangerously attempted to revise the strategy.

If the Latter Rain proved divisive, the closely related healing movement of the late 1940s and 1950s fostered a measure of unity.[70] Pentecostals of every stripe gathered in tents and auditoriums to see the power of the Holy Spirit manifested. Though some healing evangelists exaggerated claims and had questionable lifestyles, their campaigns led to thousands of converts and the establishment of many new churches. Through the ministries of William Branham, Oral Roberts, Jack Coe,

67. R.M. Riss, *Latter Rain* (Mississauga, Ont.: Honeycomb Visual Productions, 1987), pp. 53-60 (my emphasis).

68. E.g. Riss, *Latter Rain*, pp. 95-96.

69. Concerns evident in the (Assemblies of God) 'Quarterly Letter', April 20, 1949.

70. D.E. Harrell, Jr, *All Things Are Possible: The Healing and Charismatic Revivals in Modern America* (Bloomington: Indiana University Press, 1975), pp. 95-96.

Gordon Lindsay, and many more, believers professed faith for seemingly impossible problems. Overseas campaigns impacted church growth as well, with perhaps the most spectacular taking place in Buenos Aires, Argentina, in 1954 and led by Tommy Hicks. With an aggregate attendance of nearly two million people, and driven by testimonies of notable healings and deliverances, it resulted in a major breakthrough for Protestantism and Pentecostalism in particular.[71]

At the same time, the Assemblies of God and other Pentecostal denominations underwent an escalating 'Evangelicalization' in doctrine, worship and practice.[72] Precision in exegesis and theology and growing doctrinal uniformity became paramount concerns for establishment Pentecostals. Not surprisingly, their hesitations came again to the fore when the charismatic renewal arose in the 1960s and '70s and Latter Rain features reappeared in some quarters. Nevertheless, many grass roots Pentecostal ministers and laypersons attended charismatic prayer meetings and avidly read the books of well-known leaders (e.g. Dennis Bennett, Bob Mumford, Kenneth Hagin, John and Elizabeth Sherrill, Pat Robertson, and Francis MacNutt).[73] Generally speaking, charismatics often became more overtly supernaturalistic and prayed in tongues more than their Pentecostal brothers and sisters.[74] While the latter increasingly focused on methods and planning, charismatics, particularly those involved in missions, returned to the outlook of early Pentecostal missionaries.

71. A.W. Enns, *Man, Milieu and Mission in Argentina* (Grand Rapids: Eerdmans, 1971), pp. 76-78; L.W. Stokes, *The Great Revival in Buenos Aires* (Buenos Aires: Casilla De Correo, 1954). For the exaggerated claims of Tommy Hicks, see his *Millions Found Christ* (Los Angeles: Manifest Deliverance and Worldwide Evangelism, Inc., 1956).

72. R.P. Spittler, 'Are Pentecostals and Charismatics Fundamentalists? A Review of American Uses of These Categories', in K. Poewe (ed.), *Charismatic Christianity as a Global Culture* (Columbia: University of South Carolina Press, 1994), pp. 103-16.

73. For an analysis of differing perspectives of history between Pentecostals and charismatics, see C. Nienkirchen, 'Conflicting Visions of the Past: The Prophetic Use of History in the Early American Pentecostal-Charismatic Movement', in Poewe (ed.), *Charismatic Christianity*, pp. 119-33.

74. H.V. Synan, 'The Touch Felt Around the World', *Charisma and Christian Life* (January, 1991), p. 85.

The debate reached a new level of intensity after 1980 with the rise of conservative Evangelical charismatics (so-called 'Third Wavers').[75] Shying away from identification with classical Pentecostals and charismatics, leaders such as Charles H. Kraft, C. Peter Wagner and John Wimber have reformulated the radical strategy with new insights on how to minister in the Spirit's power.[76] Their interest in spiritual warfare reflects the apocalyptic vision of cosmic struggle held by their nineteenth-century precursors. Perhaps the most striking innovation has been the insistence that before effective evangelism can be accomplished, 'territorial demons' governing regions of the world must be bound (Mt. 12.29; 18.18).[77] Curiously, a religious science fiction has also materialized to alert the saints to the need for spiritual warfare (e.g. Frank E. Peretti's *This Present Darkness* [1986]).

5. *Limits to the Strategy*

Pentecostal and charismatic perspectives on the spiritual realm have proven unusually compatible with non-Western worldviews—a spiritual vision that has contributed to the gradual 'Pentecostalization' of Third World Christianity in life and worship. It has continued with great fervor in many regions of the world, from the activities of charismatic Lutherans in Ethiopia to the global missionary witness of Pentecostal and charismatic congregations in Singapore.[78]

Miracles have usually occurred where believers have expected God to heal and deliver. The contrast between the campaigns of Sunday and McPherson can be seen today in the crusades of Billy Graham and Reinhard Bonnke. Graham neither prays for the sick nor exorcises

75. For a definition of the 'Third Wave', see C.P. Wagner, *The Third Wave of the Holy Spirit* (Ann Arbor, MI: Vine, 1988).

76. Charles H. Kraft, *Christianity with Power: Your Worldview and Your Experience of the Supernatural* (Ann Arbor, MI: Vine, 1989); C.P. Wagner and F.D. Pennoyer (eds.), *Wrestling with Dark Angels* (Ventura, CA: Regal, 1990); J. Wimber and K. Springer, *Power Evangelism* (San Francisco: HarperSanFrancisco, 2nd edn, 1992).

77. See C.P. Wagner, *Confronting the Powers* (Ventura, CA: Regal, 1996).

78. On the ministry of Lutheran charismatics in Ethiopia, see L. Christenson (ed.), *Welcome, Holy Spirit: A Study of Charismatic Renewal in the Church* (Minneapolis: Augsburg, 1987), pp. 369-70; also, C.P. Wagner, 'Church Growth', in S.M. Burgess, G.B. McGee and P.H. Alexander (eds.), *Dictionary of Pentecostal and Charismatic Movements* (Grand Rapids: Zondervan, 1988), pp. 180-95.

demons in his services. Bonnke, on the other hand, both preaches and prays for signs and wonders to confirm the gospel message, offering healing to body, soul, and spirit.[79] Both constitute valid and complementary methods of evangelism.[80]

Clearly, the miracle agenda in missions has required heavenly sanctioned human procedures ('Pauline' methods) and structures to achieve long-term results, necessitating the organization of congregations, discipling of converts, establishing schools for training leaders, and even preparing Bible translations. Signs and wonders alone offered little help for necessary institutional development as the Lord delayed his return.[81] This explains why earlier Pentecostal missionaries frequently resorted to the paternalistic practices of their Protestant and Catholic counterparts to give permanence to their ministries. Following the lead of the Anglican missiologist Roland Allen, others turned to Paul's practice of planting self-supporting, self-governing and self-propagating churches. This acknowledged borrowing revealed growing appreciation of traditional mission practices. Over time, increasing successes gained through utilizing various strategies, methods, technology, training institutions and charitable ministries balanced and then gradually outweighed the original preeminence placed on direct interventions of God in some quarters of Pentecostal missions.

'Strategies', 'paradigms' and 'patterns' in evangelism depict human attempts to understand and manage God's initiative in mission. All those who have pursued the radical strategy have inevitably faced the frustration of miracles not happening as anticipated. In their theological literature, Pentecostals and many charismatics have paid little attention to the mystery that shrouds the divine will.[82] God's Word bears fruit with or without visible miracles, and he also works providentially in

79. For Bonnke's ministry, see R. Steele, *Plundering Hell—to Populate Heaven* (Tulsa: Albury, 1987).

80. Ralph R. Covell argues that the efforts of Pentecostal missionaries in China were no more successful in evangelism than those of non-Pentecostal evangelical missionaries; see his recent *Liberating Gospel in China: The Christian Faith among China's Minority Peoples* (Grand Rapids: Baker, 1995), pp. 273-74.

81. See my 'Pentecostals and Their Various Strategies for Global Mission: A Historical Assessment', in Dempster, Klaus and Petersen (eds.), *Called and Empowered*, pp. 203-24.

82. A problem brought to the attention of Pentecostals by Donald Gee in his controversial *Trophimus I Left Sick: Our Problems of Divine Healing* (London: Elim, 1952), pp. 9-10.

human affairs. In recent years, those Pentecostals and charismatics who have recognized the connection of signs and wonders to the advancing kingdom of God, have made vital theological progress in understanding the role of the miraculous in the Christian world mission.[83]

6. *Conclusion*

Prior to the Protestant Reformation, Christian missionaries believed that miracles would accompany their evangelistic activities. From the Reformation to the eighteenth century, this confidence declined due largely to anti-Catholic attitudes and skepticism. With the revival of experiential piety in the churches and desires to reform society, believers began to pray for the promised outpouring of the Holy Spirit.

The quandary over how to bring closure to the Great Commission pressed radical Evangelicals to ask daringly for the restoration of the Spirit's power as taught and illustrated in the New Testament. From this emerged an apocalyptic blueprint for end-times evangelism—the radical strategy. For some this meant praying for physical healings and power to exorcise demons, while others petitioned to receive known human languages to expedite the missionary's task. To varying degrees, Alliance and holiness missionaries, Pentecostals and charismatics, and missionaries from a broad spectrum of evangelicalism have followed this paradigm. In so doing, these practitioners have gradually increased the anticipation of divine power among evangelical Christians, moving the expectancy of signs and wonders from the periphery of the Christian world mission to a position at the center.

Research and dialogue on ministry in the power of the Spirit potentially offer Christians engaged in mission a unique oportunity to grow in mutual understanding, work together for the advancement of the kingdom of God in both Word and deed, and realize greater unity in the body of Christ.

83. E.g. G.D. Fee, 'The Kingdom of God and the Church's Global Mission', in Dempster, Klaus and Petersen (eds.), *Called and Empowered*, pp. 7-21.

BEYOND THE CLOUDS: ELIZE SCHARTEN (1876–1965),
PENTECOSTAL MISSIONARY TO CHINA

Cornelis van der Laan

1. *To the Uttermost Parts of the Earth*

From the start, the Pentecostal movement demonstrated a great zeal for missionary work. At the Hamburg Conference, December 1908, Cecil Polhill addressed the issue of foreign mission. Polhill saw the Pentecostal experience as a gift for service and for missionary service in particular: 'This Pentecostal Blessing which has come to us must go right through the world'.[1] He felt that the Welsh Revival had been quenched through lack of missionary spirit. Polhill had been a missionary to China from 1885–1900 with the 'China Inland Mission' and still was a member of their council. Upon his initiative the 'Pentecostal Missionary Union' (P.M.U.) was founded on January 9, 1909. Candidates had to be baptized with the Holy Spirit with 'the Signs and Gifts' and to believe in the infallibility of the Holy Scriptures. The educational standard required a fair knowledge of every book in the Bible and an 'accurate knowledge of the Doctrine of Salvation and Sanctification'.[2] No salaries were guaranteed. All candidates went through a training school which was soon established in London. The magazine *Fragments of Fire*, which after October 1911 continued as *Flames of Fire*, was edited by Polhill. Until G.R. Polman (1868–1932), the Dutch Pentecostal pioneer, founded the 'Nederlandsch Pinksterzendingsgenootschap' (Dutch Pentecostal Missionary Society) in 1920 all Dutch missionaries were sent by the

---

1. C. Polhill, 'The Pentecostal Movement and the Foreign Mission field', *Confidence* 2/1 (January, 1909), pp. 15-16.

2. 'The Pentecostal Missionary Union', *Confidence* 2/1 (January 1909), pp. 13-14. *Flames of Fire* stated from time to time on the back cover: 'The Mission is maintained on faith principles. No guaranteed salaries to the workers. The evangelical doctrines are held, and the baptism of the Holy Ghost (Acts 2), emphasized as the essential equipment for workers' (*Flames of Fire* [October, 1917]).

P.M.U.[3] In 1911 the P.M.U. opened a work in the capital of Yunnan province in Southwest China. Among the first P.M.U. missionaries were Arie and Elsje Kok from Holland. They were followed by Elize Scharten in 1912 and Idigje de Vries in 1914.

In Amsterdam the Immanuel Hall was opened in June 1912. The building behind the hall housed the missionary training school that commenced in October 1912.[4] From the first class, three students—Piet Klaver, Trijntje Bakker and Geertje Roos—would go to China. Instruction was given in: Bible study; Religions of heathendom; Geography; English; French; and German (optional).[5]

The Dutch Pentecostal Missionary Society, founded on October 28, 1920, was designed to 'train, send out and sustain missionaries to spread the gospel of Jesus Christ to all nations, especially those who have not yet been reached'.[6] It became incorporated as 'Vereeniging' in January 1923. Membership was open to those who

> acknowledge the true, eternal Divinity of Christ and who by their way of living testify to be redeemed by the blood of Jesus Christ, believing in the second coming of Christ for His church and the baptism with the Holy Spirit, as is written in the Holy Scriptures.[7]

3.   Dutch missionaries sent by the P.M.U. to China: Arie and Elsje Kok (1910–19); Elize Scharten (1912–26); Idigje de Vries (1914–16); Piet Klaver (1915–24). Dutch missionaries sent by the Dutch missionary society to China: Trijntje Bakker (1921–27); Geertje Roos (1921–27); Piet Klaver (second term: 1925–27). Elize remained with the P.M.U. until 1926, when the P.M.U. was merged with the Assemblies of God. In 1931 both Elize Scharten and Trijntje Bakker were associated with the German 'Vereinigte Missionsfreunde e.V., Velbert', which was founded in the same year. At that time the Dutch missionary society was in a quandary due to the resignation of Polman. To enhance communication with the Dutch sponsors, Klaver started publication of *De Vereenigde Zendingsvrienden* in May 1937.

4.   W. Polman, 'De Opening der Zendingsschool', *Spade Regen* 31 (August–November, 1912), p. 4; P.N. Corry, 'Holland: Dedication of Missionary Home', *Confidence* 5/11 (November, 1912), pp. 259-60. Upon request from German mission friends Polman had a German prospectus of the training school printed in September 1913; *Spade Regen* 34 (September, 1913), p. 136.

5.   A.A. Boddy, 'The Pentecostal Bible School in Holland', *Confidence* 7/4 (April, 1914), p. 78.

6.   G.R. Polman, 'Uit den arbeid', *Spade Regen* 13/8 (November, 1920), pp. 122-23. In 1928 Otto Karrenberg from Velbert was added to the board, who represented the Dutch Mission in Germany. G.R. Polman, 'Het Pinksterzendingsgenootschap', *Spade Regen* 21/3 (June 1928), p. 48.

7.   *Nederlandsche Staatscourant*, Supplement 74 (17 April, 1923), filed under

The mission work was financed by free gifts from members and sympathizers and by the proceeds of annual bazaars. Upon request, offering boxes were supplied to place in the houses. All Pentecostal assemblies shared in the missionary effort.

The missionary zeal was embedded in an eschatological scheme. Bringing the gospel to all nations was regarded a necessary prerequisite for the second coming of Christ. As Tibet had the reputation of being the most closed area for the gospel, it became a special target for the early Pentecostal mission. The missionaries worked along the lines of the China Inland Mission (C.I.M.). They went inland, lived among the people and had no guarantee of salary.

Not much has been published yet concerning the Pentecostal missionary work in China. Daniel H. Bays described the earliest Pentecostal missionaries (1906–1916).[8] His research is limited to the first American missionaries. They put down roots in three places which later strongly influenced the development of Chinese Pentecostalism: Hong Kong, Zhengding in the Hebei Province, and Shanghai. They were usually seen as troublemakers by the missionary establishment. These missionaries preached where they could, held healing services and expected miracles. Many if not most had no regular financial support. They published Pentecostal periodicals in the Chinese language. These papers promoted the Pentecostal message, but had no impact on non-believers. Bays concludes that the earliest Chinese participants in the Pentecostal movement were nearly all already Christians.

The P.M.U. arrived somewhat later. In 1910 the first P.M.U. missionaries settled in China. They did not live in the large cities, but like the C.I.M. moved inward. On the field they consulted with the missions present. Unlike the independent American missionaries, the P.M.U. had some institutional base, regular financial support, and a strategy to follow. Their work concentrated on reaching the non-believers. They did not publish Pentecostal periodicals in Chinese, but rather used already existing evangelistic tracts and pamphlets published by the Moravian Brethren or Bible Societies. Their converts were nearly all non-Christians.

The Dutch opened a P.M.U. station at Lijiang, near the Tibetan

'Statuten Vereenigingen 1923 no. 452'; cf. Polman, 'Het Pinksterzendingsgenootschap', *Spade Regen* 16/8 (November, 1923), pp. 125-26.

8.   D.H. Bays, 'The first Pentecostal Missionaries to China 1906–1916', Paper presented at the 18th Annual Meeting of the Society for Pentecostal Studies, Asbury Theological Seminary, Wilmore, Kentucky, November 10–12, 1988.

border. Being the oldest wooden city in South West China, Lijiang was recently chosen for the television production, 'Beyond the Clouds' (1994), in which events in the lives of four families at Lijiang portray the changing society of China.[9]

This article provides a description of one of the early Dutch Pentecostal missionaries who settled in Lijiang, Elize Scharten.

2. *Early Years*

2.1 *Birth*

Cornelia Elizabeth Scharten was born on July 5, 1876 in Amsterdam. Elize was named after her grandmother on her father's side. Her father, Karel Scharten (1836–1909), was a Lutheran minister (in the 'Hersteld Evangelisch-Luthersche Kerk'). Father Scharten came from a family with many army officers. Karel's father was a lieutenant-colonel of the infantry in Zealand. In 1862 Karel married Johanna Stumphius (1804–1908), daughter of the mayor of Beverwijk. Elize would later describe her mother as 'a true Christian'. Nine children were born to this couple, Elize arrived as the seventh. Three children died within a few years of their birth. Two brothers (Carel Theodoor and Thedoor) also become ministers in the Lutheran church. Sister Jacoba married another Lutheran minister, Karl Gramberg; while sister Jenneke married missionary Johannes Pik.[10]

2.2 *Calling*

Little is known about Elize's early years. As a girl of 18 she gave her heart to the Lord Jesus in the city mission 'Jeruël' at Rotterdam. Her conversion was accompanied by a call to missions:

> Not that I had enjoyed worldly pleasures, the Lord has always kept me from these, but the Master asked me to 'dedicate my life to Him', to which I obeyed. I believed the call was to go to the heathen world. Being Dutch I thought, it could not be anything else but 'our East', the Dutch Indies.[11]

9. 'Beyond the Clouds', River film Production for Channel Four. Co-production with the National Geographic Society and Canal, 1994.

10. K. Scharten, 'Genealogie van de familie Scharten', *Gens Nostra* 34 (1979), pp. 49-60.

11. E. Scharten, 'Gaat dan henen in de gehele wereld en predikt het evangelie aan alle schepselen', *Volle Evangelie Koerier* 10/8 (February, 1948), p. 4. A series of

Because the Lutheran mission only allowed for women who were either school teachers or nurses, this road appeared to be closed. So, Elize turned to an inner mission. In order to complete her education, she traveled to Naaes, Sweden, to be trained as an instructor of handicraft (*slöjd*).

Hereafter Elize and her sister were led to evangelize among sailors and prostitutes in the red light district of Amsterdam. More Christians joined them. They published a paper, *Rein Leven* ('Clean Living'). On Saturday nights they visited the pubs and handed out Christian literature. The work extended so much that in 1903 the Christian home, 'Welkom', was opened on the Zeedijk. It was a rough neighborhood. Policemen never walked alone. One pub-owner got converted and emptied his gin barrels on the street.[12]

2.3 *Pentecost*

During 1907 Elize received news of the Pentecostal meetings in Amsterdam. Children of God were being baptized in the Holy Spirit and speaking in foreign languages. Together with some workers from Welkom, she visited a Pentecostal gathering:

> There was speaking with other tongues, and interpretation was given. I had often read about this in the Bible and had wondered: why are these gifts of the Holy Spirit no longer seen and heard in the church? This, I was now seeing and hearing. I could not help saying a prayer of thanksgiving, because God's grace was still the same.[13]

One of the elders of the Lutheran church warned Father Scharten that his daughter had attended a 'spiritistic meeting' and had even prayed! Upon the urgent request of her mother, Elize refrained for some time from going there again, but she kept informed about the developments. The death of her mother in August 1908 took so much out of Elize that she became ill. A physician could not help her. In September 1908, Alexander Boddy visited the Pentecostal assembly in Amsterdam. Elize spoke with the Anglican minister, who advised her to search for the baptism in the Holy Spirit. From then on she visited the public and mutual Pentecostal meetings. On September 28, 1908 she received her

articles appeared under this name from February, 1948 through July, 1950.

12. E. Scharten, 'Gaat dan henen in de gehele wereld en predikt het evangelie aan alle schepselen', *Volle Evangelie Koerier* 10/8 (February, 1948), p. 4.

13. E. Scharten, 'Gaat dan henen in de gehele wereld en predikt het evangelie aan alle schepselen', *Volle Evangelie Koerier* 10/9 (March, 1948).

Spirit baptism at home: 'My mouth was filled with laughing. O grace of God, so great and rich. I was allowed to praise and glorify my Lord in foreign languages.'[14] Again Father Scharten was warned, but he replied, 'I have received a better daughter, so it is all right'.[15] Six months later Father Scharten died. Elize was transformed into a zealous co-worker in the Pentecostal assembly and had her testimony printed in a pamphlet entitled *Tot eer van God* ('To the Glory of God'). Her colleagues in Welkom were opposed to her Pentecostal leanings. Yet Elize was certain that she was following God's way.

2.4 *Call to Missions*

On Whitsuntide, Elize attended the International Conference in Sunderland, England. During one evening service, an appeal was made for missionaries to China. China was the last country in Elize's mind. However, in her heart a voice spoke, 'Now is the time that I call you to give your life to the heathen'.[16]

Elize applied to the Pentecostal Missionary Union. Upon the recommendation of G.R. Polman, she was immediately accepted. 'The Lord miraculously provided house parents to replace me in the home, Welkom'.[17] In February 1911, Elize Scharten and Trijntje Baas were sent from Amsterdam to the P.M.U. Women's Training Home in London. Trijntje Baas remained in London, but Elize left for China in April 1912 together with Elizabeth M. Biggs from Scotland and Miss M. Rönager from Denmark.

> There was much to do. Alas, one does not always meet the right advisors to know what should be taken and what should be left behind. The chairman's ideal was that a Bible and a toothbrush should suffice. Now that is too little, but I must confess that missionaries often take too much along.[18]

This was the second group sent out by the P.M.U. Among the first group in 1910 were Arie and Elsje Kok, also from Amsterdam.

---

14. E. Scharten, 'Gaat dan henen in de gehele wereld en predikt het evangelie aan alle schepselen', *Volle Evangelie Koerier* 10/10 (April, 1948).

15. E. Scharten, 'Gaat dan henen', *Volle Evangelie Koerier* 10/12 (June 1948).

16. Scharten, 'Gaat dan henen' (June 1948), p. 5.

17. Scharten, 'Gaat dan henen' (June 1948), p. 5.

18. Scharten, 'Gaat dan henen' (June 1948), p. 5.

2.5 *Arie Kok*

Arie Kok (1883–1951) and his wife Elsje Roelofje Aldenberg (born 1887 in Deventer) were the first fruits 'given to the Lord for the Foreign Mission Field'.[19] Arie and Elsje Kok had been important co-workers with G.R. Polman, their departure was certainly a loss for the work at home. In August 1909 the couple left for the P.M.U. training school in London. The Dutch Pentecostals were infused with a spirit of mission. Teenage children formed praying bands for the mission in heathen countries. A Bible class of about 20 young men and women was established for the training of evangelists and missionaries.[20] After several months of preparation in London, the Kok family left for China in early 1910. On the way they stopped for one year to work in Dorpat and Reval.[21] In February 1911, Kok arrived in Shanghai. In Shantung he met the Canadian couple H. and S. McLean, former missionaries with the C.I.M., but changing now to the P.M.U.[22] They decided to move to the province of Yunnan together. McLean planned to work among the Chinese in the large cities in the Northwest region of Yunnan Province, and Kok felt led to work among the Tibetan people along the Tibetan border in Yunnan. They reached Yunnan-fu (later called Kunming), capital of Yunnan in May 1912, shortly after Mrs. Kok has given birth to a son. One month later the three lady missionaries arrived.

3. *In China*

Elize's boat trip to Hong Kong went smoothly. Kok picked her up in Laokai, four days South of Yunnan-fu. After one week, they began the difficult task of language study. The Pentecostal missionaries received a warm welcome from the missionaries of the C.I.M. (Graham) and of the British and Foreign Bible Society (E. Amundsen) already present. There was also a Y.M.C.A. hall in the city. Yunnan (a Chinese name meaning 'South of the Clouds') Province had hardly been reached with the gospel. McLean decided to remain in Yunnan-fu, but the Dutch

19. G.R. Polman, 'Farewell Meetings with Mr. and Mrs. Kok at Amsterdam', *Confidence* 2/9 (September, 1909), pp. 208a-208b.

20. Polman, 'Farewell Meetings', 208a-208b.

21. G.R. Polman, 'Mededeelingen', *Spade Regen* 14 (January–March, 1910), p. 4.

22. Cf. S. McLean, *Over Twenty Years in China* (Minneapolis, By the author, 1927).

Pentecostals had a calling for Tibet. Since Tibet was closed to missionaries, they, in consent with the other missionaries, decided to move to
Lijiang (or Likiang) on the Tibetan border. The nearest mission post was
in Tali (or Dali), five days South of Lijiang. The C.I.M. had been praying
for 15 years for the opening of one of the cities north of Tali.[23]

3.1 *On the Tibetan Border*

Lijiang lies along the great trade route from Yunnan-fu to Lhasa, capital
of Tibet. Daily caravans pass through this outpost. Apart from the
Chinese and Tibetans, there are many Nahsi living in Lijiang. Lijiang was
the capital of the ancient Nahsi Kingdom. The Nahsi (or Nakhi, also
called Naxi) have Tibetan blood and are, like the Tibetans, despised by
the Chinese. The lady missionaries were the first European women to
visit the region. The locals were hostile and called them 'white devils'.
Initially, meetings were held on the street or in the courtyards of the
houses. Chinese songs written on cotton were placed against a wall. A
portable organ or mandolin guided the singing.

It took quite some time to win the trust of the people and to see the
first converts. The latter was due in part to the heavy demands made by
the missionaries, who insisted that converts forsake all use of opium and
alcohol. Elize viewed the use of opium as 'the curse for all of China'. In
dress, food and housing, the missionaries accommodated to the local
way of living.

Soon after some converts were gained, Kok established a Bible school
and began training capable men as evangelists.[24] His strategy to train
inland evangelists proved to be very successful. As soon as the church in
Lijiang was established, trips were made into the outlying area. From
Lijiang a number of out-stations were founded where inland evangelists
led the work. The tribes in the mountains were very open to the gospel.
Elize relates:

---

23. A. Kok to P.M.U. Council, Yunnanfu, 9 August, 1912. Letter also published
in *Flames of Fire* 7 (October, 1912), p. 3.

24. A. and E. Kok 'Een Bijbelschool op het Zendingsveld', *Spade Regen* 40
(July, 1916), p. 4. The Bible school was started by Kok in 1914 and kept in operation until 1916. Three male students were taken in. They moved into the home of the
missionaries. After two years Kok decided to add a third year to the course. Students
were taught in: Biblical History; Dogmatics; Church History; Prayer; Singing; Bible
Study; Biblical Geography; General Geography; General Knowledge. Besides the
full-time students there were other helpers, who went through a one month course.
They were instructed in singing and in the basic principles of the Christian faith.

The mountain tribes are oppressed by the Chinese, downtrodden and despised. In the beginning it was very hard for them to believe that we had come as their friends and that we meant good. Because they were received with friendship in our home; yes, that they, dressed in their sheep coat, were treated with the same courtesy as the Chinese, dressed in silk, made them trust us. This way they came nearer.[25]

The Tibetan people were not forgotten either. The missionaries gave out tracts and portions of the Bible written in the Tibetan language. The literature came from the Moravian Brethren. When the missionaries moved to a new house in 1918, the old home was turned into an inn for Tibetan travelers (like Gladys Aylward's 'Inn of the Sixth Happiness'). The Christian mother of a Tibetan evangelist took charge of the inn. Nearly every night the home was full of weary Tibetan travelers. Occasionally the missionaries were able to venture into Tibet.

3.2 *Dutch Colony*

In time, more Dutch missionaries came to Lijiang. Idigje de Vries, who had been in the P.M.U. Women's Training Home since September 1911, sailed for China in April 1914. Due to illness she had to resign in February 1916.[26] In December 1915, Piet Klaver (1890–1970) departed for China. After language study at Yunnan-fu, he proceeded on to Lijiang in 1917 to assist Kok and Scharten.[27] Later, while still in China, he married P.M.U. missionary Rose Waters from Liverpool (1918).

In 1918 Annie Kok, a sister of Arie Kok, traveled from America to Lijiang, supported by an American Pentecostal church. While learning Chinese, she taught her brother's children. Annie Kok had received her Spirit baptism in Amsterdam in 1911; later, with her parents and two sisters, she moved to Grand Rapids.[28] When in 1919 Arie Kok got over-

---

25. E. Scharten, *Uit het binnenland van China, Pinksteruitgaven* 4 (Amsterdam: G.R. Polman, 1922), p. 25.

26. G.R. Polman, 'Mededeelingen', *Spade Regen* 36 (March, 1914), p. 4, recorded that Ida de Vries's farewell from Amsterdam had been on January 11, 1914. Other references to her were found in the P.M.U. Minute Book, present in the Assemblies of God Headquarters in Nottingham, England.

27. A.A. Boddy, 'Holland: News from Pastor Polman', *Confidence* 8/12 (December, 1915), pp. 235-36, gives a description of the farewell service at Amsterdam, about 400 persons were present; cf. G.R. Polman, 'Mededeelingen', *Spade Regen* 39 (January, 1916), p. 4. After a period of language study at Yunnan-fu, Klaver arrived at Lijiang in June 1917.

28. G.R. Polman, 'Mededeelingen', *Spade Regen* 10/11 (February, 1918), p. 44;

tired and had to leave Lijiang, Klaver took over the leadership of the mission. The Kok family moved to Peking for rest, but in the end never returned to the mission field. Annie Kok remained in Lijiang until 1925. Because of his proficiency in the Chinese language, Arie Kok would later become the Chancellor of the Dutch legation in Peking. In this capacity he continued to help the missionary cause.[29]

In 1912 Trijntje Bakker (1891–1980) and Geertje Roos (born 1879) from Terschelling traveled to the newly opened missionary training school in Amsterdam. The outbreak of World War I delayed their departure for China. Finally in October 1921 the ladies Bakker and Roos were able to travel to China together with Elize Scharten, who had been on furlough. Roos and Bakker were sent out by the Dutch Pentecostal Missionary Society. Thanks to the inheritance of an uncle, Elize had become financially independent; nevertheless she remained with the P.M.U.[30]

The Dutch missionaries co-operated with other P.M.U. missionaries, some independent American Pentecostal missionaries, and later with Pentecostal missionaries from Germany. All missionaries had to leave the area in 1927 due to a civil war. Elize returned to China in 1929, followed by Trijntje Bakker in 1931.[31] Piet Klaver transferred to the Dutch Indies in 1929. Internal problems in the Amsterdam Pentecosal assembly caused the Dutch missionaries to China to associate with the German Velbert Mission beginning in 1931. Trijntje Bakker remained in China until 1938.

cf. A.C.A. Kok, 'How God Protected Christian Chinese from Bandits', *The Latter Rain Evangel* (June 1925), pp. 18-19.

29. After World War II Kok left China. In the meantime he had disassociated himself from the Pentecostal movement. In 1948 he participated in the founding of the militant 'International Council of Christian Churches' and became their General Secretary. In January 1951 he died in the U.S.A.

30. The minutes of the P.M.U. Council meeting February 6, 1918 read: 'Miss Scharten without severing connection with the P.M.U. will not require further financial support having sufficient private means to meet this', P.M.U. Minute Book 2, p. 18. In February 1921 Elize did request financial support for her trip to China, being unable to pay this personally because of the cost of her operation. P.M.U. Minute Book 2, pp. 301-302.

31. Trijntje Bakker stayed until 1938. Afterwards she was not able to return to China because of the war. Apart from a furlough between 1934–36, Elize Scharten remained in Lijiang until 1945.

3.3 *Pentecostal Mission in Yunnan*

Donald Gee gives us a good description of the Pentecostal mission in Yunnan during 1938:

> Our British assemblies may take a legitimate pride in the fact that we have taken a goodly part in pioneering the gospel in this hard field. Through many vicissitudes our British Pentecostal missionaries have continued to faithfully labor for over twenty-five years. At the present we have seventeen missionaries there. The American Assemblies of God have now joined us in the fight for Yunnan, with twenty-two missionaries. In the Northwest of the province around and beyond the Lijiang District, Dutch and German Pentecostal missionaries are operating, and also the English group known as the Tibetan Border Mission. In the South there are a few Scandinavians. Altogether there must be at least sixty Pentecostal missionaries working in the Province of Yunnan.[32]

The British P.M.U. missionaries kept working in the capital Yunnan-fu and several out-stations. Initially, Lijiang was served by Dutch missionaries, from time to time supported by British P.M.U. missionaries (Miss Elizabeth M. Biggs 1913–17, Miss Grace Agar 1917–19, Mr. Ralph Capper 1922–23, Miss Florence Ives 1923–24, Miss Ethel M. Cook, 1925–26). James H. Andrews stayed in Lijiang one year during 1922–23. In 1924 he married Jessie Biggs and replaced Klaver as leader at Lijiang.

West of Lijiang, a work among the Lisu was opened during the 1920s. In 1921 the Englishman, Alfred Lewer, married to the American Mary Buchwalter, started to work among the Lisu in the Wei Hsi area.[33] They received guidance from J.O. Fraser of the C.I.M., who already had established a successful ministry among the Lisu. In 1924 Leonard and Olive Bolton (from Bournemouth) came to assist Lewer. On the way south to meet the Boltons in Rangoon, Alfred Lewer was tragically drowned in the Mekong River. Leonard Bolton lost his wife and baby in childbirth at Tali, but nevertheless went on to Wei Hsi to continue the missionary work Lewer had begun. On furlough in 1928 Bolton married Ada Buchwalter (Mrs Lewer's sister) and returned as a missionary of the American Assemblies of God to Wei Hsi. They cooperated with Mary Lewer, working among the Lisu and Chinese until World War II.[34]

32. D. Gee, 'The Challenge of Yunnan', *Pentecostal Evangel* (5 March, 1938), p. 4.

33. R. Bolton, 'South of the Clouds: Church Planting in Yunnan Province through Lisu People Movements (1906–1949)' (term paper; Fuller Theological Seminary, Los Angeles, 1974), p. 9.

34. Bolton, 'South of the Clouds', pp. 9-11.

3.4 *Separation from the P.M.U.*

The transition of leadership from Klaver to Andrews in 1924 caused quite a stir. When Klaver was due for furlough, the P.M.U. thought it time to put a British Superintendent in charge and decided for Andrews. Klaver considered Andrews totally incapable of the job and urged the Council to put Elize Scharten in charge during his absence.[35] Likewise, Elize Scharten appealed to the Council not to send Andrews to Lijiang. The P.M.U. Council forwarded extracts of Klaver's letter to Jessie Biggs, on furlough in England and engaged to Andrews, for comment. Not surprisingly Jessie Biggs strongly defended her future husband. The Council saw no reason to alter its decision to send Andrews to Lijiang. It became even worse for Klaver when it became apparent that after his furlough he would not be allowed to return to Lijiang. A letter written by the Chinese Church at Lijiang in favor of Klaver and a letter from Florence Ives defending Klaver could not make the Council change its mind.[36] Klaver left Lijiang in January 1924, but still planned to return. In July he resigned from the P.M.U. after a conversation with Cecil Polhill. The Dutch Pentecostal Mission Council decided to send Klaver back to Lijiang 'to continue the work given them by God Himself'.[37] As Polman insisted in several letters to know the motives behind the decision to replace Klaver, secretary T.H. Mundell finally provided the information:

> The Council was much exercised about the Dutch Workers at Lijiang during the recent War with Germany when Mr. Polhill had special communications from our Government Officials in connection with the pro-German tendencies and utterances of our Dutch Missionaries at Lijiang and the Council then resolved that so soon as we could we would endeavour to have an English Superintendent over the work at Lijiang so that whilst allowing the Dutch Workers to remain, the Head of the work would be an Englishman. It was really in pursuance of that decision we ultimately decided that so soon as Mr. and Mrs. Klaver left on furlough we should replace them with Mr. and Mrs. Andrews. I am telling you candidly the reason so that we are not saying anything whatever against Mr. Klaver personally.[38]

35. P. Klaver to P.M.U. Council, Lijiang, 20 August, 1923.

36. A letter from the Lijiang Pentecostal Church written in Chinese with an English translation by Klaver was enclosed in Klaver's letter to P.M.U. Council, Amsterdam, 24 May, 1924. Florence A. Ives to P.M.U. Council, Yunnan-fu, 25 September, 1924.

37. Dutch Pentecostal Council to P.M.U. Council, Amsterdam, 11 February, 1925.

38. T.H. Mundell to G.R. Polman, London, 25 March, 1925.

This statement, however, is contrary to what Mundell wrote to Klaver in 1923:

> This decision my dear Brother, has been come to not because you are Dutch as we cannot recognize Nationalities in The Lord's work, Who has made one of all nations, but because we believe it will be entirely for The Glory of God and in His Will.[39]

No doubt the separation had serious negative effects upon the local witness. In retrospect it would seem that Klaver's conviction that Andrews was incapable of the job was more due to a clash in personalities, than to sound judgment. Apparently both possessed a rather autocratic nature. In one of Andrews's letters General Perarei is claimed to have said, 'Little Klaver is a bossy fellow, he rather sits on Mr Andrews, in fact he is ignorant and unmannerly to him'.[40] Much later, at a convention in Yunnan-fu at the time Howard Carter was visiting the area (1935), Andrews was judged as being autocratic by his co-worker C. Francis. In an angry letter to the Home Missionary Reference Council of the British Assemblies of God Andrews replied, 'As speaking of Autocracy, well, I think Mr. Carter is blessed with it too as well as brother Andrews'.[41] From the Dutch point of view there was much to be said against the decision of the P.M.U. to replace Klaver by Andrews. Yet with regard to the local witness, sending Klaver back seems to have been the wrong reply.

In November/December 1924 Andrews arrived in Lijiang where he assumed the difficult task of winning the trust of the three Dutch missionaries, Scharten, Bakker and Roos, and of the indigenous workers. Scharten had instructions from Klaver not to hand over the indigenous evangelists. The five evangelists were called to choose for themselves between Andrews and Scharten. The situation was most difficult. A letter from Scharten to W.J. Boyd at Yunnan-fu in which she informed Boyd of the separation that had taken place at Lijiang and that 'The Dutch people are leaving the P.M.U. work', was taken by the P.M.U. as

39. T.H. Mundell to P. Klaver, London, 16 November, 1923.
40. Jessie Biggs to T.H. Mundell, Glasgow, 10 October, 1923. Biggs quotes from a letter of Andrews to her written 21 August, 1923. The remark was made in the presence of Joseph Rock, who passed it on to Andrews.
41. J.H. Andrews to the Home Missionary Reference Council, Yunnan-fu, 1 May, 1936.

her resignation.[42] Elize's request to be allowed to keep two small out-stations named La-pao and Nda-zae was granted. Elize was taken by surprise that her letter to Boyd had been misunderstood: 'I must express my astonishment that you were so quick to take my resignation from a letter, which was not at all meant as a resignation'.[43] Elize went on working independently in the out-stations among the tribal people as in the past. The relationship with Andrews would gradually improve. Roos and Bakker assisted both Elize and Andrews. Their application for associate membership with the P.M.U. was never approved.

Due to the illness of Mrs Andrews, the Andrews couple had to leave Lijiang after having been there only eight months. In September 1925 they were back in England. Unfortunately Mrs Andrews died after an operation in November 1925. Klaver returned in February 1926, but had to leave again in March 1927 because of the civil war. Klaver would not come back to China again. In January 1928 Andrews arrived back in Yunnan-fu with Anna Weber, a Pentecostal missionary from Cleveland, Ohio, whom he had married the previous October. The Andrews moved to Lijiang in November 1928. Apart from a furlough Andrews, would remain at Lijiang until 1945. The years 1929–34 in particular were very fruitful. In November 1930 a large Gospel Hall was opened, built on the ground once bought by Kok. In 1931 Andrews received help from Cyril and M.H.T. Francis from Wales, and in 1934 Ray and Winifred Colley, also from Great Britain, arrived. New out-stations were opened where indigenous evangelists were put in charge. A large tent proved very effective in the village work. At night, services were held with a magic lantern showing the Life of Christ.

3.5 *Partnership with the Velbert Mission*
The German missionary endeavors in this area started after a visit of Piet Klaver to Velbert in 1925. Klaver, having just resigned from the P.M.U., was in need of help. The Velbert missionary society was formed in 1931. Several German missionaries were sent to China to work in the Yunnan area: Erich Schürmann (1931–34); Martha Horstmann (1931–40); Martha Tillmann (1933–49); Elfriede Diehl (1933–49); Oskar Siering (1934–49); Gottfried Starr (1937–49). O. Siering married M. Tillmann in

---

42. W.J. Boyd to C. Polhill, Yunnan-fu, 19 January, 1925. T.H. Mundell to E. Scharten, London, 14 March, 1925.

43. E. Scharten to T.H. Mundell, Lijiang, 30 April, 1925.

1937 and G. Starr married E. Diehl in 1940. Siering worked in Chu-Tien, Starr in Ta-ku.[44]

During the war years the German missionaries in the area were forced to move to Lijiang and were no longer allowed to travel. Elize received two German missionary families (Siering and Starr) in the large house she had obtained one year before. For this reason charges were put against her with the Dutch legation at Chung-King. Elize was requested to dismiss the German missionaries from her home.[45] After prayer, it became clear for Elize that she had to move out herself. She was received into the home of James Andrews. Because of the war with Japan, the two children of the Andrews family could not go to school. Elize instructed them at home.[46]

3.6 *Notoriety*

Elize became renowned in Lijiang and the surrounding area. Initially she worked primarily with the Nahsi tribe. After her second furlough, she also began to work with the Lisu tribe. She carefully studied the Nahsi language and became proficient enough to develop a written form of the language, teach reading and writing, prepare a dictionary, and translate the Gospel of Mark, as well as a catechism and a songbook.[47] In one of the Lisu villages she opened a school. Her various publications and dairies demonstrate her deep knowledge of the language, customs, culture and religion of the tribal people. She speaks with great affection of 'her beloved'. China had become her second home.

Elize did maintain part of her European lifestyle. She kept cows and established her own bakery. A windmill provided electricity for lighting

---

44. H. Ditthardt and T. Koch, *Velbert 50 Jahre mit Vollem Evangelium* (Erzhausen: Leuchter Verlag, 1960), pp. 42-46. *De Vereenigde Zendingsvrienden* 1937–1942 (see n. 3 above).

45. E. Scharten, 'Gaat dan henen in de gehele wereld en predikt het evangelie aan alle schepselen', *Volle Evangelie Koerier* 10/8 (February, 1948), p. 4.

46. Elize taught the children Jim and Ruth Mathematics and History. Today Jim Andrews is a missionary of the American Assemblies of God in Taiwan and writing a biography of his parents. Jim Andrews to author, 4 October 1995.

47. The Scharten family archive keeps her seven diaries. Her newsletters were printed in *Spade Regen, Confidence, Flames of Fire*, but also in the non-Pentecostal paper *Welkom* and occasionally in Lutheran papers as *Een vaste burg is onze God!, Opwaarts* and *De Wartburg*. Between February, 1948 and July, 1950 she had a series of articles published in the *Volle Evangelie Koerier*. I. van Marle, *Zij volgde haar roeping* (Hague: Gazon, 1976), contains a biography of Trijntje Bakker.

and a radio.[48] *Si Jia Si*, the church members called her. She was greatly respected.

Twice she came close to death. In 1919 she spent four months in a Hong Kong hospital with appendicitis: 'By the grace of God my life was spared'. In 1942 she broke her left leg. The leg healed slowly and, in her weakened state, a case of pneumonia almost killed her. She slowly recovered. Walking became difficult and, as a result, she fell in her home and broke her kneecap. The doctors warned her that the knee would remain stiff. Elize prayed: 'Lord, let my knee become so supple that I can again kneel before You'.[49] Her prayer was answered. Elize was indeed able to kneel again.

3.7 *Joseph F. Rock*

Between 1922 and 1945 another European frequently visited Lijiang. His name was Joseph F. Rock (1884–1962), an eccentric Austro-American botanist and explorer with 'red face, spectacles and a terrible temper'.[50] Rock's predilection for Chinese characters caused him to begin to study Chinese at the age of 15.[51] This led him to study the ancient Nahsi language. This language was no more in use, but was preserved in the pictographic literature. Rock worked in the Lijiang area as an agricultural explorer, first for the US Department of Agriculture (Washington D.C.), then for the National Geographic Society. During 1944–45 he was a consultant to the US Army Map Service.[52]

The English writer Bruce Chatwin (1940–89), who, intrigued by Rock, visited Lijiang in 1985, informs us further about this remarkable man:

> Yet, though he introduced hundreds of new or rare plants to Western gardens and sent off thousands of herbarium specimens, he never wrote a paper on the botany of China. Instead he gave his life to recording the customs, ceremonies and the unique pictographic script of his Na-khi friends. Lijiang was the only home he ever knew; and even after he was

48. These details about her European life style do not come from her own writings, but from later interviews by Hoekstra with villagers.

49. E. Scharten, 'Gaat dan heen', *Volle Evangelie Koerier* 12/3 (September 1949), p. 4.

50. B. Chatwin, 'Rock's World', in *idem, What Am I Doing Here?* (London: Jonathan Cape, 1989), p. 210.

51. J.F. Rock, *The Ancient Na-Khi Kingdom of Southwest China* (2 vols.; Cambridge, MA: Harvard University Press, 1947), p. vii.

52. Rock, *The Ancient Na-Khi Kingdom*, p. viii.

booted out, he could still write in a letter, 'I want to die among these beautiful mountains rather than in a bleak hospital bed, all alone'.[53]

Rock used Lijiang as a base for his travels along the Tibetan border. Chatwin adds,

> This then, was the meticulous autodidact, who would pack 'David Copperfield' in his baggage to remind him of his wretched childhood; who travelled '*en prince*' (at the expense of his American backers), ate off gold plate, played records of Caruso to mountain villagers and liked to glance back, across a hillside, at his cavalcade 'half a mile long'. His book, *The Ancient Na-Khi Kingdom of South-West China*, with its eye-aching genealogies and dazzling asides, must be one of the most eccenric publications ever produced by Harvard University Press.[54]

One of the villagers asked Chatwin why *Le-Ke* (as Rock was called) used to be so angry with them. Chatwin replied:

> 'He wasn't angry with you', I said. 'He was born angry.' I should perhaps have added that the targets of his anger included the National Geographic magazine (for rewriting his prose), his Viennese nephew, Harvard University, women, the State Department, the Kuomintang, Reds, red tape, missionaries, Holy Rollers, Chinese bandits and bankrupt Western civilization.[55]

In spite of his apparent anger with women, missionaries and Holy Rollers, Rock and Elize Scharten became friends. Alas, Elize's diaries (that read like field-reports) are silent about this friendship. According to J.A. Hoekstra, they left Lijiang together (1945), though this is not confirmed in Elize's report of her departure. Hoekstra writes:

> Rock and Scharten left the country together. They traveled together into India, then their ways part. Elize reached a high age in the Netherlands. Joseph Rock lived a number of years in Honolulu, embittered and disillusioned. It was not granted to him to die *among those beautiful mountains*, his own words in one of his last letters. The two never met each other again.[56]

53. Chatwin, 'Rock's World', p. 211.

54. Chatwin, 'Rock's World', p. 211. Joseph F. Rock in his two volumes, *The Ancient Na-Khi Kingdom of Southwest China,* never mentions Elize Scharten. He does mention Arie Kok (pp. 249, 267), but apparently without having met Kok personally.

55. Chatwin, 'Rock's World', p. 211.

56. J.A. Hoekstra, *Ontmoetingen in Lijiang* (Groningen: Synaps, 1991), p. 18.

3.8 *Departure*

In September 1945 the missionaries were forced to leave Lijiang. Only the German missionaries remained. The leadership of the Lijiang Assembly was turned over by Andrews to Hsi Te Ming and Chao Yi Chien.[57] Including three furloughs (1919–21; 1927–29; 1934–36) and preparations in England (1911), Elize had spent more than 34 years on the mission field. Yet, after all these years, there was hardly time to say goodbye. In her diary Elize writes:

> Everything lay behind me and much went through my soul. Yet, I knew I was in the will of the Lord. For some time I felt that my work in China was coming to an end. A part of my life was cut off with this departure. Thirty-four years of labor lay behind me and how many will there still be before me?[58]

According to her diary, Elize traveled with the Andrews to India and from there to the USA, where she stayed more than a year. In 1947 she returned to the Netherlands. She settled in Zeist and remained active in the Pentecostal movement. In Zeist she led a small gathering and was active in 'door to door' evangelism. She preached throughout the country. She donated her collection of roll paintings from Tibet to the 'Rijksmuseum voor Volkenkunde' in Leiden.[59] The last two years of her life were difficult, she was bedridden and suffered from dementia. On June 19, 1965, she died, nearly 89 years old. Her life is an example of faith and zeal for the Lord. Piet Klaver writes *in memoriam*:

> Humanly speaking, she could have had an easy, lazy and comfortable life. She had the means for this. But she chose the hard and difficult labor of being a pioneer. She did not spare herself. She was a hard worker and what she did herself, she also expected from those who worked with her.[60]

57. Jim Andrews to author, Taipei, 4 October 1995. In 1946 Ray and Winifred Colley were able to return to Lijiang, but had to leave again in 1949. Interview with W.R. and W.L. Colley, Hindhead, 19 August 1995.

58. E. Scharten, 'Reis van China naar Holland over Amerika', Diary, 1945.

59. Cf. P.H. Pott, *Introduction to the Tibetan Collection of the National Museum of Ethology, Leiden* (Leiden: Brill, 1951).

60. P. Klaver, 'In memoriam zr. E. Scharten', *Pinksterboodschap* 6/8 (1965), p. 14.

4. *Village Memories of Elize*

Since China has opened to tourism, several Dutch visitors have journeyed to Lijiang. Their contacts there reveal that some of the villagers still have vivid memories of Elize. Xuan Ke, the local teacher of Music and English, writer, story teller and keeper of the Nahsi culture and tradition, knew both Elize and Rock. His father was trained by Elize and became the first Nahsi pastor of the Lijiang assembly. Other missionaries taught Xuan Ke English, while Elize taught him Music. Because of Xuan Ke's contacts with the missionaries, he was seized by the Red Army and imprisoned for ten years, followed by another ten years of heavy labor in a tin factory. Due to the tortures during his arrest (his wrists were pierced with a sharp object), he can no longer play the piano or organ.[61] However, he has now regained a respected place in society. He owns the house where Rock once lived and serves as a guide to the 'big noses' (as Westerners are called) that visit the village. At Rock's former lodgings his bookcase, his pigeonhole desk, his wide chair ('because he was so fat') and the remains of his garden beside the Jade Stream, can still be seen.[62] A few reminders of Elize are also carefully kept: an embroidered tea-cosy and some photographs. Elize made the tea-cosy for Xuan Ke's father, who liked to rinse his throat with hot tea during his sermons. The bell that once served to announce the meetings, is now used by the elementary school to call the children inside. Jim Andrews, son of James Andrews, visited Lijiang in 1986. He had been almost 11 years old when he left the village with his parents and Elize Scharten in 1945. In the years of persecution the church and missions compound was confiscated by the authorities for a hospital. The members of the assembly had been scattered or imprisoned. Pastor Hsi Te Ming had died in prison after 18 years. Pastor Chao Yi Chien had returned to farming and died around 1980. When Jim Andrews asked Xuan Ke how many of the assembly still lived in Lijiang, the latter pointed a finger to his nose: 'Only one'.[63]

In 1988 the director of the Velbert Mission, Helmutt Timm and his wife, Hildegard, visited Lijiang.[64] Hildegard was born in Lijiang in 1940 as the daughter of Gottfried and Elfriede Starr from Velbert. Xuan Ke

61. J.A. Hoekstra, *Ontmoetingen in Lijiang* (Groningen: Synaps, 1991), p. 15.
62. Chatwin, 'Rock's World', p. 212.
63. Jim Andrews to author, Taipei, 4 October 1995.
64. H. Timm, 'Nach 39 Jahren wieder in China', *Missions Nachrichten* 5 and 6 (May and June, 1988).

asked them for the Gospel of Mark translated by Elize many years ago. All copies in Lijiang were destroyed by the communists. There is no other Bible translation in Nahsi. The archive of the Scharten family does contain a copy of the Nahsi Gospel of Mark. One year later the Timm couple delivered a photocopy to Xuan Ke. It is uncertain whether a reprint would be meaningful at this time.

J.A. Hoekstra (1932–92), lung specialist from Groningen, visited Lijiang in the early part of 1989. During his stay there, he accidentally met herb specialist Dr. Ho Shi Xin, who is proud to have been a pupil of Rock. Shi Xin told Hoekstra of Chatwin's visit in 1985. Hoekstra was taken by surprise as he greatly admired Chatwin's travel stories. Several dimensions of his life seemed to converge here: literature, travelling and medicine. On the spot, Hoekstra decided to give literary expression to this event. The same year he had Bruce Chatwin's article, 'Rock's World', reprinted, supplemented by his own impressions.[65] During his second visit to Lijiang in 1990, Hoekstra met Xuan Ke and was impressed with what he heard of Elize Scharten. Elize is remembered as a strong personality, to whom one could always make an appeal for help. Hoekstra interviewed 83 year old Wang Zhi Yuan:

> Si Jia Si, as the old Nahsi remember her, is also still alive in the memory of an 83-years old man, who was baptized by her when he was 25. After insisting, Wang Zhi Yuan sings with cracking voice, '*Yesu ling wuo, riri ling wuo*'. That is translated to me as: 'Jesus leads me, leads me every day'. The conversation with this man takes place at the farm where he lives, in the half-dark of the high stable. His son and grand-children listen. We sit on low benches around him. Does his family hear these words for the first time? More than 40 years ago the period was closed, in which this prayer could be spoken freely. Has he ever dared to sing it since? Out of precaution he destroyed everything that reminded of this period. It was dangerous to have anything at home, that could point to contact with Christianity. He tells us about the church service, the organ and the bell that sounded to announce the meetings. Then he is persuaded to speak the words of another prayer that comes to his mind. His story is touching.[66]

Another recent report of a Dutch visitor to Lijiang is from Ivo de Jong, who arrived there in 1994. Xuan Ke, now 64 years old, spoke to him about the Lisu tribe, while playing a tape recording of their singing:

---

65. J.A. Hoekstra, *Bruce Chatwin—Rock's World* (Groningen: Kemper, 1989).
66. Hoekstra, *Rock's World*, p. 17.

a minority, living three hours by bus and seven hours walking distance into the jungle from Lijiang, that after 50 years still sing the same Christian songs my father taught them. Otherwise there is nothing there, nothing of your culture. Everything which remains was transmitted by my father. In 1949 he was one of the first captured by the communists. Ten years later he died in prison. All for his faith.[67]

5. *Epilogue*

The early Pentecostal missionaries in Yunnan are impressive for their zeal, dedication and perseverance. Their memories live on. Their labor in difficult situations was not in vain, even though we cannot point to a church in Lijiang today. The church building is now part of a hospital (a warehouse where medicine is stored). No matter how communism has tried to destroy Christianity, the church in China has grown against the tide. In 1949 there were three million Catholic and one million Protestant believers. Today, conservative estimates state that there are over 50 million Christians. In the Yunnan province 95% of the Christians belong to the ethnic minorities.[68] Among these ethnic minorities are the 'beloved' of Elize: the Nahsi and Lisu.

Photographs of Li Jiang courtesy of Robert P. Menzies, 1995

67. I. de Jong, 'Wie gromt, heeft een hondeleven', *Trouw* 14 (April, 1994).
68. J.M. Taylor III, 'China', *Oost-Azië's Miljoenen* 31/2 (1987), pp. 1-2.

1. The courtyard in Li Jiang which formed part of the old church complex. This courtyard is adjacent to the old church and was originally built by the missionaries in conjunction with the church to serve as a place for instruction and training.

2. The front gate of the old missionary residence. This Chinese style complex with inner courtyard surrounded by rooms housed a number of the early missionaries, possibly including Elize Scharten.

3. A frontal view of the missionary residence (photo 2). Currently it stands next to a new hotel and its future is undoubtedly short.

4. The old church in Li Jiang, a frontal view from the street.

5. A man walking in one of the streets in the 'old town' of Li Jiang. The 'old town' has not changed much over the past several centuries.

6. Elize Scharten, 'Bidt voor mij' ('Pray for me').

INDEXES

INDEX OF REFERENCES

OLD TESTAMENT

INDEX OF AUTHORS AND PROPER NAMES